Latin America's Economic Future

To Tom, Ted and Betty

Latin America's Economic Future

edited by

Graham Bird *and* **Ann Helwege**

Department of Economics
University of Surrey
Guildford
UK

Department of Urban and
Environmental Policy
Tufts University
Medford, Massachusetts
USA

ACADEMIC PRESS
Harcourt Brace & Company, Publishers
London   San Diego   New York
Boston   Sydney   Tokyo   Toronto

ACADEMIC PRESS LIMITED
24–28 Oval Road,
London NW1 7DX

United States Edition published by
ACADEMIC PRESS INC.
San Diego, CA 92101

A catalogue record for this book is available from the British Library

ISBN 0–12–099645–6

Typeset by Columns Design and Production Services Ltd, Reading
and printed in Great Britain by T.J. Press Ltd, Padstow, Cornwall

Contents

Preface

After a decade of stalled development during the 1980s, there were signs that Latin American economies were beginning to recover in the early 1990s. Inflation rates fell dramatically, while economic growth picked up. It appeared that the debt crisis, which had dominated the 1980s, was finally over. This improvement in performance coincided with a change in policy direction, as governments in Latin America began to adopt a more market-oriented approach.

These changes raise a host of important questions. Among them, why did recovery occur, and to what extent was it due to the shift in policy? Beyond this, what factors determine whether the recovery can be converted into more sustained growth and development?

Building from a research seminar organized by the Surrey Centre for International Economic Studies (SCIES) in 1992, this book presents the findings of a programme of research to identify key steps in successful policy reform in Latin America, and the factors that may cause recovery to prove unsustainable. Contributions have been drawn from scholars with diverse ideas and a detailed knowledge of Latin America. What emerges is a well-informed and balanced assessment of the future course of Latin American economies, as well as a clear indication of the issues on which development is most vulnerable.

In preparing the book, we as editors have been greatly helped by the contributors who worked to often tight deadlines, and who responded with no discernible signs of annoyance to our comments on early drafts. We owe our gratitude to Liz Blakeway who, as the Administrative Officer of SCIES, helped organize the original seminar and subsequently helped with the administration of the research project and the preparation of this book. Thanks are also due to our home institutions, the University of Surrey and Tufts University, for the support that they have provided.

Finally, we owe a vote of thanks to our respective families: Heather, Alan, Anne, Simon and Tom in the UK, and Stephen, Simon and Olivia in the US. Although the project has conferred on us the benefits of international collaborative research, it has imposed costs on them. The fact that they have borne them happily is greatly appreciated.

Contributors

Dr Oscar Altimir *CEPAL: Naciones Unidas, Avenida Dag Hammerskjold, Casilla 179–d, Santiago, Chile.*

Professor Graham Bird *Department of Economics, University of Surrey, Guildford, Surrey GU2 5XH, UK.*

Professor Richard M. Bird *Department of Economics, University of Toronto, Toronto, M5S 1N5, Canada.*

Dr Robert Devlin *CEPAL: Naciones Unidas, Avenida Dag Hammerskjold, Casilla 179–d, Santiago, Chile.*

Professor Sebastian Edwards *Chief Economist, Latin America and the Caribbean, The World Bank, Washington D.C. 20433, USA.*

Dr José María Fanelli *CEDES, Sánchez de Bustamante 27, 1173 Buenos Aires, Argentina.*

Dr Roberto Frenkel *CEDES, Sánchez de Bustamante 27, 1173 Buenos Aires, Argentina.*

Dr Stephany Griffith-Jones *Institute for Development Studies, University of Sussex, Brighton, BN1 9RE, UK.*

Dr Merilee Grindle *Harvard Institute for International Development, 1 Eliot Street, Cambridge, MA 01238, USA.*

Professor Ann Helwege *Urban and Environmental Policy, Tufts University, Medford, MA 02155, USA.*

Dr Ana Marr *Thailand Institute of Public International Affairs (TIPIA), 1041 (Third Floor), Phaholythin Road, Phayayathai, Bangkok 10400, Thailand.*

Dr Guillermo Perry R. *Fedesarollo, Bogota, Colombia.*

Dr Alicia Puyana *St Antony's College, Oxford University, Oxford, OX2 6JF, UK.*

Dr Alicia Rodrigues *Institute for Development Studies, University of Sussex, Brighton, BN1 9RE, UK.*

Professor Lance Taylor *MIT, E52–251C, Cambridge, MA 02139, USA.*

Introduction

GRAHAM BIRD

and

ANN HELWEGE

Economic policy in Latin America has shifted sharply in the last five years from fiscal excess and protectionism to export-oriented policies that rely heavily on market mechanisms. Real devaluations and trade liberalization have opened most Latin American countries. Austerity, privatization, and monetary restraint have both reduced the economic role of the state and contained inflation. Anticipation of profitable opportunities under new neo-liberal policies has fuelled a return of capital to the region.

Rapid growth in the early 1990s has been attributed to these new policies. Output grew at 3.5 per cent in 1991, and 2.4 per cent in 1992. In six countries – Argentina, Chile, Panama, the Dominican Republic, Uruguay and Venezuela – the economy grew by more than 6 per cent. At the same time, this regional recovery has been accompanied by a marked reduction in inflation, which fell below 20 per cent in sixteen countries in 1992.

This broad characterization of regional policy might suggest that Latin America is on a track comparable to that pursued by the rapidly industrializing Asian countries in the 1970s. But even by late 1992, growth rates were slowing and some economists were arguing that few of the countries would be able to sustain growth at the rate achieved at the beginning of the decade. Thus one must ask about the foundations of economic recovery. How fast is policy really changing? Does the implementation of policy match changes in the rhetoric of Latin leaders? Do these market-friendly policies really lead to positive growth? Is the recovery durable, or it is largely the effect of short-lived speculative investment, low world interest rates, and the one-time sale of government assets? What political environment will be conducive to growth? And, who benefits from this recovery?

This book examines recent changes in economic policy in Latin America and discusses the prospects for growth. The first four contributions to the book, by Edwards, Puyana, Griffith-Jones, Marr and Rodriguez, and Graham Bird, address the importance of new trade policies and foreign investment in the region. Chapters by Helwege, Richard Bird and Perry, Devlin, and Fanelli, Frenkel and Taylor focus on recent fiscal reforms, stabilization, and the effectiveness of a smaller state in promoting growth. Altimir then discusses recent changes in income distribution, which may affect the viability of reforms. To close, Grindle addresses the changing role of the state under less restrictive economic policies.

Our goal in this book has been to identify common trends and points of vulnerability, without obscuring diversity within the region. Differences between countries emerge on closer inspection: Chile has moved farther down the road toward market-oriented policies than has Guatemala, while political consensus makes economic stability more likely in Mexico than Peru. Brazilians, who account for more than a third of regional GDP, will rightly ask 'What recovery?' before discussing the sustainability of reforms that have yet to be implemented.

Yet the trend toward trade liberalization and fiscal reform has touched most countries, raising questions about the effectiveness of these strategies. Contagious expectations drove the debt crisis and seem to have fuelled the return of capital to Latin America in the early 1990s. Thus one now wonders how vulnerable the region is to ebbing investment and to changing global economic conditions. Furthermore, growing rates of poverty in nearly all countries have made more urgent concerns about whether policies yield broad economic benefits. Contributions to this book are motivated by the hope that the current respite from recession can serve as an opportunity to secure the foundations of growth.

I THE EMERGENCE OF AN OUTWARD ORIENTATION

For the past several decades, Latin American economies have been inward-looking, with high tariffs, strict quotas, and overvalued exchange rates. Even the trade liberalizations of the late 1970s in the Southern Cone were largely reversed in the early 1980s. It is only since the late 1980s that significant efforts have been made to reduce import barriers. Average tariff rates in 1993 are less than 25 per cent in Bolivia, Chile, Costa Rica, Mexico and Peru. Where protection remains high, import licences and quotas have been replaced by tariffs, thus reducing bureaucratic delays, corruption and uncertainty. Other distorting policies, such as highly dispersed tariff rates and export taxes, have been curbed. At least between 1980 and 1987, this opening was accompanied by considerable exchange rate depreciation.

Regional export revenue grew at an extraordinary rate of 12 per cent per year between 1987 and 1990. Most of this increase was achieved through a rapid rise in export volume, suggesting that trade reforms and exchange rate policies were bearing fruit very rapidly. However, exports were virtually stagnant in 1991, and grew at a more modest rate of 4 per cent in 1992. As Edwards points out, exchange rate depreciations have been partially reversed in recent years, reducing competitiveness. One thus wonders how enduring the strong outward-orientation will be in some countries.

Weak terms of trade have also hampered export growth. As a result of several shocks in the 1980s, the regional terms of trade in 1992 were 28 per cent below the 1980 level. These difficult external conditions pose a potential threat to the recovery.

Moreover, if export growth is to be considered successful, it should be accompanied by greater productivity, and not merely a continuing reduction in real wages. Edwards points to substantial increases in factor productivity in Chile, Costa Rica, Argentina and Uruguay in the wake of trade reforms, but a decline in productivity in Mexico in recent years. Despite the sharp shift toward trade liberalization in the region, Edwards notes that distortions in agriculture, telecommunications and finance may partially explain this decline. Sustained increases in productivity also require capital, and thus investor confidence in the sustainability of trade reforms and macroeconomic stability.

The decline in protection of domestic markets has not been accompanied by an aggressive export-promotion programme as was the case in the Asian newly industrializing countries (NICs). The Chilean government has been among the most active in export-promotion, but it is far less interventionist than Asian governments that financed the start-up of new export industries. Few new non-agricultural products have emerged as major exports in the region, and export composition has not yet changed markedly. Alicia Puyana points out that Latin America's exports continue to be concentrated in fuels, minerals and foods. Although exports of manufactured goods have grown rapidly in the past two decades, they remain highly concentrated in labour-intensive goods such as clothing and leather and wood products, suggesting limited recent industrial development. A key question for the future is whether liberal economic policies will enable the region to develop new export products without more direct export promotion policies.

Latin American governments have been more active in seeking access to new markets for existing products. Yet Puyana argues that changing global trade conditions pose potential constraints on the region's export growth. Latin America remains very closely tied to the United States market. Prospects for developing closer ties with European trade partners are clouded by potential competition from emerging East European countries and more restrictive common external barriers in the Single European Market.

As a result of increasing intraregional trade, there has been renewed interest in regional trade integration, although this has had disappointing results in the past. Integration which opens domestic firms to outside competition (for example, by opening up the possibility of competition between Mexican and Venezuelan oil and oil products in their home markets) should increase efficiency, but it also increases the polarization and adjustment costs of trade liberalization. Integration efforts aimed at dampening the shock of trade liberalization by limiting its geographic scope can generate costly trade-diverting consequences, which in turn adversely affect domestic efficiency. Puyana points out that the region still lacks a common political will to share the uneven burdens of integration.

Bilateral negotiations between the United States and Latin American countries (and particularly the North American Free Trade Agreement, NAFTA) dominate regional trade prospects. Each bilateral agreement has implications for other producers in the region, which compete for access to the same markets in the US or in the negotiating Latin American country. Thus an important concern is whether the US will move toward more coherent multilateral negotiations in the region.

As export growth ebbed in 1992, rapid import growth continued. The region registered its first trade deficit ($6 billion) in several years, and the current account deficit ($33 billion) was more than half as large again as that of the preceding year. This deterioration has been attributed to trade liberaliza-tion and the appreciation of domestic currencies. While the massive inflow of capital to the region has made it possible to finance this current account deficit, it has added to the difficulty of maintaining competitive exchange rates.

Stephany Griffith-Jones, Ana Marr and Alicia Rodriguez note that between 1988 and 1991, net private capital flows to Latin America and the Caribbean increased approximately seven fold. To a large extent, this new investment reflects confidence in the macroeconomic stability achieved by sounder fiscal and monetary policies and the expectation that new trade policies will open avenues of profit. But there have certainly been signs of contagious expectations behind this investment: Brazil, for example, made very little progress either in containing inflation or in instituting structural reforms, yet it attracted a quarter of capital flows to the region in 1991. To the extent that this contagion effect is present, it makes capital flows still more unstable and unpredictable.

As current account deficits grow, one must question the extent to which these new capital inflows make Latin America vulnerable to future shocks due to a loss of external financing as investors' expectations change. Griffith-Jones, Marr and Rodriguez note that the increase in capital flows has not been due mainly to a return of bank lending. Almost 35 per cent of total flows to the region in 1991 were in the category of foreign direct investment, a much larger share of financial flows than in the early 1980s. Most Latin American countries have also sharply reduced their outstanding external debt. However, the return of capital has been fuelled by high interest rates and the privatization process, neither of which evokes confidence in the sustainability of these flows. The short maturities of bonds is also a cause for concern, particularly as investors may implicitly assume that the state will bail out private firms that default.

The challenge is to avoid massive speculative inflows that increase domestic demand without substantially increasing productive capacity, particularly in the tradeable sector. Thus the sustainability of capital flows to the region is tied to the long-term prospects for export growth. Although in theory markets anticipate future export growth, the speculative element in the current investment boom may undermine export growth through exchange rate appreciation. Efforts to cope with this appreciation have included (generally counterproductive) sterilization measures, import tariffs combined with export subsidies, and reserve requirements on capital inflows. Whether this problem is short-term and will be offset by new investment in export capacity remains unclear.

The region has a long history of vulnerability to external shocks due to changes in terms of trade, international interest rates, and the moods of foreign investors. Graham Bird raises concerns about the long-run balance of payments prospects for Latin America. Without substantial productive investment, the current mix of capital flows and trade deficits may not be sustainable. Stabilization and structural adjustment programmes, theoretically aimed at securing long-run growth, have tended to emphasize short-run results. Although privatization and liberalization have proceeded at a rapid pace in Chile and Mexico, elsewhere stabilization has been achieved through fiscal and monetary restraints that may be at odds with long-term investment.

II STABILIZATION AND MARKET-FRIENDLY POLICY REFORMS

The past several years have witnessed a substantial shift in attitudes about the need for austerity in the face of inflation. Regional inflation exceeded 1000 per cent in 1989 and 1990, as ill-conceived attempts to stop inflation without addressing its underlying causes failed. Steeped in a structuralist tradition that viewed fiscal spending as a means to overcome sectoral rigidities, many Latin American policymakers found price controls and financial regulation more appealing than austerity. Post-heterodox programmes of the late 1980s failed to contain 'inertial inflation' led by expectations, and did no better in supporting growth or easing poverty. The monetarist view that fiscal and monetary restraint are essential to curb inflation has since come to dominate the region, but it also fails to offer a growth-oriented model of stabilization, except to the extent that monetary stability is viewed as a necessary pre-condition for sustained economic growth.

Although there is now a stronger consensus about the need for contractionary stabilization, distributional issues remain the unresolved component of stabilization programmes. Ann Helwege notes that two dominant models have emerged in managing distributional aspects of stabilization: repression (associated with Chile) and consensus (achieved by Mexico). The Chilean model is not consistent with democracy and long-term stability; yet to replicate the Mexican model, other Latin American countries must build more inclusive societies that accept the need for more than token efforts to redress income inequality. Without progress on the distributional front, class conflict will continue to undermine stabilization programmes.

Even where coups and riots do not interfere with technically competent stabilization programmes, lingering questions remain about how to sequence stabilization and trade liberalization. Recent reliance on fixed exchange rates as a mechanism to gain credibility in the fight against inflation has accentuated this sequencing problem, as creeping overvaluation has contributed to trade deficits in newly opened economies. If capital flows that now finance these deficits were to ebb, Latin American countries would need to adopt more painful austerity, with little new knowledge about how to impose this on a citizenry that increasingly demands its right to democracy.

The trend toward sounder fiscal management has been accompanied by extensive tax reform. Whereas consolidated public sector deficits rose to as much as 20 per cent of GDP in the early 1980s, the debt crisis forced regimes to curtail deficits. Much of this has been achieved by cutting expenditures; however, the composition and level of revenues has also changed. Tax reform has been marked by attention to administrative aspects of tax collection, thus reducing evasion and the erosion of real revenues through collection lags. Value added taxes have taken on greater importance, in an effort to cut the distortionary effect of sectoral taxes and to reduce the role of taxes as a redistributional tool. Yet Richard Bird and Guillermo Perry argue that the value added tax remains administratively difficult to manage in developing countries. One must ask whether this tax, which has a proportionate or regressive incidence, is an appropriate tool to finance social spending. Although laissez-faire attitudes are in vogue now, the pendulum is likely to swing toward somewhat greater use of taxation to redistribute income and to shape the use of environmental resources.

Faith in the market has been most evident in a wave of privatization. The sale of public firms has been motivated by a number of factors, from the desire to signal a new ideological orientation to the urgency of reducing fiscal deficits. But to what extent have the social benefits of privatization been maximized? Robert Devlin details principles toward this end, including greater transparency in the privatization process and more systematic efforts to maximize the sale price.

Although privatization tends to increase efficiency by exposing the firm to more competition and by reducing subsidies, it carries the conundrum of compensation for displaced workers. Proposals to distribute shares to workers raise serious equity concerns, for these employed workers hold no more claim to state assets than other citizens. Despite the political appeal of assigning shares to the broad citizenry, it is unlikely that governments could administratively ensure that this process affected everyone alike. Even if it did, the benefits reaped by each individual would depend on their knowledge of equity markets. Devlin argues that it is more transparent and equitable to sell the shares at maximum price while making subsidies explicit. Revenues can then be used to finance social development.

For the most part, public firms have operated in monopolistic or oligopolistic markets. As these firms move out from under state control, few regulatory mechanisms have been put in place. The poor performance of these firms under state control has left many doubts about whether any state intervention will be productive. Yet contestability is too weak in some of these markets to ensure long-run efficiency.

Is the market-friendly approach to economic development really sound, or have Latin American regimes simply succumbed to the evangelism of neo-liberal economists? Fanelli, Frenkel and Taylor question the assumption that productivity differences between countries are largely the result of domestic policies (particularly investment in education) rather than the result of external shocks. They also challenge assertions that external openness and competition are associated with high growth and productivity, and raise doubts about whether interest rates have sufficient influence on savings to clear the market for investment capital. According to them, the market-friendly approach to policy-making is based more on ideology than hard evidence: some of the most successful cases of rapid economic growth have involved substantial government intervention through protection, subsidies and targeted incentives.

While the neo-liberal policies of the so-called "Washington consensus" have often appeared successful in recent years, some of this success has resulted from lower world interest rates and new capital flows; under different global conditions, similar shock programmes proved ruinous. Even industrialized economies such as Japan have challenged the lack of analytical subtlety which the "consensus" incorporates. While government failures have come under the lens of public choice economics, the traditional analysis of market failure has also proven resilient. Prudence dictates an open mind about the vulnerability of market-friendly reforms.

III THE POLITICAL ECONOMY OF REFORM

Will economic recovery in Latin America mitigate the growing poverty and income inequality of the 1980s? Oscar Altimir presents recent data on income distribution and poverty: for the region as a whole, the incidence of poverty rose to 46 per cent in 1990, compared to 41 per cent in 1980 and 43 per cent in 1986. With the exception of Colombia, all countries shared in this trend. Income concentration also increased in several countries: at the end of the decade, Chile, Venezuela, Argentina, Brazil, Peru and Panama had degrees of inequality that were higher than before the debt crisis. Given the extent of income concentration in the region, Altimir argues that the prospects for poverty alleviation are slim even as growth resumes, and that this may eventually undermine growth itself.

Is it possible to raise the productivity and income of poor households without upsetting the fiscal restraint and free-market principles perceived as the foundation of the current recovery? In theory, perhaps, through better targetting of social spending, access to technical training, and the extension of credit to micro-enterprises, but only a handful of countries have shown the commitment to social equity necessary to displace populism with more effective social spending.

Political reform is still a missing ingredient in most economic packages. The uncritical acceptance of a minimalist state has yet to prove itself as a wise strategy. In the long run, growth depends on the establishment of fair regulatory systems, clear property rights, and enough distributive justice to avert revolution. Weak institutions undermine investor confidence, not only about the enforcement of contracts, but about the very legitimacy of governments. Auto-coups, charges of bribery, and irregular voting procedures mar the legitimacy of at least five current regimes. Investors gauge political winds to judge the security of their investments: more secure democratic institutions would build confidence in longer-term projects.

Merilee Grindle argues that sustained recovery will require the development of the state's institutional, technical, administrative and political capacity. The recent shift to fiscal austerity focused on distortionary and counterproductive effects of state intervention. Yet the state must be able to effectively carry out laws, to set macroeconomic policy, to provide basic social services, and to mediate political conflict. On the whole, Latin American governments are now more competent in setting economic policy, less corrupt, and more committed to democracy. Nonetheless, reduced expenditures combined with rising levels of poverty have strained the capacity of the state to provide basic health and education services. Corruption within the bureaucracies that serve these needs further hinders progress. Reform, rather than mere reduction of state functions, is required. Just as it is possible to ask too much of the state in resolving the failures of the private sector, so is it possible to ask too little.

IV THE SUSTAINABILITY OF RECOVERY

The recovery of growth, the containment of inflation, and the renewal of investment in Latin America are accomplishments that should not be underrated. Rates of inflation between 1988 and 1990 were among the highest recorded, while GDP growth failed to reach 1 per cent. The sudden economic turnaround of the region has been remarkable.

Economic reforms have borne fruit rapidly. Perhaps the most dramatic accomplishment has been a new commitment to avoid financing deficits with money creation. A greater outward orientation, although evident more in trade liberalization and the aggressive pursuit of trade agreements than in exchange rate policy, has ignited hopes for long-run export expansion. More stable macroeconomic policy, relatively high interest rates and lower investment barriers have attracted a strong net inflow of foreign capital.

By mid-1992, however, it was already clear that the rapid growth achieved in the preceding year would probably not be repeated. Latin American stock markets experienced a sharp "correction", and by year end, the International Monetary Fund cut its projected regional growth rate for 1993. This caution reflects several points of vulnerability in the recovery. Key among these concerns are the impact of continued recession in OECD countries, interest rate shocks, excess exposure to primary commodity prices, and instability driven by conflicts over income shares.

We set out to identify the elements of renewed growth that are fleeting, those that are likely to endure, and what more needs to be done. The contributions in this book indicate that while substantial progress has been accomplished, there is still a long way to go to secure growth that touches all segments of society and that can be sustained with the support of democratic institutions.

1 | Trade Liberalization Reforms in Latin America: Recent Experiences, Policy Issues, and Future Prospects*

SEBASTIAN EDWARDS

I   INTRODUCTION

For many decades Latin America based its development strategy on highly protectionist policies aimed at rapidly expanding its industrial sector. In most cases, however, these policies resulted in largely inefficient firms that were unable to compete with the rest of the world and which required increasing government help to survive. Although from time to time a particular government tried to move away from protectionism, and engage in trade liberalization policies, the dominant development paradigm throughout the region was, until recently, one that emphasized inward growth, government intervention and high import barriers.[1] As Table 1.1 shows, in the mid-1980s Latin America had one of the most distorted external sectors in the developing world.[2]

Starting in the mid-1980s, however, there has been a remarkable transformation in economic thinking in Latin America. The once dominant views based on heavy state interventionism and protectionism are slowly giving way to a new approach based on market orientation, macroeconomic equilibrium and trade openness. There is also an increasing consensus on the need to redefine the role of government. Most analysts and local politicians agreed that the ever-growing government presence as a producer in the 1950–80 period had negative effects on efficiency and growth. Additionally, by focusing on their role as producers, Latin governments tended to de-emphasize

* This paper has been prepared for presentation at UCLA's Economic Forecasting and Public Policy Conference, December 16 and 17, 1992. Fernando Losada and Abraham Vela provided able research assistance. I have benefited from conversations with Ed Leamer.

Table 1.1 Import protection in the developing world, 1985.

	Total tariff protection (%)[a]	Non-tariff barriers coverage (%)[b]
South America	51	60
Central America	66	100
Caribbean	17	23
North Africa	39	85
Other Africa	36	86
East Asia	5	11
Other Asia	25	21

Source: Erzan *et al.* (1989).
[a] Includes tariffs and para-tariffs.
[b] Measured as a percentage of import lines covered by non-tariff barriers. The data on both tariffs and NTBs reported here are weighted averages.

the provision of effective social programmes to the poorest segments of society. As a result, in the early 1980s this region, which is well endowed with natural resources, had levels of poverty that surpassed those in the resource-poor Asian countries.[3]

This new market-oriented perspective on economic development has been pioneered by Chile, which in the mid-1970s embarked in a unilateral process of structural reform. The Chilean process was consolidated in early 1990 when the newly elected democratic government of President Patricio Aylwin decided to support and further the market oriented reforms initiated during the Pinochet regime. In the late 1980s and early 1990s, more and more countries in the region have followed Chile, and have implemented sweeping trade reforms. Perhaps the most ambitious liberalization project has been that undertaken by Mexico through the North American Free Trade Agreement (NAFTA).

There is little doubt that the debt crisis unleashed in 1982 played an important role in reshaping policy views regarding development strategies, growth policy and long-term growth in Latin America. Politicians sensed that the inward-oriented policies followed by the majority of the region since the Second World War were no longer sustainable. The poor performance of the Latin American countries offered a dramatic contrast to the rapidly growing East Asian countries that had aggressively implemented outward-oriented strategies (see Table 1.2). Suddenly, this difference in performance which had been documented by the academic literature on trade orientation, became a fundamental topic in the public policy debate.

In the 1980s, economists dealing with Latin America, as well as with other developing areas, began to recommend with increasing insistence development strategies based on market-oriented reforms that included as a fundamental component the reduction of trade barriers and the opening of international

Table 1.2 Growth and exports in Latin America and East Asia, 1965–1989.

	Annual rate of growth of real GDP (%)		Annual rate of growth of manufacturing (%)		Annual rate of growth of exports (%)	
	1965–80	1980–9	1965–80	1980–9	1965–80	1980–9
Selected Latin American countries						
Argentina	3.5	−0.3	2.7	−0.6	4.7	0.6
Brazil	8.8	3.0	9.8	2.2	9.3	5.6
Chile	1.9	2.7	0.6	2.9	7.9	4.9
Colombia	5.8	3.5	6.4	3.1	1.4	9.8
Mexico	6.5	0.7	7.4	0.7	7.6	3.7
Peru	3.9	0.4	3.8	0.4	1.6	0.4
Venezuela	3.7	1.0	5.8	4.9	−9.5	11.3
Latin America and Caribbean (average)	6.0	1.6	7.0	1.5	−1.0	3.6
Selected East Asian countries						
Hong Kong	8.6	7.1	n.a.	n.a.	9.5	6.2
Indonesia	8.0	5.3	12.0	12.7	9.6	2.4
Korea	9.6	9.7	18.7	13.1	27.2	13.8
Malaysia	7.3	4.9	—	8.0	4.4	9.8
Singapore	10.1	6.1	13.2	5.9	4.7	8.1
Thailand	7.2	7.0	11.2	8.2	8.5	12.8
East Asia (average)	7.2	7.9	10.6	12.6	10.0	10.0

Source: International Financial Statistics, IMF, ECLAC (1991).

trade to foreign competition. Even the staff of the United Nations Economic Commission for Latin America (ECLA), at one time the most ardent supporter of protectionist policies, began to favour outward orientation. Moreover, the World Bank, the International Monetary Fund and other multilateral institutions routinely required the developing countries to embark on trade liberalization and to open up their external sector as a condition for receiving financial assistance. The collapse of the Communist system in Central and Eastern Europe in the late 1980s and early 1990s added impetus to the analysis of policy reform and structural adjustment. The opening of the external sector and convertibility of the currency are, in fact, at the centre of almost every reform package proposed to former Communist nations.

In spite of the recent move towards trade reform in most of Latin America, there still remain some controversies regarding some aspects of trade policies. A particularly important area of disagreement refers to whether trade liberalization packages have played an important role in the performance of the outward-oriented economies. Lance Taylor (1991, p. 119) has recently offered a strong anti-trade reform view, arguing that "the trade liberalization strategy is intellectually moribund," and that there are "no great benefits (plus some loss) in following open trade and capital market strategies" (p. 141). From here he goes on to say that "development strategies oriented internally may be a wise choice towards the century's end" (p. 141).

The purpose of this paper is to analyse the recent trade reforms in Latin America. The analysis is carried out within a historical framework, and tries to isolate the lessons from successful as well as failed liberalization attempts. The paper is organized as follows: section I is the introduction; section II discusses how decades of protectionist policies affected the economic structure in Latin America, and deals with some important policy aspects of trade liberalization reforms. Especial emphasis is given to the accumulated lessons from several reform programmes. Section III addresses, in some detail, the recent Latin American trade reforms, and discusses both the policies implemented as well as the way in which these programmes have impacted the Latin economies. The discussion concentrates on Chile and Mexico, two of the early Latin reformers. Section IV analyses in some detail the recent evolution of real exchange rates in Latin America, investigating whether the recent concern among Latin observers for the massive real exchange rate appreciations in the region are warranted. In particular, section IV focuses on whether this recent trend in real exchange rate behaviour is likely to have some bearing on the future sustainability of trade reforms in the region. Finally, section V contains a discussion on the lessons that can be obtained from Latin America's history with trade reforms for the case of Mexico and NAFTA. This analysis provides a political economy-based interpretation of the benefits of the North American Agreement for Mexico.

II FROM PROTECTIONISM TO LIBERALIZATION: ANALYTICAL ASPECTS

The recent trade liberalization programmes in Latin America have sought to reverse the protectionist policies that for decades have been at the heart of the region's development strategy. In order to place these reforms in perspective it is useful to first analyse the way in which the protectionist policies affected the economic structure of Latin America, and to discuss what were the expected effects of the liberalization policies.

II.1 The economic consequences of protectionism

Latin America's long tradition of protectionist policies moulded the region's economic structure in a fundamental way. Perhaps the most important consequence of protectionism was that, from early on, high import tariffs and prohibitions generated a severe anti-export bias that discouraged both the growth and diversification of exports. In an early study using data from the 1960s, Bela Balassa (1971) found that the Latin American countries in his sample – Brazil, Chile and Mexico – had some of the most distorted foreign trade patterns in the world. These findings coincided with those obtained by Little *et al.* (1971) in their pioneer study on trade policy and industrialization in the developing world. These authors persuasively argued that the high degree of protection granted to manufacturing in Latin America resulted in a serious discrimination against exports, in resource misallocation, inefficient investment and deteriorating income distribution. They further argued that the reversal of the protectionist policies should be at the centre of any reformulation of Latin America's development strategy. However, at the time these proposals were being made, Latin America was still moving strongly in the opposite direction, pushing protectionist policies to a global level through the formation of custom unions with high common external tariffs.

The discouragement of exports activities took place through two main channels: first, import tariffs, quotas and prohibitions increased the cost of imported intermediate materials and capital goods used in the production of exportables, reducing their effective rate of protection. In fact, for years a vast number of exportable goods, especially those in the agricultural sector, had *negative* rates protection to their value added. Second, and perhaps more important, the maze of protectionist policies resulted in real exchange rate overvaluation that reduced the degree of competitiveness of exports. This anti-export bias explains the poor performance of the export sector, including the inability to aggressively develop non-traditional exports, during the twenty years preceding the debt crisis. Paradoxically, policies which were supposed to reduce Latin America's dependence on the world-wide business cycle, ended up creating a highly vulnerable economic structure where the sources of foreign exchange were concentrated on a few products intensive in natural resources (CEPAL, 1991).

A second important consequence of traditional protective trade policies was the creation of an inefficient manufacturing sector. Instead of granting short-term protection to help launch new activities, high tariffs, quotas and prohibitions became a fixture of the region's economic landscape. What originally were thought to be cases for temporary import protection – based on infant industry arguments – rapidly required permanent protective assistance in order to survive. Rapidly, the system generated a large number of lobbyists that constantly argued for privileged treatment for their particular industries. It is not an exaggeration to say that in many countries, being able to obtain special treatment on protective matters became more important than increasing productivity, developing new products, or implementing technological innovations. As a result of all of this, in most Latin American countries the rate of growth of productivity was very low during the imports-substitution epoch.[4]

An important consequence of the pressures exercised by lobbyists and interest groups was that the protective structure in Latin America became extremely uneven, with some sectors enjoying effective tariff rates in the thousands, and others suffering from negative value added protection.

The ECLA-supported policies also had serious effects on labour markets. In particular, the protection of capital-intensive industries affected the region's ability to create employment. A number of studies have shown that more open trade regimes in the developing countries have resulted in higher employment and in a more even income distribution than protectionist regimes. For example, after analysing in detail the experiences of ten countries, Krueger (1983) concluded that exportable industries tended to be significantly more labour-intensive than import-competing sectors. In the conclusions to this massive study, Krueger argues that employment has tended to grow faster in outward-oriented economies, and that the removal of external sector distortions will tend to help the employment creation process in most developing nations. These results were broadly supported by other cross-country studies, including Balassa (1982) and Michaely et al. (1991).

In terms of income distribution, the protective system generated extremely high benefits to local industrialists, in particular to those able to obtain import licences and concessions – and to urban workers. This, of course, was achieved at the cost of depressing earnings and incomes of rural workers. As can be seen in Table 1.3, during the 1970s income distribution in Latin America was significantly more unequal in Latin America than in Asia.

Table 1.3   Income distribution, historical data: Latin America and Asia.[a]

Country	Year	% of income of lowest 40%	% of income of highest 10%
Latin America			
Argentina	1970	11.1	35.2
Brazil	1972	7.0	50.6
Costa Rica	1971	12.0	39.5
El Salvador	1976–7	15.0	29.5
Mexico	1977	9.9	40.6
Panama	1973	7.2	44.2
Peru	1972	7.0	42.9
Venezuela	1970	10.3	35.7
• Median		10.1	40.1
Asia			
Hong Kong	1980	16.2	31.3
Indonesia	1976	14.4	34.0
Korea	1976	16.9	27.5
Malaysia	1973	11.2	39.8
Philippines	1970–1	14.2	38.5
Thailand	1975–6	15.2	34.1
• Median		14.8	34.1

Source: World Development Report, 1982 and 1986.
[a] The sample is restricted to the group the World Bank classifies as "middle income economies".

To sum up, although several decades of protectionist policies accomplished the goal of creating an industrial sector in Latin America, this was achieved at a high cost. Exports werre severely discouraged, the exchange rate became overvalued, employment creation lagged and massive amounts of resources – including skilled human talent – were withdrawn from the productive sphere and devoted to lobbying for ever-increasingly favourable treatment of different sectors of the economy.[5] An increasing number of comparative studies in the 1970s and 1980s made the shortcomings of the Latin American development strategies particularly apparent. In the aftermath of the debt crisis the long stagnation, and even regression, of the region's export sector – which experienced an average rate of decline of 1 per cent a year between 1965 and 1980 – became particularly painful to the local public, analysts and policy-makers.

II.2   Trade liberalization: expected result and transitional problems

The main objective of trade liberalization programmes is to reverse the negative consequencces of protectionism and, especially, its anti-export bias. According to basic theory, a trade liberalization process will result in a reallocation of resources according to comparative advantage, in a reduction of waste, and in a decline in imported goods prices.[6] Moreover, to the extent that the new trade regime is more transparent – for example, through a relatively uniform import tariff – it is expected that lobbying activities will be greatly reduced, releasing highly skilled workers from "unproductive" jobs. According to traditional theory it is expected that once the negative effective rates of protection and overvalued exchange rates are eliminated, exports will not only grow rapidly, but will also become more diversified.

From a growth perspective, the fundamental objective of trade reforms is to transform international trade into "the engine of growth". In fact, newly developed models of "endogenous" growth have stressed the role of openness.[7] For example, Romer (1989) has developed a model where by taking advantage of larger markets – the world market – an open economy can specialize in the production of a relatively larger number of intermediate goods and, thus, grow faster. Other authors have recently concentrated on the relationship between openness, technological progress, and productivity growth. Grossman and Helpman (1991) and Edwards (1992), for example, have argued that openness affects the speed and efficiency with which small countries can absorb technological innovations developed in the industrial world. This idea, based on an insight first proposed by John Stuart Mill, implies that countries with a lower level of trade distortions will experience faster growth in total factor productivity and, with other things given, will grow faster than countries that inhibit international competition.[8]

In recent papers a number of authors have tried to test the general implications of these theories using cross-country data sets.[9] Although different empirical models have yielded different results, the general thrust of this line of research is that indeed countries with less distorted external sectors appear to grow faster. As Dornbusch (1991) has recently pointed out, openness possibly affects growth not through a single mechanism, but through a combination of channels, including the introduction of new goods, the adoption of new methods of production, the new organization of industries, the expansion in the number of intermediate goods available, and the conquest of new markets that permit the expansion of exports.

The importance placed by liberalization strategists on the reduction of the anti-export bias has resulted in a significant emphasis on the role of exchange rate policy during a trade reform effort. In fact, a number of authors have argued that a large devaluation should constitute the first step in a trade reform process. Bhagwati (1978) and Krueger (1978) have pointed out that in the presence of quotas and import licences a (real) exchange rate depreciation will reduce the rents received by importers, shifting relative prices in favour of export-oriented activities and, thus, reducing the extent of the anti-export bias.[10]

Two fundamental problems have to be addressed in the transition towards freer trade: first, it is important to determine what is the adequate speed of reform. For a long time, analysts argued for gradual liberalization programmes (Little et al., 1971; Michaely, 1985). The reason for this is that, according to these authors, gradual reforms would give firms time for restructuring their productive processes and, thus, would result in low dislocation costs in the form of unemployment and bankruptcies. These reduced adjustment costs would, in turn, provide the needed political support for the liberalization programme. Recently, however, the gradualist position has been under attack. There is an increasing agreement that slower reforms tend to lack credibility, inhibiting firms from actually engaging in serious restructuring. Moreover, the experience of Argentina in the 1970s has shown that a gradual (and pre-announced) reform allows those firms negatively affected by it to (successfully) lobby against the reduction in tariffs. According to this line of reasoning, faster reforms are more credible, and thus tend to be sustained through time (Stockman, 1982).

The thinking on the speed of reform has also been influenced by recent empirical work on the short-run unemployment consequences of trade liberalization. Contrary to the traditional conventional wisdom, a study directed by Michaely et al. (1991) on liberalization episodes in nineteen countries strongly suggests that, even in the short run, the costs of reform can be small. Although contracting industries will release workers, those expanding sectors positively affected by the reform process will tend to create a large number of employment positions. The Michaely et al. (1991) study shows that in sustainable and successful reforms the net effect – that is, the effect that nets out contracting and expanding sectors – on short-run employment has been negligible. A key question, then, is what determines a successful reform? Most historical studies on the subject have shown that maintaining a "competitive" real exchange rate during the transition is one of, if not the most, important determinant of successful trade reform. A competitive, that is depreciated, real exchange rate encourages exports, and helps maintain external equilibrium at the time the reduction in tariffs has made imports cheaper.

The second problem that has to be addressed when designing a liberalization strategy refers to the sequencing of reforms (Edwards, 1984). This issue was first addressed in the 1980s in discussions dealing with the experiences of the Southern Cone (Argentina, Chile and Uruguay), when the macroeconomic consequences of alternative sequences were emphasized. It was generally agreed that resolving the fiscal imbalance and attaining some degree of macroeconomic reform should constitute the first stage of a structural reform. On subsequent steps, most agreed that the trade liberalization reform should precede the liberalization of the capital account, and that financial reform should be implemented simultaneously with trade reform.

The behaviour of the real exchange rate is at the heart of this policy prescription. The central issue is that liberalizing the capital account would, under most conditions, result in large capital inflows and in an appreciation of the real exchange rate (McKinnon, 1982; Edwards, 1984; Harberger, 1985). The problem with this is that an appreciation of the real exchange rate will send the "wrong" signal to the real sector, frustrating the reallocation of resources called for by the trade reform. The effects of this real exchange rate appreciation will be particularly serious if, as argued by Edwards (1984), the transitional period is characterized by "abnormally" high capital inflows, and the economy is characterized by high adjustment costs. If, however, the opening of the capital account is postponed, the real sector will be able to adjust and the new allocation of resources will be consolidated. According to this view, only at this time should the capital account be liberalized.

More recent discussions on the sequencing of reform have expanded the analysis, and have included other markets. An increasing number of authors have argued that reform of the labour market – and in particular the removal of distortions that discourage labour mobility – should precede the trade reform, as well as the relaxation of capital controls. It is even possible that the liberalization of trade in the presence of highly distorted labour markets will be counterproductive, generating overall welfare losses in the country in question (Edwards, 1992). Interestingly enough, the discussions on the sequencing of reform have only addressed in detail the order in which the liberalization of various "real" sectors in society should proceed. For instance only a few studies, such as Krueger (1981) and Edwards (1984), have dealt with the order of reform of agriculture, industry, government (privatization), financial services, and education. The key question here is the extent to which independent reforms will bear all their potential fruits, or whether in a broad-based liberalization process the reforms in different sectors reinforce each other.[11]

As the preceding discussion has suggested, there is little doubt that the behaviour of the real exchange rate is a key element during a trade liberalization transition. According to traditional manuals on "how to liberalize", a large devaluation should constitute the first step in a trade reform process. Bhagwati (1978) and Krueger (1978) have pointed out that in the presence of quotas and import licences a (real) exchange rate depreciation will reduce the rents received by importers, shifting relative prices in favour of export-oriented activities and, thus, reducing the extent of the anti-export bias.[12]

Maintaining a depreciated and competitive real exchange rate during a trade liberalization process is also important in order to avoid an explosion in import growth and a balance of payments crisis. Under most circumstances a reduction in the extent of protection will tend to generate a rapid and immediate surge in imports. On the other hand, the expansion of exports usually takes some time. Consequently, there is a danger that a trade liberalization reform will generate a large trade balance disequilibrium in the short run. This, however, will not happen if there is a depreciated real exchange rate that encourages exports and helps keep imports in check. However, many countries have historically failed to sustain a depreciated real exchange rate during the transition. This has mainly been the result of expansionary macroeconomic policies, and has resulted in speculation, international reserves losses and, in many cases, the reversal of the reform effort. In the conclusions to the massive World Bank project on trade reform, Michaely et al. (1991) succinctly summarize the key role of the real exchange rate in determining the success of liberalization programmes: "The long term performance of the real exchange rate clearly differentiates 'liberalizers' from 'non-liberalizers' " (p. 119). Edwards (1989) used data on thirty-nine exchange rate crises and found that in almost every case, real exchange rate overvaluation led to drastic increases in the degree of protectionism.

II.3   The determinants of successful trade liberalization policies

Two economic aspects of trade liberalization are particularly important for analysing the political economy of transition, and the likelihood of reforms to be sustained through time. First, it takes time for the structural reforms to bear fruit. This means that even though in the long run the reforms will have a positive effect on the aggregate economy, there will be some costs in the short run. These transitional costs, however, will not be even and will affect some groups more than others. Second, even in the long run, some groups will lose, seeing their real incomes diminished. These groups will be those that have benefited from the pre-reform maze of regulations and, under most circumstances, will tend to oppose the reforms from the beginning. Politically, then, trade reforms will only survive if they show some benefits early on, and if these benefits gradually expand, affecting larger and larger segments of society.

The extensive comparative studies by Little *et al.* (1970), Balassa (1971, 1982), Krueger (1978, 1980), Bhagwati (1978) and Michaely *et al.* (1991) have provided abundant evidence concerning the key determinants of a successful trade reform that persists through time, changing the trade structure of a country. These elements can serve as a guide for policy-makers who want to implement trade liberalization policies that will be sustained through time. Existing historical evidence suggests that successful (in the sense of sustained) reforms have been characterized by the following elements:

(1) Exports, and in particular non-traditional exports, expand at a rapid pace that greatly exceeds the historical rate.

(2) Productivity growth increases at a fast pace, helping to generate a rapid overall rate of growth for the economy as a whole.

(3) The trade balance does not exhibit "unreasonable" deficits. If this were to be the case, the public would be sceptical about the viability of the reform, and would speculate against the domestic currency.

(4) The overall level of unemployment stays at a relatively low level.

(5) Real wages exhibit, at least in the medium run, significant increases. In order for this increase in wages to affect a broad sector of society, trade liberalization should be supplemented by other structural reforms aimed at deregulating and liberalizing other sectors of the economy.

The historical evidence has also shown that these "success requirements" become more important in countries that have a democratic political system, than in those countries with *de facto* (military) regimes.

As was suggested in the preceding subsection, real exchange rate behaviour plays an important role in determining whether the above conditions are met. The history of the developing world is replete with trade liberalization attempts that have failed because of the inability to maintain a depreciated exchange rate, and thus because of the failure to unleash a process characterized by rapid productivity growth, export expansion and increasing wages.

III TRADE LIBERALIZATION REFORMS IN LATIN AMERICA: RECENT EXPERIENCES

During the last few years trade liberalization reforms have swept through Latin America; every country in the region has today a significantly more open trade sector than in the early and mid-1980s. The pioneer in the liberalization process was Chile, which between 1975 and 1979 unilaterally eliminated quantitative restrictions and reduced import tariffs to a uniform level of 10 per cent. After a brief interlude with higher tariffs (at the uniform level of 30 per cent) Chile currently has a uniform tariff of 11 per cent and no licences or other forms of quantitative controls. Uruguay implemented a reform in 1978, and after a brief reversal, push forward once again in 1986. Bolivia and Mexico embarked on their reforms in 1985–6, followed by a series of countries in the late 1980s. At the current time a number of countries, including Brazil, are proceeding steadily with scheduled rounds of tariff reduction and the dismantling of quantitative restrictions. However, it is still unclear whether all these reforms will be sustained, becoming a permanent feature of the Latin American economies, or whether some of them will be reversed. Recent (October 1992) developments in Argentina indeed suggest that in some countries higher tariffs might be implemented, once again, in the near future.

The Latin American trade reforms have been characterized by four basic elements:

(1) The reduction of the coverage of non-tariff barriers, including quotas and prohibitions.
(2) The reduction of the average level of import tariffs.
(3) The reduction of the degree of dispersion of the tariff structure.
(4) The reduction or elimination of export taxes.

In this section I document the extent of the recent liberalization programmes, and I provide a preliminary evaluation of the effects of these reforms on productivity growth and exports expansion.[13]

III.1 The policies

III.1.1 Non-tariff barriers

A fundamental component of the trade reform programmes has been the elimination, or at least the severe reduction, of non-tariff barriers. During the early and mid-1980s in some countries, such as Colombia and Peru, more than 50 per cent of import positions were subject to licences or outright prohibitions. In Mexico, NTBs coverage reached almost 100 per cent of import categories in 1984, as was the case in most of Central America in 1984 (Table 1.1).

Table 1.4 contains data on protectionism in 1985–7 and 1991–2,[14] shows that in almost every country the coverage of NTBs has been dramatically reduced. In fact, in a number of cases NTBs have been fully eliminated. The

Table 1.4 The opening of Latin America – selected countries.

Country	Tariff protection (tariffs plus para-tariffs, unweighted averages)		Coverage of non-tariff barriers (unweighted averages)		Range of import tariffs					
						1980s %			Current %	
	1985	1991–2	1985–7	1991–2	Year	Min	Max	Year	Min	Max
Argentina	28.0	15.0	31.9	8.0	1987	0.0	55.0	1991	0.0	22.0
Bolivia	20.0	8.0	25.0	0.0	1985	0.0	20.0	1991	5.0	10.0
Brazil	80.0	21.1	35.3	10.0	1987	0.0	105.0	1992	0.0	65.0
Chile	36.0	11.0	10.1	0.0	1987	0.0	20.0	1992	11.0	11.0
Colombia	83.0	6.7	73.2	1.0	1986	0.0	200.0	1991	0.0	15.0
Costa Rica	92.0	16.0	0.8	0.0	1986	1.0	100.0	1992	5.0	20.0
Ecuador	50.0	18.0	59.3	na	1986	0.0	290.0	1991	2.0	40.0
Guatemala	50.0	19.0	7.4	6.0	1986	1.0	100.0	1992	5.0	20.0
Mexico	34.0	4.0	12.7	20.0	1985	0.0	100.0	1992	0.0	20.0
Nicaragua	54.0	na	27.8	na	1986	1.0	100.0	1990	0.0	10.0
Paraguay	71.7	16.0	9.9	0.0	1984	0.0	44.0	1991	3.0	86.0
Peru	64.0	15.0	53.4	0.0	1987	0.0	120.0	1992	5.0	15.0
Uruguay	32.0	12.0	14.1	0.0	1986	10.0	45.0	1992	10.0	30.0
Venezuela	30.0	17.0	44.1	5.0	1987	0.0	135.0	1991	0.0	50.0

Source: World Bank, UNCTAD, and Erzan *et al.* (1989).

process through which NTBs have been eased has varied from country to country. In some cases, such as Honduras, they were initially replaced by (quasi-) equivalent import tariffs, and then slowly phased out. In other countries, like Chile, NTBs were rapidly eliminated without a compensating hike in tariffs.

As Table 1.4 shows, in spite of the progress experienced in the last few years, significant NTB coverage remains in a number of countries. In most cases these non-tariff barriers correspond to agricultural products. For example, in Mexico approximately 60 per cent of the agriculture sector's tariff positions were still subject to import licences in mid-1992. In fact, an important feature of the region's liberalization programmes is that they have proceeded much slower in agriculture than in industry. This has largely been the result of the authorities' desire to isolate agriculture from fluctuations in world prices and unfair trade practices by foreign countries.[15] However, as a recent study by Valdes has shown (1992), this approach based on NTBs entails serious efficiency costs. Slowly, however, more and more countries are addressing these concerns by replacing these quantitative restrictions by variable levies.[16]

III.1.2   Tariff dispersion

The import substitution development strategy pursued for decades in Latin America created highly dispersed protective structures. According to the World Bank (1987), Brazil, Chile and Colombia had some of the broadest ranges of effective rates of protection in the world during the 1960s. Also, Heitger (1987) shows that during the 1960s Chile had the highest rate of tariff dispersion in the world – with a standard deviation of 634 per cent – closely followed by Colombia and Uruguay. Cardoso and Helwege (1992) have pointed out that highly dispersed protective structures generate high welfare costs, by increasing uncertainty and negatively affecting the investment process. These highly dispersed tariffs and NTBs were the result of decades of lobbying by different sectors to obtain preferential treatment. As the relative power of the different lobbies changed, so did their tariff concessions and the protective landscape.

An important goal of the Latin American trade reforms has been the reduction of the degree of dispersion of import tariffs. Table 1.4 contains data on the tariff range for a group of countries for two points in time – the mid-1980s (1985–7) and 1991–2 – and clearly document the fact that the reforms have indeed reduced the degree of tariff dispersion. In many cases, reducing tariff dispersion has meant *increasing* tariffs on goods that were originally exempted from import duties. In fact, Table 1.4 shows that in many countries the minimum tariff was zero per cent in the mid-1980s. Generally, zero tariffs have been applied to intermediate inputs used in the manufacturing process.[17] From a political economy perspective, the process of raising some tariffs, while maintaining a pro-liberalization rhetoric, has not always been easy. Those sectors that had traditionally benefited from the exemptions, suddenly saw their privileged situation come to an end and tried to oppose them strongly.

An important question addressed by policy-makers throughout the region concerns the degree to which tariff dispersion should be reduced? Should the reforms implement a uniform tariff, or is some (small) degree dispersion desirable? From a strict welfare perspective, uniform tariffs are only advisable under very special cases. However, they have a political-economy appeal. In particular, a uniform tariff system is very transparent, making it difficult for the authorities to grant special treatment to particular firms or sectors (Harberger, 1990).

III.1.3 Average tariffs

Reducing the average degree of protection is, perhaps, the fundamental policy goal of trade liberalization reforms. Traditional policy manuals on the subject suggest that once the exchange rate has been devalued and quantitative restrictions have been reduced or eliminated, tariffs should be slashed in a way such that both their range and average are reduced.[18] Table 1.4 contains data on average total tariffs (tariffs plus para-tariffs) in 1985 and 1991–2. As can be seen, the extent of tariff reduction has been significant in almost every country. Even those nations that have acted somewhat cautiously in the reform front, such as Brazil and Ecuador, have experienced important cuts in import tariffs, allowing a more competitive environment, and reducing the degree of anti-export bias of the trade regime.

Countries that have embarked on trade liberalization in recent years have moved at a much faster speed than those nations that decided to open up earlier. There has, in fact, been a clear change in what we perceive as "abrupt and rapid" removal of imports impediments. What only fifteen years ago were seen as brutally fast reforms, are now looked on as mild and gradual liberalizations. When Chile initiated trade reform in 1975, most analysts thought that the announced tariff reduction from an average of 52 per cent to 10 per cent in four and a half years was an extremely aggressive move that would cause major dislocations, including large increases in unemployment. The view on the speed of reform has changed considerably in the early 1990s, when an increasing number of countries have been opening up their external sectors very rapidly. For instance, Colombia slashed (total) import tariffs by 65 per cent in one year, reducing them from 34 per cent in 1990 to 12 per cent in 1991. This rapid approach to liberalization has also been followed by Argentina, Peru and Nicaragua. This latter country eliminated quantitative restrictions in one bold move and slashed import tariffs from an average of 110 per cent in 1990 to 15 per cent in March of 1992.

III.1.4   Exchange rate policy

In the vast majority of the countries, the first step in the recent trade reform processes was the implementation of large (nominal) devaluations. In many cases this measure represented a unification of the exchange rate market. Most countries implemented large exchange rate adjustments as early as 1982 in order to address the urgency of the adjustment process. The purpose of these policies was to generate real exchange rate devaluations, as a way to reduce the degree of anti-export bias of incentives systems.

Many countries adopted crawling peg regimes, characterized by a periodic small devaluation of the nominal exchange rate, as a way to protect the real exchange rate from the effects of inflation. Although these policies helped avoid the erosion of competitiveness, they also added fuel to the inflationary process. They introduced a certain degree of inflationary inertia, and have contributed in many countries to the slow reduction of the rate of inflation. More recently, a number of countries have begun to use the exchange rate as an anchor in order to bring down inflation. This has resulted in the slowing down of the rate of crawl below inflation differentials or, in some cases, in the fixing of the exchange rate, as in Argentina and Nicaragua.

Table 1.5 contains data on real exchange rates for a group of LAC countries for 1980, 1987 and 1991. As is customary in Latin America, an increase in the index represents a real exchange rate depreciation and thus an improvement in

Table 1.5   Real exchange rates in selected Latin American countries.

Country	1970	1985=100 1980	1987	1991
Argentina	78.7	35.8	80.7	44.0
Bolivia	98.3	88.1	107.9	112.1
Brazil	51.9	70.7	78.0	51.4
Chile	29.4	55.3	94.8	83.0
Colombia	86.1	79.2	115.9	126.3
Costa Rica	58.4	65.8	94.9	97.2
Ecuador	118.6	105.6	153.3	173.7
Mexico	86.1	83.3	123.9	77.0
Paraguay	104.6	74.4	111.4	114.3
Peru	59.3	77.1	46.1	23.1
Uruguay	73.0	49.7	77.2	62.0
Venezuela	80.3	84.2	134.8	132.8

Source: International Financial Statistics, IMF.

the degree of competitiveness. As can be seen between 1980 and 1987, almost every country in the sample experienced very large real depreciations. In many cases, however, these have been partially reversed in the last few years. This has been the consequence of a combination of factors, including the inflow of large volumes of foreign capital into these countries since 1990, and the use of the exchange rate as the cornerstone of the disinflation policies. I return to this issue in Section IV of this paper.

III.2 Trade liberalization and productivity growth

The relaxation of trade impediments has had a fundamental impact on the region's economies. Suddenly, Latin America's industry, which to a large extent had developed and grown behind protective walls, was forced to compete. Many firms have not been able to survive this shock, and have become bankrupt. Others, however, have faced the challenge of lower protection by embarking on major restructuring, and increasing their level of productivity.

The ability (and willingness) of firms to implement significant adjustment depend on two main factors: the degree of credibility of the reform, and the level of distortions in the labour market. If entrepreneurs believe that the reform will not persist through time, there will be no incentive to incur the costs of adjusting the product mix and of increasing the degree of productive efficiency. In fact, if the reform is perceived as temporary, the optimal behaviour is not to adjust; instead it is profitable to speculate through the accumulation of imported durable goods. This was, as Rodriguez (1982) has documented, the case in Argentina during the failed reforms of Martinez de Hoz.[19]

In their studies on the interaction between labour markets and structural reforms Krueger (1980) and Michaely et al. (1991) found that most successful trade reforms have indeed resulted in major increases in labour productivity. In most cases where this has happened, labour markets have been characterized by some degree of flexibility. Countries with rigid and highly distorted labour markets – including countries with high costs of dismissal, limitations on temporary contracts and rigid minimum wage legislation – have generally exhibited modest improvements in labour productivity after the reform process.

Some of the early Latin American reformers have experienced important labour productivity improvements. For example, according to Edwards and Cox-Edwards (1991), labour productivity in the Chilean manufacturing sector increased at an average annual rate of 13.1 per cent between 1978 and 1981. On the other hand, the available evidence suggests that the increase in labour productivity in the Mexican manufacturing sector in the post-reform period has been more moderate. According to Sanchez (1992), labour productivity in Mexico's manufacturing sector increased at an annual rate of 3.8 per cent between 1986 and 1991. Still, this figure is more than double the historical annual rate of growth of labour productivity in the manufacturing sector between 1960 and 1982 – 1.6 per cent.

As discussed above, recent models of growth have suggested that countries that are more open to the rest of the world will exhibit a faster rate of technological improvement and productivity growth than countries that isolate themselves from the rest of the world. From an empirical point of view, this means that countries that open up their external sectors, and engage in trade liberalization reforms, will experience an *increase* in total factor productivity growth, relative to the pre-reform period.

Table 1.6 contains data on the change in aggregate total factor productivity growth in the period following the implementation of trade liberalization reform in six Latin American countries.[20] As can be seen, Chile and Costa Rica, two of the earlier reformers, experienced very large increases in TFP growth in the post-reform period. The results for Chile coincide with those obtained by Edwards (1985), who found that in the late 1970s, after the trade reforms had been completed, TFP growth was approximately three times higher than the historical average.[21] Although the outcome has been less spectacular, Argentina and Uruguay still exhibit substantial improvements in productivity growth in the period following the opening up. Bolivia, on the other hand, presents a flat profile of TFP growth. Sturzenegger (1992) argues that the very slow improvement in Bolivian productivity growth has been, to a large extent, the result of negative terms of trade shocks and, in particular, of the collapse of the tin market.

Perhaps the most interesting and puzzling result in Table 1.6 is the slight

Table 1.6 Changes in total factor productivity growth.

	% change[a]
Argentina	1.91
Bolivia	0.11
Chile	4.96
Costa Rica	3.25
Mexico	−0.32
Uruguay	2.02

Source: Martin (1992).
[a] For all countries but Chile, computed as the difference of TFP growth for 1987–91 and 1978–82. For Chile, the pre-reform period is 1972–8.

decline in aggregate TFP growth in Mexico after the reforms. Martin (1992) shows that this finding is robust to alternative methods of measuring TFP growth, including different procedures for correcting for capacity utilization. Also, Harberger (1992) has found a slowing down of TFP growth in Mexico in 1986–90 relative to 1975–82.[22] However, the aggregate nature of the TFP growth data in Table 1.6 tends to obscure the actual sectoral response to trade reform in Mexico. According to new theories on endogenous growth, faster productivity will be observed in those sectors where protectionism has been *reduced*, and not in those still subject to trade barriers or other forms of regulations.

A distinctive characteristic of the Mexican reform is that, contrary to the Chilean case, it has been uneven. In particular, while most of the manufacturing sector – with the exception of motor vehicles – has experienced a significant reduction in protection, agriculture continues to be subject to relatively high tariffs and substantial non-tariff barriers. Moreover, until very recently the Mexican land tenure system was subject to substantial legal distortions that, among other things, severely restricted the market for land – the *ejido* system. Although most agricultural sector regulations were legally eliminated in early 1992, these reforms still have to have a practical impact. The reason for this is that the titling process, where property rights are actually assigned, is only in its infancy.[23] Also, during much of the post-debt crisis period, large fragments of the services sector in Mexico – including telecommunications and financial services – were under direct government control and subject to distortions.

Table 1.7 contains data on TFP growth in Mexico's manufacturing sector for 1940–89.[24] Interestingly enough, these figures indicate that in the post-trade reform period the rate of productivity growth in the Mexican manufacturing sector has exceeded that of every sub-period since 1940, for

Table 1.7 Total factor productivity growth in manufacturing in Mexico, 1940–1990.

	Manufacturing TFP growth (%)
1940–50	0.46
1950–60	0.53
1960–70	3.00
1970–80	n.a.
1985–9	3.40

Sources: The data for 1940–80 are from Elias (1992). The figure for 1985–9 is from Ibarra (1992).

which there are data. This provides some evidence in favour of the view that, once the sectors actually subject to increased competition are considered, Mexican productivity growth has indeed improved after the trade reform. (See Table 1.8 for detailed data.)

It should be noted, however, that in spite of its improvement with respect to historical rates, recent TFP growth in manufacturing in Mexico has not been as large as in Chile's post-reform period where, as can be seen in Table 1.9, some sectors experienced growth in TFP of the order of 15 per cent in 1978–82. There are a number of possible explanations for this marked difference in behaviour between the Chilean and Mexican experiences, including the uncertainties about NAFTA's approval, which resulted in the postponement of investment in some of the key manufacturing sectors subject to increased foreign exposure.

III.2.1 Trade reforms and exports

An important goal of the reforms has been to reduce the traditional degree of anti-export bias of Latin American trade regimes, and to generate a surge in exports. In fact, based on the East Asian model, Latin American leaders have increasingly called for the transformation of the external sector into the region's "engine of growth".

It is expected that the reduction of the traditional anti-exports bias will take place through three channels: a more competitive – that is more devalued – real exchange rate; a reduction in the cost of imported capital goods and intermediate inputs used in the production of exportables; and a direct shift in relative prices in favour of exports.

Table 1.8 Disaggregated productivity growth in Mexico's manufacturing sector, 1985–1990.

Division	Labour productivity (% growth)	Total factor productivity (% growth)
Food, beverages, and tobacco	1.7	3.4
Textiles and apparel	0.7	0.4
Wood products	0.2	3.4
Paper and printing	2.3	4.8
Chemicals, rubber, and plastics	2.3	2.3
Non-metallic products	1.1	3.5
Metal products	7.5	3.5
Machinery	4.4	4.7
Other manufacturing	−4.8	n.a.
Total manufacturing	2.3	3.4

Source: Ibarra (1992).

Table 1.9   Labour productivity and TFP growth in the manufacturing sector, Chile.

Code	Industry name	% Variations in Y/L (1974–8)	TFP (1974–8)	% Variations in Y/L (1978–82)	TFP (1978–82)
High capital intensive					
353	Petroleum and coal products	14.04	16.76	16.45	14.68
372	Non-ferrous metal	−29.40	−30.27	10.89	11.78
371	Iron and steel	−18.71	−22.13	10.40	9.36
341	Paper products	10.51	12.45	11.05	3.45
369	Non-metallic products	20.17	20.37	12.75	8.92
314	Tobacco	27.13	22.76	8.30	6.54
362	Glass	13.44	12.55	16.58	6.62
351	Industrial chemical	−8.00	−13.92	20.37	12.65
Intermediate capital intensive					
311	Food products	11.21	11.32	3.09	−1.07
321	Textile	8.53	7.58	5.06	1.25
361	Pottery	11.07	9.74	−16.25	−21.31
342	Printing	21.47	20.96	6.33	3.31
313	Beverage	7.67	7.18	13.20	8.37
355	Rubber products	−4.41	−5.30	2.76	−1.04
Low capital intensive					
323	Leather products	−6.03	−5.07	0.05	−3.06
383	Electrical machinery	−8.03	−13.16	1.92	−2.73
381	Metal products	3.98	2.75	−1.01	−3.87
352	Other chemical products	0.01	−0.77	7.35	4.37
322	Clothing and footwear	10.87	10.39	6.85	4.33
382	Machinery	11.67	9.89	−4.28	−6.75
331	Wood products e.f.	20.54	17.33	11.90	4.06
332	Furniture e.m.	21.27	21.03	−0.05	−0.59

Source: Fuentes (1992).

The volume of international trade in Latin America, and in particular the volume of exports, increased significantly after the reforms were initiated.[25] For example, while for the region as a whole the volume of exports grew at an annual rate of only 2.0 per cent between 1970 and 1980, it grew at a rate of 5.5 per cent between 1980 and 1985, and at an annual average of 6.7 per cent between 1986 and 1990.[26] Although, strictly speaking, it is not possible to fully attribute this export surge to the opening-up reforms, there is significant country-specific evidence suggesting that a more open economy, and in particular a more depreciated real exchange rate, has positively affected exports growth.[27] Some countries, especially Costa Rica, have accompanied the opening-up process with the implementation of a battery of export promotion schemes, including tax credits – through the "Certificado de Abono Tributario" – duty free imports and income tax exemptions. However, some

authors, including Nogues and Gulati (1992), have argued that these systems
have not been an effective way of encouraging exports.

Table 1.10 presents detailed country-level data on the rate of growth of the
total value of exports (in constant dollars) for three different periods. Table
1.11, on the other hand, contains information on the evolution of exports
volume throughout the period. A number of facts emerge from these tables.
First, while there has been a rapid growth in exports for the region as a whole,
there are non-trivial variations across countries; in some cases there has even
been a decline in the real value of exports – this is the case, for example, of
Peru. Second, exports performance during the two sub-periods (1982–7 and
1987–90) has not been homogeneous. In the majority of the countries, exports
performed significantly better during 1987–90 than in the previous five years,
reflecting, among other things, the fact that it takes some time for exports to
actually respond to greater incentives.

An interesting fact that emerges from these tables is that in the country that
has lagged behind most in terms of trade reform – Ecuador – the performance
of exports volume has been, in the recent years, below the 1970–80 historical
average. On the other hand, in two of the early reformers – Bolivia and Chile –
exports have had a very strong performance in the 1987–90 sub-period.

The case of Chile is particularly interesting. Since most of its liberalization
effort was undertaken prior to 1980, there are enough data points to provide a
more detailed evaluation of export response to the new regime. Between 1975
and 1980 – when tariffs were reduced to a uniform 10 per cent and NTBs were
completely eliminated – the behaviour of Chilean exports was spectacular,
growing (in volume terms) at an average of 12 per cent per year – many times

Table 1.10   Value of exports of goods and non-factor services.

Country	1972–80	Annual growth rates, constant 1990 prices, US$ 1982–7	1987–91
Argentina	7.1	2.6	10.3
Bolivia	−1.8	0.6	11.4
Brazil	8.8	9.7	3.4
Chile	15.2	6.5	10.5
Colombia	4.9	10.2	6.6
Costa Rica	4.3	3.8[a]	9.1
Ecuador	6.7	3.3	9.2
Mexico	7.9	6.0	5.1
Paraguay	6.7	4.8	20.2
Peru	2.6	−3.7	0.9
Uruguay	10.0	4.2	7.1
Venezuela	−7.3	3.6	5.6

Source: World Bank, ECLAC.
[a] Changes over period 1981–7.

Table 1.11   Volume of exports.

Country	Annual growth rates 1972–80	1982–7	1987–91
Argentina	2.1	0.8	15.2
Bolivia	−1.7	−5.2	16.5
Brazil	8.2	8.0	2.4
Chile	7.4	7.6	7.5
Colombia	3.6	14.8	6.3
Costa Rica	3.8	6.2[a]	8.6
Ecuador	14.6	6.8	7.6
Mexico	10.2	6.1	5.2
Paraguay	7.3	9.2	27.1
Peru	2.3	−4.0	1.3
Uruguay	5.4	−0.5	8.1
Venezuela	−5.8	2.1	8.3

Source: World Bank, ECLAC.
[a] Changes over period 1981–7.

higher than the historical average of 1960–70 of only 2.6 per cent per annum. What is particularly impressive is that most of the exports surge has taken place in the non-traditional sector (CEPAL, 1991).

The story of Chile's success in the last few years is largely the story of the boom in agriculture exports. During the 1960–70 period, Chile was basically a net importer of agricultural goods. Today, on the other hand, agriculture exports – as well as those of forestry and fishing – are becoming increasingly important in the Chilean economy. In 1970, Chile exported US$33 million in agriculture, forestry and fishing products; by 1991 this figure had jumped to US$1.2 billion! Notice that this figure excludes those manufactured goods based on the elaboration of the agriculture, forestry and fishing sectors.

Table 1.12 contains data on agriculture exports for the 1989–91 period. Two interesting developments can be seen from this table. First, fresh fruits exports are becoming increasingly important; second, grapes are becoming a clearly dominant export. Table 1.13 contains data on the evolution of total

Table 1.12   Agriculture exports, 1989–1991.

	US$ millions 1989	1990	1991
A. Fresh fruits	343.5	740.8	991
A.1 Grapes	273.9	379.3	495.0
B. Other agriculture	153.1	142.7	144.9

Source: Banco Central de Chile.

Table 1.13 Fruit production, 1987/8–1990/1.

	Thousands of TRS			
	1987/8	1988/9	1989/90	1990/1
Plums	85.0	98.5	110.0	100.0
Apricots	14.5	16.0	19.5	11.2
Peaches	92.4	97.4	112.0	113.0
Lemons	60.0	72.5	86.0	88.0
Apples	630.0	660.0	690.0	750.0
Oranges	96.0	99.0	97.2	99.0
Avocados	28.0	39.0	37.6	39.0
Pears	99.0	119.0	139.6	165.0
Grapes	516.0	547.0	660.0	650.0

Source: Banco Central de Chile.

fruits output in the 1987–91 period. Although these figures clearly show the predominant role of grapes in Chile's fruit sector, they also indicate that other fruits are rapidly expanding. This is particularly the case for apples and plums.

However, the story of Chile's success in the agriculture sector is not relegated to fruits. Production has also increased significantly in more traditional crops, many of which are mostly devoted to domestic consumption. What is particularly interesting is that much of the increased agriculture production in the country has been the result of rapidly improving productivity. This is clearly illustrated in Table 1.14, which presents yield data for cereals, vegetables and industrial crops for the 1986–91 period. As can be seen, in almost every crop there has been a steep increase in productivity in the last few years. These figures are particularly impressive if compared with historical data. For example, in the 1969/70 agriculture year, wheat's yield was only 12.5 quintals per hectare; that of corn was 32.4 tonnes per hectare; and that of potatoes was only 95.4 tonnes per hectare.

There is little doubt that economic policy lies behind the stellar behaviour of the Chilean agriculture and export sectors in the last few years. First, the liberalization of international trade substantially lowered the costs of agriculture imported inputs and capital goods, making the sector more competitive. In fact, the liberalization of international trade put an end to a long trend of discrimination against agriculture. This, as was pointed out above, contrasts sharply with the other early Latin American reformer, Mexico, where agriculture has not yet benefited from the very recent liberalization measures, including the reform of the old *ejido* system. Second, the exchange rate policy pursued aggressively since 1985 has provided clear incentives for the expansion of exports. However, as is discussed in some detail in section IV, the current trend towards real exchange rate appreciation represents a cloud over the future of the sector. A third fundamental policy-based explanation of the agriculture success has to do with the pursuit of a

Table 1.14   Chile: Yields of most important agricultural products, 1986/7–1990/1.

	Quintals per hectare				
	1986/7	1987/8	1988/9	1989/90	1990/1
A. Cereals					
Wheat	27.1	30.1	32.7	29.5	34.1
Barley	29.5	33.9	34.6	34.8	33.7
Rice	39.3	41.7	43.1	41.7	39.4
Corn	71.2	73.2	75.3	81.4	83.9
B. Vegetables					
Beans	9.5	13.2	11.5	12.7	13.2
Peas	8.6	7.8	8.9	n.a.	n.a.
Potatoes	126.0	149.8	140.6	150.3	142.2
C. Industrial Crops					
Sugar beet	493.6	511.6	544.5	537.5	554.6
Sunflower	21.0	21.0	21.2	23.4	23.9

Source: Instituto Nacional de Estadisticas.

stable macroeconomic policy. This has given entrepreneurs confidence in the system, allowing them to plan their activities over the longer run. Many of the export-oriented agriculture activities have required sizeable investments, that are only undertaken in an environment of stability and policy continuity.

As Tables 1.10 and 1.11 show, Mexico has exhibited a slower rate of growth of total exports in the post-reform period than during 1970–80. This, however, is largely an illusion, stemming from the fact that during the 1970s Mexico's oil production increased very rapidly – at a rate exceeding 18 per cent per year. When non-traditional exports are considered, the post-reform performance is remarkable, the annual average rate of growth for 1985–91 exceeding 25 per cent (see Table 1.15).[28]

A stated objective of trade reforms has been to increase the degree of diversification of exports. Table 1.16 contains data on the share of non-traditional exports (including manufacturing exports) for a large number of countries, and shows that in the period following the trade reforms their importance has increased steadily. Also, in the majority of the countries the share of the ten more important export goods in total exports has declined significantly in the last few years (CEPAL, 1991).

IV   REAL EXCHANGE RATE BEHAVIOUR AND THE FUTURE OF TRADE REFORMS IN LATIN AMERICA

In recent years, competitive real exchange rates have been largely responsible for the vigorous performance of most of Latin America's external sectors. In fact, it is not an exaggeration to say that the trade reforms have been driven by

Table 1.15 Mexico: exports by sector of economic activity.

	Yearly rates of growth									
	1981	1982	1983	1984	1985	1986	1987	1988	1989	1990
Total	29.6	5.6	5.1	8.4	-10.5	-26.0	28.9	-0.4	10.7	17.6
Oil exports	39.6	13.1	-2.8	3.7	-11.1	-57.3	36.8	-21.5	16.3	28.3
Crude petroleum	40.8	17.4	-5.3	1.2	-11.1	-58.1	41.2	-25.3	24.0	22.3
Natural gas	16.7	-8.8	-26.8	-34.6	—	—	—	—	—	—
Oil and petroleum products	43.1	-57.3	182.8	68.6	8.6	-52.6	-1.3	-2.2	-31.4	110.4
Petrochemicals	13.7	-12.8	17.2	18.4	-33.5	-18.7	39.1	124.0	-41.0	81.9
Non-oil exports	9.1	-14.1	32.5	20.6	-9.2	41.0	23.7	14.7	7.9	12.0
Agriculture, livestock and fisheries	-3.0	-16.8	-3.6	22.9	-9.4	59.2	-26.7	8.3	5.0	23.4
Agriculture and forestry	-1.9	-20.4	-11.9	35.1	-12.5	57.0	-27.8	8.1	4.4	17.9
Livestock, hunting and fishery	-16.1	30.8	63.2	-30.6	16.9	73.3	-20.5	9.3	7.7	51.4
Extractive industry	34.2	-27.1	4.6	2.7	-4.5	-0.8	12.9	14.8	-8.5	2.3
Manufacturing	-11.4	12.2	52.3	22.1	-11.0	42.9	39.2	16.3	8.7	10.9
Food, drinks and tobacco	-11.8	4.1	2.5	13.4	-9.1	27.8	37.5	4.3	-7.4	-13.6
Textiles, apparel and leather products	-10.0	-17.1	27.3	44.0	-24.7	65.2	65.5	10.6	-0.5	1.4
Wood products	1.7	-11.9	57.7	19.5	-7.1	17.6	25.2	35.8	8.2	-14.7
Paper, printing and publishing	-5.8	-3.7	-3.8	29.3	2.1	40.4	59.7	45.9	-17.0	-24.5
Chemicals	-21.6	-3.3	42.1	20.4	-10.6	21.3	33.3	27.8	10.0	9.3
Plastic and rubber products	9.5	13.0	69.2	47.7	-23.1	60.0	40.0	39.3	14.7	-29.1
Non-ferrous mineral products	-3.1	12.0	50.0	37.6	9.0	19.4	18.9	17.9	7.6	-7.4
Iron and steel industry	-11.1	75.0	184.8	18.5	-34.9	81.7	40.9	20.5	14.2	12.3
Metallurgy	-42.1	440.0	48.7	-9.3	-21.0	17.6	32.9	29.8	26.3	-6.8
Metal products, machinery and equipment	-4.7	-0.6	87.1	24.7	10.2	32.0	53.1	14.8	9.1	22.9
Other manufacturing industries	4.2	-30.0	114.3	0.0	21.3	-7.7	-19.0	41.2	12.5	17.6

Source: Estadisticas del Comercio Exterior de Mexico.

Table 1.16   Composition of exports of goods.

Country	Non-traditional exports/total				
	1980	1982	1985	1987	1990
Argentina	0.27	0.31	0.28	0.31	0.39
Bolivia	0.15	0.09	0.05	0.19	0.47
Brazil	0.57	0.59	0.66	0.69	0.70
Chile	0.38	0.22	0.35	0.39	na
Colombia	0.41	0.42	0.41	0.55	0.64
Costa Rica	0.36	0.38	0.37	0.42	0.54
Ecuador	0.24	0.09	0.12	0.14	0.10
Mexico	0.13	0.20	0.18	0.38	0.43
Paraguay	0.58	0.71	0.82	0.68	0.65
Peru	0.21	0.23	0.24	0.27	0.29
Uruguay	0.61	0.58	0.66	0.67	0.63
Venezuela	0.04	0.07	0.09	0.13	0.19

Source: ECLAC, *Economic Survey of Latin America*, several issues.

highly competitive real exchange rates, which have made Latin American products very attractive in world markets. Recently, however, in most of these countries real exchange rates have experienced rapid real appreciations, leading to losses in competitiveness (Figure 1.1). These developments have generated considerable concern among policy-makers and political leaders.[29]

These real appreciations (and losses in international competitiveness) have been the result of two basic factors: first, the use, in many countries, of the exchange rate policy as an anti-inflationary tool and, second, massive capital inflows into Latin America that made foreign exchange "over-abundant".

In the late 1980s some analysts, including the staff of the IMF, argued that the crawling peg regimes adopted in most of Latin America after the debt crisis had become excessively inflationary. In particular, it was argued that crawling pegs introduce substantial inflation inertia. According to this view, exchange rate policy in the developing countries should move towards greater rigidity – and even complete fixity – as a way to introduce financial discipline, provide a nominal anchor, and reduce inflation.[30]

A number of Latin countries have, in fact, decided to use an exchange rate anchor as a way to reduce inflation. In practice they have done this by either slowing down the rate of the crawl – as in Mexico and Chile, to some extent – or by adopting a completely fixed nominal exchange rate – as in Argentina and Nicaragua. Much of the recent enthusiasm for fixed nominal exchange rates is intellectually rooted on the modern credibility and time consistency literature.[31] According to this approach, which was pioneered by Calvo (1978) and by Kydland and Prescott (1977), governments that have the discretion to alter the nominal exchange rate – as in the crawling peg system – will tend to abuse their power, introducing an inflationary bias into the economy. The reason for

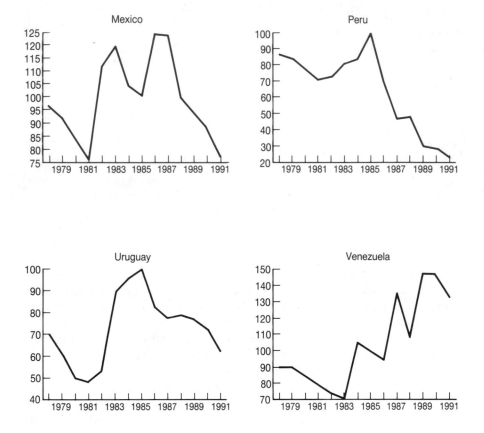

Figure 1.1   Real exchange rates in Latin America (1985 = 100).

this is that under a set of plausible conditions, such as the existence of labour market rigidities that preclude the economy from reaching full employment, it will be optimal for the government to "surprise" the private sector through unexpected devaluations.[32]

However, if the government can credibly precommit itself to maintaining a fixed exchange rate, it will effectively eliminate the temptation to surprise the private sector through unexpected devaluations. Promises of fiscal discipline will become credible and private sector actions will not elicit successive rounds of inflationary actions (Aghevli *et al.*, 1991). In particular, it has been argued that fixed exchange rates provide a reputational constraint on government behaviour. The authorities know that if they undertake an overly expansive credit policy, they will be forced to abandon the parity and devalue. As the recent (mid-1992) crisis of the ERM has shown, exchange rate crises can indeed shatter the reputations of politicians.

In spite of its elegant appeal, this view has, in its simplest incarnation, some serious problems.[33] One of the most serious limitations of the nominal exchange rate anchor policy is that, under almost every circumstance, once the exchange rate is fixed, other prices – including wages – will continue to increase, generating a change in relative prices in favour of non-tradables. This has indeed been the case in both Argentina and Nicaragua, the two countries in the region that have adopted strictly fixed exchange rates as a way to drastically reduce inflation. In both cases the stabilization programmes were based on a severe fiscal correction that virtually eliminated the fiscal deficit, in restrictive credit, and in a nominal exchange rate anchor. Although this policy succeeded in both countries in greatly reducing inflation, it has resulted in serious relative price misalignment. In Argentina this has been reflected in the fact that wholesale price inflation, which is heavily influenced by tradables, is only 3 per cent per year, while consumer price inflation – highly dependent on non-tradables – exceeds 18 per cent per year. In Nicaragua, tradable-related inflation rates have been very low (in the order of 2–3 per cent), while non-tradable inflation has exceeded 30 per cent in the last twelve months.

Mexico followed a variant of the exchange rate anchor policy, announcing a predetermined rate of devaluation at a pace deliberately below ongoing inflation. The purpose of this policy has been to both anchor tradables prices and reduce expectations. However, since domestic inflation has systematically exceeded the predetermined rate of devaluation, Mexico has experienced a sizeable real appreciation which exceeded 35 per cent between 1985 and mid-1992. The Mexican authorities have recently tried to face this problem by accelerating the daily rate of devaluation of the peso from 20 cents to 40 cents. A number of observers, however, have argued that this is not enough, and that in order to restore the required level of international competitiveness to Mexican exports, the rate of nominal devaluation should be significantly faster than 40 cents a day.[34]

The second cause behind the recent generalized real appreciations in Latin America has been the recent large increase in capital inflows into the region. As Table 1.17 shows, after eight years of negative resource transfers, there was a significant turnaround in 1991–2. This increased availability of foreign funds affected the real exchange rate through increased aggregate expenditure. A proportion of the newly available resources has been spent on non-tradables – including real estate – putting pressure on their relative prices and on domestic inflation. An interesting feature of the recent capital movements is that a large proportion corresponds to portfolio investment, and relatively little is direct foreign investment. Table 1.18 provides net capital inflows data by country. As can be seen, Mexico has been the most important recipient of foreign funds in the region in the last years. It has indeed been this very large availability of

Table 1.17 Capital inflows and net resource transfers in Latin America, 1981–1992.

	Net capital inflows	Interest and profit income	Net resource transfers
1982–5	55.3	−111.7	−56.4
1986–9	33.5	−138.7	−105.2
1990	17.0	−35.7	−18.7
1991	36.3	−31.1	5.2
1992[a]	42.8	−21.2	21.6

Source: Jaspersen (1992).
[a] Projection.

Table 1.18 Net capital inflows as a percentage of GDP in selected Latin American countries, 1982–1991.

Country	1982	1983	1984	1985	1986	1987	1988	1989	1990	1991
Argentina	2.4	0.5	3.0	2.9	1.8	2.6	3.9	0.2	1.0	6.3
Brazil	4.2	2.1	1.8	0.1	0.6	1.3	−0.5	0.4	1.3	0.2
Chile	4.4	2.3	8.3	5.0	3.0	3.7	3.7	4.3	7.8	2.5
Colombia	6.5	4.1	2.6	5.9	2.9	0.0	2.1	1.0	0.0	2.8
Mexico	5.6	−1.5	−0.6	−1.2	0.7	−0.7	−0.8	0.8	5.0	10.6
Peru	5.7	2.4	3.4	1.1	2.1	2.3	3.5	1.5	2.4	9.5
Venezuela	−2.5	−6.6	−3.6	−1.8	−1.9	0.8	−1.5	−5.7	−4.1	4.9

Source: IDB, *Economic and Social Progress in Latin America*, 1992.

foreign financing which has allowed that country to have a current account deficit of the order of 5–6 per cent of GDP. An important question, however, is whether the situation will be sustainable through time, or if a decline in the level of funds available is foreseen for the near future.

Real exchange rate appreciation generated by increased capital inflows is not a completely new phenomenon in Latin America. In the late 1970s most countries in the region, but especially the Southern Cone nations, were flooded with foreign resources that led to large real appreciations. The fact that this previous episode ended in the debt crisis has added drama to the current concern on the possible negative effects of these capital flows.

Whether these capital movements are temporary – and thus subject to sudden reversals, as in 1982 – is particularly important in evaluating their possible consequences. In a recent study, Calvo *et al*. (1992) argue that the most important causes behind the generalized inflow of resources are external. In particular, their empirical analysis suggests that the recession in the industrialized world and the reduction in US interest rates are the two main reasons that have triggered these capital movements. These authors suggest that once these world economic conditions change, the volume of capital flowing to Latin America will be reduced. This means that at that point, the pressure over the real exchange rate will subside and a real exchange rate depreciation will be required.

The countries in the region have tried to cope with the real appreciation pressures in several ways. Colombia, for instance, tried to sterilize the accumulation of reserves by placing domestic bonds (OMAs) in the local market in 1991.[35] However, in order to place these bonds the local interest rate had to increase, making them relatively more attractive. This generated a widening interest rate differential in favour of Colombia, which attracted new capital flows that, in order to be sterilized, required new bond placements. This process generated a vicious cycle that contributed to a very large accumulation of domestic debt, without significantly affecting the real exchange rate. This experience shows vividly the difficulties faced by the authorities wishing to handle real exchange rate movements. In particular, this case indicates that real shocks – such as an increase in foreign capital inflows – cannot be tackled successfully using monetary policy instruments.

Argentina has recently tried to deal with the real appreciation by engineering a "pseudo-devaluation" through a simultaneous increase in import tariffs and export subsidies. Although it is too early to know how this measure will affect the degree of competitiveness in the country, preliminary computations suggest that the magnitude of the adjustment obtained via a tariffs-cum-subsidies package may be rather small. Mexico has followed a different route, and has decided to postpone the adoption of a completely fixed exchange rate. In October of 1992 the pace of the daily nominal exchange rate adjustment was doubled to 40 cents. As in the case of Argentina, it is too early to evaluate how effective these measures have been in dealing with the real appreciation trend. However, as pointed out earlier, a number of analysts of the Mexican scene have already argued that this measure clearly was not enough.

Chile has tackled the real appreciation by implementing a broad set of measures, including conducting exchange rate policy relative to a three currencies basket, imposing reserve requirements on capital inflows, and undertaking limited sterilization operations. In spite of this multi-front approach, Chile has not avoided real exchange rate pressures. Between December of 1991 and July 1992 the Chilean bilateral real exchange rate appreciated almost 10 per cent. As a result, exporters and agriculture producers have been mounting increasing lobbying pressure on the government for special treatment, arguing that by allowing the real exchange rate to appreciate, the government has broken an implicit contract. This type of political reaction is, in fact, becoming more and more generalized throughout the region, adding a difficult social dimension to the real exchange rate issue.

Although there is no easy way to handle the real appreciation pressures, historical experience shows that there are, at least, two possible avenues that the authorities can follow. First, in those countries where the dominant force behind real exchange rate movements is price inertia in the presence of nominal exchange rate anchor policies, the adoption of a pragmatic crawling peg system will usually help. This means that, to some extent, the inflationary targets will have to be less ambitious, as a periodic exchange rate adjustment will result in some inflation.[36] However, to the extent that this policy is supplemented by tight overall fiscal policy, there should be no concern regarding inflationary explosions.

Second, the discrimination between short-term (speculative) capital and longer-term capital should go a long way in helping resolve the preoccupations regarding the effects of capital movements on real exchange rates. To the extent that capital inflows are genuinely long-term, and especially if they help finance investment projects in the tradables sector, the change in the RER will be a "true equilibrium" phenomenon, and should be recognized as such by implementing the required adjustment resource allocation.

V   WHAT DOES ALL OF THIS MEAN FOR MEXICO?

The analysis presented above has documented the dramatic change in foreign trade policy in Latin America during the last few years. The region, which for many decades had followed strict protectionist policies, has opened up significantly to the rest of the world. Tariffs have been slashed, NTBs have been eliminated in many countries and the dispersion of protective measures has been greatly reduced. The purpose of these policies has been threefold: first, by eliminating distortions, it is expected that resources will be allocated in a more efficient way, reducing the waste that for many years plagued the region. Second, lower protectionism is expected to reduce the traditional anti-export bias, encouraging exports growth and diversification. And third, the trade reforms are expected to increase productivity growth and help modernize the region. This, in turn, will help improve income distribution over the longer run.

The data analysis presented above shows that, in general, trade reforms in Latin America have helped expand exports and increase productivity growth. This has particularly been the case for Chile, the pioneer Latin American reformer. What is surprising, however, is that our analysis shows that in Mexico, another of the early reformers, the expected positive effects of the reforms have not materialized fully. In fact, comparisons between the Chilean and Mexican cases shows an important difference in export growth and diversification, and productivity improvements. Moreover, when other elements are brought into the analysis – including real wage performance, trade balance evolution and overall real GDP growth – the contrast between the two countries is even more marked (see Tables 1.19, 1.20 and 1.21).

There are several possible explanations for the performance of the Mexican

Table **1.19** Real wages, Chile and Mexico (1980 = 100).

Year	Chile	Mexico
1982	109.1	102.2
1983	97.2	80.7
1984	97.4	74.8
1985	93.5	75.9
1986	95.0	71.5
1987	94.7	71.3
1988	100.9	71.7
1989	102.9	75.2
1990	104.8	77.9
1991	109.5	77.2
1992 (June)	115.2	n.a.

Source: ECLAC.

Table **1.20** Trade balance, Chile and Mexico (US$ millions).

Year	Chile	Mexico
1989	1,578	−645
1990	1,273	−3,026
1991	1,576	−11,063
1992 (May)	857	−7,585

Source: ECLAC.

Table **1.21** Real GDP growth, Chile and Mexico (%).

Year	Chile	Mexico
1988	7.5	1.4
1989	9.8	3.1
1990	2.0	3.9
1991	5.7	4.0
1992[a]	9.7	2.9

Source: ECLAC and author's estimates.
[a] Preliminary.

economy and, in particular, for its contrast with the case of Chile. First, the Chilean reforms have been in place for a much longer period of time – roughly since 1976–7. Second, in Chile the reforms were credible from early on, and towards the late 1970s investment in export-oriented sectors began to boom. Ibarra (1992) has argued that this has not been the case in Mexico. In fact, he documents a very low level of new investment in those sectors with greater comparative advantage. This could reflect the uncertainty introduced by NAFTA into the future of Mexico's trade policy. Investors decided to "wait and see" whether NAFTA was actually implemented before committing themselves to major projects. And third, the fact that in Chile the reforms were broad, affecting many sectors which reinforced each other, contrasts with the piecemeal approach followed by Mexico.

An analysis of the "determinants" of successful trade reforms presented in Section II.3 shows that, in the case of Mexico, some of these requirements have not been met:

(1) Although non-traditional exports have grown rapidly, the actual rate of expansion has not been as spectacular as in Chile and Costa Rica. In fact, after expanding fast in 1983–7, non-oil exports as a percentage of GDP seem to have levelled off at around 6.7 per cent.

(2) As was shown above, aggregate factor productivity growth in Mexico has not increased in the post-reform period. And the rate of

acceleration of productivity growth in manufacturing, although positive, has been only modest.

(3) A positive factor is that unemployment has stayed low – below 3 per cent in the last few years. Additionally, the *Programa de Solidaridad Social* has provided an effective safety net for the poorer segment of society. As a result of this, the transformation of the economy has not been associated with employment dislocations.

(4) Real wages, however, have stayed practically stagnant in the economy as a whole, as well as in manufacturing (see Table 1.20). This, of course, is the reflection of the slow growth in productivity.

(5) The trade balance has become increasingly negative (Table 1.21). This has been possible thanks to the large inflow of foreign capital experienced in the last few years, which has allowed the country to finance the widening gap between imports and exports. There is, however, a clear danger that the public might perceive this large trade deficit as unsustainable in the medium run. This may indeed lead to a loss of credibility in the programme as a whole. As was indicated in the preceding section, the rapid real appreciation experienced by the peso in the last few years has contributed to this widening trade imbalance, affecting overall credibility.

In many ways, the picture described above does not conform with the successful and sustained liberalizations identified in the economics literature.[37] In fact, under "normal" conditions, analysts could be tempted to argue that Mexico's reform would not be long-lived and, under heavy political pressure, would be reversed. However, Mexico is not a "normal" case. It is politically unique and, by promoting NAFTA, the Mexican authorities have been able to provide credibility to the trade reform programme. In particular, by legally tying the government's hands, the approval of NAFTA indicates that, even if the programme has not borne fruits (yet), there will be no turning back towards protectionism and isolationism. By signing NAFTA, the Mexican government has effectively bought credibility, and hopes to greatly reduce the degree of speculation on the possible reversibility of the reforms. In other words, the Mexican government has obtained additional time to show that trade liberalization indeed works and is the appropriate route for the new century.

NOTES

1 On the evolution of economic thinking in Latin America, see the comprehensive review by Fishlow (1985).

2 However, as I have argued in Edwards (1988), in many of the countries in the region this extremely high degree of import protection was the result of the need to cope with the sudden halt in capital inflows following the eruption of the debt crisis in 1982.

3 In the 1970s the poorest 40 per cent of society received 10 per cent of total income in the Latin countries. The corresponding figure for Asian nations was almost 15 per cent.

4 See Elias (1992).

5 Most authors agree that the import substitution process rapidly ran into difficulties once low-technology consumer goods had been "substituted". As countries tried to move towards producing more sophisticated goods – including capital goods and machinery – they faced an increasingly uphill battle. See Hirschman (1968) and Fishlow (1985).

6 Of course, this amounts to the important textbook notion that freer trade increases the level of domestic welfare. However, modern approaches go beyond this goal and also consider the acceleration of growth as a goal of trade policy.

7 Traditional neoclassical growth models concentrated on the effect of national economic policies on the level of income per capita. The new generation of endogenous growth models have shifted attention to the relationship between different policies and the rate of growth of the economy. See Lucas (1988).

8 In Chapter 17 of his *Principles of Political Economy* (1848) Mill said that "a country that produces for a larger market than its own can introduce a more extended division of labour, can make greater use of machinery, and is more likely to make inventions and improvements in the process of production". Arthur Lewis makes a similar proposition in his 1955 classical book on economic growth.

9 See Tybout (1992) for a general survey on empirical models on the relationship between trade orientation and growth of total factor productivity. See also Edwards (1992) and de Gregorio (1992).

10 See Krueger (1978, 1981) and Michaely et al. (1991).

11 Of course, this discussion is related to second-best analysis of policy measures. See Edwards (1992) for a formal multisector model to analyse the welfare consequences of alternative reform packages.

12 See Krueger (1978, 1981) and Michaely et al. (1991).

13 This section is partially based on Edwards (1992).

14 These are *unweighted* averages, and thus are not comparable to those presented in Table 4.1. There has been a long discussion in applied international trade theory on whether tariffs and NTBs should be measured as weighted or unweighted averages. Both views have some merits and some limitations. An obvious problem of the weighted average approach (where the weights are the import shares) is that more restrictive distortions will tend to have a very small weight. In the extreme case, prohibitive tariffs that effectively ban the importation of a particular item will have a zero weight! Corden (1966) provides an early, and still highly relevant discussion on these issues.

15 The issue of protecting local producers from "dumping" is an important one in the design of the new liberalized trade regimes. The crucial problem is to enact legislation that is able to distinguish true cases of unfair trade practices from simple cases of increased foreign competition stemming from more efficient productive processes. At this time the approval of a dynamic and flexible anti-dumping legislation should be high in the region's agenda for legal and institutional reform.

16 See Valdes (1992).

17 This system with very low (or zero) tariffs on intermediate inputs and high tariffs on final goods generated very high rates of effective protection or protection to domestic

value added. In recent years a number of authors have argued that the use of effective protection is misleading. The reason for this is that ERPs are unable to provide much information on the general equilibrium consequences of tariff changes (Dixit, 1986). In spite of this, ERP measures are still useful, since they provide an indication on the degree of "inefficiency" a country is willing to accept for a particular sector.

18 However, "tariffs" is sometimes a misleading term, since many countries have traditionally relied on both import duties (that is tariffs proper) and import duty surcharges or para-tariffs.

19 See Corbo *et al.* (1985) for a detailed microeconomic account of the process of adjustment in a large group of Chilean manufacturing firms.

20 The original TFP growth data comes from Martin's (1992) study on sources of growth in Latin America. The countries in Table 1.6 are those that initiated the reform before 1988. In order to compute series on total factor productivity (TFP) growth, Martin analysed the contributions of capital and labour, and explicitly incorporated the role of changes in the degree of capital utilization. The countries considered in this study are Argentina, Bolivia, Chile, Colombia, Costa Rica, Dominican Republic, El Salvador, Guatemala, Honduras, Mexico, Nicaragua, Panama, Peru, Uruguay and Venezuela. Harberger (1992) presents data on TFP growth before and after a series of historical trade reform episodes. He finds that in the majority of the cases, productivity growth increased after the liberalization process.

21 It may be argued, however, that the major increase in TFP growth in Chile has been the result of the complete structural reform package implemented in that country.

22 It should be noted that this result regarding TFP growth is independent of the date chosen as the first post-reform year. If 1986 – a very bad year for oil exporting countries – is excluded, the overall flavour of the results reported above is still maintained: Mexico's TFP growth has not increased in the post-reform period.

23 A number of observers have argued that the titling process will, by itself, take between five and ten years.

24 Since these figures come from two different sources they may not be fully comparable and, thus, should be interpreted with care.

25 Trade liberalization aims at increasing a country's total volume of trade. Under textbook conditions it is expected that at the end of the reform, trade will be balanced. However, there are a number of circumstances, including the need to pay the country's foreign debt, under which trade will not grow in a balanced way after a reform. This has been the case in the majority of the Latin American countries.

26 The real *value* of exports, however, has evolved at a somewhat slower pace. The reason for this is that terms of trade experienced, in every sub-group of countries, a significant deterioration during 1980–91 (see CEPAL, 1992). These data are from ECLAC (1991).

27 See, for example, Nogues and Gulati (1992).

28 A large percentage of this growth, however, has been in the *maquiladora*, or in-bond sector.

29 See Calvo *et al.* (1992).

30 For a flavour of the discussion within the IMF see, for example, Burton and Guillman (1991), Aghevli *et al.* (1991), Flood and Marion (1991) and Aghevli and Montiel (1991). In Edwards (1992b) I deal with some of these issues.

31 The new impetus for fixed rates has emerged strongly in the International Monetary Fund. See Aghevli *et al.* (1991).

32 This assumes that wages are set before the government implements the exchange rate policy, but after it has been announced.

33 See, for example the discussion in Edwards (1992).

34 Rudi Dornbusch, for example, has recently argued that the daily rate of devaluation of the peso for the next year should be at least 120 cents. See *Excelsior*, Monday, November 23 1992, page 1.

35 An important peculiarity of the Colombian case is that the original inflow of foreign exchange came through the trade account.

36 More specifically, with this option the single-digit inflationary goal will be postponed.

37 As pointed out, the most comprehensive study on the subject is Michaely *et al.* (1991).

REFERENCES

Aghevli, P., M. Khan and P. Montiel (1991) "Exchange Rate Policy in Developing Countries: Some Analytical Issues", *IMF Occasional Paper* **78**.

Balassa, Bela (1971) *The Structure of Protection in Developing Countries*, Baltimore, Johns Hopkins University Press.

Balassa, Bela (1982) *Developing Strategies in Semi-Industrial Economies*, Baltimore, Johns Hopkins University Press.

Barro, R. (1991) "Economic Growth in a Cross Section of Countries", *Quarterly Journal of Economics* **106**(2), 407–43.

Barro, R. and X. Sala-i-Martin (1991) "Convergence across States and Regions", *Brookings Papers on Economic Activity* **0**(1), 107–58.

Behrman, J.R. (1976) *Foreign Trade Regimes and Economic Development: Chile*, Columbia University Press for NBER, New York.

Bhagwati, J. (1978) *Anatomy and Consequences of Exchange Control Regimes*, Ballinger Publishing Co. for NBER, Cambridge MA.

Bianchi, A., *et al.* (1987) "The Adjustment Process in Latin America, 1981–86", in V. Corbo, M. Goldstein and M. Hkan (eds), *Growth-Oriented Adjustment Programs*, IMF and the World Bank, Washington DC.

Bianchi, A., *et al.* (1988) Latin America 1981–1984: Crisis, Adjustment, and Recovery", in M. Urrutia (ed.), *Financial Liberalization and the Internal Structure of Capital Markets in Asia and Latin America*, United Nations University, Tokyo.

Burton, D. and M.G. Guillman (1991) "Exchange Rate Policy and the IMF", *Finance and Development* **28**(3), 18–21.

Calvo, G. (1978) "On the Time Consistency of Optimal Policy in a Monetary Economy", *Econometrica* **46**(6), 1411–28.

Calvo, G., L. Leiderman and C. Reinhart (1992) "Capital Inflows and Real Exchange Rate Appreciation", *IMF Working Paper* 92/62, August.

Cardoso, E. and A. Helwege (1992) *Latin America's Economy: Diversity Trends and Conflicts*, MIT Press, Cambridge MA.

CEPAL (1991) *Equidad y Transformacion Productiva: Un enfoque integrado*, CEPAL, Santiago, Chile.

CEPAL (1992) *Equidad y Transformacion Productiva: Un Enfoque Integrado*, Santiago, CEPAL.

Corbo, V. (1985) "Reforms and Macroeconomic Adjustments in Chile during 1974–84", *World Development* **13**(8), 893–916.

Corbo, V., T. Condon and J. de Melo (1985) "Productivity Growth, External Shocks, and Capital Inflows in Chile: A General Equilibrium Analysis", *Journal of Policy Modeling* 7(3), 379–405.

Corbo, V., and J. de Melo (1985) "Liberalization with Stabilization in the Southern Cone of Latin America: Overview and Summary", *World Development* 13(8), August, 863–6.

Corden, Warner Max (1966) "The Structure of a Tariff System and the Effective Protective Rate", *Journal of Political Economy* 74(3).

Corden, W.M. (1969) "Effective Protective Rates in the General Equilibrium Model: A Geometric Note", *Oxford Economic Papers*, July, 135–41.

Cox-Edwards, A. (1992) "Labor Markets and Structural Adjustment", working paper.

Cukierman, A., S. Edwards and G. Tabellini (1992) "Seigniorage and Political Instability", *American Economic Review*, forthcoming.

de Gregorio, Jose (1992) "Economic Growth in Latin America", *Journal of Development Economics* 39(1).

Diaz-Alejandro, C. (1975) *Essays on the Economic History of the Argentine Republic*, Yale University Press, New Haven, CT.

Diaz-Alejandro, C. (1978) *Foreign Trade Regimes and Economic Development: Colombia*, Columbia University Press for NBER, New York.

Dixit, A. (1985) "Tax Policy in Open Economies", in A. Auerbach and M. Feldstein (eds), *Handbook of Public Economics*, North-Holland, New York.

Dixit, A. (1986) "Trade Policy: An Agenda for Research", in P. Krugman (ed.), *Strategic Trade Policy and the New International Economics*, MIT Press, Cambridge, MA.

Dornbusch, Rudiger (1991) "Policies to Move From Stabilization to Growth", *Proceedings of the World Bank Conference on Development Economics*, Washington, D.C., The World Bank.

ECLAC (1991) *Statistical Yearbook of Latin America*, Santiago, CEPAL.

Edwards, S. (1984) *The Order of Liberalization of the External Sector in Developing Countries*, Princeton University Press, Princeton NJ.

Edwards, S. (1987) "Sequencing Economic Liberalization in Developing Countries", *Finance and Development* 24(1), 26–9.

Edwards, S. (1988) "Structural Adjustment Policies in Highly Indebted Countries", in J. Sachs (ed.), *The Developing Country Debt Crisis*, Chicago University Press, Chicago IL.

Edwards, S. (1989) *Real Exchange Rates, Devaluation, and Adjustment: Exchange Rate Policy in Developing Countries*, MIT Press, Cambridge, MA.

Edwards, S. (1992a) "Trade Orientation, Distortions and Growth in Developing Countries", *Journal of Development Economics* 39(1), 31–58.

Edwards, S. (1992b) *The Sequencing of Structural Adjustment and Liberalization*, ICS Press, San Francisco CA.

Edwards, S., and A. Cox-Edwards (1991) *Monetarism and Liberalization: The Chilean Experiment*, University of Chicago Press, Chicago, IL.

Elias, V. (1992) "Sources of Growth in Latin America", unpublished manuscript.

Erzan, Refik, Kiroaki Kuwahara, Saratino Marchese, and Rene Vossenar (1989) "The Profile of Protection in Developing Countries", *UNCTAD Review* 1 (1).

Fischer, S. (1987) "Economic Growth and Economic Policy", in V. Corbo, M. Goldstein, M. Kahn (eds), *Growth Oriented Adjustment Programs*, IMF and the World Bank, Washington DC.

Fischer, S. (1988) "Symposium on the Slowdown in Productivity Growth", *Journal of Economic Perspectives* 2(4), 3–7.

Fishlow, A. (1985) "Revisiting the Great Debt Crisis of 1982" in K.S. Kim and D.F. Ruccio (eds), *Debt and Development in Latin America*, University of Notre Dame Press, Notre Dame IN.

Fishlow, A. (1991) "Liberalization in Latin America" in T. Banuri (ed.), *Economic Liberalization: No Panacea*, Oxford University Press, Oxford.

Flood, R.P., and P. Isard (1989) "Monetary Policy Strategies", *International Monetary Fund Staff Papers* 36(3), 612–32.

Fuentes, J.R. (1992) "Economic Policies, Human Capital and their Importance in the Process of Growth: Theoretical and Empirical Implications", UCLA Ph.D. Dissertation.

Garcia-Garcia, J. (1991) "Liberalization Foreign Trade: Colombia" in Michaely *et al.* (eds), *Liberalizing Foreign Trade*, Volume 4.

Grossman, G. and E. Helpman (1989) "Product Development and International Trade", *Journal of Political Economy* **97**(6), 1261–83.

Grossman, G. and E. Helpman (1991a) "Quality Ladders in the Theory of Growth", *Review of Economic Studies* **58**(1), 43–61.

Grossman, G. and E. Helpman (1991b) *Innovation and Growth in the Global Economy.* MIT Press, Cambridge MA.

Grossman, G. and E. Helpman (1991c) "Trade, Knowledge Spillovers, and Growth", *European Economic Review* **35**(2–3), 517–26.

Harberger, A. (1985) "Observations on the Chilean Economy, 1973–1983", *Economic Development and Cultural Change* **33**(3), 451–62.

Harberger, A. (1990) "Towards a Uniform Tariff Structure", University of Chicago, mimeo.

Harberger, A. (1992) "The Sources of Economic Growth and Economic Liberalization: With Application to Mexico for the 1990s", UCLA, mimeo.

Heitger, B. (1987) "Import Protection and Export Performance – Their Impact on Economic Growth", *Weltwirtschaftliches Archiv* **123**(2), 249–61.

Hirschman, Albert (1968) "The Political Economy of Import-Substituting Industrialization in Latin America", *Quarterly Journal of Economics* **82**(1).

Ibarra, L. (1992) "Credibility and Trade Reform in Mexico", UCLA, mimeo.

Jaspersen, F. (1992) "External Resource Flows to Latin America: Recent Developments and Prospects", IDB Working Paper.

Krueger, A. (1978) "Alternative Trade Strategies and Employment in LDCs", *American Economic Review* **68**(2), 270–4.

Krueger, A. (1980) "Trade Policy as an Input to Development", *American Economic Review* **70**(2), 288–92.

Krueger, Anne (1981) *Trade and Employment in Developing Countries*, Chicago, University of Chicago Press.

Krueger, Anne (1983) *Exchange Rate Determination*, Cambridge, U.K., Cambridge University Press.

Kydland, F., and E. Prescott (1977) "Rules Rather Than Discretion: The Inconsistency of Optimal Plans", *Journal of Political Economy* **85**(3), 473–91.

Lewis, A.W. (1955) *The Theory of Economic Growth*, Allen & Unwin, London.

Little, I., T. Scitovsky and M. Scott (1971) *Industry and Trade in some Developing Countries*, Oxford University Press for OECD, Oxford.

Lucas, R. (1988) "On the Mechanics of Economic Development", *Journal of Monetary Economics* **22**(1), 3–42.

Martin, R. (1992) "Sources of Growth in Latin America", World Bank, mimeo.

McKinnon, R. (1982) "The Order of Economic Liberalization: Lessons from Chile and Argentina", *Carnegie Rochester Conference Series on Public Policy* **17**, 159–86.

Michaely, M. (1982) "The Sequencing of Liberalization Policies: A Preliminary Statement of The Issues", unpublished manuscript.

Michaely, Michael (1985) "The Demand for Protection Against Exports of Newly Industrialized Countries", *Journal of Policy Modelling* **7**(1).

Michaely, M. (1988) "Liberalizing Foreign Trade: Lessons from Experience", unpublished manuscript.

Michaely, M., A. Choski and D. Papageorgiou (1991) (eds) *Liberalizing Foreign Trade*, Blackwell, Oxford.

Mill, J.S. (1884) *Principles of Political Economy*, D. Appleton and Co., New York.

Nogues, J. (1991) "Liberalizing Foreign Trade: Peru" in Michaely *et al.* (1991), *Liberalizing Foreign Trade*, Volume 4.

Nogues, Julio, and Sunil Gulati (1992) "Economic Policies and Performance Under Alternative Trade Regimes: Latin America During the 1980s", LAC Technical Department Report No. 16, Latin America and the Caribbean Region, Washington, D.C., The World Bank.

Persson, T., and G. Tabellini (1990) "Macroeconomic Policy, Credibility and Politics", *Fundamentals of Pure and Applied Economics* **38**.

Rodriguez, C. (1982) "The Argentine Stabilization Plan of December 20th", *World Development* **10**(9), 801–11.

Romer, P. (1989) "Capital Accumulation in the Theory of Long-Run Growth", in R. Barro (ed.), *Modern Business Cycle Theory*, Harvard University Press, Cambridge, MA.

Roubini, N. and X. Sala-i-Martin (1991) "Financial Development, Trade Regime and Economic Growth", *Center Discussion Paper* 646, Economic Growth Center, Yale University, New Haven, CT.

Roubini, N. and X. Sala-i-Martin (1992) "A Growth Model of Inflation, Tax Evasion and Financial Repression", *Center Discussion Paper* 658, Economic Growth Center, Yale University, New Haven, CT.

Sanchez, Manuel (1992) "Entorno Macroeconomico Frente al Tratado de Libre Comercio" in ITAM, *Mexico y el Tratado de Libre Comercio*, Mexico City, ITAM/McGraw-Hill.

Sturzenegger, F. (1992) "Bolivia: Stabilization and Growth", UCLA, mimeo.

Summers, R. and A. Heston (1988) "A New Set of International Comparisons of Real Product and Price Levels Estimates for 130 Countries, 1950–1985", *Review of Income and Wealth* **34**(1), 1–25.

Taylor, L. (1991) *Varieties of Stabilization Experience: Towards Sensible Macroeconomics in the Third World*, World Institute for Development Economics Research, Studies in Development Economics, Oxford, New York, Toronto and Melbourne.

Tybout, James (1992) "Linking Trade and Productivity: New Directions", *The World Bank Economic Review* **6**(2).

Valdes, A. (1992) "The Performance of the Agricultural Sector in Latin America", The World Bank, mimeo.

World Bank, *World Development Report 1982*, Washington, D.C., World Bank.

World Bank, *World Development Report 1986*, Washington, D.C., World Bank.

World Bank (1987) *World Development Report*, Washington, D.C., The World Bank.

2 | The External Sector and the Latin American Economy in the 1990s: Is There Hope for Sustainable Growth?

ALICIA PUYANA*

I INTRODUCTION

There is evidence of economic recovery in Latin America, at least if only the major macroeconomic variables are considered. Fresh data corroborate the fact that inflation, the secular malady of the region, was fading to just 23 per cent in 1992, down from nearly 1,000 per cent in the early 1990s. For the first time since the debt crisis exploded, capital flows are positive. Trade reforms have been instituted to eliminate the distortions of the import substitution model, while in many Latin American countries, foreign reserves are accumulating and per capita domestic income has started to increase.

Some doubts arise, nevertheless, about the robustness of the recovery and the sustainability of growth. First, capital inflow has been attracted by relatively high interest rates and may reverse when the United States and other developed countries come out of recession. Furthermore, in many countries currency overvaluation counteracts export promotion, and the debt overhang restricts public expenditure and investment. Finally, it is not clear how long the strict adjustment model can continue to contract employment and domestic demand, aggravating the conditions of poverty.

This chapter will concentrate on the role that Latin American foreign trade policies and the international trade environment will play in sustaining economic growth in the region. As a framework for the analysis of foreign trade prospects for Latin America, this paper will consider the early effects of economic reforms on trade patterns, relevant new factors in the international

* The author thanks Ana Maria Mendez for her help in gathering and processing basic data and for discussing the content of this chapter. The author takes sole responsibility for its content.

trading system, and finally, new elements that will affect programmes of regional economic integration.

II RECENT TRENDS

Latin American exports have grown far more rapidly since the debt crisis began than was the case in the preceding decade. Indeed, as Table 2.1 suggests, the average rate of growth in export volume since 1984 has been more than twice that in the period 1974–83. This stands in contrast to slower rates of growth in gross domestic product. Although export growth has been strong, real export earnings have been held back by deteriorating terms of trade. Thus success in export expansion has not gone far to finance modernization, nor to regain the lost growth in employment experienced during the last decade.

In the context of Latin American export potential, it is important to note that commodity export prices have fallen in real terms so far that, today, relative prices of commodities are estimated to be at the lowest levels ever recorded. It is widely believed that prices will not recover their pre-1982 levels and that they may even drop further. The extensive decline in relative commodity prices since the mid-1980s has been on an unprecedented scale and cannot be seen as simply a continuation of earlier tendencies (Boughton, 1991).[1]

Along with the decline in relative prices, exports of commodities have suffered from price volatility. In the period 1970–90, the standard deviation of changes in commodity prices was twice as large as that for manufactured goods. The liberalization of international markets for commodities and the increased number of suppliers may make this instability even more pronounced. The decline in relative prices has been reinforced by an increase in price volatility, and both phenomena together aggravated balance of payments problems precisely when the debt crisis was at its most severe. At the same time, trade liberalization stimulated imports.

To some extent, the weak terms of trade reflect recession in the OECD

Table 2.1   Latin America: output and foreign trade.

| | Annual changes (%) | | | | | |
	1974–83	1984–8	1988	1990	1992	1994–7
Export volume	2.0	4.0	8.1	4.6	5.0	5.7
Real GDP	3.1	2.9	0.7	−0.1	2.7	5.0
Terms of trade	1.4	−3.6	−0.7	−1.2	−0.6	0.5

Source: IMF (1992) *World Economic Outlook*, May.

countries. Output growth in the developed countries is an important element in the determination of commodity prices. It has been estimated, for example, that an annual increase of 1 per cent in industrial countries' output will push up prices of non-fuel commodities by 2 per cent in real terms (Gilbert, 1990). During the last twenty years, the economies of the major developed countries were negatively affected by four periods of recession in the United States (1973–4, 1979–80, 1981–2 and 1990–1), during which highly volatile exchange rates and inflationary pressures coincided. Furthermore, increases in interest rates tend to depress prices of some commodities, and the dollar's depreciation has weakened the value of many commodities (and manufactures) originating and sold outside the United States that trade at dollar prices. The collapse of commodity agreements was an additional element. Some of these agreements (coffee, cocoa, sugar) had helped to avoid extreme oscillations, both up and down, in prices.

III THE NEW EXPORT-ORIENTED MACROECONOMIC MODEL: IS THERE MORE OPENNESS?

The new economic model pursued by Latin American countries introduces a combination of two different processes that do not necessarily have to coincide in time: adjustment and stabilization policies, and the liberalization of foreign trade. The import substitution policies pursued by Latin American countries (and elsewhere) during several decades were dismantled in a couple of years. As Rodrick (1992) notes, "Since the early 1980s, developing countries have flocked to free trade as if it were the Holy Grail of economic development." As the same author argues, the deep macroeconomic crisis of the early 1980s enabled policy-makers to introduce controversial trade reforms. The high distributional costs that such reforms brought about were overshadowed by the crisis itself:

> desperate policy-makers packaged reforms in the fiscal, monetary and exchange rate areas – which were intimately linked to the crisis – with reforms in commercial policies – which were by and large only incidental. The depth of the crisis reduced distributional considerations to second-order importance and eliminated previous resistance.[2]

The objectives of the reforms in general and of those in the trade regimes are manifold: to reverse the loss of competitiveness in international markets in order to regain export dynamism and larger shares of world trade; to overcome the inefficient allocation of productive factors and to reduce unemployment; to advance to a new industrialization process at higher levels of productivity; to create an environment conducive to domestic and foreign private investment and to increase the rate of capital formation; to sustain macroeconomic stability and to reduce inflation. As in the import substitution model, economic integration is presented as a complementary element of the general strategy.

Successful liberalization of trade policies ("to put prices right") will presumably bring about sustained growth in the coefficient of imports and exports to GDP, considered a proxy for the degree of openness of an economy. Thus, the ratio should be larger than during the inward-looking model. It can be assumed that lower import tariffs and export taxes will have the effect of reducing the domestic prices of importables and exportables. As a result, the degree of openness of an economy is inversely associated with changes in relative prices (the ratio of local prices of importables to exportables). The more open an economy (that is, the smaller the level of import substitution), the smaller the relative price. Production and export structures should move towards comparative advantage and, if the exchange rate is properly established, no excessive trade deficit will occur.

In principle, if the export sector has higher productivity than the rest of the economy, in those countries which are reallocating resources toward exports, the export–GDP ratio should increase and these economies should grow faster. Although the impact of exports on GDP growth is not as strong as is frequently assumed,[3] the relationship could be strong in the case of relatively industrialized Latin American countries, such as Argentina, Brazil, Mexico, and perhaps Colombia. However, stronger trade orientation could actually result in a lower rate of output during a period of weak world demand.

Although tariffs were drastically reduced for some sectors, in several Latin American countries maximum nominal tariff levels still approach 35–40 per cent. Effective tariff levels might be even higher than this, as a relatively large set of non-tariff barriers remain, such as quotas (for vehicles and parts in Argentina and Mexico) and health regulations or import licences for some agricultural or basic products (Mexico, Colombia). Additionally, strong revaluation has been taking place since 1985 in the majority of countries, which reinforces the effect of dismantling import restrictions but does not advance export production.

In a long-term view, the picture that emerges in Latin America is rather surprising. The ratio of imports and exports to GDP has tended to fall, so that the value of trade for 1991 is lower than in 1960, despite the export push of the 1980s aimed at financing debt obligations and a minimum level of imports. (See Table 2.2.) The ratio of imports to GDP in 1990 was 68 per cent lower than in 1960 or 1980. With the exception of Chile, no country has substantially increased its import coefficient. The debt crisis and the fall of export commodity prices negatively affected the import capacity of Latin American economies. The persistent economic slowdown of imports in developed countries and the resulting deceleration of world trade help to explain the drop

Table 2.2   Latin American trade, 1960–1990.

Ratio exports–GDP	1960	1970	1980	1985	1990
World	9.0	10.2	17.7	15.1	14.4
USA	4.0	4.3	8.2	5.4	6.9
Latin America	13.9	10.7	12.9	13.5	12.1
Argentina	8.9	7.5	5.2	12.8	13.2
Brazil	8.6	6.4	8.4	11.2	7.5
Chile	13.4	16.7	16.9	23.9	30.8
Colombia	11.5	10.2	11.8	10.2	16.4
Ecuador	15.5	11.3	30.1	11.8	18.0
Peru	21.8	16.6	22.6	20.7	16.9
Mexico	6.1	3.9	8.4	12.5	11.2
Venezuela	30.1	27.0	32.5	19.8	35.6

Ratio imports–GDP	1960	1970	1980	1985	1990
World	9.6	10.7	18.2	16.0	15.0
USA	3.2	9.3	13.3	18.7	9.6
Latin America	14.0	11.0	14.0	9.6	9.6
Argentina	10.4	7.1	6.8	5.8	4.4
Brazil	10.0	6.7	10.4	6.3	5.4
Chile	14.5	12.6	18.6	17.1	25.2
Colombia	12.9	11.7	14.0	11.9	13.6
Ecuador	12.1	16.4	19.2	11.1	13.1
Peru	18.6	10.0	14.5	14.1	16.2
Mexico	9.5	6.9	10.4	7.9	11.8
Venezuela	15.5	15.9	20.0	13.3	13.2

Ratio total trade–GDP	1960	1970	1980	1985	1990
World	18.6	20.9	24.9	21.1	29.4
USA	7.2	13.6	21.5	24.1	16.5
Latin America	27.9	21.7	26.9	23.1	21.7
Argentina	19.3	14.6	12.0	18.6	17.6
Brazil	18.6	13.1	18.8	17.5	12.9
Chile	27.9	29.3	35.5	41.0	56.0
Colombia	24.4	21.9	25.8	22.1	30.0
Ecuador	27.6	27.7	99.3	22.9	31.1
Peru	40.4	26.6	37.1	34.8	32.1
Mexico	15.6	10.8	18.8	20.4	23.0
Venezuela	45.6	42.9	52.5	33.1	48.8

Source: International Financial Statistics, Supplement on Trade Statistics (Washington 1987) World Bank World Development Report 1992.

in the export ratio to GDP. Paradoxically, Latin America is not more open now than it was in 1960 or 1970 when import substitution was fully implemented and the region's trade/GDP ratio was higher than the world ratio. Moreover, the share of imports in the total trade/GDP ratio is lower now than in the period 1960–80, indicating that there are forces preventing an increase in competition in domestic markets.

The "reinsertion of Latin America in the world economy" also looks rather elusive. In 1991, the share of Latin America in total world exports was 4.2 per cent, slightly higher than the period 1987–90 but significantly lower than the whole 1950–80 period. (See Table 2.3.) It looks like the "outward-looking, export growth model" has not yet been established. The slow-down of the world economy, the contracting world demand for commodities, and the structure of Latin American exports could explain this outcome.

III.1   Changes in the composition of exports

As a result of the reduction in the level of protection and decreased dispersion in tariffs, we expect the composition of production to change, since sectors or sub-sectors with higher productivity should grow faster. If, in the meantime, the currency is overvalued, as is now the case in the majority of Latin American countries,[4] liberalization could induce contraction in the industrial sector. If devaluation occurs, sectors in which a particular country has a comparative advantage will grow faster than the rest of the economy, and will become more competitive in domestic and international markets.

It is perhaps too early to register substantial changes in the structure of production and the sectoral composition of GDP as a result of liberalization and adjustment. At the two-digit level, the composition of GDP in 1990 was identical to that of fifteen years ago. Nonetheless, the product structure of

Table 2.3 Latin American participation in global commerce, 1950–1990.

Year	Exports[a]	Imports[a]
1934–8	9.4	6.3
1948	12.5	10.1
1950	11.1	9.6
1960	7.7	7.7
1970	5.5	5.7
1980	5.5	5.9
1985	4.5	6.1
1987	4.0	4.7
1989	3.9	4.8
1990	3.8	4.5
1991	4.2	4.3

Source: IMF, *Direction of Trade Statistics* (various issues).
[a] As a percentage of total world exports or imports.

exports has experienced a transformation that started in the 1970s and accelerated in the last decade. Exports of manufactured goods today represent 32.2 per cent of total exports, registering the highest growth rate for the period 1979–89, while minerals and fuels accounted for 34.5 per cent of earnings. (See Table 2.4.) During the last two years, there have been signs that exports of food products, agricultural raw materials and minerals expanded in relative terms, thanks to the contraction of fuels.

It has been suggested that in those countries in which liberalization started in the 1970s – Argentina, Chile and Uruguay – a recomposition of the industrial sector took place in favour of "Ricardian"-type products. There was significant growth in food products, furniture, wood and wood products, paper and paper products, food products, leather products and non-metallic mineral products and in the chemical, aluminium and steel sectors, which were

Table 2.4 Latin American market structure of exports by main products, 1970–1989 (%).

	World total	EC	USA	Japan	SE Asia	Latin America
Food						
1965	42.0	52.4	38.8	17.7	13.1	19.0
1970	40.9	51.8	38.3	35.4	29.7	17.6
1980	29.1	38.2	21.3	19.2	39.8	12.1
1989	28.3	42.1	17.5	21.6	23.4	15.4
Agriculture/raw minerals						
1965	8.2	11.1	4.4	38.9	53.6	6.0
1970	5.8	7.5	1.9	18.5	44.6	5.6
1980	3.1	5.0	1.1	8.3	11.3	2.4
1989	4.0	5.1	2.1	5.6	13.3	4.6
Ores/minerals						
1965	14.4	17.4	18.9	32.1	2.4	5.9
1970	17.7	26.2	16.7	38.4	0.7	4.8
1980	9.5	15.7	5.8	36.1	20.3	5.0
1989	11.8	17.8	6.8	38.5	20.5	7.9
Fuels						
1965	29.9	16.7	3.16	10.2	25.0	55.3
1970	24.7	8.2	32.4	3.9	10.8	46.0
1980	42.4	29.1	61.4	25.3	12.1	49.4
1989	22.7	11.9	36.7	15.7	1.6	23.8
Manufactures						
1965	5.2	2.4	5.7	0.9	6.0	13.4
1970	10.6	6.2	10.2	3.7	13.5	25.0
1980	14.7	11.0	9.9	10.7	16.3	30.3
1989	32.2	22.1	36.1	18.4	41.2	48.1

Source: Unctad, *Handbook of International Development Statistics*, 1992.

relatively more protected. In all three countries, a relative or absolute contraction took place in capital goods, textiles, clothing, footwear, metal products, machinery and rubber products.

New patterns of comparative advantage in manufactures seem to be emerging in the processing of natural resourccs and labour-intensive products. In the larger and higher-income countries (Brazil and Mexico), the production of relatively more technology-intensive goods appears to be expanding. In a few of the smaller countries, in which natural resources are less abundant, comparative advantage may eventually emerge in high-tech services, such as data processing, communications and exclusive tourism. Population size and the level of industrial development will dictate the eventual product mix.

The resource endowment of the region provides information about the products in which comparative advantage, in static terms, could lay. In theory these products will lead the economic growth of the region. Apart from oil and oil products, which represent the single largest export from Latin America, accounting for 45 per cent of total exports, the region supplies 15 per cent of the world demand for refined metal. The main products (in world order) are: silver, tin, iron, antimony, molybdenum, fluorite, copper and bauxite. There is potential for increasing the production of these minerals and metals above world rates, since the region's share of world mineral reserves is higher than its share in world production, particularly in the case of bauxite, copper, lithium, mercury, molybdenum, nickel and zinc.

The extent to which this potential is realized will be determined by the capacity of the region to attract foreign investment, which in turn depends on world demand for mineral and global markets for capital. As in the past, new investments in minerals could turn out to be highly concentrated, both in terms of products and countries. Worldwide, some 75 per cent of investment in this sector is projected to go to only three minerals – bauxite-aluminium, copper and iron-steel – and in Latin America, 70 per cent of these metals are found in Brazil, Chile and Peru.

After oil and minerals, Latin America has an important potential in agricultural products, with exports amounting to around 25 per cent of total earnings. The actual trade pattern of agricultural exports is heavily concentrated in sales of agricultural raw materials and unprocessed food products. There is an important margin for new lines of specialization, for example, in edible oils and their derivatives, fresh and processed fruit and vegetables, tobacco, fish and fish products, paper and wood products.

After more than forty years of attempted import substituting industrialization (ISI) and almost fifteen years of export promotion policies, the region's record in exports of manufactured goods has been at best mixed. Exports of manufactured goods grew at annual rates of 12.8 per cent during 1970–9 and 9.8 per cent for 1980–7. But the share in world exports remained low – 2.3 per cent in 1987, and by 1989 it dropped to just 1.8 per cent.[5] In ten countries of the region, manufactured exports in 1987 had a smaller share in total external sales than five years earlier. Finally, exports of manufactures are extremely concentrated, and increasingly so. Around 80 per cent of the Latin American total exports of manufactured goods in 1987 originated in Brazil, Mexico and Argentina – up from 65 per cent in 1975. The manufacturing sectors in which exports grew most dynamically were machinery and transport equipment, basic manufactures and chemicals.

Latin America's real comparative advantage lies in labour-intensive products, such as leather and footwear; in technology-intensive goods, it is also competitive in iron and steel, explosives, fertilizer, wood products and inorganic chemicals. This product mix reflects the fact that the region has not fully developed its potential for processing minerals and metals, in which the region is rich.

Table 2.5 shows the main product groups in which the region demonstrates "revealed comparative advantage", that is, a capacity to expand shares in the importing countries' markets. An interesting overlap exists, indicating that countries are competing in international markets in a rather small range of products, the majority of which are labour-intensive, standardized and final non-durable consumption goods. Leather and wood products have been identified as highly competitive in nine countries; clothing appears in eight. This high degree of similarity suggests a common range in factor endowments and a relatively low level of industrial development.

It is perhaps not yet possible to detect important changes in the structure of exports as a result of liberalization policies, since in the short run, exports will continue to rely primarily on the existing productive and export capacity. New investments are needed to develop new export products, but it is well known that during the last decade no important investment flow took place and domestic savings were almost nil. Foreign capital has started to flow into the region, but with no clear sign that it will go to finance long-term investment.

The concentration of Latin American exports in raw materials (mainly fuels and food) and labour-intensive goods makes it more difficult to increase the export/GDP ratio, since the price and income elasticity of demand for those goods is low, especially in the developed countries to which Latin America exports. Dependence on minerals and primary goods during a period of slow or no growth in the world economy will retard Latin America's recovery. Moreover, given the linkages from export instability to short-term income and macroeconomic instability,[6] it is probable that Latin America will continue to confront shocks due to the instability of commodity prices and high dependence on their exports.

IV THE IMPACT OF GLOBAL TRADE CONDITIONS

Latin American economic growth, trade expansion, and integration programmes will be affected by the economic prospects of the developed countries, the

Table 2.5 Latin American revealed comparative advantage in manufactures, 1987.

Product group	Arg	Bol	Col	Guat	Mex	Par	T&T	Bah	Bra	C.Ric
Leather (61)	20.96	0.52	2.74			11.3			2.42	
Inorganic chemicals (52)	3.47	0.10								
Textiles/yarn/fabrics (65)	0.68									
Wood/cork (63)		1.27			0.73	1.05	1.98		0.92	
Travel goods (83)			4.47							
Clothing (84)			1.27							
Essential oil, perfumes				2.05						
Plumbing/heating/light (81)				0.65	1.13					
Non-metal mineral products (66)					1.13					
Dyes, tanning products (86)						1.04				
Fertilisers (56)							14.41			
Iron/steel (67)							1.20		3.70	
Medical/pharmaceutical (54)						1.96				
Plastic materials (58)								-0.05		
Explosives (57)									17.68	
Footwear (85)									7.87	
Furniture (82)										0.69
Organic chemicals (51)							5.05	7.34		

Product group	Hond	Nic	Per	Uru	Bar	Chi	Ec	Jam	Pan	E.Sal	Ven
Leather (61)	0.11			26.05	−0.11						
Inorganic chemicals (52)									−0.03		
Textile/yarn/fabrics (65)			2.65						−0.28		
Wood/cork (63)	3.59	0.13				2.98	1.1				
Travel goods (83)		−0.15		3.55							
Clothing (84)			0.90	5.01	−0.13		0.8	1.2	1.12	0.09	
Essential oil, perfumes										0.07	
Plumbing/heating/light (81)						0.37					0.05
Non-metal mineral products (66)											
Dyes, tanning products (86)											
Fertilisers (56)							186.2				
Iron/steel (67)											
Medical.pharmaceutical (54)											0.27
Plastic materials (58)											
Explosives (57)			5.74			0.59					
Footwear (85)										0.92	
Furniture (82)	0.7	−0.14						0.34			−0.02

Source: Lord and Bounturi (1992).

outcome of the Uruguay Round of GATT negotiations, the completion of the Single European Market and the possibility of economic recovery in ex-socialist countries. After a period of strong growth during the 1970s and 1980s, in which trade expanded faster than output, the growth of international trade in goods decelerated, and the difference between world trade and GNP growth declined. (See Table 2.6.) Forecasts suggest that although trade will expand faster than GNP, there will not be a return to the sort of differentials which existed before the 1970s. As the latest projections of the IMF for 1992–3 suggest, the increased difference between the two growth rates is first a result of the slow-down in GDP growth.

Expansion of trade during the 1950–70 period was assisted by the reduction of barriers to trade, low world inflation and interest rates, and by the huge transfers of financial capital from developed to developing countries. These forces weakened from the mid-1970s onwards, and are unlikely to recover fully in the medium term.

As a defensive response to the export effort of developing countries, the industrialized world has resorted to non-tariff barriers to trade, which at present cover nearly 20 per cent of OECD imports. Anti-dumping actions, rules of origin and local content, voluntary export restraints and export quotas affect those sectors in which Latin American countries are most competitive: textiles, clothing, steel products, beverages, travel goods, shoes and several agricultural products.

IV.1   The Uruguay Round

The current Uruguay Round of the GATT is the most complex and ambitious round ever attempted. It covers areas which were largely neglected in past negotiations, such as agriculture, or which were relegated to special regimes, such as clothing and textiles, which fell under the Multifibre Arrangement (MFA). It also involves a variety of new sectors and issues, such as trade-related investment measures (TRIMS), trade in services and trade-related aspects of intellectual property (TRIPS).

Difficulties in the Uruguay Round have strengthened the trend toward

Table 2.6   World trade and GDP growth.

Growth rate (%)	1950–60	1960–70	1970–80	1980–88	1990	1992	1993
World trade	6.5	8.3	5.2	4.0	3.0	4.5	6.3
World GDP	4.2	5.3	3.6	3.0	2.2	1.4	3.6
Difference	2.3	3.0	1.6	1.0	1.9	3.1	2.7

Sources: For 1950–88: World Bank (1991) *The World Economy and the Prospects for Developing Countries*, Washington DC. For 1990–3: IMF (1992) *World Economic Outlook*, May.

bilateral or multilateral trade negotiations. The problems that have made it impossible to reach any substantive agreement can be better understood if the historical context in which the round took place is considered. In the first place, the massive character of the negotiations (more than one hundred negotiators, rather than selected groups, as was the case in previous rounds), necessarily reduces the speed and scope of the agreements. Second, the United States, with its universal trade relations and high trade deficit, finds it more convenient to solve trade conflicts bilaterally than in the larger arena of the GATT table (Fishlow and Haggard, 1991). Third, since the round was launched, the world economy has suffered instability and recession, which make it difficult to agree on topics such as the elimination of agricultural subsidies and the dismantling of the MFA. The integration of the ex-socialist countries and China into the international financial institutions of the post-war world will also necessarily affect world trade, since those countries will play a different role as trade partners.

It now looks clear that the negotiations will end with a rather poor result. Such an outcome will leave Latin America with few gains, if any, in crucial areas such as agriculture and textiles, and will commit the region to a progressive opening of its domestic economies to external competition. Latin America will have to compete with the subsidized exports of the EC and the USA. The announcement in October 1992 by President Bush that 30 million tonnes of subsidized American wheat would be put on the market was only the most recent signal of the protectionist mood in developed countries.

IV.2 European integration and its implications for LDCs

The advantages derived by the European Community (EC) from its closer integration are clear. In macroeconomic terms, it should provide the basis for growth, lower inflation and lower unemployment. Comparative advantages and economies of scale can be better exploited, while greater specialization and competition should lead to lower costs, higher productivity and greater innovative potential.

All these factors could imply both positive and negative effects for Latin America. On the positive side, if it leads to higher EC incomes, it will provide growing demand for extra-EC imports. Some authors estimate that this income growth effect could increase developing countries' primary exports by as much as $5.1 billion. Of this increase, $4.0 billion would relate to fuels and $1.0 billion to agricultural products. The income effect of the Single European Market (SEM) for member countries could mean 1.5 per cent extra GDP growth, which would in turn translate into a 0.1 per cent induced growth for Latin America – much less than the 0.5 per cent calculated for Asian countries. This is because it is the United States, and not the EC, which is Latin America's main trade partner.

The elimination of national trade restrictions and preferential bilateral arrangements should also help to redistribute trade towards the most competitive suppliers. The case of bananas is illustrative. Elimination of national restrictions would cause serious losses to a number of Caribbean and African countries, but benefit Latin American suppliers.

But there will also be negative effects. First, there is concern over the possible emergence of more restrictive common external barriers which will protect otherwise adversely affected "sensitive" sectors and which may postpone internal adjustment. This is likely to be the case in agriculture, which will continue to be heavily protected from external competition. In particular, for Latin American countries it will become more difficult to penetrate export markets with labour-intensive products. At the same time, raising the level of EC minimum standards, like technical and health requirements, will serve to exclude certain products.

Economic relations between Latin America and the EC, however, have weakened over the long term[7] and Latin America has received scant attention in terms of the EC's scheme of regional economic preferences. This means that the region may suffer more than the rest of the world if the economic effects of 1992 turn out to be negative for the countries outside the Community. By the same token, if those effects are positive, Latin America will probably gain less.

IV.3   Changes in Eastern Europe and LDCs

Recent developments in Eastern Europe are likely to have a significant effect on the trade relations between the EC, the USA and developing countries. The countries of Eastern Europe are better placed than LDCs to penetrate the EC market. On the other side, increased income growth in these countries (due to economic restructuring, increased market access and lower defence spending) should encourage LDC exports. It is widely acknowledged, however, that the magnitude of the current economic crisis in the region means that this effect is unlikely to take place in the near future.

Developments in Eastern Europe and the former Soviet Union could have a negative trade impact on Latin America. First, the former Soviet bloc was Latin America's third largest trading partner, after developed market economies and Latin America itself. Moreover, it was one of the few regions in which Latin America had a positive trade balance.[8] In the medium term, factor endowments and geographic proximity to the EC are likely to give Eastern Europe a good competitive position to export goods, especially manufactures similar to those exported by Latin America.

V   LATIN AMERICAN INTEGRATION: A NEW VERSION OF AN OLD DREAM?

Through liberalization of trade policies and the dismantling of the import substituting industrialization (ISI) policy, it is expected that, parallel to changes in the product composition of exports, the geographic pattern of trade will change in the direction of stronger links to countries with different factor endowments. Thus we should see an increase in the share of industrialized countries and a decreased share of developing countries in total regional exports. In effect, two main modifications in the geographical structure of trade have been taking place in the last two decades: first, reduction of the share of trade with the EC, which started in the early 1970s, and second, the increase in the importance of the USA.

In the context of new patterns of external trade linkages, the questions that emerge concern what role, if any, regional economic integration would play. How could the complementarity between an externally-oriented model and regional integration be constructed? And what would be the effects on integration of a more intense trade relationship with the USA, in the form of free trade agreements?

It is interesting to establish whether trade linkages within Latin America have been modified, both in intensity and product structure, as a result of trade liberalization. Additionally, if integration is gaining new momentum as the intensity of signing agreements should suggest, intraregional exchange should grow faster than total exports. It is also probable that changes in the composition of intraregional trade along the lines of comparative advantage will emerge.

Latin American intraregional exports have oscillated at around 12–13 per cent of total exports since the record levels registered during 1975–82. (See Table 2.7.) In relative terms, the region is more important as an origin of Latin America imports than as a destination for its external sales. (See Table 2.8.) It is worth mentioning that the share of intraregional imports in total imports has constantly increased since 1960. However, intraregional exports have fallen in relative terms since 1980. In 1991, the share of intraregional sales was 13 per cent of total exports, down from 16 per cent in 1980. The import side of the regional exchange has been more stable, growing from 13 per cent to 17 per cent. Nevertheless, if the analysis considers a shorter period (1985–90), the weakening of Latin American intraregional trade linkages is substantial.

In the last three years, Latin America has been the scene of an intense integrationist effort. Bilateral and multilateral trade agreements are signed and new timetables to fulfil commitments twenty or more years overdue – such as common external tariffs – are drawn up. The North American Free Trade Agreement (NAFTA) and the Enterprise for the Americas Initiative (EAI) have come on the scene, with the shining promise of a new partner in the long history of Latin American attempts at economic integration. If it is difficult to conclude whether this integrationist effort is mainly political and will fade away in time; it is even more complex to attempt to measure the impact of the Bush initiative on Latin America's external relations.

Table 2.7 Latin America: total exports by market of destination, 1960–1990 (%).

Exporter	Latin America	Arg.	Brazil	Chile	Colomb.	Ecuador	Mexico	Peru	Venez.
Importer									
EC									
1960	31	69	36	52	28	26	11	40	16
1970	31	53	40	56	31	3	7	37	13
1980	24	30	31	37	37	8	15	20	17
1990	23	29	31	34	26	9	14	28	12
Japan									
1960	3	3	2	6	1	5	7	7	1
1970	6	6	5	12	3	16	5	13	1
1980	5	3	6	11	4	12	4	9	4
1990	6	4	8	15	4	3	6	13	3
United States									
1960	38	9	44	37	64	61	59	36	43
1970	31	9	25	14	36	38	60	33	38
1980	30	9	17	13	27	32	65	32	28
1990	39	13	33	17	46	45	68	22	55
Latin America									
1960	9	16	7	8	3	8	3	10	11
1970	12	21	11	12	9	10	9	7	8
1980	16	24	18	24	16	20	6	21	12
1990	13	25	11	14	12	26	5	15	15
Other									
1960	19	8	11	19	4	—	20	7	29
1970	20	11	19	5	21	33	20	7	40
1980	25	34	28	15	16	28	9	18	39
1990	19	30	26	20	11	17	8	22	15

Source: UNCTAD, *Handbook of International Trade and Development Statistics*, several issues, United Nations, New York.

Table 2.8 Latin America: imports by country of origin, 1960–1990 (%).

Importer	Latin America	Arg.	Brazil	Chile	Colomb.	Ecuador	Mexico	Peru	Venez.
Exporter									
EC									
1960	32	35	34	33	31	40	28	36	35
1970	27	33	30	30	26	27	20	26	28
1980	19	30	17	20	20	9	15	18	24
1990	18	32	21	20	20	13	13	20	28
Japan									
1960	4	4	4	3	3	4	5	—	4
1970	6	5	6	3	6	9	4	8	8
1980	7	9	5	7	9	12	5	8	8
1990	6	4	6	7	9	8	4	6	5
United States									
1960	45	26	30	45	57	48	27	44	52
1970	40	35	22	37	48	39	64	32	49
1980	34	23	19	29	40	36	62	30	48
1990	41	24	21	19	37	38	69	30	44
Latin America									
1960	9	13	14	17	2	6	—	8	2
1970	13	22	11	21	10	10	3	15	4
1980	15	21	12	25	16	14	4	15	9
1990	17	27	18	26	21	18	4	30	10
Other									
1960	10	22	18	2	7	2	40	12	7
1970	14	15	20	10	11	15	10	19	12
1980	15	17	48	20	15	29	14	29	12
1990	19	13	33	27	12	23	9	16	14

Source: UNCTAD, *Handbook of International Trade and Development Statistics*, several issues, United Nations, New York.

Since 1984, there has been a renewed interest in promoting integration in Latin America, partly in response to the apparent global tendency toward the formation of large economic blocs and as a defensive response to the economic recession in developed countries. Nevertheless, the 1990s started with many unresolved questions about the future of economic integration in Latin America, due to persistent crises in the Andean Group and the Central American Common Market, the ambiguous signal of success in the new Southern Cone Common Market (Mercosur), and the promises of President Bush's Enterprise for the Americas Initiative.

For almost forty years the Latin American experience in integration shows that neither the more liberal models of integration, based mainly on market forces, (ALALC-ALADI) nor those with strong planning and redistribution elements (ANCOM-CACM) have been able to solve the problems of diverging national interests and conflicting perceptions about the distribution of benefits and costs of integration which emerge due to differences in economic development and industrial potential.

The results thus far of regional economic integration have been rather disappointing. All agreements have passed through constant reforms. Despite the fact that a considerable increase in intraregional trade took place during the first years in all programmes, the dynamic effects of trade, especially the promotion of new areas of production and the mobilization of investment, have been so limited as to be virtually imperceptible. Other dynamic effects of freer markets, such as an improvement in installed capacity use, an increase in industrial employment, or a change in income distribution were also extremely limited. Part of the explanation lies in the fact that integrated markets continued to be limited to relatively small, high income groups. No measures that substantially alter the supply side (productivity, supply structure) or the demand side (income distribution, employment policies) were put in motion.

Moreover, the experience of the commercial programmes, which offered special trade concessions to the relatively less developed members, demonstrates the strength of polarization effects. These less developed countries remained net importers of manufactured goods and exporters of basic goods. The North–South pattern of trade was reproduced.

The process stagnated because supranational objectives common to all member countries were unclear, and no advance was made toward the creation of supranational levels of decision-making. The unequal distribution of cost and benefits of integration made consensus impossible.

What could be the effects of economic liberalization and adjustment policies upon the prospects for regional integration?[9] In the first place, it is important to ask whether the emerging degree of macroeconomic homogeneity between Latin American countries, without which economic integration has proven unlikely to prosper, will allow integrated markets to overcome the problems of contradictory national interests. Are the probable new national productive structures a more solid basis for integration than old import substitution industrialization?

A policy of maintaining stable real exchange rates will prevent changes in relative competitiveness through massive devaluations, to which countries resorted as a response to external shocks and deterioration in the balance of payments situation. By dismantling the system of subsidies to promote industrialization and exports, prices are closer to their costs of production, thus the negative trade diversion effects are reduced, as are the disagreements about subsidized export and unfair competition. The reduction of state intervention in the market also means that state enterprises will not be granted special privileges such as favourable import rates, preferential prices, or tax exemptions, and national producers will not have the same priority in public sector procurement policies.

As a result of the drastic reduction in import tariffs, countries will be more competitive in international comparative terms. It also means that the preferences that each country offers are reduced to an important degree, but at the same time, they are now more uniform. Therefore, the costs of trade diversion are reduced and so the perception of unbalanced trade concessions. There remains no answer, however, to the problems of polarization effects resulting from the initial disequilibria in economic development.

V.1   New strategies for regional integration

To gauge the potential for regional economic integration in Latin America, it is necessary to bear in mind the emerging new structure of production, the profile of exports and the evolution of regional external trade patterns discussed in earlier sections. As a complement to the "new outward export-oriented" model, integration should be less protectionist and more of a trade-creating mechanism than before. Preferences should be given in the import-competing sectors (and not exclusively in the complementary ones). Tariff reductions should benefit those products for which domestic production costs are higher, in which differences in costs between member countries are larger, and in which countries have an international comparative advantage.

For integration to act as a complement to the externally-oriented export model, two strategies could be pursued: first, to speed up structural changes with the aim of productivity increases and faster development of production in sectors with international comparative advantage, or second, to reduce the adjustment costs of trade liberalization.

An emphasis on the first goal should have a trade creation effect, that is, preferences should be given first and faster in import-competing sectors, in those with low productivity levels and in those in which production cost differs significantly from country to country. Preferences would be given in those sectors in which actual protection is relatively high. Regional trade preferences should be complemented by a reduction in the level of tariffs for imports from non-member countries.

The above strategy would imply, for instance, that Mexico and Venezuela ought to open fully their oil and oil products markets between themselves and to other countries with export potential such as Colombia. Argentina, Brazil and Mexico should reciprocally open their imports of transport equipment. All Latin American countries should reciprocally open the agricultural, textile, leather and food sectors, that is, the goods in Table 2.5 which indicate the highest levels of "revealed comparative advantage". The costs of the "apertura" will increase, and perhaps the opposition to reforms will gain an advantage.

In the manufacturing sector, Latin American countries have reached some level of revealed comparative advantage in a relatively small group of products in which they compete with each other and with other developing countries. These are mainly labour-intensive standardized goods. If regional integration is to induce higher levels of efficiency in the production of those manufactured goods, reallocation of production from the less to the more efficient producers should take place. The latter will gain a larger share of the regional as well as of the international market. This strategy will increase the cost of trade liberalization. Relatively less developed countries, with limited capital resources and less qualified labour, and probably small domestic markets, will absorb a larger share of the adjustment costs. As Latin American experiences with integration suggest, the coherence and stability of an integration scheme requires means to overcome the structural problems that impede shared gains in growth.

In the second strategy, integration is meant to buffer the effects of trade reforms. Preferences would be given especially in sectors in which economies are complementary rather than competitive. As in the case of the NAFTA, sectors such as textiles, food production, oil, and beverages, in which employment is concentrated, or those such as petrochemicals, paper, plastics, oil products or transport equipment, which are relatively more modern with large economies of scale and perhaps suffering from idle capacity, could be excluded from preferences. In this alternative, the enlargement of the market through regional integration would not be followed by a reduction in tariffs to non-member countries. Although integration will allow greater competition at the regional level, it will make it possible to maintain protection vis-à-vis third countries. As a result, trade-creation effects will be partially prevented and, consequently, the costs derived from reallocation of production upon employment will be reduced. But if the regional preferences are granted in order to preserve a relatively high level of protection, trade-diverting effects will appear. A pattern of interindustry trade will appear, duplicating the experience of the past, although now the trade diversion effects will be smaller, since the general level of tariffs has been sharply reduced. NAFTA is a recent example of a protective type of integration, in which sensitive sectors, such as textiles, food and oil, will be open to competition at a considerably slower pace.

V.2   Limits to the expansion of integration in Latin America

In our opinion, several factors could hamper progress towards the creation of an economically integrated region: differences in economic development, macroeconomic instability and divergence, and finally, the effects of NAFTA and similar agreements with the United States.

The existing level of economic disequilibrium between countries, reflecting a lack of economic homogeneity, and the competitive structure of their economies, might push countries in the direction of defensive trade agreements. Latin America is divided by intense disparities in economic development and income and, what is more serious, in the capacity of individual countries to achieve and maintain high rates of growth. It is generally accepted that blocs with wide disparities in national income face difficulties in integration because of the costs derived from the redistribution of income and employment as trade flows change.[10] In these conditions, the tendency is to abandon the objectives of deeper economic and political integration and to prefer looser, non-binding preferential arrangements with little economic impact (Langhamer, 1992). Economic differences multiply if the participation of the United States in regional integration is considered.

Difference in income level and in total GDP are today as large as forty years ago, when moves towards regional integration were first put in motion. No significant convergence has taken place. For instance, Brazilian GNP per capita is 4.5 times higher than that of Honduras, but 8.6 times smaller than that of the United States. (See Table 2.9.)

At the sectoral level, the gaps between agricultural and industrial value-added per capita are larger than in other regions. These indices are considered an important measure of potential political conflict between member countries, since they suggest differences in elasticity of supply as market conditions change (Puyana, 1982). Per capita industrial value-added in Brazil in 1990 reached $810, while in Colombia and Mexico, it was only $250 and $593 respectively, and in the USA it was $4,710. In the agricultural sector, disequilibria are smaller but still important. These differences also show important gaps in productivity which result from differences in capital stock, in the capacity for technology generation and appropriation, and in investment in human capital. These structural problems are hardly solved when only, or mainly, trade and tariff policies are used. In these circumstances, in the absence of compensatory mechanisms, the distribution of the dynamic effects of trade will be highly concentrated in the more developed countries.[11]

Integration can reinforce the "polarization" effect, in which a participating nation or specific region experiences a decay in its economic situation due to the reassignment of resources resulting from integration. Initial differences in

Table 2.9 Latin America and the United States: basic indicators of uneven development.

	Population (millions)	(%)	GNP per capita	Value added ($ millions) Agriculture	Manufacturing	Exports 1990 ($ millions)	(%)	Imports 1990 ($ millions)	(%)	Value added ($ millions) Agriculture	Manufacturing
Honduras	5.1	0.8	590	546	461	916	0.2	1,028	0.2	107	90
Bolivia	7.2	1.1	630	1,069	585	923	0.2	7,160	—	149	81
Dom. Rep.	7.1	1.1	830	1,273	925	7,340	—	2,057	0.3	177	130
Guatemala	9.2	1.4	900	1,978		1,211	0.2	16,260	—	215	
Ecuador	10.3	1.5	980	1,435	2,298	2,714	0.5	1,862	0.3	130	223
El Salvador	5.2	0.8	1,110	605	1,042	550	0.1	1,200	0.2	116	200
Paraguay	4.3	0.6	1,110	1,462	933	959	0.2	1,113	0.2	340	217
Peru	21.7	3.2	1,160	2,420	7,730	3,277	0.7	3,230	0.5	112	356
Colombia	32.3	4.8	1,260	6,876	8,177	6,766	1.4	5,590	0.9	213	253
Jamaica	2.4	0.3	1,500	209	783	1,347	0.3	1,685	0.3	88	326
Panama	2.4	0.3	1,830	482	352	321	0.1	1,539	0.1	202	147
Costa Rica	2.8	0.4	1,900	915	1,065	1,457	0.3	2,026	0.3	327	380
Chile	13.2	2.0	1,940	—	—	8,579	1.7	7,023	—	125	—
Argentina	32.3	4.8	2,370	12,405	22,024	12,353	2.5	4,077	0.7	384	—
Nicaragua	3.9	0.6	—	—	759	379	0.1	750	0.1		—
Mexico	86.2	12.8	2,490	21,074	51,138	26,714	5.4	28,063	4.6	244	593
Venezuela	17.9	2.9	2,560	3,671	9,064	17,220	3.5	6,364	1.0	135	460
Uruguay	3.1	0.5	2,560	893	2,202	1,696	0.3	1,415	0.2	288	710
Brazil	150.4	22.4	2,680	42,288	120,845	31,243	6.3	22,459	3.7	281	803
Trin/Tob	1.2	0.2	3,610	124	540	2,080	0.4	1,262	0.2	103	450
United States	252.0	37.3	21,790	170,844	1,186,824	371,466	75.4	515,635	84.4	678	4,710
Total	670	100		269,569	1,417,747	492,905	—	610,720	—	—	—

Source: World Development Report 1992.

productivity and economic development, or simply a displacement in demand for goods produced by a region, can lead to an increasing polarization between regions.

This constitutes one of the main problems and is a determining factor in the continuity of any integration process. In fact a more equitable redistribution of costs and benefits of integration among its member states can be considered an indicator of the political and social cohesion of the new system.[12] This is mainly so because redistribution is above all a political decision, as it implies significant concessions and transfers of resources toward regions of less relative development, and in many cases countries of greater development are not disposed to assume that cost. Nonetheless, attempts to redistribute costs and benefits of integration have had limited effect, even in integrationist schemes as advanced as that of the EC. As Tables 2.10–2.11 indicate, smaller countries, including Bolivia, Ecuador and Chile, are much more dependent on intraregional trade than Mexico, Brazil or Argentina.

Second, there is still divergence in policies and macroeconomic objectives: the structure of protection and the remaining non-tariff barriers suggest that some sectors face positive discrimination for development purposes. Labour-intensive products, some agricultural and food goods, and resource-based goods (for example, transport equipment, coffee, and petrol products) receive more protection. This implicit sectoral strategy will affect the political will to establish a common external tariff. Recent conflicts in the Andean Group that led Peru and Bolivia to threaten to leave the pact were the result of disagreement on the level and structure of the sub-regional common external tariff. Similar conflicts exploded in Mercosur as a result of the overvaluation of Argentina's currency and growing trade deficit.

In addition to the levelling of macroeconomic policies resulting from adjustment programmes and from the liberalization of commerce regimes, there remain other elements that can undermine progress towards regional integration. If the necessary measures are not taken to accommodate these issues at the outset, it would be Utopian to talk about the creation of a common market, as would be discussion of hemispheric integration.

Exchange rate management varies in the region. Certain countries have opted for a revaluation or have fixed their currency to only one currency, the dollar. Others maintain a constant real exchange rate, accelerate devaluation, and use a basket of currencies for reference. Logically the exchange rate will be managed by considering international interest rates, commerce with the United States, the exchange rate of the dollar, goals on inflation, fiscal and current account deficits, and the prices of basic products in international markets. Regional or sub-regional trade will play a secondary role, if any, but will be considerably affected by relative exchange rate movements.

The margin and necessity of co-ordinating macroeconomic policies in Latin American countries would depend on the intensity of commercial, financial and capital flows, and by relative exchange rate movements. In reality, it is

Table 2.10 Latin America: exports as a percentage of GDP of exporting country.

Exporting country	Total 1970	1980	1990	Market of destination United States 1970	1980	1990	Latin America 1970	1980	1990
Argentina	7.5	5.2	13.2	0.7	0.5	1.7	1.6	1.3	3.3
Brazil	6.4	8.4	7.5	1.6	1.4	1.7	0.7	1.5	0.8
Chile	16.7	16.9	30.8	2.4	2.2	5.2	2.0	4.1	4.3
Mexico	3.9	8.4	11.2	2.3	5.5	7.6	0.4	0.5	0.5
Bolivia	18.3	18.8	13.8	6.4	6.2	3.8	1.5	5.1	7.5
Colombia	10.2	11.8	16.4	3.7	3.2	7.5	0.9	1.9	2.0
Ecuador	11.4	21.8	18.0	4.8	7.6	8.1	1.5	4.4	4.7
Peru	15.4	20.1	15.9	4.5	6.6	3.9	1.4	4.6	2.3
Venezuela	27.0	32.5	35.6	10.3	0.1	19.6	2.2	3.9	5.3
Andean Pact	19.0	25.0	21.0	8.4	8.5	9.9	1.7	3.8	4.0
Latin America	10.7	12.9	12.1	3.3	3.9	4.7	1.3	2.1	1.6
United States	4.3	8.2	6.9	—	—	—	0.6	1.4	0.9

Source: IMF, *International Financial Statistics* and *Direction of Trade Statistics* (several issues).

Table 2.11 Latin America: imports as a percentage of GDP of importing country.

Importing country	Total 1970	1980	1990	Market of origin United States 1970	1980	1990	Latin America 1970	1980	1990
Argentina	7.1	6.8	4.4	1.8	1.6	1.4	1.6	1.4	1.2
Brazil	6.7	10.4	5.4	2.1	2.0	1.3	0.7	1.3	1.0
Chile	12.5	18.6	25.2	4.7	5.4	4.8	2.6	4.7	6.6
Mexico	6.9	10.4	11.8	4.4	6.5	8.1	0.2	0.3	0.5
Bolivia	15.3	15.1	17.4	5.4	4.4	3.6	2.9	4.1	7.0
Colombia	11.7	14.0	13.6	5.6	5.7	5.1	1.2	2.2	2.9
Ecuador	16.4	19.8	13.1	6.4	6.1	4.9	2.6	2.8	2.8
Peru	9.0	15.8	16.2	3.1	6.0	4.2	1.3	2.5	4.5
Venezuela	15.9	20.0	13.2	7.8	9.6	5.8	0.6	1.8	1.3
Andean Pact	12.5	16.7	13.0	5.6	7.2	4.7	1.1	2.2	2.3
Latin America	11.0	14.0	9.6	4.4	4.8	3.9	1.4	2.1	1.6
United States	9.3	4.3	6.9	—	—	—	1.3	2.0	1.3

Source: IMF, *International Financial Statistics* and *Direction of Trade Statistics* (several issues).

mainly (perhaps only) in the exchange of goods where intra-Latin American relations have acquired some weight, although the resulting interdependence is still relatively small. Intra-Latin American investments, financial or direct, represent a limited fraction of the whole. On the other hand, in commerce as well as in financial flows, the region is becoming progressively more integrated with the United States, Japan, and the European Community.

As theories of monetary union suggest, the co-ordination of monetary and exchange rate policies requires that one country, the "anchor" country, pulls and maintains the co-ordination, as a result of its greater macroeconomic stability. It is difficult to visualize which Latin American country could assume this role (as does Germany in Europe). In the context of integration with the United States, the question is whether the USA would be willing to act in this way. Moreover, co-ordination of exchange policies requires the existence of product and factor mobility, integration of capital markets and total convertibility of currencies, a non-existent situation in Latin America.

V.3   Economic relations with the United States

As financial, commercial and exchange relations with the United States grow, it is evident that it is this economy which will most profoundly affect the evolution of the Latin America economies. Latin America is increasing its trade linkages with the USA, while the US is driving in the opposite direction, producing an asymmetric trade pattern which is reinforced by the degree of geographic diversification in US foreign trade. While 39 per cent of Latin America's exports and 41 per cent of its imports are with the US, the participation of Latin America in the total foreign trade of the US represents 13.7 per cent for exports and 11.8 per cent for imports. No country represents more than 15 per cent of the US external trade transactions. Additionally, the differences in the export–GDP ratios in Latin America and the United States suggest that the former is much more dependent on exports to the latter, than the other way round. Latin American exports to the US account for a share of regional GDP that is five times the corresponding ratio for exports from the latter to the region.

Latin America is progressively integrating with the country that today exercises the greatest influence on the world's economy. If the US government is willing to assume only a certain level of co-ordination (which could be called "indicative") in the G7, it is unlikely that it will do more with Latin America. None of the other countries of the region, nor the region as a whole, has the strength to impose this type of co-ordination. Argentina can fix its currency to the dollar, as it has done, but the opposite will not happen. The likeliest scenario would be that the countries of the region will try to maintain their real exchange rates and low inflation rates to conserve their competitiveness in the North American market.

Latin American integration and more generally, the region's foreign trade, will have to adjust to the impact of NAFTA and the Enterprise for the Americas Initiative. In fact, the presence of the United States as a new partner in the negotiations for trade preferences introduces new elements into the integration process in Latin America that are not fully understood.

Since the United States is looking only for free trade agreements, FTAs, and not for any kind of integration with political implications, the integrationist component in the intraregional programmes will be further weakened. The interests of Latin American countries in signing agreements with the United States are seen as being served by the creation of a "safe haven"[13] by means of which to preserve their market shares in the US in the event of resurging protectionist pressures there. It is clear that the fear of being marginalized from NAFTA-type arrangements with the US has led Latin American countries to propose and procure bilateral trade agreements as quickly as possible, giving the US an exceptionally strong bargaining position.

US motives are, in the first place, support of economic reforms, particularly in Mexico. As a result, a web of bilateral agreements will emerge, and not a free trade zone in a strict sense. The final result would be an indeterminable number of bilateral agreements which will respond to the particular interests of each country. Furthermore, the United States will not modify the direction of its macroeconomic policy in its role as a global economic actor in order to fully integrate itself into the Latin American economies. The latter have had to accept these conditions to enter negotiations with the United States.

A growing perception is that as an effect of NAFTA-type agreements, Latin American exporters will face a double problem: some countries will be displaced from the USA market as a result of trade preferences given to others, while competing exports from the USA will displace intraregional exports. The urgency for signing treaties with the USA reflects the fear of being displaced from the North American market. On the other side, the intensification of the regional agreements shows the will to preserve intraregional Latin American trade.

As there is a wide range of products in the structure of intra-Latin American trade in which regional exporters compete with exports from the USA, the tariff concessions that are negotiated in the FTAs may provide the US with preferences that convey a major competitive advantage over other countries of the region, prejudicing a substantial share of intraregional trade. It has been calculated, for example, that 92 per cent of Mexican exports to Brazil, or even 100 per cent of Chilean sales to Venezuela, will be affected.

To prevent such negative effects, a customs union rather than free trade agreements should be negotiated. But as is evident in the Enterprise for the Americas Initiative and the NAFTA treaty, the US has no plans to move even to a multilaterally negotiated free trade zone. Thus to avoid giving the US still larger preferences, Latin American countries could shift tariff levels to the level of the US and set a similar structure of non-tariff barriers. That would be a *de facto* "customs union" without engaging the United States in a costly bargaining process.

In addition to trade costs, it is expected that NAFTA will generate other costs for the region. Some are particularly concerned about the costs of foreign investment diversion as investors plump for Mexico rather than anywhere else.

In any case, a strong free trade relation with the United States gives new life to the old debate about uneven development and the conditions that make convergence possible. Recent studies suggest that polarization effects and uneven development are a likely result of freer trade in which the initial advantages are duplicated, becoming in some cases "self-perpetuating".[14] Sectoral development policies and measures to prevent the concentration of dynamic effects of trade in the more developed countries and/or to compensate backwards regions have to be put in place. In that context, it is notable that new approaches to growth theory of developed economies in the post-war era suggest that the liberalization of international trade was only one of several elements explaining convergence and productivity growth, the others being an active fiscal policy, capital formation, controlled inflation, low commodity prices, a carefully timed sectoral policy, investment in human capital, the size of domestic markets and the structure of the industrial sector.

In the case of Latin America, it has been suggested that the main growth factors seem to be investment, primarily in machinery and equipment (especially direct foreign investment), political stability, investment in human capital and, finally, macroeconomic stability. Economic openness and the terms of trade were only marginally significant.[15] The above findings support arguments in favour of relatively active policies aimed at strengthening factors that explain growth. It is not clear how far it will be possible to include growth policies in the integration process. The problems that such an approach would imply, in both theory and policy development, are an important challenge.

NOTES

1 This view is sustained by the World Bank: "The volatility and decline in real primary commodity prices, especially during the last decade, have posed serious problems for low-income primary producers." (World Bank, 1991.)

2 (Rodrick, 1992, p. 6.) According to Rodrick, the reduction of protection will reduce the income of industrialists, organized labour and import licence holders, while devaluation will benefit both import-competing and export-oriented interests, and will "squeeze" unorganized labour and reduce real wages in terms of tradables. Commercial liberalization benefits importers and pushes down import-competing producers.

3 See Sheeby (1992).

4 From 1985 to 1991, a strong revaluation took place, with the exception of Brazil, Mexico, Paraguay and Peru, in all countries. See CEPAL (1991).

5 During the same periods, OECD exports of manufactures grew at 6.9 per cent and 4.0 per cent, and exports from Asian NICs at 17.0 per cent and 9.8 per cent, respectively. See Lord and Bounturi (1992).

6 See Love (1992).

7 According to Izam (1991), Latin America (compared to industrialized Asian countries and Africa) is the only region whose share as a supplier to the EC has gone

down during the last fifteen years. The region has also registered a low increase in the share of direct foreign investment from the EC.

8 Between 1980 and 1989, around 7 per cent of total annual exports from Latin America went to Eastern Europe and the Soviet Union. Latin America was also the main developing exporting region to the Eastern bloc, accounting for an annual average share of more than 48 per cent of the total imports from developing countries. During 1980–8, Latin America exported $73.9 billion of goods to the Eastern bloc and imported $62.3 billion. Latin America mainly exported agricultural goods and industrial raw materials, and imported machinery and fuels. Cuba was by far the most important trade partner in the region, followed by Argentina and Brazil. See United Nations, *World Economic Survey*, 1991.

9 A more detailed analysis of these aspects can be found in Oxford Analytica's (1992) *Economic Prospects for Latin America*, a study prepared for the InterAmerican Development Bank.

10 M.G. Plummer (1991) found "high and nontrivial" short-term detrimental effects to the Greek economy from membership in the EC, which might be compensated in the long run.

11 See Robson (1984) and El Agraa (1988).

12 See Tsoukalis (19XX, p. 203). For a detailed analysis of the impact of differences in economic development on the evolution of the integration programmes in Latin America, see Puyana (1982).

13 The term is from Whalley (1992).

14 For a modern example which demonstrates that "uneven development" is not a "necessary outcome" in free market conditions, and in which relative advantages based on inequalities are not necessarily self-destructive, see Chichilnisky (1981) and Krugman (1981).

15 J. De Gregorio, "Economic Development in Latin America", *IMF Working Paper*, WP/91/71.

REFERENCES

Boughton, J.M. (1991) "Commodity and Manufactures Prices in the Long Run", *IMF Working Paper* No. WP/91/47, Washington.

CEPAL (1991) "Preliminary Overview of the Economy of Latin America and the Caribbean", ECLAC, United Nations, December.

Chichilnisky, G. (1981) "Lessons of Trade and Domestic Distribution", *Journal of Development Economics* 8.

El Agraa, A.M. (1988) *International Economic Integration*, Macmillan, London.

Fishlow, A. and S. Haggard (1991) "The United States and the Regionalization of the World Economy", OECD, Room Document, November.

Gilbert, C. (1990) "Primary Commodity Prices and Inflation", *Oxford Review of Economic Policy* 6(4), 77–99.

Izam, M. (1991) "Europe 1992 and the Latin American Economy", *CEPAL Review* 43, April.

Krugman, P. (1981) "Trade Accommodation and Uneven Development", *Journal of Development Economics* 8.

Langhamer, R.J. (1992) "Developing Countries and Regionalism", *Journal of Common Markets Studies* **XXX**(2).

Lord, M. and M. Bounturi (1992) "Latin American Trade in Manufactures: An Empirical Study", in Interamerican Development Bank, *Economic and Social Progress in Latin America*, Washington, DC.

Love, J. (1992) "Export Instability and the Domestic Economy: Questions of Causality", *Journal of Development Studies* **28**(4).

Plummer, M.G. (1991) *Weltwirtschaftliches Archiv* **127**, 171.

Puyana, A. (1982) *Economic Integration Among Unequal Partners: The Case of the Andean Group*, Pergamon Press, New York.

Robson, P. (1984) *The Economics of International Integration*, Allen & Unwin, London.

Rodrick, D. (1992) "The Rush to Free Trade in the Developing World: Why So Late? Why Now? Will It Last?" *NBER Working Paper*, 3947, January.

Sheeby, E.J. (1992) "Exports and Growth: Additional Evidence", *Journal of Development Studies* **28**(4).

Tsoukalis, L. (19XX) *The New European Community*, Oxford University Press, Oxford.

Whalley, J. (1992) "CUSTA and NAFTA: Can WHFTA be Far Behind?", *Journal of Common Market Studies* **XXX**(2), June.

World Bank (1991) *Global Economic Prospects and the Developing Countries*, Washington.

3 | Private Capital Returns to Latin America*

STEPHANY GRIFFITH-JONES

with

ANA MARR

and

ALICIA RODRIGUEZ

I INTRODUCTION

This chapter discusses the massive and rather surprising return of private capital flows to Latin America. This is both a very new and a very old phenomenon. It is very new in that only three years ago (when focus was mainly on the foreign exchange constraint and debt overhang of the region), such a massive return of private capital flows to Latin America would have seemed totally unlikely to most policy-makers, market actors and observers. And it is a very old phenomenon in that private capital has flown in great abundance to the region on many previous occasions, since the early nineteenth century.

This chapter will first (section II) analyse the international context of changing international private flows. It will then examine in some detail what and how much is happening in private capital flows to Latin America. As this phenomenon is so recent, it seems essential first to learn as much as possible about its magnitude and its features – not easy, given the limitations of existing data and data collection. The next section (III) attempts an explanation of recent developments, focusing both on supply and demand factors. Section IV tries to develop an analytical framework for evaluating the effects of these flows in Latin American countries; some further empirical evidence is

* This chapter was first published in J.J. Teunissen (ed.) *Fragile Finance*, FONDAD, Holland, 1992. We thank Nicholas Georgiadis for valuable research assistance. We are particularly grateful to Mohammed El-Erian, Ricardo Ffrench-Davis and John Williamson for their valuable comments.

provided in that context. Section V presents conclusions, preliminary policy suggestions and some suggestions for further study.

II   THE INTERNATIONAL CONTEXT AND PRIVATE CAPITAL FLOWS TO LATIN AMERICA

II.1   International trends

The return of private capital flows to Latin America needs to be understood in the context of major changes in international capital flows at a global level. During the 1980s, financial markets became characterized by:

(1)   their growing integration among different countries, market segments, institutions and financial instruments;
(2)   liberalization;
(3)   the spread of innovative financing instruments and techniques.

The factors explaining these trends are related first to the policy of deregulation of financial services in a number of areas, such as prices, interest rates, fees and commissions. This policy began in earnest in the 1980s, and is now almost complete in industrial countries. Furthermore, the restrictions on the range of financial institutions' activities have also continued to dwindle, both through market practice and through legislative and regulatory action. Indeed, in the three major economies with traditionally segmented systems – Canada, Japan and the United States – there have been moves toward a relaxation of functional barriers. Movement towards geographic integration of financial markets has been particularly marked in recent years within the European Community, especially in the context of the 1992 Single Market programme. Indeed, as the IMF reports (IMF, 1991), many market participants in Europe (both EC member and non-member countries) view the overall process of European integration as the single most important influence on their activities and strategies for the 1990s. Within the EC, progress in integration of financial services has been accompanied by discussion of more integrated supervision and regulation, particularly in the field of banking. However, progress in the latter, in certain key sectors such as securities, has been relatively slow, which could perhaps be a cause for concern.

It should be stressed that other factors have also contributed to the globalization of capital markets: these include important technological advances in telecommunications and computing, which accelerate and reduce costs both of operations and exchange of information at a global level. Also, the sharp current account imbalances in major industrial countries during the 1980s led to large flows of funds from surplus to deficit countries, and especially to the US; this latter trend seems to be diminishing somewhat as Germany's current account surplus disappears and the US current account deficit declines.

Finally, there are two somewhat related trends, which seem important to highlight in this context. One is the far more rapid growth of securitized forms of lending (such as bonds) than of bank loans. (See Table 3.1.) The second is that institutional investors (such as pension funds, insurance and mutual funds) have played an increasingly dominant role in world capital markets; institutional investors have a greater ability to analyse in depth the changing conditions in different markets than individual investors; this has led many of them to a greater geographical diversification in their investments, with the aim of improving their profits and diversifying their risks.

Table 3.1 reflects the evolution of the international capital markets since 1982. A first trend to observe is the very rapid increase in total global borrowing, from $179 billion in 1982 to $439 billion in 1991. A particularly large increase (of almost 20 per cent) occurred in 1991, after a contraction in 1990 related to a significant reduction in some of the Japanese bonds. A second trend to observe is the increased importance of bonds in total borrowing; bonds, which represented around 42 per cent in 1982, increased their share to around 67 per cent in 1991. This increase in the share of bonds in total borrowing has been accompanied by a decline in the share of syndicated loans, and a contraction in 1991; this was mainly caused by the attitude of leading international banks towards extending new loans other than to prime borrowers. This attitude reflects greater emphasis on containing asset growth within boundaries set by new capital adequacy requirements and on improving quality of loan portfolios. On the other hand, the past and the future situation of the international securities markets is clearly more favourable. Market observers point to the fact that the availability of funds remain ample on a global basis. According to the OECD (OECD, 1992), this positive underlying trend in international securities markets is strengthened by two factors: first, the process of asset diversification may intensify as several "emerging" segments of the Eurobond market have reached a critical size, justifying a heavier weighting in institutional investors' portfolios. Second, the maturing of

Table 3.1 Borrowing on the international capital markets.

$ billion

Instruments	1982	1984	1987	1988	1989	1990	1991
Bonds	75.5	111.5	180.8	227.1	255.7	229.9	297.6
Equities	n.a.	0.3	18.2	7.7	8.1	7.3	21.6
Syndicated loans	98.2	57.0	91.7	125.5	121.1	124.5	113.2
Note issuance facilities	5.4	28.8	29.0	14.4	5.5	4.3	1.8
Other back-up facilities			2.2	2.2	2.9	2.7	4.5
Total securities and committed facilities	179.1	197.6	321.9	376.9	393.3	368.7	438.7

Source: OECD *Financial Market Trends*, February 1992, and previous issues.

the Eurobond market implies an increase in bond redemptions, which provides investors with an increasingly large source of liquidity that needs to be profitably reinvested.

If Eurocommercial paper lending and other non-underwritten facilities are added, total borrowing on international capital markets increased from $392 billion in 1987 to $518 billion in 1991. The share of developing countries in this total borrowing, though still relatively low, increased significantly, going up from 5.0 per cent of the total in 1988 to 8.1 per cent in 1991. Indeed, the overall recourse to private international markets by developing countries rose in 1991 by nearly 50 per cent (to $42 billion), the highest level in abolsute nominal terms since the early 1980s (OECD, 1992). Particularly noticeable in this expansion was the very strong growth in borrowing by a number of Latin American countries, which we will discuss next.

II.2   New private flows to Latin America

II.2.1   Dramatic change of direction and increase

As is well known, in the 1980s, net resource transfers to Latin America and the Caribbean (LAC) were strongly negative (see Table 3.2). One of the key reasons for this was a sharp fall in private flows to the region, caused mainly by a large decline in private bank lending, which had reached high levels prior to 1982. Indeed, according to El-Erian (1992), the total amount of voluntary loan and bond financing flows to Latin American countries during the whole 1983–8 period was considerably smaller than that for 1982 alone.

Starting in 1989, and continuing in 1990 and 1991, there was a dramatic increase in voluntary new private flows to Latin America and the Caribbean. According to ECLAC (see again Table 3.2), net total private flows to LAC increased in the period since 1988 almost sevenfold. As a result of this dramatic increase, and to a lesser extent due to a decline in net payments of profits and interest, 1991 was the first year since 1981 that the net transfer of financial flows reversed direction and turned positive. Thus, the net outward flow of $16 billion in 1990 was transformed into a net inflow of nearly $7 billion in 1991 (see again Table 3.2); this represented a turnaround of $23 billion in the net transfer in one year, an amount equivalent to 15 per cent of the region's exports of goods and services.

As can be seen in Table 3.3, Salomon Brothers (1992) estimated even a somewhat more rapid increase than ECLAC, with private capital flows to Latin America calculated to have increased eightfold between 1989 and 1991 and by almost 200 per cent in 1991 alone, reaching over $40 billion.

II.2.2   Country distribution

For 1991, according to Salomon Brothers, there was quite a large concentration of private flows in those going to the two largest countries in the region (Brazil and Mexico), which received almost 70 per cent of inflows (see

Table 3.2 Latin America and the Caribbean: net capital inflow and transfer of resources.

	(1) Net capital inflow ($ billions)	(2) Net payment of profits and interest ($ billions)	(3) = (1) – (2) Transfer of resources ($ billions)	(4) Transfer of resources – exports of goods and services (%)
1975	14.3	5.6	8.7	21.2
1980	32.0	18.9	13.1	12.5
1981	39.8	28.5	11.3	10.0
1982	20.1	38.8	–18.7	–18.2
1983	2.9	34.5	–31.6	–30.9
1984	10.4	37.3	–26.9	–23.7
1985	3.0	35.3	–32.3	–29.7
1986	9.9	32.6	–22.7	–24.0
1987	15.4	31.4	–16.0	–14.8
1988	5.5	34.3	–28.8	–23.4
1989	9.6	37.9	–28.3	–20.8
1990	18.4	34.4	–16.0	–10.6
1991	36.0	29.3	6.7	4.4

Source: UN ECLAC *Preliminary Overview of the Economy of Latin America and the Caribbean 1991*, December 1991, Santiago, Chile.

Table 3.3 Private capital flows to Latin America and to selected Latin American countries ($ billion).

	1989	1990	1991
Argentina	1.4	0.5	5.1
Brazil	0.2	0.4	11.6
Chile	1.1	2.0	1.7
Mexico	0.7	8.4	16.1
Venezuela	1.0	1.8	4.8
Regional	0.6	0.2	0.8
Total	5.0	13.4	40.1

Source: Salomon Brothers (1992).

Table 3.4). For Mexico (which accounted for 40 per cent of total flows to Latin America in 1991), this represented around 6 per cent of its GDP, while for Brazil it represented 2.7 per cent of its GDP.

In 1991, inflows to Venezuela (at $4.8b) are estimated to have reached 10 per cent of the country's GDP, while inflows to Argentina reached 7.6 per cent of GDP and to Chile 5.8 per cent of GDP (see again Table 3.4). The country composition was somewhat different in 1990, when the largest flows went to Mexico and Chile, the two countries which, according to Salomon Brothers, received above 75 per cent of total inflows to Latin America. In 1990, inflows to Chile represented 7.4 per cent of the country's GDP and inflows to Mexico represented 3.6 per cent of that country's GDP.

It is very interesting that in 1991, not only Chile and Mexico (which had pursued prudent macroeconomic policies and had reduced their debt overhang significantly in the late 1980s) had access to private capital markets, but also countries like Brazil, where important macroeconomic imbalances and a large debt overhang still persisted. However, the terms on which Brazilian borrowers have access to the capital markets are somewhat less attractive. We will return to this issue in Section III.

II.2.3 Types of flows

It is important to emphasize that the increase in net capital flows to Latin America and the Caribbean has been due not mainly to a return of bank lending, but to the region's re-entry to capital markets (especially bonds, private placements and medium-term notes), portfolio investments, and foreign direct investment. It is in this sense noteworthy that the process of the region's market re-entry is done via a wide range of financing instruments, and involves a wide range of markets, investors and lenders.

Table 3.4 Types of private capital flows to Latin America, 1991.

(% of type of flow)	Total	Argentina	Brazil	Chile	Mexico	Venezuela	Regional
Borrowing							
Bonds, private placements and medium-term notes	100.0	13.0	41.2	2.3	54.1	6.9	−17.4
Commercial paper	100.0				24.1	4.9	71.0
CDs	100.0	27.2	69.1		3.7		
Trade financing	100.0		65.8		34.2		
Term bank lending	100.0	4.2	70.0	13.7	10.6	1.4	
Sub-total	100.0	8.8	42.7	3.3	38.6	4.7	1.9
Total portfolio investment							
Funds	100.0	7.4	16.2	3.4	12.5		60.4
ADRs[a]	100.0	12.9			87.1		−0.0
Sub-total	100.0	11.6	3.7	0.8	69.9		13.9
DFI[b]							
Cash inflows from privatization	100.0	39.1		10.5	60.9		
Other DFI	100.0	9.1	12.4		52.6		15.4
Sub-total	100.0	16.7	9.2	7.9	39.3	15.4	11.5
Other flows	100.0	15.9	84.1				
Sub-total	100.0	15.9	84.1				
Grand total	100.0	12.7	29.0	4.2	39.9	7.2	7.0
% of GDP		7.6	2.7	5.8	5.9	10.0	

Source: Table elaborated by Alicia Rodriguez on the basis of data in Salomon Brothers (1992).
[a] ADRs = American depository receipts.
[b] DFI = Direct foreign investment.

Table 3.5 offers a decomposition of private flows to Latin America in 1991. We can see that 39 per cent of the total flows ($15.7 billion) took the form of borrowing, with most of this borrowing being in the form of bonds, private placements and medium-term notes. Borrowing was a particularly important source of funds in 1991 for Brazil (see again Table 3.5). Furthermore, as can be seen in Table 3.4, in 1991 a very high proportion of short-term flows to Latin America (via for example CDs and trade financing) went to Brazil.

Another important category in 1991 was foreign direct investment, which at $14 billion represented almost 35 per cent of total flows into the region. Direct foreign investment is reported to have been a particularly high proportion in Venezuela (where it went mainly for privatization), Chile (for new investments) and to a lesser extent in Argentina, mostly for privatization, but also in a smaller proportion for new investment (see again Table 3.5). Portfolio investment flows represented a smaller share – 16 per cent – of private flows in 1991, with fairly significant proportions in Mexico and in other Latin American countries. In previous years, 1989 and 1990, Mexico and Chile were the Latin American countries that obtained a particularly large share of portfolio investment in Latin America (West, 1991). Indeed, it was a Chilean firm, CTC (Chilean Telephone Company), which was the first Latin American company since 1963 to sell shares on the New York Stock Exchange, via ADRs.

Also of interest in this context is the Telmex (Mexican Telephone Company) privatization, which involved the issuance of some $2.3 billion on several equity markets. This equity offering was reported[1] to have been the sixth largest placement of shares in the world (in nominal values).

II.2.4   Length of period and cost

As regards the length of time for which these amounts of capital are entering, it is encouraging that for some countries, such as Mexico and Chile, and to a lesser extent Venezuela, 1991 was characterized by increased levels of longer-term capital flows.

Thus, for Chile, over 65 per cent of the private flows entering in 1991 were via direct investment, all of which was for new investment; for Mexico, almost 35 per cent of private flows entering in 1991 were via direct investment, again all for new investment. Furthermore, Mexico established a new benchmark and reportedly broke a psychological barrier with a ten-year, $150 million Eurobond issue for NAFINSA (the national development bank). However, on average, Mexican international bond issues have not improved their maturities that much. According to the IMF (IMF, 1991), for secured issues average maturities went up only from a 5-year average in 1989 to a 5.5-year average for 1991 (see Table 3.6); for unsecured issues in the private sector, there has been a more important lengthening of maturities (from 2 to 4.4 years), but still to fairly short periods. On the other hand, public sector unsecured issues saw

Table 3.5 Types of private capital flows to Latin America, 1991.

(% of total flows)	Total	Argentina	Brazil	Chile	Mexico	Venezuela	Regional
Borrowing							
Bonds, private placements and medium-term notes	21.2	21.6	30.2	12.0	28.7	20.2	−53.1
Commercial paper	6.3				3.8	4.3	63.7
CDs	1.6	3.4	3.8		0.1		
Trade financing	4.2		9.4		3.6		
Term bank lending	5.9	1.9	14.1	19.3	1.6	1.2	
Sub-total	39.1	27.0	57.6	31.3	37.8	25.7	10.6
Total portfolio investment							
Funds	3.7	2.2	2.1	3.1	1.2		32.0
ADRs[a]	12.3	12.5			26.8		
Sub-total	16.0	14.6	2.1	3.1	28.0		32.0
DFI[b]							
Cash inflows from privatization	8.8	27.0					
Other DFI	26.0	18.7	11.1	65.7	34.2	74.3	57.4
Sub-total	34.8	45.7	11.1	65.7	34.2	74.3	57.4
Other flows[c]							
Argentina	1.6	12.6					
Brazil	8.5		29.3				
Sub-total	10.1	12.6	29.3				
Grand total	100.0	100.0	100.0	100.0	100.0	100.0	100.0

Source: Table elaborated by Alicia Rodriguez on the basis of data in Salomon Brothers (1992).
[a] ADRs = American depository receipts.
[b] DFI = Direct foreign investment.
[c] Identified by the countries' central banks.

Table 3.6 Average terms on international bonds (Mexico).

| | 1989 | | 1990 | | 1991 | |
	Spread[a]	Maturity (years)	Spread	Maturity (years)	Spread	Maturity (years)
Secured issues	165	5	304	4.4	150	5.5
Unsecured issues:						
Public sector	820	5	379	4.9	246	4.2
Private sector	800	2	613	3.6	542	4.4

Source: IMF.

[a] Spread = premium in basic points, defined as the difference between the bond yield at issue and the prevailing yield for industrial country government bonds in the same currency and of comparable maturity.

their average maturity decline slightly. (It is noteworthy, however, how significantly spreads have come down in Mexico, especially for unsecured public issues (see again Table 3.6)).

Aside from direct investment, some bonds and possibly some portfolio investment, the majority of private capital flows to the region have been short-term, especially in short-term money market instruments, where local Latin American interest rates have tended to be significantly higher than in the US. Thus, many American, Latin American and European investors and lenders have been attracted to CDs, treasury bills, bonds and commercial paper that offer yields at two to four times LIBOR for short-term investments. Table 3.7 shows estimated benchmark real domestic interest rates and compares them to US$ LIBOR.

The dramatic drop in short-term US real interest rates during 1991 to a level which (by 1980s' standards) was very low, drastically increased the attractiveness of Latin American investment instruments, with far higher yields. It is interesting that US investors, faced with lower interest rates at home, increase their investments in Latin America to such an extent, even

Table 3.7 Benchmark real domestic interest rates, 1990–1991.

	1990	1991
Argentina (intercompany lending rate)	47.4%	22.0%
Brazil (monthly rate – LTN/BBC)	25.4%	32.4%
Chile (90–365-day real annual deposit rate)	9.5%	5.5%
Mexico (28-day CETES rate)	34.7%	15.9%
Venezuela (91-day zero coupon rate)	33.8%	35.5%
US$ LIBOR (6-month average)	8.4%	4.4%

Source: Salomon Brothers, based on national and international sources.

though European interest rates are far higher than US ones. This shows that world financial markets are still not fully integrated.

As Kuczynski (1992) correctly suggests, the fact that in 1991 private capital inflows took place even into countries such as Peru, which were suffering from significant financial and other problems, suggests that the external causes of inflows of funds, driven by sharply lower interest rates in the US markets, were a very powerful explanation of such short-term flows. As we will discuss in more depth in the next section, other factors (including not just high Latin American interest rates but also better economic prospects in the region) have also played a major role.

II.2.5 Sources of funds

It is also encouraging that the investor base of flows going to Latin America has broadened significantly, particularly in 1991, to include money managers, pension funds, mutual funds, insurance companies, finance companies, as well as Latin American investors, the latter either returning capital home or investing in other countries in that region. Furthermore, multinational companies are increasing their direct investments in the region. According to the World Bank, Mexico and Brazil were the top two destinations for investment in developing countries in the period 1981 to 1991. The prospect of trade integration between Latin American countries, the US and Canada, is further encouraging the formation of strategic alliances between US and Latin American companies.

An interesting issue is to what extent the capital flowing into Latin America is from Latin American investors returning home their assets previously held abroad. As can be seen in Table 3.8, estimated repatriation of capital flight in 1990 reached $7 billion (for five major countries in the region); this would be

Table 3.8 Estimated capital flight (−) and repatriation (+), 1983–1990.

(US$ billion)	Argentina	Brazil	Chile	Mexico	Venezuela	Total
1983	−1.7	−4.3	+0.2	−1.8	−4.5	−12.1
1984	+0.9	−6.4	+1.2	−3.1	−1.6	−9.0
1985	+0.4	−1.3	+1.0	−4.1	+0.4	−3.6
1986	+1.6	−0.4	+0.6	−2.1	+1.2	+1.0
1987	−1.8	−1.0	+0.2	−1.6	+0.9	−3.2
1988	+0.8	−1.5	−0.6	−5.3	+1.8	−4.7
1989	−1.3	−1.7	0.0	+5.2	+1.2	+3.4
1990	+0.3	−1.0	+1.4	+5.5	+0.7	+7.0
1983–90	−0.7	17.6	+4.1	−7.3	+0.2	−21.3

Source: Chartered West LB (1991) *Developing Country Investment Review*, London, March.

around 40 per cent of total capital inflows into the whole region during that year (see again Table 3.2). For 1989, the proportion would be similar. This would seem to give some credibility to the perception of those observers who believe that more than 50 per cent of the capital entering Latin America is from Latin American investors. However, it would seem[2] that a growing proportion of capital flowing into the region originates from investors outside the region, as the potential and profitability of such flows becomes more broadly known.

In any case, the return of capital which had previously fled is an important and positive trend emerging since 1989. According to Chartered West LB estimates for five major Latin American countries (Mexico, Chile, Venezuela, Brazil and Argentina), there was a total net capital repatriation for 1989–90 of $10.5 billion, which is in sharp contrast with the 1987–8 period when there was a capital flight of $8.0 billion, implying a turnaround of $18.5 billion in a short period.

As can be seen in Table 3.8, the situation was quite heterogeneous across these five countries, in 1989–90. Some countries (Mexico, Venezuela and Chile) saw important levels of repatriation, while other (Brazil and Argentina) saw capital flight; indeed, Brazil – once held as an example of a country to have avoided capital flight – was consistently losing capital between 1983 and 1990. On the other hand, Mexico – a country which traditionally suffered considerable capital flight – had a massive return (estimated at $10 billion) in the 1989–90 period; the Mexican government estimates that a further $5.5 billion returned in 1991. Of the five, the only country that has had a significant net repatriation of capital for the whole 1983–90 period is Chile. This seems to have been due both to so-called economic fundamental factors (strength of macroeconomic policy, good relations with external creditors, private sector orientation, low inflation, positive real interest rates and a welcoming attitude to foreign direct investment) and to institutional factors (debt conversions and dollar-swap mechanism). It is noteworthy that the apparently more sustainable stability given by a successful democratic government (in 1990) resulted in that year in the highest capital repatriation of the period for Chile (see again Table 3.8). It is important to stress that, at least in the Chilean case, a return to democracy has had a favourable effect on capital repatriation.

III CAUSES OF LARGE PRIVATE INFLOWS INTO LATIN AMERICA

It is important to understand the causes of large private inflows into Latin America, not only because this is of interest in itself, but also because such an understanding throws light on two relevant policy issues: one is whether the scale of these private flows is likely to be sustained; the other concerns what other countries (in the rest of Latin America, in the rest of the developing

world and in Eastern Europe) should do to be equally or at least partly as successful as some Latin American countries have been in attracting new flows.

One set of factors relates to overall supply conditions. We have already
mentioned above two key supply factors that have encouraged flows to Latin
America; these are the rapid growth and globalization of world capital markets
(especially of bonds and equities) and the dramatic decline in US dollar short-
term interest rates. Continued recession or slow growth in the US and Europe
further discourage investment there, as do serious debt problems in important
sectors, e.g. real estate, in those countries. The decline in budget deficits in
certain countries (e.g. in the UK) in the 1980s also implied smaller demand
from traditional alternative investment sources, e.g. gilts;[3] a reduction in the
US budget deficit could have a similar effect.

More generally, it should be stressed that net private capital flows to the
Latin American region do not and will not just depend on conditions and
policies in those countries, but also on the savings and investment balances in
the rest of the world, interest rate differentials, and on the efficiency and
stability of international financial and capital markets.

Before continuing our analysis, it seems worthwhile to stress that it is very
encouraging that certain LAC countries have regained access to international
financial and capital markets at a time (1990/91) when several international
factors (declining German current account surplus, increased demands from
Eastern Europe and the former Soviet Union, fragility of some international
banks) were either problematic and/or highly uncertain.

We will now examine the factors which attracted flows specifically to certain
Latin American countries. Clearly improved domestic policies and economic
prospects in Latin American countries played a key role in attracting new flows
to some of the biggest countries in the region, as did other important factors
which we discuss below.

III.1 Improved domestic policies and prospects

There is consensus that one of the key preconditions for access to foreign flows
(as well as encouragement of return capital by nationals) is the reduction of
domestic financial imbalances – where these existed – due to improved
budgetary performance and prudent monetary policies. Among the relevant
factors are reinforcement of fiscal revenue effort and positive real interest rates.
Secondly, policies that enhance the supply response of the economy are clearly
important, including that of production of tradables. As, for example, the
Chilean experience in the 1980s clearly shows, a competitive exchange rate
plays a key role in promoting production of tradables. A third area where
domestic policies seem important is improving economic efficiency through
structural reforms, such as trade liberalization, tax reform, rationalization of
legal and other procedures ruling foreign investment, etc. It should, however,
be emphasized that some of these structural reforms, and in particular trade

liberalizations, initially have high costs, especially if carried out very rapidly and during periods of foreign exchange scarcity, as is well illustrated by the Chilean experience during the 1970s. Latin American countries have made particularly significant efforts also to relax restrictions on foreign ownership, as a way to attract foreign direct investment. As Lustig (1992) emphasizes for the Mexican case, "after 1982 it was no longer possible to wait for foreign investment to follow growth. Foreign investment had to come before growth was in place. It became a needed ingredient for growth"; therefore major efforts were made to attract it. Two types of measures that have clearly encouraged foreign capital inflows are privatization (and the high rates of return associated with it) and development of the domestic capital markets, especially but not only stock exchanges.

There are two areas not so frequently stressed in the academic literature which nevertheless seem important factors to explain both foreign capital inflows and return of flight capital. One is economic growth or the prospect of increased growth. The former was initially illustrated by the Chilean case and the latter illustrated by the Mexican case, where prospects of growth are not only bolstered by recent figures, but also very crucially by the prospects of the Free Trade Agreement (FTA) with the US and Canada. Furthermore, in 1991, for several Latin American countries growth prospects both improved and were seen to improve significantly. However, serious problems remain partly inherited from the 1980s, such as still relatively low levels of investment and a heavily concentrated distribution of income. A second additional factor is political stability, preferably in the context of a relatively consensual and democratic political process. The increase in capital inflows into Chile during the first year of democratic government provides evidence for the importance of this factor.

III.2   Restructuring of existing debt

There is now also agreement in the economic literature[4] that for many countries it is a precondition for renewed capital flows that the "old debt overhang" be eliminated or significantly reduced. There is now strong evidence (for example from Mexico) that at least for some countries there can be a strong complementarity between some debt reduction (as in Mexico, via its Brady deal) and increased capital inflows. As had been hoped by the Mexican government,[5] the positive indirect effects of Mexico's Brady deal became more important than the direct effects. The multi-annual Mexican Brady deal, which not only reduced debt service but also shifted amortizations forward for a significant number of years, reduced uncertainty and provided confidence, contributing to indirect benefits (including significantly increased capital flows and return of capital flight), which are estimated – at least in the short-term – to have been more important than the cash flow effects of the Brady package.[6]

In the case of Venezuela, there is preliminary evidence that also its Brady deal has contributed to increased capital flows. The case of Chile is somewhat different, as its debt overhang was dealt with through pure market-based techniques (mainly via debt–equity swaps) and – in 1990 – a more conventional rescheduling of commercial debt. However, also in this case, the reduction of the debt overhang (together with rapidly growing exports) was an important factor in encouraging new private flows.

It should be mentioned here that rather surprisingly, some countries – like Brazil and Argentina – which had not reached an agreement with the commercial banks and (in the case of Brazil) which had not yet managed to restore macroeconomic equilibrium, nevertheless since 1991 have had access to new capital flows (though at less attractive financial terms). It is interesting that these new private flows may, in the case of Brazil, contribute to a reduction in the debt overhang, thus reversing the causality observed in other countries! Indeed, the sharp increase in Brazil's foreign exchange reserves in 1991, partly caused by these large inflows, may help the Brazilian government put together a Brady-type debt reduction package, as some of these reserves could be used to provide collateral required by banks for this purpose.

These flows seem to have arisen partly[7] on the basis of the expectation that Brazil and Argentina would follow the same path as Chile, Mexico and Venezuela (a sort of positive regionalization of expectations), and partly in view of the fact that it is highly creditworthy companies (allowed unrestricted access to foreign exchange and with a good payment record in the past) which have been attracting these flows. However, in the medium-term, for companies in those countries to borrow significant amounts and at cheaper and longer terms, it seems to be an important prerequisite that the countries' macroeconomic situations should improve and that the debt overhang should have some kind of definite settlement.

Nevertheless, it is important to stress that the "quality" of the companies attracting the flows (whether public or private, or – as often occurred recently – in the context of privatization), is a very significant element in attracting new flows. Large, well-known, creditworthy companies, especially if they are exporters, will find this task much easier. It seems to be the case that the size and reputation of the companies, rather than particular sectors, is what attracts foreign flows. Indeed, foreign flows have been attracted by companies in sectors as diverse as oil, paper, tourism, banks, telephone companies and copper mines; perhaps the main common feature is their ability to generate foreign exchange income via their sales. It is unclear whether small countries in the region (with fewer and less well-known companies in that category) will be equally able to attract in such a large scale the type of new private inflows that are now coming into Mexico, Chile, Venezuela, Colombia and may continue to enter Argentina and Brazil. Their task is made even more difficult if they still have an unresolved debt overhang, as several (e.g. Ecuador) do. In this sense, it seems important if that is the case that:

(1) they get – where necessary – relatively more debt reduction than those countries which can attract new flows.
(2) They get strong support from the IFIs in reaching a rapid favourable debt settlement (as commercial banks may be less keen in those cases to do so, and as they may require more debt reduction).
(3) They continue to have significant access to official flows.
(4) That special efforts are made by IFIs and industrial governments to help those countries attract private flows.

III.3   Reduced transaction costs

Though perhaps somewhat less important, but also of significance, is the fact that there has been a reduction in transaction costs for developing countries to access international capital markets, especially that of the USA. The 1990 approval of Regulation S and Rule 144A has reduced transaction costs and liquidity problems for LAC countries tapping US markets.[8] Regulation S exempts securities from registration and disclosure requirements (with costs for first-time LDC issues estimated formerly in the order of $500,000 to $700,000); simultaneously, the adoption of Rule 144A reduced the loss of liquidity associated with private placements (in the past, buyers of securities through private placements had to hold them for at least two years after the initial offering). Since 1990, "qualified institutional buyers" (e.g. entities managing and owning at least $100 million in securities) have had the two-year holding requirement relaxed. These changes have also reportedly reinforced the possibilities offered by the American Depository Receipts (ADR) programme without meeting the full costs of offerings/listings. This has helped LAC countries (e.g. Chile and Mexico, as described above) to place shares in the US market.

Also, access to bond markets for LAC countries has led to and has been helped by established market-credible credit ratings, thus reducing investors' costs, and allowing access by LAC countries to new segments of the international capital markets, with Mexico receiving its first credit rating by Moody's Investors in December 1990. The ceiling rating for Mexico debt was set at B a 2, just below investment grade, but there seem to be good possibilities for an upgrading. Indeed, it could be argued that the market is already giving investment grade to Mexico and the credit ratings are lagging behind.

These improvements in access to US capital markets should also be accompanied by similar (or equivalent) changes, if necessary, in European and/ or Japanese markets. Some steps have already been taken. For example, in Japan, in June 1991, the authorities lowered the minimum credit rating standards for public bond issues on the Samurai market (from single A to triple B). In Switzerland, steps are being taken to abolish minimum credit requirements.

III.4 Possibility of customizing financial instruments

One option for improving access to capital markets, especially by countries at a stage when they are re-establishing (or establishing) fully their reputation in those markets, is to provide explicit credit enhancements, via either collateralization (e.g. on the basis of existing assets, such as deposits abroad) or an expected stream of receivables (such as Telmex's attracting investors by providing them a claim on payments due to it by the US company AT&T on account of international communications). Another technique recently used by LAC borrowers has been enhancement by early redemption options, and particularly by a "put option" which provides the holder with the discretion to resell (put) the bond to the borrower at a predetermined price.

Such mechanisms have been innovatively used in recent years by Mexican, Venezuelan and other LAC companies; their use could be broadened, if necessary, to companies and countries that need to offer this type of "comfort", and to investors still somewhat worried about credit and transfer risk. However, possible costs of extensive use of this mechanism need to be carefully evaluated, and should be a cause of some concern. These costs include in particular the reduction of flexibility for the country and the company on use of its future income, as well as costs associated with legal and technical arrangements. These should be compared with the advantage of initially helping restore market access and of possibly obtaining funds more cheaply than would otherwise have been possible. More broadly, the proliferation of explicit or implicit government guarantees should be avoided, unless they are essential.

III.5 Other structural elements

As regards foreign direct investment, besides the factors outlined above, there seem to be additional, more structural elements, which influence its level. Thus, a 1992 IFC study[9] concludes rather categorically that recent research suggests that the traditional determinants of FDI levels, such as labour costs and country risk, have become far less important than was the case in the past. On the contrary, structural factors – such as the availability of an educated and highly skilled work-force, market size, quality of infrastructure, level of industrialization and the size of the existing stock of FDI, as an indicator of the quality of the business climate in the country – play an increasingly important role.

IV SUGGESTIONS FOR AN ANALYTICAL FRAMEWORK FOR EVALUATING EFFECTS OF RETURN OF PRIVATE CAPITAL FLOWS TO LATIN AMERICA

Undoubtedly, the fact that private capital flows are flowing back to certain major countries in Latin America is a very positive trend, reflecting international recognition of those countries' improved growth performance, international competitiveness, and declining inflation. Both policy-makers and major social actors in those countries clearly deserve praise for having achieved such important turnarounds in their economies, having encouraged such rapid renewed access to private capital markets so soon after the major debt crises of the 1980s.

In clearly welcoming these trends, certain policy-relevant questions need to be asked. Are the current high levels of net private flows to those countries likely to be sustainable for a long period? Are the terms, in relation to maturities, costs and guarantees particularly of borrowing, not too onerous for the recipient economies? Are the risks taken by lenders/investors not eventually going to become too high? Are the external resources being productively invested in the country? Is a sufficiently high proportion of this investment in foreign exchange generating/saving economic activity, that will help service the debt or generate other flows abroad? Are these large flows not having undesirable, as well as clearly desirable, macroeconomic effects on the recipient economies? What measures are being taken by governments of recipient economies to counteract such problematic effects, and how effective are they? It seems a rather urgent task to conduct fairly detailed empirical research which will provide a more informed basis for answering such questions.

On a more positive note, questions need to be asked on what lessons can be learnt from such countries as Chile and Mexico by other developing countries, as well as by East European countries and the republics of the former Soviet Union, on how they can regain or gain access to international private capital markets. Is it likely that other countries (in Latin America, but also in poorer parts of the world, such as Africa) can gain/regain access to new private flows? Or are there structural reasons which make it more difficult? If so, what can be done, within and outside those countries, to help them gain access to private capital markets? What role should be played by guarantee mechanisms, for example via the World Bank and/or regional banks to encourage new private flows to the poorer, less creditworthy countries?

Returning to the Latin American countries that have regained market access, policy questions need to be asked in countries both where flows originate and are received. At one level, what can be done to improve, deepen and make sustainable access by those countries to developed countries' flows? What can be done especially for improving access to flows that are more long-term, and have lower as well as less variable cost? At another level, should regulators and supervisors in developed and developing countries increase their monitoring, supervision and possibly regulation, especially of the new categories of flows that are coming in, such as for example portfolio investment? How best can a balance be achieved which satisfies prudential needs without unduly constraining access to LDCs?

The need to ask this type of question arises both out of economic history and out of economic analysis. Writers such as Bagehot (1873), and far more recently Kindleberger (1978), have pointed out that private capital markets tend to be characterized by successive periods of over-lending and under-lending, often resulting in costly financial crises. Kindleberger analyses the pattern of boom (usually in times of upward movement in the business cycle) and over-contraction of lending, usually in times of slow-down of economic activity, and has illustrated this pattern with historical examples, going as far back as the South Sea Bubble. Marichal (1988) and others have described the five great debt crises resulting from previous lending booms that have occurred in Latin America since independence, in the mid-1820s, in the mid-1870s, in early 1890s, in the 1930s and in the 1980s.

A particularly useful framework of analysis for current new flows is suggested by a recent paper by Corden (1990), and by John Williamson's comments on it,[10] focused on lessons of experience from lending booms in the 1970s and the debt crises of the 1980s. Based on empirical analysis, Corden examines phenomena of increased spending in developing countries, whether on consumption and investment, caused mainly by ready availability of funds from world capital markets; he stresses the importance of public spending booms, but recognizes that private sector booms have in practice similar effects (as illustrated by the Chilean experience in the 1970s and early 1980s). Two effects of the booms need to be carefully distinguished: the first is the Keynesian effect, which reflects itself via higher demand for home-produced goods and a reduction of the foreign exchange constraint, in a short-term rise in the growth rate; to the extent that the increase in demand (and the inflows of capital) are temporary, this Keynesian boom is temporary. Not only the rate of growth of output initially rises, but to the extent that the boom was financed by foreign flows, spending can grow even faster. Once – and if – a debt crisis starts, investment and growth of output fall, often drastically; debt service payments are rising very fast, the rate of growth – or the level of national income – fall even more. Usually in the first phase, there is an appreciation of the exchange rate, as the capital inflows create a "Dutch disease" type of pressure, often welcomed by governments understandably anxious to lower inflation or avoid its increase. The second type of effect of lending booms (that needs to be carefully distinguished from the former) is on growth of capacity (on the supply side). What is crucial here is the proportion of external flows going to investment in the country, how productive it is, and what proportion of it is – directly and/or indirectly – converted into tradables. If enough efficient investment takes place and output rises sufficiently (and is converted into tradables in a large enough proportion), it is more likely that future debt service or other flows generated by the original inflows can be financed without problem.[11] The rise in debt or foreign investment will not have been a problem; indeed, it will have temporarily increased the rate of growth and made the country permanently better off. What Corden surprisingly does not mention is that, if other positive effects are unchained (such as increased productivity of investment and/or increase in domestic saving and investment), the long-term effects on growth can be even bigger and more sustainable.

However, there is also a less rosy scenario. If increased investment proves insufficient and/or inefficient (the latter, either because it was *ex-ante* inefficient or because unexpected adverse movements of international interest rates, terms of trade or other changes occur) and if insufficient production of tradables is generated, then the initial output growth is followed by a debt problem, leading possibly to reductions in total absorption below levels that could have been sustained in the absence of the earlier boom. Thus, particularly the total effect (through time) of such flows on the country's retained income can be negative, even if the effect on output may have been positive.

The rosy scenario is more likely to materialize if the modality of flows is better suited for long-term growth. This implies preferably long-term, low-cost modalities, or even better, mechanisms where outflows are linked to results. In this sense, it is important that LDC borrowers make use of instruments available on the market, that reduce vulnerability to variables such as commodity prices and international interest rates, and that they contribute to the further development of such instruments. Short-term lending at variable interest rates is, on the other hand, particularly undesirable, as the experience of the 1980s so dramatically shows.

Because of the risk of the less rosy scenario occurring, precautions would seem essential to minimize such risks and to maximize the likelihood that both investors, lenders, as well as recipients and borrowers, obtain not just short-term but also sustainable benefits from such flows. A strengthening of international public compensatory mechanisms (e.g. via enlargement of the IMF facility for this purpose) could give an additional layer of protection against instability in international variables, such as commodity prices and interest rates.

It should be stressed that the renewal of private flows to Latin America in the early 1990s has played a key positive role in helping to kick-start economic recovery, in reviving domestic private sector confidence and increasing government revenues, thus making the funding of urgently needed social spending possible in reviving domestic private sector confidence and increasing government revenues. The value of this initial, positive Keynesian effect of foreign flows should therefore not be under-estimated, especially in a region which is emerging from a "lost decade" in terms of growth and development.

More problematic has been, possibly, the appreciation of real exchange rates during 1991. Of eighteen Latin American countries, fifteen had their exchange rate appreciate by between 5 and 20 per cent during 1991. Though partly in the correct direction, compensating for massive real devaluations in the 1980s, these revaluations in 1991 and early 1992 pose the risk of growing increasingly unsustainable trade deficits, especially in some countries.

V CONCLUSIONS AND POLICY SUGGESTIONS

Drawing on this framework, it seems important to stress the following:

(1) As regards the scale of private flows, and especially debt-creating ones, it seems desirable that all involved should err on the side of prudence. It is when international private flows represent a very large proportion of developing countries' GDP or (particularly) exports, that their impact on borrowers and lenders is more likely to become problematic.

(2) Some type of flows seem more desirable than others, and where possible, recipient and originating countries' governments should encourage a desirable mix. Foreign direct investment on the whole seems more desirable than lending, as it tends to imply more careful cost-benefit calculation by investors, is more likely to bring additional efficiency gains, and because profit remittances tend to be more closely linked to the success of the project than debt servicing. However, in some cases the rates of profit remittance may surpass the cost of debt servicing. This is a subject where more recent analysis of empirical trends may be required. Within borrowing, longer maturities are obviously preferable to short-term ones; fixed interest instruments are preferable to variable interest ones, unless expectations of declining interest rates are strong, and – obviously, but often forgotten – unless the country has no other option, borrowing at very high cost may be less desirable than not borrowing at all.

The evidence presented in Section II seems to indicate that most of the private flows of the early 1990s have a better profile than those of the 1970s, in that a higher proportion (e.g. in Chile and Mexico) comes in the form of foreign direct investment, and a higher proportion of lending to some countries (e.g. Mexico) comes via fixed interest bonds. Furthermore, as discussed above, the conditions on bonds, particularly for Mexico have improved rather significantly, especially in terms of large reduction in risk premiums. In the case of other countries, e.g. Brazil and Peru, a large proportion of flows seem to come in via rather short-term and high-cost lending, which is far more problematic.

This leads to two preliminary conclusions. One is the need by the recipient countries and by international institutions, such as the IMF and BIS, to monitor carefully and precisely all capital inflows into different Latin American countries, as well as their conditions. This is no easy task, as some of the flows may not be currently registered and as there are methodological problems (such as, for example, to calculate effective yields on bonds rather than initial yields, which are normally recorded). Efforts need to be made in this direction, to avoid the problems of the mid to late 1970s, when there was insufficient information on private flows, contributing to incorrect decision-making. A second conclusion is that it may be necessary for recipient countries in particular to discourage excessive inflows, particularly of certain types of inflows. In this sense, recent measures (through different mechanisms by the Chilean, Mexican and Brazilian governments, either to discourage all flows or more short-term ones) were clearly well taken. Further measures may be required in those or other countries if flows continue at excessive levels.

As regards types of flow, it has been argued in certain circles that there is a smaller risk of negative effects if the flows originate in and go to the private sector. In relation to bonds, for Mexico (in 1991) and Brazil (1991), Tables 3.9 and 3.10 clearly indicate that most of the bond finance flowed into the private sector, though in the case of

Table 3.9   Mexico: issue of bonds, by type of borrowers.

	Number of issues			Amount in %		
	1989	1990	1991[a]	1989	1990	1991[a]
Public						
Sovereign			2			
Banks		4	1	29.9	21.9	5.1
Development banks		2	1		4.4	6.4
Eximbank	1	1	2		6.6	8.9
PEMEX		4	3		11.0	14.0
TELMEX	1	2		47.8	22.6	
CFE		1			10.3	
Sub-total	2	14	9	77.6	76.7	34.4
Private						
Banks		1	2		2.2	4.8
Cement	1	1	2	22.4	4.4	29.3
Mining		2			6.6	
Telmex			1		0.0	29.0
Tobacco		1			2.9	
Oil		1	1		1.4	2.5
Steel		1			2.2	
Others		2			3.6	
Sub-total	1	9	6	22.4	23.3	65.6
Total	3	23	15	100.0	100.0	100.0

Source: Data based on Banco de Mexico information.
[a] Prior to September 1991.

Table 3.10   Brazil: issue of bonds, by type of borrowers, 1991.

	Issues	Amount (US$ million)	%
Public			
Sovereign			
Banks			
Development bank	1	55	1.61
Eximbank			
PETROBRAS	5	842	24.72
TELEBRAS[a]	2	225	6.61
Sub-total		1,122	32.94
Private			
Steel	1	200	5.87
Bank	2	130	3.82
Celulose	1	40	1.17
Computers	1	100	2.94
Deriv. oil	1	50	1.47
Chemical	3	120	3.52
Others	4	186	5.46
Others (US$ 20m.)		1,458	42.81
Sub-total		2,284	67.06
Total		3,406	100.0

Source: Data based on Salomon Brothers (1992).
[a] It was expected that Telebras would start being privatized in 1993.

Mexico, the situation was different in 1989 and 1990 (see again Table 3.9). Though this should provide some comfort, as the private sector is likely to be more efficient than state enterprises, it needs to be remembered that some of the previous boom–bust lending cycles have also involved private actors as both lenders and borrowers.

While private actors may be more efficient at taking decisions and managing enterprises at a microeconomic level, governments and public international organizations do have an advantage in analysing trends at a macroeconomic level, to evaluate whether the sum of microeconomic decisions taken by private actors is efficient and sustainable in the present and future. Hence, the need for government monitoring, supervision and regulation of private flows.

Furthermore, as regards private investors, especially in bonds, it is interesting that the risk is not wholly taken by them, as most bond issues (particularly to private sector borrowers) are either collateralized by receivables and by letters of credit, or have put options; this transfers part of the risk to the borrower. Though attractive and ingenious as a mechanism for helping re-entry to capital markets, it implies that investors may not evaluate the risk as fully as they would in other circumstances, and as a result of these conditions, the supply of finance does not reflect pure market risk/ reward ratios.

More broadly, private lenders and borrowers (and especially large ones) may assume, based on past experience, that there are implicit government guarantees or forms of insurance on their flows; this may further increase supply beyond levels that pure market considerations would determine. This provides a particularly strong, theoretical and practical reason for government supervision and regulation, at the stage when new flows are expanding, as governments may be brought in anyway at a later stage, if things go wrong, to bail out the private sector at the taxpayers' expense. Even more generally, it can be argued that because financial markets are prone to over-react, in both directions, and this may have severe costs for the society as a whole, the need to avoid such market failures justifies the need for regulation and supervision.

(3) It is necessary that the projects which new flows are to finance should be evaluated carefully, using cost-benefit techniques which compare the present value of estimated total costs and revenues, and examining in particular the estimated foreign exchange cost-benefit balance of individual projects, as well as the overall sum of costs and benefits for all inflows. As Corden (1990) and Williamson (1990) correctly point out, in such evaluations due account needs to be taken of future likely devaluations, if and when the lending boom diminishes.

As risks tend to be distributed in an unclear fashion among private lenders/investors and borrowers, and among private and public institutions (both in originating and recipient countries), it seems important that at least one actor carries out rigorous and careful cost-benefit analysis. In this sense, it would seem desirable that governments in recipient countries either carry out such analysis themselves or verify strictly that the private sector is doing so, providing the necessary technical assistance if required.

It is naturally essential that such evaluations, and other necessary supervisory or regulatory measures (e.g. of local stock exchanges) are not done in a way that would stifle such flows with unnecessary red tape. The need for agility should, however, be combined with a minimum of prudence. Such a balance is not easy, given the speed with which booms of lending/investment originate and develop, as well as the large scale on which they often take place. Relevant timely and independent technical assistance (from IFIs, developed country regulators, from other LDC regulators) may be very valuable; rapid exchange of information among regulators of different sectors (banking, securities, others) and different countries may need to be organized on a systematic basis. Regulatory and information gaps need to be filled quickly, to the extent that the creation of new markets may not yet have been accompanied by appropriate supervisory and regulatory institutions.

In the case of developed countries, the need for more appropriate regulation and supervision of flows to developing countries in certain sectors (e.g. insurance companies, pension funds) needs to be put in a broader context of appropriate regulation of all these institutions' investments.

(4) Difficult issues of macroeconomic management are raised for recipient countries, especially as regards their levels of spending, control of the money supply and exchange rate.

As Williamson (1990) and Corden (1990) both clearly conclude, countries should try to restrict their spending to the level of their permanent income. Equally, they need an exchange rate that is consistent with long-term equilibrium in the balance of payments. However, in practice, these are complex matters, as for example the level of permanent income or of an "equilibrium exchange rate" crucially depends (among other factors) on how large and how permanent private capital flows will be, on future evaluation of terms of trade, international interest rates, etc. Again, erring on the side of prudence may be advisable, as regards some counter-cyclical policy and avoiding excessive over-valuation.

Further policy-relevant research is required that studies the policy dilemmas in the new circumstances (both internationally and nationally), taking into account the far more deregulated international environment and the greater openness and reliance on market forces of recipient economies. Interchange of policy experiences among countries and an analysis of their effectiveness will be valuable; European experiences, for example, in the case of Spain in the late 1980s, may provide interesting lessons for LAC countries receiving massive inflows of capital.

(5) Finally, it should be emphasized that creditors and investors do have very good long-term reasons to channel funds into certain Latin American countries. These have made major and costly efforts at very successfully restoring macroeconomic equilibrium, under very difficult circumstances; they have also introduced a number of structural reforms, which have increased dramatically the ability of those countries to augment exports. Partly as a result of such efforts, growth has in some countries increased (though investment levels are still relatively low) and inflation has come down. More importantly,

perhaps, there is strong consensus within these countries for continuation of such policies.

There is, however, perhaps need for a final word of warning. This is for both lenders/investors to beware of euphoria; also, successful governments in Latin American countries would probably do well to remember Williamson's (1990) wise though apparently conservative suggestion, that all positive shocks should be treated as though they were transitory and all negative shocks as though they were permanent. The most hopeful element about the new situation is perhaps precisely that in many respects, many Latin American governments (though clearly not all) seem to be taking such advice seriously. If this continues, perhaps the new private capital inflows to them may be sustainable in the medium term, and the "rosy scenario" may materialize, as it has in some selected developing countries, such as South Korea.

Besides prudence in financial and macroeconomic matters, as well as the other elements discussed above, a precondition for the "rosy scenario" may be sustained efforts, e.g. by increases in government social spending, in education and health to improve the welfare of the poorest groups in Latin American countries. Besides it being equitable, such measures would both improve political stability and sustainability and contribute to human capital development, essential both for growth and for attracting long-term capital flows. Furthermore, given the current macroeconomic situation, such increases in social spending could be more easily funded in a non-inflationary manner. Indeed, for example, the very fact that international and domestic interest rates are declining for many Latin American governments, as well as the revaluation of their currencies, eases the domestic currency cost for those governments to service their debt, both domestic and foreign. This allows them some scope for non-inflationary increases in social spending.

NOTES

1 See El-Erian (1992).
2 Interview material.
3 "Pension Fund Investment", *Financial Times*, May 7, 1992.
4 Among those stressing the direct link between debt reduction and new capital flows, see Dooley (1990) and van Wijnbergen (1991). Sachs, Krugman and others have argued in a similar way.
5 See Aspe (1990).
6 For a more detailed discussion, see S. Griffith-Jones (1991), "Is there still a Latin American debt crisis?", paper prepared for CEPAL.
7 Interview material.
8 See Pfefferman and Madarassy (1992).
9 See Pfefferman and Madarassy (1992).

10 See Williamson (1990).
11 For a more detailed discussion, see Griffith-Jones (1991).

REFERENCES

Aspe, P. (1990) "The Renegotiation of Mexico's External Debt", in M. Faber and S. Griffith-Jones (eds), *Approaches to Third World Debt Reduction*, IDS Bulletin 21(2), April.

Bagehot, W. (1873) *Lombard Street: A Description of the Money Market*, J. Murray, London.

Corden, M. (1990) "Macro-economic Policy and Growth: Some Lessons of Experience", in World Bank, *Proceedings of the World Bank Annual Conference on Development Economics*, Washington DC.

Dooley, M. (1990) "Market Valuation of External Debt", in J. Frenkel, M. Dooley and P. Wickan (eds), *Analytical Issues in Debt*, IMF, Washington DC.

El-Erian, M.A. (1992) "Restoration of Access to Voluntary Capital Market Financing", *IMF Staff Papers* 39(1).

Griffith-Jones, S. (1991) "International Financial Markets; A Case of Market Failure", in C. Colclough and J. Manor (eds), *States or Markets? Neo-liberalism and the Development Policy*, Clarendon Press, Oxford.

IMF (1991) *International Capital Markets, Developments and Prospects*, World Economic and Financial Surveys, Washington DC.

Kindleberger, C. (1978) *Manias, Panics and Crashes: A History of Financial Crisis*, Macmillan, Basingstoke.

Kuczynski, P.P. (1992) "International Capital Flows into Latin America: What is the Promise?", *World Bank Annual Conference on Development Economics*.

Lustig, N. (1992) "Mexico's Integration Strategy with North America", in C. Bradford (ed.), *Strategic Options for Latin America*, OECD Development Centre and IADB, Paris.

Marichal, C. (1988) *Historia de la deuda externa de América Latina*, Alianza Editorial, Madrid.

OECD (1992) *Financial Market Trends* 51, February.

Pfefferman, G. and A. Madarassy (1992) *Trends in Private Investment in Developing Countries*, Discussion Paper, IFC, Washington DC.

Salomon Brothers (1992) *Private Capital Flows to Latin America: Volume Triples to US$ 40b in 1991*, February 12, New York.

van Wijnbergen, S. (1991) "Mexico and the Brady Plan", *Economic Policy*, April.

West, P. (1991) "El regreso de los países latinoamericanos al mercado internacional de capitales privados", *Revista de la CEPAL*, September, Santiago, Chile.

Williamson, J. (1990) "Comment on Corden's Paper", in World Bank, *Proceedings of the World Bank Annual Conference on Development Economics*, Washington DC.

4 | Latin America's Balance of Payments: Pessimism or Cautious Optimism?

GRAHAM BIRD

While viewed as a "lost decade" in terms of economic development in Latin America, the 1980s have illustrated that it is dangerous in the short run and impossible in the long run to ignore the balance of payments. Ultimately the balance of payments acts as a binding constraint on economic development. Benefits associated with relaxing the constraint at one moment in time carry with them costs in terms of imposing a stricter constraint in the future; there is a strong intertemporal dimension. It may be human nature, and it is certainly politically expedient to place a high discount rate on future costs, but it is simply unwarranted optimism to assume that tomorrow never comes.

The fundamental nature of the balance of payments is implicit in the more conventional emphasis put on domestic saving and foreign exchange gaps. From a national income accounting perspective, the balance of payments reflects the difference between domestic investment and domestic saving, with excess investment revealing itself in a payments deficit. By the same token, an excess of import payments over export revenue effectively defines a current account deficit. Even three-gap analysis which additionally accentuates the fiscal gap between government expenditure and tax revenue has an external connotation, in the sense that fiscal deficits are strongly and positively associated with balance of payments deficits.

If the binding nature of the balance of payments is accepted, it follows that economic recovery in any country will only be as strong as the underlying balance of payments. Weakness here will in the long run undermine economic development. In the short run, pessimistic expectations generated by this long-term weakness will induce a behavioural response that brings economic problems forward in time. Living for the day in a macroeconomic world dominated by expectations, credibility, and time inconsistency may simply be ineffective as well as inefficient.

Adopting this view raises some well-focused and strategic questions about the nascent economic recovery that some observers have identified in Latin

American countries at the beginning of the 1990s. To what extent are Latin American economies free from the secular deterioration in the balance of payments which is frequently associated with adverse movements in developing countries' terms of trade? Is their balance of payments vulnerable to external shocks emanating from export shortfalls, or import and interest rate excesses; and, leading on from this, to what extent does the balance of payments performance of Latin America depend on economic growth in the major industrial countries? Has domestic macroeconomic management secured stabilization, or will fiscal and monetary excesses continue to fuel the inflation which is often viewed as endemic or inertial within Latin America? What are the prospects for appropriate economic adjustment; will relations with the international financial institutions be harmonious and result in successful programmes? Will the availability of international finance enable Latin American economies to select the optimum blend of financing and adjustment, or will evaporating creditworthiness force countries to pursue stricter and more anti-growth adjustment paths? Has the external debt crisis been overcome, or has the debt overhang left Latin America with an economic hangover, as well as acute balance of payments vulnerability?

The very length and significance of this litany of questions must raise considerable doubts about the chances of prolonged economic success in Latin America. Even if the outlook across a broad range of determinants were to be bright, the vulnerability of the balance of payments to unforeseen shocks of both domestic and foreign origin counsels against unbridled optimism.

The remainder of this chapter briefly examines the questions raised above, drawing on individual country examples where appropriate. While there are clearly many important differences between the balance of payments circumstances of specific Latin American economies, there are also significant similar and unifying themes and it will be upon these that the chapter concentrates. A short statistical appendix giving data on key aspects of Latin America's balance of payments is provided to help illustrate some of the issues raised.

I   AN ANALYTICAL FRAMEWORK

Any general theory of the balance of payments must comprise a number of elements, although this does not imply that each element will be equally important in every particular case. It is unhelpful to see balance of payments theories as competing and conflictual. A general theory will include structural, absorption, monetarist, and portfolio components.

Structural elements incorporate the type of goods and services produced and exported and by implication therefore not produced (or only produced at prohibitive costs) and imported. Where exports possess a lower income elasticity of demand than do imports and appropriate assumptions are made about national and world income growth, a secular deterioration in the balance of payments will result. Although conventionally used to illustrate the structural balance of payments weakness of economies that depend heavily on primary products, this so-called Houthakker-Magee effect (Houthakker and Magee, 1969) has also been found to make an important contribution towards explaining the current account problems of more developed economies such as the US.

Structural problems also emanate from the pattern of trade and the efficiency of production, which then impacts on international competitiveness. Inefficiency, however, is merely an intermediate explanation – the ultimate question is why inefficiency exists. In this connection, as well as in others, structural elements of the balance of payments relate to the supply side of the economy.

The absorption approach concentrates instead on the balance between aggregate domestic supply and aggregate domestic demand, viewing balance of payments deficits as the consequence of excess demand (or deficient supply). A Keynesian income–expenditure model for an open economy is used to express current account disequilibria in terms of domestic macroeconomic imbalances. Assuming an economy is operating at full capacity, it will be excess expenditure in the form of private consumption, investment and government spending which results in BoP deficits; in Keynesian tradition, inept fiscal policy is deemed to be at the heart of the problem.

It is important to note, however, that the absorption approach is quite consistent with a supply-side orientation. It is clearly preferable to correct BoP deficits by raising aggregate supply than by lowering aggregate demand, the adjustment with growth alternative.

Increasing national income will also dampen monetary pressures on the BoP, since it will increase the demand for money. The monetary approach highlights domestic monetary disequilibria as the root cause of BoP disequilibria, with excess growth in the domestic money supply creating BoP deficits. However, monetary influences on the balance of payments cannot be isolated from fiscal impulses, since it is likely to be fiscal pressures which lead to monetary excesses in the first place.

The sources of BoP disequilibria discussed above have their primary impact on the current account. By contrast, portfolio factors exert primary influence over the capital account. Here, capital movements reflect the correction of portfolio imbalances which are themselves created by divergent interest rates, disequilibrium real exchange rates and the expectations to which these give rise.

Since the theory of the balance of payments is multi-faceted, with disequilibria being a function of many, frequently interrelated, components, it would be unwise for governments in Latin America or analysts of the region to ignore any potentially significant cause. From a full appraisal of the possible sources of disequilibria identified by BoP analysis, an appreciation may be gained of the likely course of Latin America's balance of payments during the 1990s and beyond, or, more accurately, of the scope for variability in the course that will be followed.

The uncertainty surrounding Latin America's BoP prospects is heightened by two further considerations. First, how vulnerable are Latin American economies to export and world interest rate instability, and how sensitive is economic growth to such instability? Second, where BoP deficits arise, how well-equipped are the economies of Latin America to implement effective policy action to deal with such deficits?

It is in the context of stabilization and adjustment policy that the political economy of the balance of payments assumes central importance. Some socio-political-institutional structures will provide a more conducive environment in which to pursue BoP correction than others. Where there is powerful political resistance to measures designed to raise international competitiveness which invariably carry with them at least short-term sacrifices in terms of domestic living standards, the balance of payments becomes much more of a problem than in countries where the political impediments are less pronounced. The economic history of the region, as well as contemporaneous studies of the factors which contribute to political uncertainty, such as the degree of income inequality, suggest that the balance of payments will continue to create considerable difficulties for many Latin American economies.

While political factors will influence both stabilization and adjustment policies, it is important to retain an analytical distinction between them. Economic adjustment involves a change in the level or distribution of productive resources within an economy, whereas stabilization involves correcting imbalances between aggregate demand and aggregate supply, which reflect themselves in inflation and/or exchange rate disequilibria by means of reducing the level of aggregate demand.

An important question relates to the connection between stabilization and economic adjustment. There can be little doubt that it is difficult to achieve adjustment in an economy suffering from chronic macroeconomic instability. In such an environment, relative price changes are difficult to disentangle from the "noise" of absolute price changes, and resource allocation stands the risk of being inefficient. At the same time, however, there is a fundamental intertemporal inconsistency between reducing aggregate demand now and raising aggregate supply in the future. Unless there are spare resources, it will always be difficult to raise aggregate supply in the short run, and the emphasis will therefore be placed on lowering aggregate demand. But investment and capital expenditure by the government are unlikely to be insulated from such demand deflation. If they were to be, this would mean that cuts in demand would be concentrated on current consumption, and this is probably the most politically sensitive area of domestic aggregate demand. A strategy which focuses on reducing current consumption is likely to have a self-destruction element in societies that are politically volatile.

Cutting capital expenditure as a means of avoiding these short-term political constraints carries with it longer-term economic and political problems, since reduced capital accumulation will have an adverse effect on future aggregate supply. This analysis suggests that stabilization has to be treated as part of an overall adjustment programme, the essential components of which are protected as far as possible from the adverse effects of macroeconomic stabilization.[1]

A different angle on the underlying problems associated with BoP adjustment is provided by focusing directly on the current account and on exports and imports. In principle, countries may clearly exert an impact on their export performance through measures designed to influence competitiveness and the composition of exports. But the success of such an adjustment strategy will be constrained by the level of demand in principal markets. Moreover, there is always the theoretical danger that success in increasing the volume of exports may induce an adverse commodity terms of trade effect, with this translating itself into an adverse effect on the income terms of trade and therefore on export revenue. Are Latin American economies international price takers, or do they face price-inelastic demand? Raising export supply will, in the latter case, drive down export earnings. The question is whether the adverse terms of trade effect is just a theoretical abstraction or a practical reality.[2]

With such theoretical uncertainties, but perhaps even more so given the practical difficulties in achieving export expansion in the short run, it is not surprising to find BoP policy emphasizing import compression. But according to our earlier definition, such a strategy is more a matter of stabilization than of adjustment. Indeed it is within this context that short-term stabilization may threaten long-term economic adjustment, since imports may be strategic inputs which make a significant contribution to economic development, exports, and long-run increases in an economy's productive potential.[3]

The above analytical discussion identifies a range of pitfalls surrounding the future evolution of any economy's balance of payments. It also confirms that once an economy begins to suffer from macroeconomic instability and disequilibrium, the restoration of a new stable equilibrium is painful and difficult to achieve, whatever policies are adopted. In the next section we move on to apply aspects of our analytical framework to Latin America.

II   LATIN AMERICA'S BALANCE OF PAYMENTS: EXPERIENCE AND EVIDENCE

Wherein lie the threats to Latin America's future BoP performance? Do structural, absorption and monetary factors point to an underlying strengthening in the region's balance of payments, or are pessimistic prognostications in fact more realistic?

To what extent will Latin America enjoy continuing access to the financing option, or will it be forced to implement a blend of policy which is heavy on stabilization and light on international financing?

What form will stabilization and adjustment take, and what are the chances of success? While the balance of payments acts as a constraint on economic development, there are other factors which in turn constrain balance of payments policy.

A great deal of detailed evidence on the structure and pattern of the trade of Latin American economies is provided by Chapter 2 in this book, by Alicia Puyana. She shows that many Latin American economies still rely heavily on minerals, metals and agricultural goods for their export earnings, and that for ten Latin American economies, the share of manufactured goods in total exports actually fell during the mid-1980s. She also observes the high degree of concentration of manufactured exports within Latin America, with 80 per cent of the region's total exports of manufactured goods originating in Brazil, Mexico and Argentina. Even for these countries, exports of manufactures are less important than exports of non-manufactured goods. (Summary data on Latin America's BoP are provided in Tables 4.1, 4.2, 4.3 and 4.4 in the statistical appendix to this chapter.)

There is, moreover, little evidence to support the claim that the shift away from import substituting industrialization (ISI) and towards export promotion has had much discernible impact on the pattern of exports, or that the investment necessary to change the structure of exports is likely to be forthcoming in the foreseeable future. This means that Latin America will not be exempt from the primary product syndrome that is more normally seen as characterizing the low income countries of Africa and Asia, even if it suffers from the syndrome in a less acute form. Latin America's concentration on the export of raw materials which have traditionally been found to exhibit both low price and low income elasticities of demand makes export expansion difficult. The lower income elasticity of demand that has regularly been found for primary products as compared with manufactured goods further implies that Latin American economies will indeed be exposed to the Houthakker-Magee effect.[4] Moreover, the impact of this effect will be exaggerated by recession among the industrial countries of the world which provide the principal markets for Latin American exports. In 1990, almost 70 per cent of exports from Latin America were destined for the United States, member-countries of the European Community, and Japan; although the relative importance of these specific markets varied between individual Latin American economies, with, for example, Argentina and Chile having a relatively strong orientation towards Europe, and Mexico and Venezuela being strongly oriented towards the US.

Given the significance of raw material exports, it is relevant to note that in the year running from the third quarter of 1991 to the third quarter of 1992, industrial production rose by only 0.8 per cent in the US, and fell by 2.3 per cent in Germany, 0.8 per cent in France, 1.2 per cent in Italy and 0.6 per cent in the United Kingdom. In the same period industrial production fell by 6.1 per cent in Japan. Future export growth in Latin America must surely depend on how strongly and quickly the major industrial economies move out of recession.

The sensitivity of Latin American economies to economic policy and performance in OECD countries is also confirmed by simulation models of North–South macroeconomic interactions. Modelling contractionary monetary policy in the G3 countries (the US, Germany and Japan) for the early 1980s, Allen, Currie, Srinivasan and Vines (1992) discovered that there is a pronounced adverse effect on Latin American output, domestic prices, investment, and consumption. In the case of output, the deviation from trend is between −5.0 and −5.5 per cent over the first two years, but the effect on investment, which initially falls by 10–14 per cent, is particularly strong and of considerable significance, given the importance of investment in terms of future aggregate supply, and therefore the future balance of payments. The immediate effect of the G3's contractionary monetary policy on Latin America's current account balance of payments was, according to the model, to create an additional deficit of $14.2 billion.[5]

Other econometric studies examining the 1970s have confirmed that the balance of payments in developing countries is significantly and importantly influenced by externally caused movements in the terms of trade, as well as by variations in world interest rates (Khan and Knight, 1983) and preliminary findings from regression analysis of the balance of payments of developing countries in the 1980s seem to support a similar conclusion.[6]

If these results are accepted, it becomes clear that the Latin American balance of payments, and economic performance in general, is vulnerable to external influences and shocks, and that this in turn creates great uncertainty for BoP forecasting. It also becomes relevant to ask whether, apart from adverse secular movements, variations in export earnings or interest payments about the trend generate instability for Latin America's balance of payments, and whether such instabilities have adverse long-term consequences for economic development. While the evidence on the consequences of commodity price instability for those countries whose exports are concentrated on primary commodities is far from being unambiguous, there is strong evidence to suggest that undiversified export mixes do create BoP difficulties.[7]

Moreover, for the highly-indebted Latin American economies, the balance of payments will be exposed to the consequences of variations in world interest rates in terms of both their effect on debt repayments and their effect on capital flows. The effects of changes in interest rates may of course either reinforce or offset the effects of changes in export earnings. Examining the causes of changes in debt service ratio (DSR) during 1980–85, Gibson and Thirlwall (1988) found that the relative effects of changes in interest rates and export earnings varied across Latin American economies. In Brazil the interest rate effect contributed 9.2 percentage points to the fall in the DSR, whereas the effect of rising export earnings contributed 10.3 percentage points. In Venezuela, where the DSR also fell, falling interest rates contributed 3.8 percentage points, whereas falling export earnings served to raise the DSR. A similar pattern existed in Peru. In Mexico, Argentina and Chile the DSR rose. In Mexico both interest rate and export earnings effects served, in part, to offset the effects of a rising volume of debt. In Argentina both served to push up the DSR, and in Chile the interest rate effect was weakly negative while the export earnings effect was strongly positive. In Bolivia a negative interest rate effect was also outweighed by a positive export earnings effect. Taking Latin and Central America together, the data show that for 1980–2 the fall in export earnings contributed more than twice as much as the increase in interest rates to the increase in the region's DSR. For 1982–5, however, the fall in interest rates was eight times as important as the rise in export earnings in accounting for the fall in the DSR.

Although such evidence is primarily directed towards providing information on the structure of the debt crisis, it also shows the significance of variations in world interest rates for the balance of payments of highly indebted Latin American economies. Debt concentration as well as export concentration imposes a structural constraint on the balance of payments of many Latin American economies. While falling world interest rates strengthen the balance of payments of highly indebted countries by reducing interest rate payments and perhaps by opening up interest rate differentials which generate positive new capital inflows as well as the repatriation of flight capital, rising world interest rates may equally swiftly cause capital inflows to evaporate and place an additional burden on the balance of payments. Until it becomes possible to forecast world interest rates with some precision it remains impossible to forecast precisely the future evolution of Latin America's balance of payments. It is only possible to anticipate its vulnerability to changes in the world economic environment.

Not only is it exogenous factors which create uncertainty for the balance of payments of Latin American economies. Absorption and monetary models highlight the significance of maintaining domestic macroeconomic equilibrium and therefore the importance of the fiscal and monetary balance. Killick and Malik (1992) argue that in the case of both Brazil and Mexico, external factors only reinforced domestic macroeconomic weaknesses. In Brazil they argue that international bank credit was used as an alternative to the economic adjustment that oil shocks required. In the presence of substantial macro imbalances, expansionary fiscal and monetary policies were pursued, and even though the currency depreciated in nominal terms the real rate appreciated. Their conclusion is that, "the rise in world interest rates and weakening world demand for the country's exports merely executed the *coup de grâce*, precipitating in 1982–83 a crisis of macroeconomic management which had seemed only a matter of time in any case" (p. 603).

In the Mexican case, Killick and Malik argue that the government did not comprehend the economy's vulnerability to "Dutch disease". The rise in oil prices was seen as permanent rather than temporary, short-term bank borrowing was resorted to, and the real exchange rate allowed to appreciate. At the same time the country's own nationals, with less confidence in the future, engaged in capital flight. Again it is suggested that outside developments merely "tipped an imbalanced economy into crisis" (p. 603). Lack of confidence relating to fiscal and monetary policy clearly translates into a lack of confidence with respect to the BoP. The additional problem is that lack of confidence concerning the future performance of the BoP and the domestic debt accumulation associated with fiscal deficits, converts via its capital account consequences to an immediate deterioration in contemporaneous BoP performance. Moreover, expectations in a BoP context are likely to be self-fulfilling. A loss of creditworthiness based on pessimistic expectations curtails the international financing which may be of vital importance in filling savings and foreign exchange gaps.

A derivative of the absorption approach focuses on the balance between domestic saving and domestic investment. The main instrument through which governments seek to influence these balances is fiscal policy, incorporating government capital and current expenditure and tax revenue as well as other forms of revenue as may come from the sale of state-owned assets (privatization).

Several chapters in this book allude to the severe fiscal difficulties that Latin American economies face. Richard Bird and Guillermo Perry discuss the problems of extending the tax base and Latin America's disenchantment with income taxes. Merillee Grindle provides evidence to show how Latin American countries have, in general, failed to increase taxation as a proportion of GDP and illustrates the complex political economy of fiscal policy. Lance Taylor and his collaborators show how domestic fiscal policy may be derailed by trade liberalization measures which eliminate an important source of tax revenue, or by a combination of a large debt overhang and rising world interest rates or exchange rate depreciation which increases the domestic currency costs of servicing a given stock of external debt. Even where fiscal imbalances have been alleviated, the evidence suggests that this may be a temporary consequence of state divestiture, rather than an underlying shift in fundamental fiscal factors. If this is perceived to be the case, and if, in addition, there is little confidence that privatization will increase efficiency and raise aggregate supply, the beneficial effects of the improved fiscal balance will be muted and short-lived.

While the analytical connections between fiscal deficits and balance of payments deficits are broadly understood and accepted, and while econometric evidence confirms that fiscal excesses are reflected in BoP disequilibria, the policy problem is found in the economic and political complexities of actually eliminating fiscal deficits. If we are not sanguine about the possibilities for overcoming these complexities, we cannot be sanguine about eliminating fiscal pressures on the balance of payments.[8]

If BoP deficits reflect an excess of investment over and above domestic saving, should Latin American economies depress investment in order to strengthen their balance of payments? There is little doubt that, in effect, this is what many of them did during the 1980s, when the evidence shows just such a decline in investment.[9]

While it may legitimately be observed that the fall in investment was associated with an increase in the marginal efficiency of capital, this is hardly the point. It is more relevant to focus on the long-term implications of falling investment for economic growth and the balance of payments. The imbalance between savings and investment should more appropriately be corrected by raising domestic saving. An important element in domestic saving is public saving, and this brings us back to the role played by taxation policy. If savings cannot be raised, a conventional savings gap exists which either has to be filled by foreign borrowing, or alternatively eliminated by lowering investment to comply with the predetermined savings constraint. As far as Latin America is concerned, the prospects for increasing domestic savings, and reversing the trend of the 1980s, are probably rather slim. Securing BoP equilibrium in the near term therefore implies reduced capital accumulation, but this does not augur well for the long term. Again, the intertemporal nature of the balance of payments is aptly demonstrated.

To the extent that there is a proclivity towards fiscal deficits in many Latin American economies, there will also be a proclivity towards the consequences of such deficits. First of all there are the monetary repercussions. Where bond markets are relatively well developed, there is the opportunity for excess government expenditure to be financed by domestic borrowing, which will push up interest rates. As far as the BoP is concerned there will be beneficial short-run effects on both the current and capital accounts as higher interest rates depress domestic expenditure and attract capital from abroad (unless higher interest rates are perceived to increase risk). However, where higher interest rates deter investment the longer-term adverse consequences for aggregate supply need to be considered. Where domestic capital markets are not so well developed, governments will be under pressure to monetize fiscal deficits and in these circumstances the short-run effects on the BoP will be negative. Moreover, in as much as monetary expansion results in accelerating inflation and an appreciation in the real exchange rate, there will be further adverse consequences for the BoP in the longer run.

The scenario of fiscal indiscipline, monetary expansion, inflation and ensuing currency overvaluation is almost a caricature of the "typical" Latin American economy. For many years the statistically suspect view that developing countries experienced much faster rates of inflation than developed countries was associated with the rapid rates observed in a narrow range of largely Latin American countries, including Argentina, Bolivia, Brazil, Chile and Uruguay (the so-called ABC countries).

As evidence presented elsewhere in this book illustrates, some Latin American economies demonstrated a degree of success towards the end of the 1980s and in the early 1990s in reducing inflation below the very rapid rates experienced earlier in the 1980s, but, given the historical background, is it reasonable to doubt whether such reductions are firmly established? If not, and if the fundamental factors that have caused inflation in the past are still present, there will continue to be pressures on both the current and capital accounts of Latin America's balance of payments, both directly through the erosion of competitiveness, and indirectly through the expectations generated for future demand management (which will be contractionary) and exchange rate policy (where currency depreciation will occur). It is in Latin America that the inflation–devaluation–inflation spiral has been most pronounced, and the difficulties that a country faces in extricating itself from such a vicious downward spiral should not be underestimated. On top of this, and again as discussed elsewhere in this volume, inflation in Latin America is associated with adverse fiscal consequences – government expenditure rises but tax revenue falls as greater evasion takes place (Tanzi, 1989). Here the neutralizing fiscal drag experienced in industrial economies is replaced by a reinforcing fiscal thrust, and therefore an additional spiral between fiscal deficits, inflation, and further fiscal deficits, is created. According to this analysis, Latin American economies are corkscrew economies. Once there is a departure from macroeconomic equilibrium, forces are generated which push the economies still further away from equilibrium.

Firm policy commitments and the use of nominal anchors in the form of quasi-fixed exchange rates may present a theoretical possibility for breaking out of such downward spirals, but they will be difficult to implement effectively where the credibility of the government has already been undermined by previous policy failures and a track record of announcing and then abandoning strong policy stances and of cutting loose from anchors.[10]

Chapter 1 in this volume, by Edwards, demonstrates how the use of quasi-fixed exchange rates as a counter-inflationary device can result in the appreciation of real exchange rates and currency overvaluation which then has a negative effect on both the current account, via relative prices, and the capital account, via the expectations of future devaluation which are created. Short-term measures such as higher interest rates designed to offset the impact of such expectations on the overall BoP can easily undermine its longer-term strength by discouraging investment and reducing the growth of aggregate supply.

In summary, a realistic assessment of the future course of Latin America's balance of payments is that disequilibria will occur. A combination of unhelpful structural phenomena along with domestic fiscal and monetary pressures will combine to create BoP difficulties. Will Latin American economies be able to cushion themselves against such unfavourable developments by international financing?

III INTERNATIONAL FINANCING: FEAST, FAMINE OR BALANCED DIET?

As suggested above, international financing may have had a perverse effect on the balance of payments of some Latin American economies, with the easy and inexpensive availability of finance in the 1970s allowing domestic economic policies to be excessively relaxed. The scarcity of finance in the 1980s, on the other hand, often forced countries to implement strict adjustment measures. The behavioural responses to the availability of international financing depend on aspects of political economy which are particularly significant in Latin America.

It is, in principle, inappropriate to regard international financing as a substitute for adjustment, unless BoP deficits are temporary and self-correcting. Financing should permit countries to choose the optimum speed of adjustment and it should enable them to opt for adjustment policies which place greater emphasis on longer-run increases in aggregate supply than short-run reductions in aggregate demand. In this sense, the imposition of an effective availability constraint imposes welfare losses on potential capital-importing countries. The central theoretical question relates then to the optimum blend of financing and adjustment during a period of transition from BoP disequilibrium to equilibrium. The short answer to this question comes easily, in theory: the optimum blend is where the marginal rate of transformation between current and future sacrifices in expenditure (adjustment and financing respectively) equals the marginal rate of substitution transformation between them, and therefore depends largely on a country's rate of time preference. International financing enables contemporaneous sacrifices in expenditure to be avoided, but at the same time carries with it the need to make such sacrifices in the future when loans have to be serviced and repaid. In practice it is difficult to apply this nostrum in any precise and scientific fashion, because it is difficult to measure social discount rates. Instead, loosely defended claims are made that Latin American economies over-borrowed in the 1970s, paying insufficient attention to adjustment and their future capacity to repay, and under-borrowed as a result of the imposition of an externally imposed lending constraint in the aftermath of the debt crisis, thereby being forced to place too much emphasis on adjustment policies which had a severe negative impact on domestic living standards.

Looking to the future, two questions may be identified as being fundamentally significant. First, is it more likely that the governments of Latin American countries will select the optimum blend of financing and adjustment, and second will they be able to attract in the appropriate form the level of international financing that this implies?

Analysis undertaken elsewhere in this book suggests that Latin America will face a foreign exchange constraint during the 1990s and that international financing will be needed in order to foster economic development and restore some growth in living standards. But from where is such financing likely to come?

Data presented in Chapter 3 of this book by Stephany Griffith-Jones suggests that some Latin American economies have shown considerable success in restoring creditworthiness in the eyes of international creditors. Another recent study by El-Erian (1992) also reports and examines the restoration of capital market financing in Latin America. However, as he points out, the restoration has applied much more to bonds and equities, foreign direct investment and capital repatriation than to commercial bank lending – all forms of borrowing that have less adverse implications for debt. Moreover, it has applied much more to some countries than to others. El-Erian distinguishes between two groups of Latin American countries. The first group (Chile, Mexico and Venezuela) have "solid footholds" in the markets, whereas the second group (Argentina and Brazil) are at an earlier stage of market re-entry. Of course this classification excludes many Latin American countries, reflecting the fact that the international financing of BoP deficits is not an option available to all countries in the region. (Table 4.5 in the statistical appendix provides data on foreign direct investment.)

Historically, bond and equity financing has been available to only a narrow sub-group of Latin American economies and, if there is little prospect of significantly resuscitating bank lending, the concentration of international financing will tend to be accentuated in the future. This having been said, it also needs to be recognized that Latin American experience during the 1970s illustrated the inappropriateness of short-term bank lending for the financing of longer-term BoP and development purposes. It was not simply a matter of the volumes being wrong but also, and more importantly according to some analysts, of the wrong instruments being used (Llewellyn, 1990). Although he makes no attempt to estimate their quantitative significance, El-Erian attributes the enhanced access of some Latin American countries to voluntary capital market financing to four elements: successful implementation of economic adjustment policies, appropriate restructuring of existing debt, reduced transaction costs, and greater customization of financing instruments to market conditions.

Identifying these elements also serves to identify the vulnerability of international financing to Latin America. Slippage in implementing required policies, or lack of policy success, a deterioration in the Latin American debt position, and the greater availability of indicators of creditworthiness could combine to convert re-entry into exit. Moreover, it needs to be recognized that measures designed to collateralize existing debt by effectively giving it seniority may have adverse effects on future inflows which will be needed to finance investment (Snowden, 1992). Measures designed to alleviate short-term problems may therefore carry longer term costs.[11]

Unavoidably, considerable uncertainty must surround renewed international financing and its BoP repercussions. One scenario has capital inflows being associated with policies that will create the resources necessary to service obligations. International financing will then enhance creditworthiness. The balance of payments out-turn is beneficial not only because a trend improvement is established, but also because greater creditworthiness strengthens the ability of countries to deal with short-term instabilities.

However, a second and more pessimistic picture may be painted. This has capital inflows reflecting a once-and-for-all change in the ownership of formerly state-owned assets, a temporary differential between interest rates in Latin America and, in particular, North America, and an inappropriately high degree of confidence in the likely success of the more market-friendly approach to economic development which has led to the temporary erosion of risk premia. As the process of privatization slows down and industrial efficiency fails to increase, as interest rate differentials narrow or are reversed, and as expectations regarding future economic performance reveal themselves to be irrational, capital inflows will quickly evaporate.[12]

If fiscal deficits, monetary expansion, inflation and the threat of currency devaluation remain uncorrected in the longer term, creditworthiness will unavoidably be adversely affected. Rather than flight capital being repatriated and new inflows being generated, the incentives for capital flight will be re-created and new capital will go elsewhere.[13]

The availability of international finance will become a yet more effective constraint, and countries will be forced to select sub-optimal blends of adjustment and financing, with more emphasis being placed on short-term stabilization. As noted earlier, a strategy of this type, while leading to some short-term reduction in BoP deficits, may achieve this at a high cost in terms of other aspects of economic performance and at the cost of weakening the underlying balance of payments in the long term.

Which of these two scenarios is the more realistic? If the conventional view of Latin American economies and societies as experiencing strong elements of inertia and hysteresis is broadly accurate, it is difficult to find clear scientific reasons for being optimistic. After all, the last time Latin America received a wave of international financing it was followed by the debt crisis and by the prolonged erosion of living standards. There has to be very considerable confidence in the superiority of the instruments through which lending is occurring and of the adjustment policies which are now in place over those that accompanied foreign borrowing in the 1970s, in order to believe that the 1990s will be significantly better.[14]

IV   THE ROLE OF THE INTERNATIONAL FINANCIAL INSTITUTIONS

But what if the financing is formally connected to economic adjustment via the intermediation of the international financial institutions (the IMF and the

World Bank) – will this increase the chances of success?[15] Even here, the grounds for optimism are weak. While Latin American governments appear more sympathetic to the Fund's conventional wisdom than they were at the beginning of the 1980s, and while few would openly suggest that the need for economic stabilization can be ignored, there still remain concerns about policy-based lending by the IFIs in Latin America. Are the programmes they support the most appropriate ones? And, if they are appropriate and necessary, are they sufficient to secure longer-term improvement in the balance of payments?

Unfortunately, neither theory nor empirical evidence provides straightforward answers. Allowing the real exchange rate to become overvalued confers few benefits outside the possible counter-inflationary effects of lower import prices, but imposes large costs on both the current account and the capital account of the balance of payments.[16]

Depreciation of the nominal exchange rate may be the best single means of correcting such over-valuation (Edwards, 1988) and it is on exchange rate policy that the IMF appears to have had its most discernible effect (Killick with Malik, 1992). But, by the same token, for depreciation to be at its most effective, other conditions have to be met not only in terms of familiar Marshall-Lerner conditions, but also in terms of the extent of the inflation "pass-through" effects which can negate the impact of devaluation on competitiveness,[17] the degree of real wage resistance, and the nature of accompanying fiscal, monetary and trade policies. As noted earlier, it is important to move away from partial analysis. Trade liberalization may for example adversely affect the fiscal deficit. More modern open economy macroeconomic theory also counsels against the frequent use of devaluation, on the grounds that this undermines economic credibility and destroys the counter-inflationary "nominal anchor" to which macroeconomic policy may be attached.[18] A track record of devaluation encourages private agents to anticipate it and to mark up prices ahead of it. The inflation thereby caused itself forces the government to devalue. Expectations are thereby ratified and a self-perpetuating dynamic is established. In such circumstances the dilemma facing governments is that both devaluation designed to correct currency overvaluation, as well as the absence of devaluation, which leaves the real exchange rate over-valued, may in principle have damaging effects on the credibility of economic policy.

Other anachronisms tend to complicate economic adjustment in Latin America. Wage indexation will cushion the impact of Fund programmes on the urban poor and will therefore make them politically more acceptable. At the same time, effective BoP correction usually relies on reducing real wages, and any measure which gets in the way of this will therefore dilute the BoP benefits. Indexation, in effect, institutionalizes real wage resistance and the domestic inflationary consequences of exchange rate depreciation, and therefore dampens its impact as an expenditure switching device.

Similar problems are associated with the debt overhang in highly indebted developing countries. Debt exaggerates the need for economic adjustment, yet it also reduces the domestic return on adjustment, with the principal beneficiaries often being foreign creditors (Sachs, 1989a, 1989b). The incentive to adjust is reduced most therefore in circumstances where the adjustment is most needed. Add to this the extreme income-inequality found in Latin America, which creates considerable political problems for stabilization and economic adjustment, and one can understand why correcting BoP deficits is an extremely difficult task, whether under the auspices of the Fund or not.

In analysing the likely course of Latin America's balance of payments, the inescapable conclusion is that, if it is so difficult to define with any precision the most appropriate BoP strategy and, beyond that, yet more difficult to carry political support for it, the chances of the most effective and efficient policy being adopted and thereafter fully implemented will be severely reduced.

The available empirical evidence on the involvement of the IMF and indeed the World Bank in the design of adjustment programmes is not very reassuring. It has to be recognized that there are considerable methodological problems in assessing the impact of IFI-backed programmes. It also needs to be noted that different studies using different methodologies, different country samples, and different time periods, find somewhat different results and reach different conclusions (Edwards, 1989; Khan, 1990; Killick with Malik, 1992). It also has to be accepted that the past is not a perfect guide to the future.

This having been said, researchers not normally regarded as antipathetic towards the Fund have argued strongly against both the macroeconomic analysis which they claim to underpin Fund advice, and have suggested that the evidence of the 1980s, drawn largely from Latin America, confirms the resulting expectation that Fund-backed programmes will be relatively unsuccessful. Edwards (1989), for example, claims that during the 1980s there was a greater emphasis than before on demand deflation and devaluation, that the degree of compliance with intermediate targets fell, and that there was little positive impact on ultimate targets.[19] Although Edwards found little clear reason to believe that the devaluation component of IMF-approved programmes has the effect of widening income inequalities, other research focusing exclusively on Latin America has made precisely the claim that IMF programmes have had this effect, while also claiming that the evidence suggests that they have adverse effects on both inflation and economic growth (Pastor, 1987). In these circumstances it would not be very surprising to find that the programmes are politically unsustainable and that non-compliance is common.

In a recent study of the non-completion of IMF-backed programmes, Killick, Malik and Manuel (1992) discovered that 52 per cent of the forty-seven programmes adopted by Latin American economies during 1980–90 remained incomplete according to their measure, a somewhat higher non-completion rate than that found in the developing economies of either Asia

(44 per cent) or even Sub-Saharan Africa (48 per cent). Killick and his collaborators attribute Latin America's relatively poor record to the implicit tax on economic adjustment which is associated with a debt overhang – a hypothesis that is further supported by the finding that non-completions among severely indebted middle-income countries were higher than for any other country grouping as classified by debt status, and by the similar conclusion reached by Edwards (1989). It is also found that the rate of non-completion rose sharply for developing countries as a whole in 1987–90 as compared with previous sub-periods – a finding which raises interesting questions, given the apparently growing acceptance of the wisdom of Fund advice in Latin America reported earlier.

Studies of the World Bank's structural and sectoral adjustment lending in developing countries have produced results which are similar in some respects (Mosley, Harrigan and Toye, 1991). A high rate of slippage is observed, and while the impact of the programmes on some macroeconomic variables seems to be positive, such as on export growth and the balance of payments, there are also negative effects, particularly on investment, and possibly, though more ambiguously, on economic growth. The adverse effect of policy-based lending by the IFIs on investment is shared between the Bank and the Fund (Killick, Malik and Manuel, 1992). Such results lead to worries concerning the long-run evolution of the balance of payments, in which context it would be preferable to see increases in aggregate supply and domestic saving.

World Bank policy-based lending has, however, not been as widespread among Latin American countries as it has been among some other regional groups. Where it has occurred, case study evidence provides a rather mixed picture. Examining the Bank's Agricultural Sector Adjustment Loan to Ecuador in 1985, for example, Mosley (1991) concludes that it did a great deal to help negate an economic crisis which had been caused by a collapse in export revenues. At the same time he argues that with a lower political profile and some modifications to the terms of conditionality, its impact could have been even greater.[20]

To what extent are the IFIs responding to such negative evidence and modifying the programmes which they support? Is there reason to believe that the involvement of the IFIs will have a more beneficial influence on Latin America's balance of payments in the future?

Part of the IMF's response has been to challenge the scientific legitimacy of the studies which accentuate the negative effects of Fund programmes, and, as noted earlier, there are, and will remain, legitimate grounds for doing so, since all current methodologies have their imperfections – not least those used by the Fund itself. But another part of the Fund's response has been to modify its rhetoric, with greater emphasis being placed on economic growth as a primary objective of programmes, more concern being expressed for the impact of programmes on "vulnerable groups" in society, and a greater willingness to get involved in the composition of government expenditure, including military expenditure, rather than simply its total amount.

Changes in rhetoric have been accompanied by observable changes in practice. The Fund now channels more of its resources through the Extended Fund Facility than it did for most of the 1980s. According to its own rubric, the EFF has a more pronounced supply-side orientation, and the evidence is that EFF programmes have a superior record in terms of their impact on economic growth, although a less good record in terms of the BoP (Killick *et al.*, 1984). Moreover, the number and range of specified performance criteria included in Fund-supported programmes has increased. Yet the suspicion still remains that the forces of continuity are stronger than those of change, and that, at heart, Fund-backed programmes remain founded on restrictive monetary and fiscal policy and exchange rate depreciation. Where there have been apparent and significant variations, as in the case of Mexico in 1986, when there were important automatic contingency arrangements built into the agreement relating to petroleum export earnings and the growth of the economy, and Bolivia, when the Fund soft-peddled on further devaluation, these seem to be essentially individual departures from the norm, rather than a change in the norm itself. Other programmes negotiated more recently with Latin American and Caribbean economies reveal only limited evidence to support the change in Fund rhetoric. In Argentina's 1990 stand-by there was indeed a larger "structural" element than might have been expected some years earlier, with provisions for privatizing and reforming public enterprises, liberalizing interest rates and reforming taxes. However, performance criteria remained quite conventional, although there were eight of them. There was little or nothing in the programme which gave it a clear growth orientation, nor were there any measures to protect poverty groups. Some such protection was at least accommodated in the programmes negotiated with the Dominican Republic and Jamaica in 1991, but here again the programmes were based on more familiar elements.[21]

In certain ways the involvement of the IFIs highlights the fundamental BoP problems that most, if not all, Latin American economies face. Structural deficiencies require supply-side changes to diversify production and exports, and to increase efficiency and become more competitive.[22] The BoP in the long run depends on the ability of countries to earn additional foreign exchange, and this depends ultimately on increasing tradable aggregate supply. However, it is also important to avoid fiscal and monetary excesses which lead to inflation and the appreciation of real exchange rates, and, in the short run, it will be these factors which tend to be the dominant ones. The difficulty is how to address the short-run BoP disequilibria in a way that does not adversely effect longer-term growth prospects. It seems logical to assume that sustained economic development will only be achieved if macroeconomic stability is maintained, yet at the same time the empirical evidence suggests that stabilization has a negative impact on economic growth, at least in the short run. If aggregate supply declines, this puts further immediate pressure on the BoP, which may result in further measures of demand deflation. The trick for policy-makers is to escape from this vicious circle. Not only do they need to have the ability to escape, but they need to be able to generate the expectation that they will do so.

V LATIN AMERICA'S EXTERNAL DEBT

During the 1980s there can be little doubt that external debt was a dominant determinant of the poor overall economic performance of the highly indebted Latin American countries. Indeed it was in the context of debt that the IMF became involved with them, having been largely bypassed during the 1970s. However, the general perception now seems to be that although Latin America's debt problem still remains, it is no longer a crisis. The debt service ratio for Latin American economies fell at the beginning of the 1990s and, as noted earlier, capital inflows have been regenerated for at least some countries, with the result that Latin America's net resource transfer became positive at the beginning of the 1990s for the first time since the early 1980s. (Table 4.6 in the statistical appendix provides data on DSRs.)

To the extent that, first, Latin American economies contrive to be net importers of external savings, and second, external savings alleviate the constraint on economic growth and development imposed by a shortage of domestic savings and can be used to raise net foreign exchange earnings in the future, the debt crisis may indeed have been overcome. Inadequate domestic saving has already been identified as an underlying problem from the viewpoint of raising aggregate supply in the long run, and therefore of strengthening the long-term balance of payments. Where a significant proportion of inadequate savings are exported as a consequence of debt service this will have a further adverse impact. Analysis by Fanelli, Frenkel and Taylor in Chapter 8 of this volume certainly suggests that it is unlikely that Latin American economies will be able to generate the increases in domestic savings that will be needed to restore economic growth and that increased domestic saving will have to be augmented by the use of foreign savings. Once more, therefore, we encounter intertemporal trade-offs which imply that some short- to medium-term capital importation will be necessary in order to strengthen the long-term basic BoP.

In principle, there are essentially two routes via which the burden of external debt may be lightened. The first involves reducing the volume of debt through initiatives such as the Brady Plan.[23] It is interesting to note that during both 1980–2 and 1982–5 it was the increasing volume of debt which put most pressure on the debt service ratio of Latin and Central American countries. During the former period, additional pressure was exerted on the ratio by raising interest rates and by falling export earnings, but taken together, these were less than half as significant as the increase in debt volume. In the latter period, interest rates and export earnings combined to help pull down Latin America's DSR, but their continued effect was only half as strong as the effect of rising debt volume which pulled in the opposite direction. It was only the renegotiation of the rate of amortization which, along with helpful interest rate and export earnings effects, overcame the upward pressure exerted by increasing debt volume. (The relative importance of these influences for individual Latin American economies which rescheduled their external debt between 1982 and 1985 varied somewhat.)

The second way of alleviating an external debt burden is by enhancing the manageability of a given volume of debt. This may be achieved by renegotiating the structure and time profile of the debt, so that the problem of annual debt service payments is modified, or by increasing economic growth and exports with the result that debt/GNP and debt/export ratios fall. It is in this context that increasing debt volumes may still be associated with diminishing debt problems.

This brief review raises a series of relevant questions concerning the future external debt and BoP of Latin America, but fails to provide straightforward answers.

It is certainly feasible to imagine a set of circumstances in which external debt is no longer a problem and in which its further acquisition contributes positively to the long-term BoP. These circumstances would be as follows: Latin American economies remain creditworthy in the eyes of private creditors; capital inflows are used productively to generate domestic (exportable) output; world interest rates keep relatively low and the world demand for Latin America's exports strengthens; and temporary liquidity or cash flow problems are avoided.

The threat comes from the fact that it is just as easy, and empirically perhaps more likely, to imagine that at least some of these favourable circumstances will not exist. Capital inflows, as noted earlier, may be transitory, they may not be productively used so that the growth in the capacity to deal with debt does not match the growth in debt, and the world economic environment may quickly turn hostile, as was demonstrated in the early 1980s – a reasonable argument can be made that the debt crisis of the 1980s could have been avoided had it not been for external pressures on the DSRs of Latin America.

If the debt crisis were to flare up once again, it is more likely that adjustment pressure would be put back on the indebted nations than that an internationally orchestrated and quantitatively significant strategy of debt reduction would be adopted. While there is evidence drawn from Latin America to suggest that more advantageous debt deals can be negotiated by countries that have designed credible adjustment strategies (Griffith-Jones, 1989), there must be doubts about the political durability and long-term economic wisdom of policies that accentuate reductions in aggregate demand, especially where these also imply reductions in capital accumulation.

Issues of creditworthiness also return us to the question of domestic economic management, credibility and reputation discussed earlier. Evidence drawn from regression studies confirms the theoretical expectation that there is a link between external debt problems and internal fiscal imbalances (Sachs, 1989). Armed with such information, creditors are unlikely to continue to lend to Latin American economies if fiscal deficits remain uncorrected. But what are the prospects for fiscal correction, given the acute political economy of government expenditure and taxation in Latin American economies; many Latin American societies do not seem to offer themselves to easy fiscal rectitude. Imagine, however, that governments committed to establishing fiscal balance are in place. What expectation will this create in the minds of potential lenders or investors? The expectational effects could, in principle, be positive and self-fulfilling. However, it could equally well be that creditors will anticipate political instability, as fiscal measures are forced through, with adverse economic consequences for economic growth, at least in the short term. With such expectations, will those with funds to lend want to lend them in Latin America? There may of course be differences in the prospects of individual countries, but an apparently durable, even if unscientific, aspect of commercial bank lending has been the regionalization phenomenon. Lenders do not seem to distinguish clearly between individual Latin American economies but implicitly assume a high degree of covariance between them, with a form of leadership-spillover mechanism at work. Concern about economic performance in one large Latin American economy can quickly have an adverse effect on the creditworthiness of others.

A slightly cautionary stance on Latin America debt is also suggested by data which show an increase in the region's DSR from 28.8 per cent in 1991 to 33.7 per cent in 1993. This again at least raises the question of whether we have been observing a temporary respite in Latin America's debt problems, rather than a permanent cure.

IV   CONCLUDING REMARKS

Both analysis and experience suggests that while it is possible to circumvent it temporarily, the balance of payments ultimately becomes an effective constraint on economic performance and domestic economic policy. During the 1980s, most Latin American economies made sacrifices in terms of economic growth and development, in order to secure the strengthening in their net trading position that was necessitated by their external debt.

The resurrection of economic growth that may be observed at the beginning of the 1990s can, in principle, avoid being brought to an abrupt end by BoP difficulties, provided the appropriate balance between aggregate demand and (rising and tradable) aggregate supply is maintained. It sounds simple, but, in practice, it is very hard to achieve. Data from the IMF's *World Economic Outlook* show that a current account deficit which was on average $8.5 billion during 1988–90 had increased to $24 billion by 1992. We have seen that Latin America is unlikely to gain much BoP support from movements in its commodity or income terms of trade. Export diversification and promotion may be desirable and may be increasingly seen as desirable, but this does not make it easy to bring about.

On top of these secular problems is the problem of BoP instability, which is conveniently illustrated by the difficulties that Mexico encountered during the 1980s arising from the fall in the world price of oil. The problem of BoP vulnerability, which is further exaggerated for such highly indebted countries, is widely encountered in Latin America.

Against this structural background, additional pressures on the BoP come from fiscal and monetary excesses which are especially difficult to correct within a Latin American context where political volatility and income equality impose limitations on stabilization policy to an extent that does not exist in many other economies.

The costs associated with economic adjustment may be reduced where international finance is available. But Latin America cannot count on such availability, and must avoid being tempted into trading off too much economic adjustment against financing, should it be available. Adjustment must be supported by financing, rather than be replaced by it.

Countries can almost always avoid BoP deficits if they are able and willing to make sufficient domestic sacrifices, but this strategy implies equilibrium at a lower level of economic activity and trade. Although Latin America pursued this strategy during the 1980s, largely because it had no alternative, it may be a strategy that is unsustainable. Increased growth and the return of capital provides an opportunity for an alternative strategy during the 1990s and beyond, but success is extremely conditional and depends not only on appropriate policies being pursued domestically but also upon the existence of a conducive world economic environment. There is a great deal that can go wrong, and things do seem to have a tendency to go wrong in Latin America. This is part of the problem. Latin American economies find it difficult to disassociate themselves from their past. With a poor record of macroeconomic management and a depleted stock of credibility it is difficult for anyone other than an extreme risk-taker to be wildly optimistic. Cautious optimism or pessimism will, however, generate a wait-and-see attitude, and this will induce behavioural responses which in themselves lower the chances of success. It is imperative that Latin American governments seek to build the confidence that will be required in order to secure the lasting BoP improvements which will then permit a more permanent economic recovery to be maintained.

VII STATISTICAL APPENDIX

All data in the following tables appear in US$m, except for Table 6 which is in per cent, and have been drawn from the IMF's *International Financial Statistics*.

Table 4.1 Current account balance.

Country	1982	1983	1984	1985	1986	1987	1988	1989	1990	1991
Argentina	-2,353	-2,436	-2,495	-952	-2,859	-4,235	-1,572	-1,305	1,903	-2,667
Bahamas	-63	-35	-46	-149	-27	-166	-128	-158	-190	-201
Barbados	-36	-42	19	40	-16	-53	2	-3	-16	-30
Bolivia	-173	-138	-174	-282	-384	-423	-255	-264	-192	-262
Brazil	-16,312	-6,837	42	-273	-5,304	-1,450	4,159	1,025	-3,788	-377
Chile	-2,304	-1,117	-2,111	-1,328	-1,137	-808	-167	-767	-598	142
Colombia	-3,054	-3,003	-1,401	-1,809	383	336	-216	-201	700	2,551
Costa Rica	-267	-280	-151	-126	-80	-256	-179	-415	-424	-88
Dominican Republic	-443	-418	-163	-108	-186	-364	-22	-199	-9	-58
Ecuador	-1,196	-134	-264	114	-553	-1,131	-505	-514	-273	-467
El Salvador	-120	-28	-54	-29	117	136	26	-174	138	-168
Guatemala	-399	-224	-377	-246	-18	-443	-414	-367	-213	-184
Guyana	-141	-158	-95	-97	-141	-110	-94	-114	-148	-136
Haiti	-99	-111	-103	-95	-45	-31	-40	-63	-39	-11
Honduras	-228	-219	-316	-204	-147	-150	-175	-197	-110	-220
Jamaica	-403	-355	-332	-302	-38	-136	34	-295	-328	-198
Mexico	-8,307	5,403	4,194	1,130	-1,673	3,968	-2,443	-3,958	-7,117	-13,283
Nicaragua	-514	-507	-597	-726	-688	-679	-715	-370	-305	-5
Panama	-207	241	218	286	355	204	766	448	251	135
Paraguay	-375	-248	-317	-252	-365	-490	-210	318	4	-323
Peru	-1,609	-872	-221	137	-1,077	-1,481	-1,091	362	-949	-1,871
Suriname	-57	-161	-79	-12	-22	75	63	163	33	-35
Trinidad and Tobago	-845	-1,003	-523	-83	-442	-239	-110	-56	440	-17
Uruguay	-235	-60	-129	-120	45	-134	34	155	236	105
Venezuela	-4,248	4,427	4,651	3,327	-2,245	-1,390	-5,809	2,161	8,279	1,663
Latin America	-43,988	-8,315	-824	-2,159	-16,547	-9,450	-9,061	-4,788	-2,715	-16,005

Table 4.2 Exports of goods (fob).

Country	1982	1983	1984	1985	1986	1987	1988	1989	1990	1991
Argentina	7,623	7,835	8,100	8,396	6,852	6,360	9,134	9,573	12,354	11,972
Bahamas	213	225	262	296	293	273	274	259	308	320
Barbados	208	272	340	301	244	131	145	147	151	144
Bolivia	828	755	725	623	546	519	543	724	831	760
Brazil	20,173	21,898	27,002	25,634	22,348	26,210	33,773	34,375	31,414	31,624
Chile	3,706	3,831	3,650	3,804	4,191	5,224	7,052	8,080	8,310	8,929
Colombia	3,114	2,970	4,273	3,650	5,331	5,661	5,343	6,031	7,080	7,572
Costa Rica	869	853	998	939	1,085	1,107	1,181	1,333	1,354	1,491
Dominican Republic	768	785	868	739	722	711	890	924	735	658
Ecuador	2,327	2,348	2,621	2,905	2,186	2,021	2,202	2,354	2,714	2,851
El Salvador	700	758	726	679	778	590	611	498	580	588
Guatemala	1,170	1,092	1,132	1,060	1,044	978	1,073	1,126	1,211	1,230
Guyana	241	193	217	214	210	241	215	205	204	239
Haiti	177	187	215	223	191	210	180	148	160	163
Honduras	677	699	737	790	891	833	875	883	848	808
Jamaica	787	686	702	569	590	708	883	1,000	1,158	1,145
Mexico	21,230	22,312	24,196	21,663	16,031	20,655	20,566	22,765	26,838	27,121
Nicaragua	406	452	412	305	258	295	236	319	332	268
Panama	392	343	1,686	1,974	2,366	2,492	2,347	2,681	3,318	4,154
Paraguay	396	326	361	466	576	597	871	1,242	1,376	1,268
Peru	3,293	3,015	3,147	2,978	2,531	2,661	2,691	3,488	3,231	3,329
Suriname	429	367	374	336	337	339	358	549	466	397
Trinidad and Tobago	2,229	2,027	2,111	2,111	1,363	1,397	1,453	1,535	1,935	1,751
Uruguay	1,256	1,156	925	854	1,088	1,182	1,405	1,599	1,693	1,605
Venezuela	16,332	14,571	15,878	14,283	8,535	10,437	10,082	12,915	17,444	14,892
Latin America	89,544	89,956	101,658	95,792	80,587	91,832	104,383	114,753	126,045	125,279

Table 4.3 Imports of goods (fob).

Country	1982	1983	1984	1985	1986	1987	1988	1989	1990	1991
Argentina	4,859	4,119	4,118	3,518	4,406	5,343	4,892	3,864	3,726	7,400
Bahamas	755	822	866	922	1,013	1,155	1,059	1,204	1,229	1,154
Barbados	507	572	606	559	523	458	518	599	623	618
Bolivia	496	496	412	463	597	646	591	730	776	804
Brazil	19,395	15,429	13,916	13,168	14,044	15,052	14,605	18,263	20,661	21,004
Chile	3,643	3,485	3,288	2,920	3,099	3,994	4,833	6,502	7,037	7,354
Colombia	5,358	4,464	4,027	3,673	3,409	3,793	4,516	4,557	5,108	4,535
Costa Rica	805	894	993	1,001	1,045	1,245	1,279	1,572	1,797	1,698
Dominican Republic	1,257	1,279	1,257	1,286	1,352	1,592	1,608	1,964	1,793	1,729
Ecuador	2,187	1,421	1,567	1,611	1,643	2,054	1,583	1,693	1,711	2,207
El Salvador	800	832	915	895	902	939	967	1,090	1,180	1,294
Guatemala	1,284	1,056	1,182	1,077	876	1,333	1,413	1,484	1,428	1,673
Guyana	254	226	202	209	236	238	196	193	227	229
Haiti	302	326	338	345	303	311	284	259	247	300
Honduras	681	756	885	879	874	813	870	835	870	864
Jamaica	1,209	1,124	1,037	1,004	837	1,065	1,240	1,606	1,680	1,551
Mexico	14,435	8,550	11,255	13,212	11,432	12,222	18,898	23,410	31,271	38,184
Nicaragua	724	742	735	794	677	734	718	547	570	688
Panama	1,380	1,270	2,509	2,731	2,907	3,058	2,531	3,084	3,804	4,981
Paraguay	711	551	649	659	864	919	1,030	1,016	1,473	1,680
Peru	3,721	2,772	2,140	1,806	2,596	3,182	2,790	2,291	2,891	3,494
Suriname	460	402	392	310	304	274	239	331	374	396
Trinidad and Tobago	2,487	2,233	1,705	1,355	1,209	1,058	1,064	1,045	948	1,210
Uruguay	1,038	740	732	675	815	1,080	1,112	1,136	1,267	1,544
Venezuela	13,584	6,409	7,246	7,501	7,886	8,870	12,080	7,283	6,807	10,101
Latin America	82,332	60,970	62,972	62,643	63,849	71,428	80,916	86,558	99,498	116,692

Table 4.4 Capital account balance, excluding reserves.

Country	1982	1983	1984	1985	1986	1987	1988	1989	1990	1991
Argentina	2,085	426	2,716	2,513	1,665	2,430	3,595	206	761	5,638
Bahamas	83	0	-34	-13	22	-19	65	97	69	177
Barbados	24	40	-17	-6	19	101	42	0	45	-1
Bolivia	167	108	305	57	362	200	165	191	221	231
Brazil	11,486	5,532	4,928	292	2,006	4,417	-1,621	1,495	5,330	512
Chile	1,034	520	2,014	1,229	797	1,021	1,102	1,409	3,255	942
Colombia	2,232	1,434	944	2,236	1,160	-1	939	478	-161	-600
Costa Rica	228	249	8	43	77	163	196	352	171	317
Dominican Republic	327	268	231	-5	145	-32	175	389	145	112
Ecuador	1,084	-169	334	-128	1,542	1,295	699	636	318	448
El Salvador	153	102	112	33	69	-61	62	151	20	-28
Guatemala	379	312	373	314	63	462	275	384	147	655
Guyana	98	100	131	105	78	37	51	83	165	166
Haiti	91	91	114	56	52	55	55	70	17	32
Honduras	153	159	335	224	174	262	219	281	156	94
Jamaica	268	223	418	314	81	215	149	339	391	183
Mexico	9,526	-2,445	-1,071	-2,096	1,127	-1,003	-1,355	1,362	8,530	20,406
Nicaragua	539	632	885	929	660	764	707	495	448	6
Panama	76	137	72	-151	79	277	466	-3	-538	-654
Paraguay	338	287	286	81	181	189	-156	-20	9	164
Peru	1,927	718	1,037	347	736	867	1,215	447	547	1,525
Suriname	13	50	-10	15	1	-51	-66	-173	-15	10
Trinidad and Tobago	439	381	-123	20	-196	78	-55	77	-231	-104
Uruguay	1,082	250	165	-75	18	333	241	24	70	-356
Venezuela	-1,528	-3,830	-2,012	-1,035	-1,112	520	-1,027	-3,447	-3,594	3,128
Latin America	32,304	5,575	12,125	5,299	9,806	12,519	6,138	5,323	16,276	33,003

Table 4.5 Private sector: direct investment.

Country	1982	1983	1984	1985	1986	1987	1988	1989	1990	1991
Argentina	257	183	268	919	574	-19	1,147	1,028	2,008	2,439
Bahamas	3	-6	-5	-30	-13	11	37	25	-16	0
Barbados	4	2	-2	3	5	5	11	5	10	0
Bolivia	31	7	7	10	10	36	-12	-25	26	50
Brazil	2,534	1,373	1,556	1,267	177	1,087	2,794	744	236	209
Chile	384	132	78	114	116	230	141	184	249	576
Colombia	337	514	561	1,016	642	293	159	547	483	420
Costa Rica	27	55	52	65	57	76	121	95	160	137
Dominican Republic	-1	48	69	36	50	89	106	110	133	145
Ecuador	40	50	50	62	70	75	80	80	82	85
El Salvador	-1	28	12	12	24	18	17	14	13	25
Guatemala	77	45	38	62	69	150	330	76	48	91
Guyana	4	5	5	2	...	...	...	...	...	...
Haiti	7	8	5	5	5	5	10	9	8	14
Honduras	14	21	21	28	30	39	48	51	44	45
Jamaica	-16	-19	12	-9	-5	53	-12	57	138	127
Mexico	1,655	461	390	491	1,160	1,796	635	2,648	2,548	4,742
Nicaragua	0	0	0	0	0	0	0	0	0	0
Panama	3	72	10	59	-62	57	-52	36	-30	-60
Paraguay	37	5	5	1	1	5	8	13	68	80
Peru	48	38	-89	12	22	32	26	59	41	-7
Suriname	-6	46	-40	-7	-34	-73	-96	-168	-43	
Trinidad and Tobago	204	114	110	-8	-22	35	63	149	109	169
Uruguay	-14	6	3	-8	33	55	45	0	0	0
Venezuela	253	86	-3	57	-444	-16	21	77	96	1,767
Latin America	5,881	3,274	3,113	4,168	2,465	4,039	5,627	5,814	6,411	11,054

Table 4.6 Debt service ratio.

Country	1982	1983	1984	1985	1986	1987	1988	1989	1990	1991
Argentina	53.1	73.3	54.1	60.6	79.9	76.7	45.4	37.0	34.8	40.3
Bahamas		3.3	4.2	3.4	8.9	3.2	4.2	3.2	2.5	4.2
Barbados	5.1	6.3	6.7	10.2	13.0	20.5	16.3	11.9	17.3	17.5
Bolivia	59.8	53.8	65.6	50.8	37.6	34.3	50.5	31.9	40.6	33.7
Brazil	86.9	56.8	48.3	40.8	48.9	42.8	49.2	30.8	21.4	28.3
Chile	79.2	56.9	64.3	50.8	43.3	37.5	24.0	27.7	26.8	26.6
Colombia	33.7	42.2	31.3	44.2	35.3	39.3	46.0	50.8	42.7	41.4
Costa Rica	21.8	61.6	33.2	43.1	35.8	23	24.8	18.7	25.7	23.8
Dominican Republic	34.7	30.1	19.3	22.8	26.6	19.7	18.2	15.1	11.9	21.1
Ecuador	79.0	29.8	38.4	33.3	43.8	34.1	40.4	36.7	33.4	32.8
El Salvador	15.8	22.5	26.5	28.6	28.0	28.6	21.6	18.6	24.1	18.9
Guatemala	11.6	16.1	22.2	28.8	32.7	30	29.6	21.0	13.4	16.5
Guyana	20.9	24.3	24.2	25.3	30.3	25.5	24.6	28.6	120.5	29.6
Haiti	9.2	7.8	9.7	13.2	16.0	19.1	21.5	21.9	14.4	19.1
Honduras	31.8	25.3	23.3	25.2	29.6	35.2	36.4	12.8	43.7	40.4
Jamaica	29.0	32.3	34.9	43.6	51.0	49.1	43.9	33.5	31.9	30.1
Mexico	60.3	54.6	56.5	55.8	59.2	43.8	53.3	43.5	31.6	33.7
Nicaragua	45.1	21.5	18.6	18.6	13.8	12.2	9.7	4.3	4.2	81.8
Panama	44.2	31.5	38.5	29.5	31.5	29	1.9	0.8	15.4	21.0
Paraguay	27.4	21.9	23.8	25.5	29.4	12.1	6.4	6.9	11.2	30.1
Peru	56.8	40.5	33.7	31.2	24.9	12.1	6.4	6.9	11.2	30.1
Suriname	0.6	0.6	0.8	0.9	1.6	1.5			...	...
Trinidad and Tobago	5.8	13.1	8.6	11.0	20.0	25.2	18.2	12.2	14.7	15.3
Uruguay	33.4	28.8	38.8	45.4	33.9	39.9	41.4	32.4	46.0	21.7
Venezuela	33.8	29.4	43.3	28.2	53.8	42.6	50.3	27.3	23.2	27.7
Latin America	55.0	47.0	43.6	42.2	48.5	41.3	43.0	32.1	27.1	30.6

NOTES

1 Recent studies which have attempted to identify the principal sources of economic growth in Latin America have isolated investment as a particularly significant contributor (De Gregorio, 1992). This finding is not only empirically sound but is also consistent with many if not most theories of economic growth, including the so-called new endogenous theories.

2 Outside factors will also influence both the availability and price of international financing and will thereby have an important impact on the range of BoP options open to Latin America.

3 The significance of imports in terms of generating future exports is emphasized, for example, by Khan and Knight (1988).

4 Much of this evidence has been summarized elsewhere by the author (Bird, 1978, 1984).

5 It is interesting to note that the simulation exercise undertaken by Allen *et al.* (1992) also reveals that US fiscal expansion has a mixture of expansionary and contractionary consequences for Latin America, with the latter effect dominating. An initial beneficial effect on Latin American exports is subsequently overtaken by the depressing effects of dollar appreciation. Meanwhile the induced increase in US interest rates weakens Latin America's current account and has an adverse effect on investment and the capital stock.

   In examining the relationship between exports and growth in GDP, Sheehey (1992) discovers that when bias is removed, the evidence reveals how a stronger trade orientation can result in lower output growth during periods of weak world demand.

6 Twomey (1992) finds that changes in the terms of trade have a significant effect on real exchange rates in Latin America. Changes in real exchange rates will in turn influence the BoP.

7 A summary and evaluation of most early studies is presented in Bird (1978). A recent study by Love (1992), using modern causality tests, claims to have found strong evidence that export instability induces short-term macroeconomic instability. It may also be noted at this point that for some of the more developed Latin American economies a switch towards manufactures has not arrested the decline in their terms of trade.

8 Berg and Sachs (1988), as well as other work surveyed by Sachs (1989a), show that fiscal deficits have an important bearing on the BoP and the incidence of debt difficulties. However, as they recognize, deeper political factors will lurk behind such regression results. Their own work, which attempts to identify proxies for political instability (such as income inequality and the size of the agricultural sector) confirms this, as does other work which attempts more directly to measure political factors (Li, 1992).

9 It may also be noted that the investment ratio in Latin American and Caribbean countries during 1988–90 stood at 20.1 per cent, as compared with 30.2 per cent in the developing countries of Asia (*World Economic Outlook*, IMF, January 1993).

10 It is relevant to note in this context that while a nominal anchor may increase the effectiveness of a counter-inflationary policy, it appears to do little to reduce the costs of such a policy in terms of lost output. Having examined the existing

literature, as well as having undertaken a number of case studies, including Mexico where some reliance was placed on an exchange rate anchor in bringing down inflation, Dornbusch and Fischer (1993) conclude that "none of the evidence . . . establishes firmly that the exchange rate commitment significantly reduced the costs of disinflation" (p. 40). They also draw attention to the role of indexation and disindexation in Latin American inflation, but agnostically conclude that "whether disinflation is easier in the absence of indexation or whether the absence of indexation indicates a government's commitment not to live with inflation, is difficult to say at this point" (p. 40).

Having devised a procedure for estimating the size and diffusion of credibility effects in the context of stabilization policies in high inflation countries, Agénor and Taylor (1993) apply it to the Cruzado Plan which was implemented in Brazil during 1986. They find that the Plan initially had positive credibility effects but that these rapidly eroded as the Plan failed to eliminate unsustainable macroeconomic imbalances. An interesting question is the extent to which a series of similar plans gradually erodes the initial "honeymoon period" credibility gain. The supposition must surely be that a rising incidence of failure will secularly reduce the degree of expected success.

11 For a further discussion of foreign direct investment in Latin America, see, for example, Birch (1991).

12 After a detailed investigation of international capital flows to Latin America, Kuczynski (1993) reaches similar agnostic conclusions, suggesting that, "given the size of external debt owed by the region and the amount of capital still held abroad, the prospects for sustained investment flows depend to a significant extent on global interest rates, the development of domestic fixed-income capital markets and political and social reforms." In particular he emphasizes that any failure in directing new saving into improving the economic conditions of (urban) low income groups will not only threaten the sustainability of capital inflows but will also tend to reactivate capital flight.

13 Capital flight has been a significant problem for some Latin American economies. Casual estimates put the scale of capital flight at 30–40 per cent of total net borrowing in Argentina, Mexico and Venezuela. The implications of this include a decline in domestic investment, the erosion of the tax base, growing income inequality, and reduced incentives for additional financing. These implications will have further consequences of their own for economic growth, economic adjustment and the balance of payments. However, it is in the nature of capital flight that it cannot be easily measured, and it is not surprising that different studies have made different estimates of its size, and have therefore come up with different results when trying to explain it (Anthony and Hughes-Hallet, 1992). There can be little doubt, however, that measures which generate incentives for capital repatriation would make an important contribution to alleviating any financing constraint encountered by those Latin American economies in which capital flight is generally acknowledged to have been a problem, and would in this regard take some pressure off their future BoP.

14 An alternative way of financing temporary BoP deficits is through decumulating international reserves which are held as an inventory. A problem here is that reserve levels may contribute positively to creditworthiness. Latin American countries fairly uniformly and heavily depleted their reserves during 1989–91. A question that arises

from this is whether reserves are now at a sub-optimal level. Certainly Latin America's reserve import ratio was lower at the beginning of the 1990s than it had been in the mid-1980s, although still higher than that found in African, European and Middle Eastern developing countries. If current reserve levels are sub-optimal, reserve accumulation will place an additional burden on Latin America's balance of payments.

15 The IMF has become much more heavily and widely involved in making loans to Latin American countries since 1982 than it was before. It was a net provider of credit to the region up until 1986, but a net recipient during 1987–91 (with the exception of 1990). In absolute terms, Fund lending to Latin America has been dominated by loans to Mexico, Brazil, Argentina and Chile, although loans to Venezuela became significant after 1989. Whereas the IMF has lent to Mexico, Brazil, Chile and Venezuela under its Extended Fund Facility, it has lent to Argentina and the smaller Latin American countries under its normal stand-by arrangements. Purchases from the Fund as a percentage of current account BoP deficits in Latin America were a meagre 1.1 per cent in 1983 and a staggering 432.4 per cent in 1984. They fell back to between 9.0 per cent and 28.0 per cent between 1986 and 1989, rose to 61.4 per cent in 1990, and fell rapidly to only 6.5 per cent in 1991.

16 Keeping import prices low may help provide some explanation as to why Latin American economies tend towards currency over-valuation where it is claimed that importers of capital goods are powerful political lobbyists (Mahon, 1992).

17 Bahmani-Oskooee and Malixi (1992) find that changes in effective exchange rates make a significant contribution towards explaining inflation in the LDCs in their sample. The effect is more pronounced in the more open economies, such as Brazil, than in the less open ones such as Peru. They find that small but continuous changes in effective exchange rates, as well as large changes, have inflationary consequences, a result which is at odds with some earlier studies of Asian economies.

18 Sachs (1989b) provides a clear annunciation of this view in the context of Latin America.

19 See Edwards (1989) for a presentation of the evidence. Edwards examines thirty-four upper tranche programmes approved in 1983 with developing countries, the vast majority of which had serious debt problems. He finds that "almost every programme contained credit ceilings and a devaluation component" (p. 32), arguing that "this contrasts sharply with previous Fund programmes". Edwards uses two methods for assessing the programmes. The first is a simple before-and-after comparison. He finds that "on average, the current account improved somewhat, while inflation increased quite significantly. With respect to output growth, after a steep reduction in 1983, there was a small improvement in 1984 and 1985". He notes that "countries that did not have Fund programmes also experienced major current-account improvements" (p. 34). Second, he compares targets and outcomes. His results show a rather low rate of compliance, both in absolute terms and by comparison with previous periods.

Sachs (1989b) argues that "the evidence presented in the IMF's 1988 review of conditionality also suggests that, since 1983, the rate of compliance has been decreasing sharply, down to less than one-third compliance with programme performance criteria in the most recent years" (p. 107). Edwards notes that "a serious consequence of the low rate of compliance has been that in recent years there had been a significant increase in the number of programmes that have been interrupted as well as in the number of waivers approved by the Fund" (p. 36).

Of course, the evaluation of IMF-supported programmes is fraught with methodological problems. Khan (1990) reviews these problems in considerable detail but, on the basis of his own tests covering Fund-supported programmes during 1973–88, concludes that they have generally been associated with an improvement in the balance of payments. The improvement was particularly marked for the current account, where the implementation of a programme led, on average, to about a 1 percentage point improvement in the ratio of the current account to GDP. In contrast to Edwards and Sachs, Khan claims that the evidence indicates that Fund-supported programmes have been more effective in improving the external balance in the 1980s than they were in the 1970s. Indeed he suggests that while "we do not as yet have the final word on the effects of programmes, . . . it does appear that these effects are more positive than has previously been reported" (p. 224). Although Khan does not take into account the degree of policy implementation (since he maintains that it is "not easy" to do so), he suggests that exclusion of this factor may lead to an under-estimation of effectiveness. "Had the tests been restricted to only those countries that successfully implemented the recommended policies, it is conceivable that an even more positive picture would emerge" (p. 223). This view again differs from that of Edwards and Sachs, who argue that the degree of compliance should itself constitute a measure of effectiveness. Clearly there is still some way to go before a broad consensus emerges on the effectiveness of Fund-supported programmes. For a yet more recent assessment of the effects of Fund programmes, see Killick with Malik (1992) and Killick, Malik and Manuel (1992).

20 Harrigan (1991) provides a useful review of World Bank involvement in Jamaica and Guyana. Bacha and Feinberg (1986) argue that with appropriate modification to its conditionality and enlarged resources, the World Bank could play an "increasingly critical" role in Latin America.

21 For a detailed assessment of the ways in which IMF conditionality has and has not changed over the 1980s and 1990s, see Killick (1992).

22 Mahon (1992) argues that during the 1960s Latin American countries would have faced politically unacceptable currency devaluations had they sought to compete with East Asian countries. The income sacrifice associated with reorienting economies away from relatively high productivity primary exporting to low productivity manufacturing was simply too high. In one sense, the decline in real wages brought about by the debt crisis during the 1980s has created a better platform upon which export growth in manufactures might be erected. At the same time, however, Mahon claims that the debt crisis has accentuated the regressive pattern of income distribution and, along with others, he suggests that extreme income inequality will generate further pressures for "populist" solutions which will erode any sustained drive for exports based on low wages. An outlook of political unrest will not help the investment required to raise productivity and will do nothing to attract capital from abroad.

23 We do not examine in detail debt reduction schemes as applied to countries in Latin America either under (Mexico, Venezuela, Uruguay, Costa Rica) or outside (Chile) the auspices of the Brady Plan. A number of useful studies exist, such as Reisen

(1991), Griffith-Jones (1992) and van Wijnbergen (1991). A broader treatment of how such schemes contribute to a new economic trajectory for Latin America is provided by Bulmer-Thomas (1992). Economic theorists have, however, identified ways in which debt reduction may have negative consequences for the countries pursuing it (Bulow and Rogoff, 1991). A recent critical analysis of Chile's programme of debt conversion is, for example, provided by Lagos (1992). The finding by Hofman and Reisen (1991) that a fall in highly indebted countries' investment has more to do with falling capital inflows than with the existence of a debt overhang is of interest in relation to the long-term balance of payments. Their conclusion is that the credit constraint dominates the debt overhang in explaining investment behaviour, and that a debt strategy which emphasizes debt reduction in place of new money will have negative investment effects. Arguing from a rather different point of view, and having stressed the heterogeneity of debt management in Latin America, Griffith-Jones (1992) suggests that a particularly strong case for debt reduction can be made for countries that are unable to attract private capital.

REFERENCES

Agénor, P.R. and M.P. Taylor (1993) "Analysing Credibility in High Inflation Countries: A New Approach", *Economic Journal* **103**.

Allen, C., D. Currie, T.G. Srinivasan and D. Vines (1992) "Policy Interactions Between the OECD Countries and Latin America in the 1980s", *The Manchester School*, June.

Anthony, M. and A.J. Hughes-Hallett (1992) "How Successfully Do We Measure Capital Flight: The Empirical Evidence for Five Developing Countries", *Journal of Development Studies* **28**(3).

Bacha, E.L. and R.E. Feinberg (1986) "The World Bank and Structural Adjustment in Latin America", *World Development* **14**(3).

Bahmani-Oskooee, M. and M. Malixi (1992) "Inflationary Effects of Changes in Effective Exchange Rates: LDCs' Experience", *Applied Economics* **24**.

Berg, A. and J. Sachs (1988) "The Debt Crisis: Structural Explanations of Country Performance", *Journal of Development Economics* **29**.

Birch, M. (1991) "Changing Patterns of Foreign Direct Investment in Latin America", *Quarterly Review of Economics and Business*, Autumn.

Bird, G. (1978) *The International Monetary System and the Less Developed Countries*, Macmillan, London.

Bird, G. (1984) "Balance of Payments Policy", in T. Killick *et al.*, *The Quest for Economic Stabilisation: The IMF and The Third World*, ODI with Heinemann Educational Books, Oxford.

Bulmer-Thomas, V. (1992) "Life After Debt: The New Economic Trajectory in Latin America", Inaugural Lecture, 5 March, Queen Mary and Westfield College Dicussion Paper No 255.

Bulow, J. and K. Rogoff (1991) "Sovereign Debt Repurchases: No Cure for an Overhang", *Quarterly Journal of Economics* **CVI**, November.

De Gregorio, J. (1992) "Economic Growth in Latin America", *Journal of Development Economics* **39**.

Dornbusch, R. and S. Fischer (1993) "Moderate Inflation", *The World Bank Economic Review* **7**(1).

Edwards, S. (1988) *Exchange Rate Misalignment in Development Countries*, The World Bank Occasional Paper, No 2, The Johns Hopkins University Press, Baltimore MD.

Edwards, S. (1989) "The International Monetary Fund and the Developing Countries: A Critical Evaluation", *Carnegie Rochester Conference Series on Public Policy* **31**.

El-Erian, M.A. (1992) "Restoration of Access to Voluntary Capital Market Financing: The Recent Latin American Experience", *IMF Staff Papers* **39**(1).

Gibson, H. and A.P. Thirlwall (1988) "An International Comparison of the Causes of Changes in the Debt Service Ratio, 1980–85", *Studies in Economics* **88**(13), University of Kent.

Griffith-Jones, S. (1989) "The Bargaining Position of Debtor Nations" in G. Bird (ed.) *Third World Debt: The Search For a Solution*, Edward Elgar Publishing, Aldershot.

Griffith-Jones, S. and R. Gottschalk (1992) "Is There Still a Latin American Debt Crisis?" in G. Bird (ed.) *International Aspects of Economic Development*, Surrey University Press with Academic Press, London.

Harrigan, J. (1991) "Jamaica" and "Guyana", in P. Mosley *et al.* (eds) *Aid and Power*, Volume 2, Case Studies, Routledge, London.

Hofman, B. and H. Reisen (1991) "Some Evidence on Debt-Related Determinants of Investment and Consumption in Heavily Indebted Countries", *Weltwirtschaftliches Archiv.* **127**.

Houthakker, H.S. and S. Magee (1969) "Income and Price Elasticities in World Trade", *Review of Economics and Statistics* **51**.

Khan, M.S. (1990) "The Macroeconomic Effects of Fund-Supported Programmes", *IMF Staff Papers*, June.

Khan, M.S. and M.D. Knight (1983) "Determinants of Current Account Balances of Non-Oil Developing Countries in the 1970s: An Empirical Analysis", *IMF Staff Papers*, December.

Khan, M.S. and M.D. Knight (1988) "Import Compression and Export Performance in Developing Countries", *Review of Economics and Statistics*, May.

Killick, T. (1992) *Continuity and Change in IMF Programme Design, 1982–92*, Overseas Development Institute Working Paper **69**.

Killick, T. with M. Malik (1992) "Country Experiences with IMF Programmes in the 1980s", *The World Economy* **15**(5).

Killick, T. *et al.* (1984) *The Quest for Economic Stabilisation: The IMF and The Third World*, Heinemann in association with the Overseas Development Institute, London.

Killick, T., M. Malik and M. Manuel (1992) "What Can We Know About the Effects of IMF Programmes", *The World Economy* **15**(5).

Kuczynski, P.-P. (1993) "International Capital Flows to Latin America: What is the Promise?", *Proceedings of the World Bank Annual Conference on Development Economics, 1992*, World Bank, Washington DC.

Lagos, R.A. (1992) "Debt Relief Through Debt Conversion: A Critical Analysis of the Chilean Debt Conversion Programme", *Journal of Development Studies* **28**(3).

Li, C. (1992) "Debt Arrears in Latin America: Do Political Variables Matter?", *Journal of Development Studies* **28**(4).

Llewellyn, D.T. (1990) "The International Capital Transfer Mechanism of the 1970s: A Critique", in G. Bird (ed.) *The International Financial Regime*, Surrey University Press with Academic Press, London.

Love, J. (1992) "Export Instability and the Domestic Economy: Questions of Causality", *Journal of Development Studies* **28**(4).

Mahon, J.E. (1992) "Was Latin America Too Rich to Prosper? Structural and Political Obstacles to Export Led Industrial Growth", *Journal of Development Studies* **28**(2).

Mosley, P. (1991) "Ecuador" in P. Mosley *et al.*, op. cit.

Mosley, P., J. Harrigan and J. Toye (1991) *Aid and Power: The World Bank and Policy-Based Lending*, 2 Volumes, Routledge, London.

Pastor, M. (1987) "The Effects of IMF Programmes in the Third World: Debate and Evidence from Latin America", *World Development*, February.

Reisen, H. (1991) "The Brady Plan and Adjustment Incentives", *Intereconomics*, March/April.

Sachs, J. (1989a) "Conditionality, Debt Relief and the Developing Country Debt Crisis" in J.

Sachs (ed.) *Developing Country Debt and Economic Performance, Volume 1, The International Financial System*, University of Chicago Press, for the National Bureau of Economic Research, Chicago IL.

Sachs, J. (1989b) "Strengthening IMF Programmes in Highly Indebted Countries", in C. Gwin, R. Feinberg *et al.*, *The International Monetary Fund in a Multipolar World: Pulling Together*, US–Third World Policy Perspectives, No 13, Overseas Development Council.

Sheehey, E.J. (1992) "Exports and Growth: Additional Evidence", *Journal of Development Studies* **28**(4).

Snowden, P.N. (1992) "Reviving Capital Inflows After Debt Reduction – Seniority and Incentives Under the Brady Strategy" in G. Bird (ed.) *International Aspects of Economic Development*, Surrey University Press with Academic Press, London.

Tanzi, V. (1989) "Fiscal Policy, Growth and the Design of Stabilisation Programmes" in M.I. Blejer and K.Y. Chin (eds) *Fiscal Policy, Stabilization and Growth in Developing Countries*, International Monetary Fund, Washington DC.

Twomey, M.J. (1992) "Terms of Trade, Foreign Exchange Booms and Real Exchange Rates in Latin America", *The International Trade Journal* **VI**(3).

van Wijnbergen, S. (1991) "The Mexican Debt Deal", *Economic Policy*, April.

5 | Stabilization Policy in Latin America: Debates about Growth and Distribution

ANN HELWEGE*

The 1980s left a legacy of lessons for macroeconomic policy in Latin America. As we reconstruct the elements of success and failure in stabilization programmes of the past decade, we change our underlying assumptions about what governments can do to promote growth. Growth offers the promise of overcoming poverty, yet we do not have a model for growth-oriented stabilization. Thus we must deal with the distributional aspects of stabilization.

This chapter looks at how recent stabilization experiences in Latin America have substantially narrowed the debate about the need for austerity in the face of inflation. The successful containment of inflation in Latin America in the early 1990s has affirmed many of the principles in market-friendly approaches to stabilization. But behind much of the opposition to orthodox stabilization plans has been an unresolved concern about the distributional impact of austerity. A decade and a half of experiments with monetarism and heterodoxy have demonstrated that neither offers an option of using rapid growth to circumvent distributional issues. Debates such as whether exports are responsive to exchange rates or whether inflation is principally inertial now seem a distraction from the task of understanding distributional conflicts in Latin America.

The first section of this chapter addresses a long-standing debate about whether contraction and fiscal austerity are essential steps in the stabilization process. Structuralists, who dominated Latin American policy from the 1950s to the 1970s, viewed fiscal policy as an important tool for overcoming rigidities on the supply side of the economy. Thus contractionary approaches to stabilization were seen as undesirable. During this era, monetarists argued that

* The author thanks Marisela Montoliu and Graham Bird for helpful comments on earlier versions of this paper, and Manual Pastor, John Sheahan, and Miguel Kiguel for generously sharing research materials.

government intervention was a cause of inefficiency and inflation in Latin America. Some issues in the old monetarist/structuralist debate now seem resolved, if not by compelling econometric work, by hard experience. Yet monetarist models of stabilization (often referred to as "orthodoxy", a subset of which includes the more extreme neo-conservatism applied in the Southern Cone) failed to provide a growth-oriented alternative to the old interventionist model.

Demand-driven Keynesian models, which were not seen as applicable to developing countries in the 1960s, were tested with heterodox experiments in the mid-1980s. Heterodoxy sought to contain prices by stopping inflationary expectations, while averting a recession. These policy experiments thus carried forward the structuralist position that contraction is counterproductive. Although heterodoxy failed, its emphasis on inertial inflation was incorporated into exchange rate based stabilization programmes. These programmes have proven successful only insofar as the regime is able to bring fundamental macroeconomic imbalances under control.

An important lesson of the past decade is that fiscal restraint and contraction are inevitable steps in stabilization. Juan Carlos de Pablo accurately notes: "The essential distinction to be made is not between countries that have fiscal deficits and those that have surpluses, but one between countries that can finance their imbalances and those that cannot."[1] Countries that reach the point of implementing a stabilization programme are typically unable to finance deficits.

Given that fiscal restraint and contraction seem integral to successful stabilization, the second section of this chapter emphasizes the need to develop mechanisms to ameliorate the distributional consequences of austerity. Even where rapid growth has taken off, as in the case of Venezuela, distributional conflict threatens to undermine progress. There are two dominant models in managing distributional aspects of stabilization: repression (associated with Chile) and consensus (achieved by Mexico). The Chilean model is not desirable; the Mexican model may not be replicable. Clearly, distribution is not the only lingering open question in the design of stabilization policies, but it is an important one.

I OLD ISSUES: THE DEBATE BETWEEN MONETARISM AND STRUCTURALISM

Forty years ago, structuralism served as the foundation for import substituting industrialization (ISI) policies. Structuralists adopted elasticity pessimism. Exports were assumed to be unresponsive to devaluations because of rigidities in agriculture, inelastic international demand for minerals and fuels, and the technological inferiority of industry. Low elasticity models suggested that devaluations can even make balance of payments matters temporarily worse, as foreigners pay less hard currency for a marginally larger volume of exports.

Industrialization became synonymous with development, as agriculture and mining offered little promise of absorbing labour and expanding output. Instead of using prices to resolve economic imbalances, structuralism turned to government intervention. Protectionism was justified on classic infant industry grounds. Governments invested heavily in industry to promote backward and forward development linkages; price controls were implemented to reduce the real cost of labour in industry; and overvaluation was used to subsidize imports of industrial inputs. Fiscal deficits and their inflationary consequences were discounted as the inevitable price of overcoming structural rigidities.[2]

Structuralism was certainly not a Keynesian underconsumption model. In the structuralist model, an expansion of demand alone would mainly raise prices. Fixed coefficient models of development, such as the two-gap model, worked on the assumption that growth was supply constrained.[3] Deficit spending was productive mainly insofar as it alleviated supply bottlenecks. In the long term, successful stabilization depended on making progress toward industrialization. In the short run, stabilization programmes that required fiscal restraint were often thought to be at odds with the promotion of long-run growth.

Despite structuralism's liberal reputation, its social welfare programmes tended to favour workers in the formal sector, rather than the politically disenfranchised poor. A pro-urban distributional agenda prevailed. Minimum wages and social security programmes supported wage-earners, and industrialists benefited from protectionism. Price controls on basic foods subsidized urban workers (including informal workers) at the expense of agriculture. The rural poor were targeted with the rhetoric if not reality of land reform, while industrialization was sought as a long-term solution to rural poverty.

Monetarist critiques of this paradigm stressed the link between fiscal deficits and inflation, the role of trade barriers and overvaluation in external imbalances, and the negative effect of price controls on output. The issues in this debate were: How much real output growth can be gained by liberalizing prices? How elastic is the supply of exports with respect to the exchange rate? Does money alone drive inflation, or is it the consequence of supply rigidities and inertial mechanisms such as indexation? Does protection advance industrial growth? Can government effectively substitute for private production?

Not all of these issues were resolved with the abandonment of ISI in the early 1960s. A general consensus emerged that government-owned enterprises tended to be grossly inefficient, and that protectionism led to a lack of competitiveness, rather than to more rapid movement up the learning curve. While Asian countries had used protectionism and state-led development effectively, there was no doubt that the Latin versions of these policies were failures. On the other hand, little consensus emerged about the responsiveness of exports to devaluations, the effectiveness of price liberalization, or the role of inertial forces in driving inflation.

The path to reverse obvious distortions caused by government interventions was also debated. Ramos (1986, p. 175) noted:

> [A]s interventions became widespread, it became increasingly difficult to determine whether a specific intervention further distorted the market or simply offset an existing distortion; hence it was also unclear whether eliminating it would lessen or accentuate existing distortions.

Moreover, the distributional consequences of dismantling ISI created powerful interests opposed to liberalization. Although little progress occurred in the direction of privatization and trade reform, the trend toward greater state intervention stopped.

In hindsight, the old structuralist model offered neither a model that could sustain growth without inflation and external imbalances, nor an especially progressive distributional agenda. By the 1970s, structuralist policies were increasingly seen as unsustainable, but easy external financing staved off the need to reverse state intervention.

I.1   Monetarists at the helm: neo-conservatism and orthodoxy

Orthodox stabilization programmes are derived from monetarist theories of inflation. Among orthodox programmes, I include programmes supported by the International Monetary Fund and the extreme neo-conservative experiments in the Southern Cone. These programmes share the assumption that stabilization requires contraction. Few orthodox economists expect the growth-oriented aspects of these programmes, including the supply response to lower wages and price liberalization, to take effect before stabilization is achieved.[4]

Neo-conservative experiments in Argentina, Chile and Uruguay in the late 1970s put an extreme emphasis on free markets and sought to control inflation through fiscal austerity and monetary restraint. A combination of sharp devaluation, trade liberalization, and wage repression were used to reduce trade imbalances and increase long-run competitiveness. These programmes culminated in widespread bankruptcies, growing external indebtedness, and a marked deterioration in income distribution. The three countries had become more export-oriented, but export growth did not keep up with import demand. Trade deficits were financed by borrowing. When the debt crisis struck, Chile's dependence on foreign loans became evident as GNP fell by 14.5 per cent in 1982. Moreover, while inflation was reduced, it remained high in the three cases.

Ongoing orthodox stabilization programmes supported by the International

Monetary Fund also yielded uneven results. Neo-conservatism suffered from the combination of using a fixed exchange rate as a benchmark to set inflationary expectations, while rapidly liberalizing trade and capital accounts. Increasing overvaluation then fuelled trade deficits and high external debt. By contrast, orthodox programmes did not use fixed exchange rates to manage expectations, and they moved more slowly in the liberalization process. Yet they did (and do) rely principally on austerity and devaluation as means to reduce the role of government, to slow monetary growth, and to increase competitiveness.

Critics such as Pastor (1987) argued that IMF programmes based on austerity and devaluation had mixed effects on growth, stabilized the balance of payments mainly through capital inflows rather than an improved current account, and tended to accelerate rather than contain inflation.[5] Orthodoxy appeared to neither stop inflation nor resolve external imbalances. Moreover, to the extent that any growth occurred, its rewards were reaped disproportionately by upper income groups. Pastor marshalled evidence that IMF programmes were significantly and consistently associated with declines in labour's share of output.

By the mid-1980s, there were still wide differences among economists about the links between deficits and inflation, devaluation and export growth, and trade liberalization and competitiveness. Even where there was considerable consensus about the logic of theoretical relationships in formal models, there was discord over the extent to which institutional factors tend to overwhelm these relationships in policy application.

I.2   The Bolivian experience: is it enough to restrain demand?

For many Latin American economists, Bolivia serves as a canonical example of orthodoxy's failure to stimulate growth, even when distributional concerns are cast aside.

Bolivian prices rose 11,857 per cent in 1985. Hyperinflation was the result of several factors. The debt crisis cut off external financing for large fiscal deficits, and the decision to continue debt service exacerbated the reversal of capital flows. The price of tin plummeted 29 per cent between 1980 and 1985, cutting export earnings by a third. In addition, a bitter struggle over income shares, unresolved since the revolution of 1952, created political instability. Unions demanded and got real wage increases, but capitalists divested and sent their wealth abroad. At the peak of the hyperinflation, the government lost its ability to tax, and the real value of seigniorage (revenues raised by printing money) vanished as the economy became dollarized.

The orthodox stabilization programme of 1985 reduced monthly inflation from 66 per cent to a slight disinflation within two months. Imports were liberalized, and the official exchange rate was devalued from 75,000 pesos to the dollar to 1,000,000 pesos overnight. The government then committed itself to a "dirty float". Public sector salaries were frozen, petrol subsidies were cut, and a value added tax was implemented to cut fiscal deficits. Perhaps most visible was a 75 per cent reduction in the labour force of the government mining corporation, COMIBOL, and the arrest of union leaders. Wages fell sharply.[6]

Pastor (1992, p. 167) describes the role of distributional conflict:

> In Bolivia, distributional conflict played a crucial role in triggering and sustaining the hyperinflation of the first half of the 1980s. . . . Any government seeking to end the inflation had to break the class stalemate and force one group to accept both lower incomes *and* higher taxes.
>
> The architects of the 1985 Bolivian stabilization program did just that. Real wages were depressed and labor union leaders were arrested and exiled. A new regressive value-added tax was announced and then implemented. Controls on prices and productive activity were lifted and the government dramatically reduced the size of public enterprise. This pro-capitalist character of the program played a crucial role in establishing "credibility".

Financial capital was enticed back with a tax amnesty on flight capital, a no-questions-asked approach to drug money, and extraordinarily high interest rates (averaging 4.3 per cent per month between mid-1986 and mid-1987). Yet as of the early 1990s, there had been little productive investment. Investment was just 10 per cent of GDP between 1985 and 1991. To some extent, this reflects weak tin prices and austerity in the government's capital budget. However, significant dynamic sectors failed to emerge in the economy. In 1989, J. Sachs remarked, "Bolivia has gone from being a poor country with hyperinflation to a poor country without inflation."[7]

Keynesian explanations attribute orthodoxy's failure to generate growth in Bolivia to weak demand caused by lower real wages, but other factors were also at work. Tin prices (and taxes from tin) continued to fall sharply after the stabilization programme was implemented, and the price of coca paste, a major export, fell from about $1,500 to $700 per kg between 1987 and 1989. Despite substantial increases in volume, weak prices of zinc, tin, lead, coffee, and sugar prevented a full recovery of export earnings, and a contract to sell natural gas to Argentina was renegotiated at a lower price.

The Bolivian economy lacks idle capacity, the basis for a rapid recovery of growth. Its infrastructure is primitive, its workers are poorly educated, and unresolved class conflict continues to hinder new investment. Unless the price of a primary export surges suddenly, the country can at most hope for a gradual recovery as new export products emerge.

Sturzenegger (1992) contends that while structural reform is needed and beneficial, "What the numbers indicate from the 'model' case of Bolivia is that policymakers should not expect wonders from price liberalization or trade reform. Even less so that they will become engines of growth." Improvements in education and infrastructure, the resolution of class tensions, and investment in non-traditional exports are long-term development tasks. While fiscal restraint and getting prices "right" through devaluation may be necessary to end inflation and to restore external balances, they are insufficient to achieve growth.

I.3 Heterodoxy: the Keynesian counter to orthodox austerity

In the mid-1980s, the results of orthodoxy raised the question of whether policy-makers might not do better. Heterodox programmes of the mid-1980s, including the Austral Plan in Argentina, the Inti Plan in Peru, and the Cruzado Plan in Brazil, sought to contain inflation without incurring a recession. Two principles guided these programmes: the assumption that capacity constraints were not binding at the aggregate level, and the belief that inflation is principally inertial. Thus heterodox programmes set out to stop the self-perpetuating cycle of inflationary expectations without restricting demand and thereby causing a collapse in economic growth.

Heterodoxy, like structuralism, viewed contraction as a counterproductive element in stabilization. However, its underlying assumptions differed considerably from this earlier paradigm. Structuralist models assumed fixed coefficients and low supply elasticities, but heterodox policymakers took the existence of idle capacity as a signal that output could be maintained in the

Table 5.1 Bolivian economic data.

	Price of tin	Tin taxes as % of GDP	Inflation	GDP growth
1980	761	1.5	47.2	—
1981	642	0.6	32.1	0.9
1982	582	0.4	123.5	−4.4
1983	589	0.1	275.6	−4.5
1984	555	0.7	1,282.4	−0.6
1985	523	0.2	11,857.1	−1.0
1986	294	0.0	276.3	−2.5
1987	316	0.1	14.6	2.6
1988	331	0.1	16.0	3.0
1989	395	0.1	15.2	2.8
1990	281	0.1	17.1	2.6
1991	254		14.5	4.1
1992			13.0[a]	3.2[a]

Source: Sturzenegger, A. (1992) "Bolivia: From Stabilization to What?", NBER Conference on Stabilization, Economic Reform and Growth, Washington DC, December; International Monetary Fund (1992) *International Financial Statistics*, Washington DC; *The Economist* (1992) Country Profile: Bolivia, No. 3.
[a] *The Economist* forecast, third quarter 1992.

stabilization process. Structuralism stressed the importance of fiscal policy in overcoming supply constraints; heterodoxy emphasized the importance of maintaining aggregate demand.

Key steps in heterodoxy were wage and price controls, a fixed exchange rate, and monetary reform. New currencies were introduced to change expectations. Easy monetary policy was adopted to avoid credit shortages caused by rising demand for local currency as inflation ebbed. With an eye toward fairness, the Brazilians used a complicated "tablita" to ensure that existing contracts would reflect past inflationary expectations. Real wages were increased by 8 to 15 per cent in Brazil.

Inflation briefly receded in all three heterodox cases, only to return at even higher rates within a few years (see Table 5.2). Heterodoxy's failure could be largely explained by a lack of fiscal discipline, rapid monetary growth, and an excessively expansive incomes policy. Although policy-makers had hoped to take advantage of idle capacity by maintaining aggregate demand, it became apparent that the use of idle capacity requires complementary imported inputs and wage goods.

The initial success of the heterodox programmes led to renewed applications of the basic model, none of which lasted. Argentina cycled through the Plan Primavera, the February Plan, the Austral II Plan, and another Plan Primavera, while Brazil created the Bresser Plan, the Summer Plan, and the Collor Plan. The Summer Plan of 1989 repeated several measures used in the Cruzado Plan: a new price freeze, the creation of yet another currency, and

Table 5.2 Inflation and growth in post-heterodox economies.

| | Argentina | | Brazil | | Peru | |
	Inflation	GDP growth	Inflation	GDP growth	Inflation	GDP growth
1982	163.2	−4.9	98.1	0.6	64.4	0.2
1983	345.0	3.0	142.0	−3.4	111.2	−12.6
1984	627.5	2.7	196.7	5.3	110.2	4.8
1985	672.2	−4.4	226.9	7.9	163.4	2.3
1986	90.1	5.7	145.3	7.6	77.9	9.2
1987	131.3	2.2	229.7	3.6	85.8	8.5
1988	343.0	−2.6	682.3	−0.1	667.1	−8.3
1989	3,079.2	−4.5	1,287.0	3.3	3,398.7	−11.6
1990	2,314.0	0.4	2,938.0	−4.0	7,482.6	−4.9
1991	172.8	4.5[a]	440.8	1.2	409.5	2.2
1992	18.0	9.0[b]	1,131.5	−1.0[b]	56.6	−2.0

Source: Interamerican Development Bank (1992) *Economic and Social Progress in Latin America*, Washington DC; United Nations Commission on Latin America and the Caribbean (1993) *CEPAL News*, Washington DC.
[a] *The Economist* (1992) Country Profile: Argentina, No. 3.
[b] Preliminary estimates.

measures to de-index the economy. As in earlier programmes, fiscal provisions were ignored, and total public sector borrowing requirements rose from 48 per cent to 73 per cent of GDP. A lack of confidence compounded the crisis by forcing the government to displace borrowing with seigniorage. Hyperinflation took off once Brazilians anticipated a repudiation of domestic debt.

These expansionist policies indicated that priming the pump, a powerful tool in the developed countries, fails in Latin America. Keynes (1936, p. 300) cautioned:

> It is probable that the general level of prices will not rise much as output increases, so long as there are available efficient unemployed resources of every type. But as soon as output has increased sufficiently to begin to reach the "bottle-necks", there is likely to be a sharp rise in the prices of certain commodities.

In Latin America, the foreign exchange constraint is met too quickly, and supply elasticities are too low, to assume that growth will be achieved by increasing effective demand. It would seem we knew this in the 1950s, when structuralists cautioned against simple expansionism. Heterodox experiences of the 1980s suggest it is a lesson only recently learned.

Ironically, heterodox programmes which sought to stabilize prices by resolving conflicts over income shares may have worsened distribution. Brazil, with one of the highest Gini coefficients in the world, experienced a further deterioration in income distribution between 1987 and 1989 (Cardoso, Paes de Barros and Urani, 1992).

The economic agenda set out by the Brazilian president, Itamar Franco, in late 1992 suggests that stabilization-cum-Keynesian expansion has not entirely run its course in Latin America. Attacking austerity as a "false modernization" scheme that contributed to Brazil's falling per capita GDP, Franco advanced a proposal to pay government workers more, to double and possibly quadruple the country's minimum wage, and to create four million new jobs over two years through public projects. The agenda also criticized the use of high interest rates and tight monetary policy to contain inflation, then running at 1,132 per cent. The lack of enthusiasm that met this programme is perhaps an indication that Brazilians expect high fiscal deficits and easy money to fuel instability and make life harder.

I.4 Inertial inflation and exchange rate-based stabilizations

Although heterodoxy failed to restore fundamental balances, it drew attention to the role of inertial inflation. In examining inflation in Argentina and Brazil, Kiguel and Liviatan (1992) argue:

> it is more difficult and costly to demonstrate a regime change in countries that

have a tradition of high inflation. Balancing the budget for a year or two is not enough to convince the public that the economy is departing from a long history of high inflation.

Hyperinflation in these countries is attributed to a gradual deterioration of domestic and external conditions over two decades, leading to the entrenchment of progressively higher rates of inflation. Kiguel and Leviatan claim that by 1989 in Argentina and Brazil, "Anything short of a major stabilization package capable of changing inflationary expectations in a dramatic way would have been insufficient to avoid hyperinflation."

Fixed exchange rates, or very slow crawling pegs, are currently used to establish the credibility of stabilization plans. As a tool for gaining public confidence, fixed rates have been used both by orthodox proponents of contractionary adjustment and by economists who emphasize inertial inflation and hope to avoid contraction.

Rudiger Dornbusch wrote in 1982:

> Success at disinflation depends on a combination of two factors. Within the overall consistency of the programme it is important that there be domestic slack and that there be an expectation of price stability beyond the period of a wage freeze. There are only two sources of such assurance. One is fiscal reform that eliminates budget deficits as a source of inflation. The other is longer term exchange rate policy into which the government is literally locked by announcement and the taking of forward positions.

By committing to a given exchange rate, the government is theoretically forced to use fiscal discipline to avoid a balance of payments crisis in the absence of capital controls and import licensing. The credibility of the programme hinges on the government's ability to avoid inflationary fiscal deficits and wage increases that would undermine the exchange rate.

Yet Sachs (1987) has noted that when inflation is less extreme than it became in Bolivia, fixed exchange rates can lull policy-makers into mistaken confidence that the rate can be maintained without contractionary adjustment. According to Sachs, setting the exchange rate yields positive initial results as long as the government holds reserves. Inflation is then temporarily brought under control. Although everyone understands that the economic programme will break down when reserves run out, they know it will not break down immediately. Holdings of real money increase in the short run, and assets are brought in from abroad, but investors fully prepare to reverse the process before the fixed rate breaks down. Reserves may temporarily increase, but eventually the unsustainable rate collapse to a speculative attack on the central bank, a collapse of the exchange rate and resurging inflation.[8]

The commitment to a fixed exchange rate in Chile and Argentina in the late 1970s led to current account deficits financed by external borrowing prior to the debt crisis. Since 1989, successful experiences with exchange rate-based stabilization plans have been supported with capital inflows, particularly portfolio investment, that shift more of the risk of failure to investors. However, these capital inflows may partly result from speculative bubbles and an unsustainable privatization process, rather than sound management of macroeconomic fundamentals. This money can then sustain mistakes that are not necessarily made apparent by an immediate collapse of the exchange rate.[9] Thus the initial success of exchange-rate based stabilization programmes should not be mistaken for the discovery of a simple growth-oriented stabilization scheme.

Argentina reflects both the promise and vulnerability of exchange rate-based stabilization plans. In mid-1989, the Menem regime fixed the exchange rate. Unsupported by fundamental changes necessary to contain inflation, the exchange rate proved unsustainable and inflation exploded. More serious adjustment efforts were made beginning in March 1990 with a floating (but stable) exchange rate. Despite a commitment to austerity, the government succeeded in bringing inflation below 10 per cent per month for only four months.

In March 1991, the Argentine government guaranteed the convertibility of pesos into US dollars at a fixed exchange rate and resolved not to print money without buying dollars in the foreign exchange market. For two years, the central bank maintained its commitment not to finance budget deficits by printing money. Annual inflation declined to approximately 20 per cent in 1992. The success of this programme, in contrast to the exchange rate-based stabilization of 1989, may lie in the fiscal track record established by the government even as it attempted stabilization under floating rates in 1990. In other words, a fixed exchange rate only serves as a nominal benchmark as long as the public has confidence in the overall consistency of macroeconomic policy.

Despite the implementation of a sweeping economic reform package, however, the Argentine fiscal budget remains in deficit and the trade deficit has soared. Revenue from privatization, capital repatriation and external credit close the gap, but none is a sustainable financing mechanism. Having set a rigid standard for itself, the Argentine government has few options. As Dornbusch (1992) points out, it can abrogate its convertibility commitment and face a loss of public confidence, or it can maintain its commitment and allow growth to collapse because of accompanying fiscal restraint or an inevitable loss of confidence in the economy's fundamentals. In the context of rising expectations set off by an overdue recovery and frustration with wages that remain a quarter below the level of 1986, fiscal discipline may be politically infeasible.

Advocates of exchange rate-based stabilization programmes hope this highly visible standard will force Latin American policy-makers to avoid populist policies that ultimately damage the economy. Yet pegged exchange rates are not much different than price and wage controls: without a shift in the fundamental causes of instability, the rate cannot last. Setting the exchange rate alone does not solve the distributional tension and excess demand that contributes to instability.

I.5   Liberalization: compounding conflict

Stabilization programmes are now closely linked with liberalization schemes to open trade, free price controls and privatize state enterprises. To the extent that there is a growth-oriented agenda in orthodox stabilization programmes, it is found in the long-run efficiency consequences of price stability and liberalization. But even among those who support a dismantling of state intervention, there is little agreement on how to practically implement reforms. The sequencing debate in the stabilization literature asks whether all reforms can be implemented at once, and if not, where should policy-makers begin?

There are important technical questions in the sequencing debate. Eliminating subsidies is a step toward "getting prices right", but to the extent that inflation is inertial, an explosion of prices for basic commodities can intensify inflation. Liberalizing trade while fixing the exchange rate to anchor prices can also lead to a surge in imports and the bankruptcy of firms that are unable to adjust to this influx. Tight monetary policy to control inflation also interferes with liberalization: high interest rates draw in financial capital and contribute to currency appreciation, while inhibiting investment that would enable firms to adjust to external competition. Since no Latin American country now has complete control over its capital account, success in stabilizing prices can be at odds with trade promotion. At least in the early 1990s, adding privatization to this equation accelerated capital inflows, further raising currency values.

At the same time, liberalization is a distributional minefield: raising bus fares to just seven cents provoked the Venezuelan riots of March 1989. Is it appropriate to add the unevenly shared adjustment costs of liberalization to the distributional conflict of stabilization? Increasingly, the "cold shower" approach is seen as destabilizing, because it gives domestic firms too little time to adjust to new conditions. But going too slowly risks the loss of an opportunity for reform as the economic crisis creates political support for decisive change. Moreover, liberalization may be an important step toward building a credible macroeconomic programme that eases inflationary expectations.

In theory, firms and workers that benefit from liberalization can compensate losers because efficiency increases. In practice, governments in the midst of a stabilization programme cannot hope to finance programmes that soften the adjustment to new relative prices. The pace at which liberalization can accompany stabilization is thus significantly determined by the extent to which its distributional consequences can be managed politically.

II THE UNSOLVED PUZZLE: DISTRIBUTION

If one accepts the apparent lesson that contraction – forcing demand to conform to the economy's capacity, rather than rapidly increasing output – is essential to overcome high inflation and external imbalances, one must inevitably turn to the distributional aspects of stabilization programmes.

Orthodoxy tackles the roots of inflation directly by ensuring that the sum of shares demanded in the economy do not exceed the size of the total pie. Diminishing expectations are thus integral to orthodox stabilization. Heterodox policy-makers were unwilling to accept this, preferring to hope that growth could avert the need for more than a temporary arbitration of income shares.

Orthodox programmes use wage repression as a means to resolve conflicts over income shares, to restrain aggregate demand, and to increase the external competitiveness of the economy. This anti-labour approach can stop inflation: the question is whether it is consistent with political stability and economic growth.

Labour repression has been used repeatedly in Latin American stabilization programmes. Fairness and human rights issues aside, we still lack a clear sense of how low wages need to go to attract investment. In Bolivia, austerity and low wages proved insufficient for macroeconomic take-off. Very low wages may be less important to capital than political stability. Even where growth takes off, as it has in Venezuela, violent distributional conflicts can undermine success.

II.1 Venezuela: the importance of political stability

Venezuela's orthodox stabilization programme set the stage for the fastest growth rate in Latin America in 1991. Yet fantastic growth trickled down too slowly for many Venezuelans, and conflict emerged.

The structural reform package of 1989:

- sharply devalued and unified the exchange rate;
- liberated trade by cutting tariffs and import licences;
- eliminated price controls on basic goods and reduced fertilizer subsidies;
- increased public sector prices, including those of utilities and transportation; and
- increased interest rates.

The fiscal deficit was brought down from 9.8 per cent of GDP in 1988 to a small surplus in 1990 and 1991.

Gross domestic product fell 7.8 per cent in 1989. Austerity had immediate political consequences. Riots broke out in 1989 in response to higher fares on public buses, and continued in response to a precipitous slide in real wages.

Fortuitous external factors spurred a rapid recovery. The suspension of OPEC's quota system the outset of the Persian Gulf War enabled the state oil company to produce at near full capacity – in 1990, petroleum revenues were 71 per cent higher than in 1988. Export revenues declined in 1991, but were still half again the earnings of 1988. Foreign capital was drawn to Venezuela by high interest rates, the oil boom, and extensive privatization. Real GDP grew by 9 per cent in 1991.

Despite rapid growth, the Venezuelan programme is seen by many as a failure, because of the political instability it engendered. Two coup attempts in 1992 reflected popular claims that the reforms were inequitable. Bankruptcies among small producers were blamed on high interest rates, while wealthy Venezuelans brought home capital to take advantage of favourable interest rates. With the highest per capita GDP in Latin America, 57 per cent of Venezuelans were said to be able to afford just one meal a day.

Evidence of corruption also fuelled public anger, ultimately forcing the president out of office in 1993. Instability in turn prevented the regime from more actively pursuing tax reform to contain inflation, pushing it toward greater reliance on tight monetary policy.

Venezuela has taught us that even "successful" orthodox programmes must deal with distributional issues. Moreover, one cannot hope to build support for

Table 5.3   Venezuelan economic data.

	Inflation (consumer prices)	Real wage growth	GDP growth
1982	9.6	−0.4	0.7
1983	6.2	−4.8	−5.6
1984	12.2	−11.2	−2.1
1985	11.4	−5.7	1.4
1986	11.5	0.0	6.3
1987	28.2	−9.2	4.5
1988	29.5	−8.4	6.2
1989	84.3	−10.6	−7.8
1990	40.8	−3.9	5.7
1991	34.2	5.0	9.2
1992	31.9[a]		9.0[a]

Source: Interamerican Development Bank (1992) *Economic and Social Progress in Latin America*, Washington DC.
[a] Preliminary estimates.

a programme based on austerity if policy-makers have their hand in the till. The conditions for growth have been much stronger in Venezuela than in Bolivia, but political collapse has threatened the entire stabilization programme.

IMF economists, known for their orthodox views, now emphasize the need for more social sensitivity in structural reform programmes. Michel Camdessus, Managing Director of the IMF, recently stressed: "Social measures must not be included in economic adjustment programs simply to make them more attractive; rather, thay must be an *intrinsic component* of the overall strategy for economic adjustment."[10] Yet economists know little about how to build political support for recessionary policies. Chile and Mexico offer two strikingly different approaches.

II.2   Repression and growth: the Chilean model

Rapid growth in Chile under the Pinochet regime leads some to wonder whether most Latin American countries might not need repression to resolve their distributional conflicts. But if repression works, is the sacrifice of political freedom for economic growth acceptable? And does it work?

The first question is entirely normative. For those who believe repression is unacceptable because it is inconsistent with democracy, the task of stabilization involves restructuring an entrenched political culture that supports inequality and despotism. This task is no less pressing, and no easier to achieve, than the technical aspects of structural adjustment.

The second question, whether repression facilitates stabilization, is still widely debated. Chile offers a less compelling case than many Latin Americans believe. High growth rates in the late 1970s were thought to justify the brutal years of repression in 1974–6, but growth collapsed with the debt crisis. High interest rates, overvaluation and liberalization had badly damaged the economy. Between 1974 and 1983, growth averaged 1.8 per cent. To point to high growth in the late 1970s as a success would be as inaccurate as declaring heterodoxy a triumph because it led to brief periods of growth: each experiment contained the seeds of its own failure.

Beginning in 1984, Chilean policy-makers adopted more moderate policies. These included a pragmatic exchange rate, lower interest rates, improved credit for agriculture, and selective intervention to promote exports and foreign investment. The drastic trade liberalization of the 1970s was temporarily reversed to revive the economy, and gradual tariff reductions were introduced.

Nonetheless, there is no denying that Chile's path was orthodox in the 1980s. The fiscal deficit, at 4.3 per cent of GDP in 1984, was eliminated by 1989. Devaluation and foreign investment incentives contributed to export growth (in volume) of 10.5 per cent per year between 1985 and 1989.

Austerity imposed social costs. Real wages declined in the public sector and automatic adjustment of social security to inflation was eliminated. The public work programme designed to ease unemployment (at more than 24 per cent between 1982 and 1985) paid just $25 per month. Per capita spending on health, housing and education declined by more than 20 per cent in the crisis of the 1980s. A radical reduction in the tax rate on corporate earnings and personal investment income, intended to promote savings, accentuated the regressive nature of Chile's adjustment.[11]

By all accounts, the number of Chileans living in poverty increased, particularly in the early 1980s.[12] Real wages fell 40 per cent between 1981 and 1985. Income distribution deteriorated, as the income share of the highest quintile rose from 51.9 per cent in 1978 to 59.5 per cent in 1989. As of early 1990, the real minimum wage was 35 per cent lower than its value for 1980, and family allowances were just one-third of their 1980 value. Subsidies for the extremely poor had declined 50 per cent in real terms between 1981 and 1989.[13]

Chileans slowly acknowledged that austerity was wrecking the social fabric. Across the political spectrum that coalesced against Pinochet, there was agreement that the new Aylwin government would need to deal with the "social debt" overhang. Real social spending rose an accumulated 20.5 per cent during 1990–1, and the real minimum wage was increased, although it remained 12 per cent below its 1980–1 value as of March 1992.

The question was how to finance reconciliation. Rather than adopting drastic measures, the government implemented a combination of modest tax increases. The corporate tax base was expanded from distributed earnings to total earnings, and the tax rate was temporarily increased from 10 per cent to 15 per cent. Although this was a substantial relative increase, the corporate tax rate remains very low by international standards, and corporate tax payments can be credited against personal income taxes. Secondly, personal income taxes were raised by narrowing income brackets rather than by raising the top rate. Finally, the value added tax rate was increased from 16 per cent to 18 per cent. Together, these measures raised revenue for social spending by almost 2 per cent of GDP.

Chile belatedly shows modest progress in building a social consensus around income shares. Does this tell us that redistribution must follow stabilization, or that Chile was simply slow to figure out how to reach compromises?

II.3 "Concertación" as the distributional solution: the Mexican model

Concertación, social pacts and incomes policies attempt to base stabilization on political consensus. The problem is that it is easy to build a consensus by giving everyone what they want, even if the economy cannot support it – this was the heterodoxy trap. Negotiating shared sacrifice has proven difficult in a region fraught with social conflict and highly unequal distribution of income.

Mexican stabilization has combined political acumen and economic realism. The Solidarity Pact of 1987 is credited with creating a stable environment for liberalization. Labour and industry agreed to accept restraint of wages and prices, with the understanding that the government would slow the pace of devaluation and begin an earnest structural adjustment programme. Privatization and negotiation toward the North American Free Trade Agreement were then parlayed into an investment boom which softened the blow of adjustment. Inflation fell from 132 per cent to 20 per cent by 1989; by 1992, policy-makers hoped to bring the rate below 10 per cent.

An ambitious anti-poverty programme, known as *Solidaridad*, has undercut protests about the inequity of structural adjustment. *Solidaridad* uses revenue from privatization to spur poor communities to pave roads, extend water pipes and build schools. The government provides materials and technical advice, while the communities themselves identify priorities and supply labour. Although the programme no doubt helps the ruling political party to shore up its electoral support, there are few complaints that money is misdirected to communities that do not need help. Careful targeting of social expenditure has muted arguments by the opposition that the stabilization programme lacks a social conscience.

On the surface, Mexico looks like a model of painless stabilization, particularly as industry and labour agreed to a truce on distributional conflicts. But wages fell 23 per cent in 1983, and continued to decline until shortly after the social pact (see Table 5.4). One cannot deny that wage repression may be an important element of Mexico's success. Nonetheless, political repression has not been as harsh as that in Chile.

Can the Mexican model be replicated? The political environment in Mexico has historically been far more consensual than elsewhere in Latin America: there has not been a coup in seventy years, and while abuses of power occur, there is no comparison between Mexico and the dirty wars of the Southern

Table 5.4 Real wages in Mexico, percentage change.

1982	0.7
1983	−22.8
1984	−7.1
1985	−2.7
1986	−5.9
1987	−1.9
1988	−1.3
1989	9.0
1990	2.9
1991	2.4

Source: Interamerican Development Bank (1992) *Economic and Social Progress in Latin America*, Washington DC.

Cone, the Central American crises, or Andean racial tensions. To adopt a consensual approach to stabilization, other countries must face the daunting challenge of social change.

II.4 Targeting taxes and social expenditures

In the short run, stabilization requires a cut in the income of some, if not all, classes. Who shall bear this burden? Workers are bound to lose, although one can argue about how far wages need to fall to gain external competitiveness and contain demand. Can fiscal policy soften this blow?

Imposing the burden of fiscal adjustment on low income groups presumes that investment is closely tied to the overall tax rate on the rich. Yet we know that tax policies can more directly target investment. Changes in marginal tax rates on profit and capital gains, for example, are more likely to influence investment than would changes in personal income or real estate tax rates. Moreover, fiscal subsidies that favour the middle and upper classes, such as cheap petrol and free university education, are very weakly related to investment rates. Workers need not bear the full burden of fiscal adjustment, even if they must share in it. Current changes in tax policy in Latin America, however, reflect a trend away from progressive to proportional taxation.[14]

It is easy to argue for more careful targeting of redistributive programmes. As in many policy areas, the quality of government intervention is as important as its overall level. Targeting would favour basic health clinics in slums over middle-class hospitals, primary education over university education, sanitation programmes and potable water over meticulously tended middle-class streets. These priorities carry strong moral weight.

However, the poor are poor because their political voices are weak. Pragmatically speaking, careful anti-poverty targeting does not solve the conflict between well-organized (and thus higher income) workers and capitalists that often derails stabilization programmes. The minimum wage is a central point of struggle in stabilization programmes, but this distributional conflict has little to do with poverty, because the poorest workers are in the informal sector.

Small budget changes to target the poor create the image that a regime is sensitive to issues of inequality. Modest programmes are clearly good propaganda. More substantial redistribution requires financing, or the elimination of programmes that serve the middle and upper classes. How large an additional burden will these classes accept in the midst of a contractionary stabilization programme? With the exception of Cuba (and that may change), all radical redistribution schemes in Latin America have been overturned.

In most Latin American countries, the highest 20 per cent income group earns more than half of national income. Meller (1992) points out that total direct taxes represent around 3 per cent of GDP in many Latin American countries, compared to more than 10 per cent in OECD countries. By levying a flat 20 per cent tax on the upper quintile of income, Meller argues that Latin American countries could raise revenues by more than 3 per cent of GDP to finance social expenditures. Yet Latin Americans have shown no tolerance for redistribution in times of growth, much less in times of crisis.

III CONCLUSION

A growth-oriented model for stabilization has yet to emerge. The Latin American economies which contained inflation and launched growth in the 1990s first endured austerity programmes. Recovery has been aided by revenues from privatization and a speculative investment boom, driven by high interest rates and the prospect of new trade agreements, but as Brazil demonstrates, stabilization does not occur until a regime addresses basic macroeconomic imbalances.

The current recovery in the region is fragile. One cannot dismiss the possibility of renewed stagnation. Is Latin America better prepared for future shocks? Some mistakes may not be repeated. Heterodoxy has proven that expansion of demand in the face of rapid inflation is unwise, even if idle capacity creates the illusion that austerity is unnecessary. Recent experiences with exchange rate-based stabilization plans also suggest that inertia alone does not explain inflation.

Distributional conflict, at the root of instability in Latin America, will not be solved by focusing solely on growth, either through populist expansion or stark structural adjustment. The 1980s yielded consensus on the need for contraction in the face of inflation and external imbalances, even if the Brazilian government still prefers to hand out entitlements to five quarters of a pie. Elsewhere in Latin America, orthodox economists have taught policy-makers to make sure the shares of the pie add up to one, but they have done

Table 5.5 Income ratio of highest 20 per cent of households to lowest 20 per cent, 1980–1988.

Brazil	26.1
Colombia	13.3
Costa Rica	16.5
Guatemala	10.0
Peru	11.8
Venezuela	10.8

Source: United Nations (1992) *Human Development Report 1992*, Oxford University Press, New York.

little to solve the political problem of allocating shares. Modest anti-poverty programmes will not suffice to dispel conflict if the current expansion collapses.

Stabilization programmes polarize Latin American societies that are already deeply divided. Successful stabilization without repression requires building more inclusive societies which accept the need to share the burden of adjustment. This cultural reform is a formidable task that should not wait for the next crisis to begin.

NOTES

1 "Comment" in M. Bruno *et al.* (1991, p. 187).
2 Current neo-structuralist analyses differ from these structuralist models of the past. Both emphasize the importance of institutional factors that create supply-side rigidities and weaken the impact of price incentives. However, neo-structuralists tend to seek government policies that set the institutional context for private sector growth, rather than extensive government ownership of industry *per se*. See Chapter 8 by Fanelli, Frankel and Taylor in this volume for a neo-structuralist perspective.
3 A classic reference on the two-gap model is H. Chenery and M. Bruno (1962) "Development Alternatives in an Open Economy", *Economic Journal* 72, 79–103.
4 In the 1990s, some orthodox stabilization programmes have achieved early growth with the support of revenues generated through privatization and capital inflows attracted by high interest rates. In general, orthodox economists have cautioned against using these unsustainable revenues to circumvent the wage and fiscal restraint necessary to secure stabilization.
5 See Graham Bird's chapter in this volume for a discussion of IMF adjustment programmes.
6 By 1991, the International Labour Organization estimated that real wages were 26.6 per cent of their 1980 level. This is probably an overstatement, as it conflicts with Interamerican Bank estimates that point to nearly a full recovery of 1985 wages by 1991. For a discussion of conflicting wage estimates, see Pastor (1992, p. 97).
7 Presentation for the Boston Area Consortium on Latin America, Harvard University.
8 In Bolivia, the full stabilization scheme designed by Sachs began with a fixed exchange rate but then moved toward a flexible exchange rate, and more importantly, the exchange rate was pegged in the context of deep fiscal reforms.
9 Massive inflows of speculative capital raise the problem of how to prevent excessive currency appreciation which undermines structural adjustment. In the early 1990s, the Chilean central bank found it costly to sterilize foreign exchange purchases by selling bonds at interest rates above international rates. To slow inflows, Chile has adopted taxes and reserve requirements that reduce the gap between Chilean interest rates and international rates.
10 "Social Dimensions of Economic Restructuring in Latin America", *IMF Survey*, December 14, 1992.
11 Laban and Larrain (1992).
12 See O. Altimir's estimates in this book.

13 Laban and Larrain (1992).
14 See Chapter 6 by R. Bird and G. Perry in this book for a discussion of recent tax reforms.

REFERENCES

Bruno, M., S. Fischer, E. Helpman, N. Liviatan and L. Meridor (1991) *Lessons of Economic Stabilization and Its Aftermath*, MIT Press, Cambridge MA.

Cardenas, M. and M. Urrutia (1992) "Macroeconomic Instability and Social Progress", NBER Conference on Stabilization, Economic Reform and Growth, Washington DC, December.

Cardoso, E., R. Paes de Barro and A. Urani (1992) "Inflation and Unemployment as Determinants of Inequality in Brazil: the 1980s", NBER Conference on Stabilization, Economic Reform and Growth, Washington DC, December.

Corbo, V., M. Goldstein and M. Khan (1987) *Growth-Oriented Adjustment Programs*, The International Monetary Fund and The World Bank, Washington DC.

Dornbusch, R. (1982) "Stabilization Policies in Developing Countries: What Have We Learned?", *World Development* 10(9), 701–8.

Dornbusch, R. (1992) "Progress Report on Argentina", NBER Conference on Stabilization, Economic Reform and Growth, Washington DC, December.

Fanelli, J.M., R. Frenkel and G. Rozenwurcel (1990) "Growth and Structural Reform in Latin America: Where We Stand", *Documento CEDES* 57, Buenos Aires.

Fanelli, J.M. and R. Frenkel (1992) "On Gradualism, Shock and Sequencing in Economic Adjustment", *Documento CEDES* 81, Buenos Aires.

Fischer, S. (1991) "Growth, Macroeconomics and Development", in S. Fischer (ed.), *NBER Macroeconomics Annual 1991*, Cambridge MA.

Harberger, A.C. (1992) "Tax Lore for Budding Reformers", NBER Conference on Stabilization, Economic Reform and Growth, Washington DC, December.

Hausmann, R. (1990) "The Big Bang Approach to Macro Balance in Venezuela: Why So Sudden? Why So Painful?", mimeo, Instituto de Estudios Superiores de Administracion, Caracas.

Interamerican Development Bank (1987–92) *Economic and Social Progress in Latin America*, Washington DC.

Keynes, J.M. (1936) *The General Theory of Employment, Interest and Money*, republished by Harcourt, Brace and World, New York, 1964.

Kiguel, M.A. and N. Liviatan (1988) "Inflationary Rigidities and Orthodox Stabilization Policies: Lessons from Latin America", *The World Bank Economic Review* 2(3), 273–98.

Kiguel, M.A. and N. Liviatan (1992) "Stopping Three Big Inflations: Argentina, Brazil and Peru", NBER Conference on Stabilization, Economic Reform and Growth, Washington DC, December.

Laban, R. and F. Larrain (1992) "Continuity and Change in the Chilean Economy", NBER Conference on Stabilization, Economic Reform and Growth, Washington DC, December.

Meller, P. (1992) "Latin American Adjustment and Economic Reforms: Issues and Recent Experience", mimeo, United Nations, UNCTAD/OSG/DP/53, December.

Pastor, M. (1987) "The Effects of IMF Programs in the Third World: Debate and Evidence from Latin America", *World Development* 15 (February), 249–62.

Pastor, M. (1992) *Inflation, Stabilization, and Debt: Macroeconomic Experiments in Peru and Bolivia*, manuscript, forthcoming from Westview Press.

Ramos, J. (1986) *Neoconservative Economics in the Southern Cone of Latin America*, Johns Hopkins University Press, Baltimore MD.

Sachs, J. (1987) "Trade and Exchange Rate Policies in Growth-Oriented Adjustment", in Corbo, Goldstein and Khan (1987).

Sheahan, J. (1991) *Conflict and Change in Mexican Economic Strategy*, Center for US–Mexican Studies, University of California, San Diego, Monograph No. 34.

Sheahan, J. (1992) "Peru's Return to an Open Economy: Macroeconomic Complications and Structural Questions", Latin American Studies Association Meeting, mimeo, September.

Silber, S.D. and A.A. Zini, Jr. (1992) "Trade Reforms in Brazil and the Collor Plan", mimeo, Latin American Studies Association Congress, September.

Sturzenegger, F.A. (1992) "Bolivia: From Stabilization to What?", NBER Conference on Stabilization, Economic Reform and Growth, Washington DC, December.

Taylor, L. (1988) *Varieties of Stabilization Experience: Towards Sensible Macroeconomics in the Third World*, Oxford University Press, New York.

Taylor, L. (1991) *Income Distribution, Inflation and Growth: Lectures on Structuralist Macroeconomic Theory*, MIT Press, Cambridge MA.

Thorp, R. (1991) *Economic Management and Economic Development in Peru and Colombia*, University of Pittsburgh Press, Pittsburgh PA.

Wise, C. (1992) "In Search of Markets: Latin America's State-Led Dilemma", mimeo, Claremont CA, November.

6 | Tax Policy in Latin America: In Crisis and After

RICHARD M. BIRD

and

GUILLERMO PERRY R.

The last decade has been a difficult one for most Latin American countries. That this period has also been one of major tax reform in the region is no coincidence. In the 1970s and early 1980s, fiscal developments in many countries aggravated the effects of such external shocks as the rise in real interest rates and the fall in commodity terms of trade. Later, fiscal reforms, including major changes in tax policy and administration, similarly played an essential role in the recovery process. An important question for the 1990s is whether the new tax systems now in place will prove better able to cope with the external and internal pressures that continue to shape fiscal policy in the region, or whether still further changes lie ahead.

To answer this question, we proceed as follows. The next section reviews briefly some of the major factors that have influenced tax policy in most major Latin American countries in recent years: external shocks and internal pressures on the one hand, and the fiscal requirements of adjustment and structural reform on the other.[1] Against this background, the third section of the chapter considers briefly some of the major changes that have taken place in tax policy (and tax administration) as a result of these factors, including the rise of the value added tax (VAT), the lowering of income tax rates, and the renewed interest in various forms of simplified taxation.[2] Finally, the last section of the chapter discusses several issues that seem likely to shape future tax policy in the region, such as the regional and global competition for capital and the continuing debate on incentives and redistribution.[3]

I FISCAL POLICY, STABILIZATION, AND STRUCTURAL ADJUSTMENT

Fiscal disequilibrium played a central role in the general economic deterioration that occurred in most Latin American countries in the early 1980s.[4] At the extreme, the deficit of the consolidated public sector (including the quasi-fiscal deficit arising from central bank operations) rose to more than 20 per cent of GDP in Argentina and Mexico in some years.[5] This marked fiscal imbalance arose from three distinct, though interrelated, causes:

(1) external shocks, in particular the deterioration of the terms of trade and the increase in the real rate of interest;

(2) the accumulation of external debt as a result of current account deficits in the late 1970s and early 1980s; and

(3) in some countries, the adoption of expansionary fiscal policies at the end of the 1970s and in the early 1980s.

The direct fiscal effects of these factors were aggravated by the ensuing economic crisis and in some instances by the accumulation of a large stock of public internal debt issued to finance the fiscal and quasi-fiscal deficits. Both the timing and importance of these factors varied considerably from country to country and period to period, however, depending upon the structure of public revenues and expenditures, the composition of imports and exports, the initial state of macroeconomic disequilibrium and external indebtedness, the precise nature of the external shock, and the nature and timing of policy reactions.

The external shocks were undoubtedly the most dramatic: interest on the public debt, for example, rose to close to 19 per cent of GDP in Mexico in 1987, while at the same time the operating surplus of Pemex, the state oil company, fell by 7 per cent of GDP compared to 1980. The effects of such shocks on the public finances of many countries in the region were magnified by the accelerating inflation, the economic recession, the sharp reductions of imports, the financial crisis, and the capital flight that resulted from the addition of the external shocks to the initial macroeconomic disequilibrium arising from earlier expansionary policies. Some of the policy actions taken in response to the deepening crisis also made matters worse in some countries.

For example, tax bases were eroded by inflation in both legal and illegal ways: legally, as a result of inappropriate policies (especially the deduction of nominal interest expenses), and illegally, as the reward for evasion increased and the resources – e.g. well-paid tax auditors – available to block evasion decreased. At the same time, owing to collection lags, tax collections fell in real terms, as did surpluses from public enterprises (whose prices were often controlled as part of anti-inflationary policy), while quasi-fiscal deficits increased as nominal interest rates rose. Similarly, the compression of imports adversely impacted on indirect tax revenues both from tariffs and equally importantly from the value added tax (VAT), much of which in many countries is collected from imports. On the other hand, devaluation *per se* boosted revenues and provided net fiscal relief in countries in which the public sector was a net exporter of goods and services, such as Chile (copper) and Mexico and Venezuela (oil), although it added to the fiscal pain in other countries, such as Argentina and Brazil.[6]

In addition, at certain periods some countries (e.g. Argentina 1977–80, Mexico 1980–2, and Colombia 1980–4) exacerbated the fiscal situation by following deliberately expansionary fiscal policies. In the end, however, virtually every country had to take action, often very strong action, to restore fiscal balance as an essential element of restoring sustainable internal and external balance. Most countries did so in the first instance by cutting expenditures rather than raising taxes.

Expenditure cuts were particularly dramatic in public investment, which fell by almost 6 per cent of GDP in Chile from 1984 to 1989 and by over 4 per cent in Argentina from 1983 to 1991. On the other hand, as Tanzi (1992) emphasizes, public investment was much higher in the early 1980s as a proportion of GDP than it had been a decade earlier, and the really dramatic long-run decline was more in private than in public investment, reflecting in large part the adverse effects of higher instability and uncertainty, as well as the reduction of total savings.

When increased tax revenues did contribute to restoring fiscal balance, those revenues often came from such sources as foreign trade taxes (e.g. in Chile and Colombia), fuel taxes (e.g. in Bolivia,[7] Argentina, and Mexico), or minor, and in principle undesirable taxes on financial transactions (e.g. in Argentina prior to 1991). In many Latin American countries, VAT had been introduced, and income taxes substantially reformed, in the 1970s. It was only towards the end of the 1980s, however – by which time most relevant political groups had accepted that some more permanent and credible changes had to be made in the fiscal system to avoid continued crisis – that significant steps were finally taken in some countries to improve collection of the major "modern" taxes – notably VAT, but also income taxes.[8] Before discussing in more detail changes in tax policy and administration, however, we consider two distinct, though related, factors that have shaped fiscal policy in Latin America in recent years: the needs of stabilization and the needs of structural reform.

I.1 Fiscal policy and stabilization

One lesson almost every Latin American country has learned with a vengeance in recent years is that fiscal policy is the key to economic stabilization, especially in the more open economies now characterizing most countries (Bahl, 1992). No matter whether one follows the traditional (in Latin American "development" circles) *dirigiste* paradigm or the more recently popular supply-side (competitive small open economy) approach, sustainable fiscal policy is required for success, and inadequate fiscal policy means failure (Felix, 1992). The contrast between the failure of the stabilization effort in the early 1980s and its success at the end of the decade in Mexico and, in the early 1990s, in Argentina illustrates the point. As Bacha (1992) and others (e.g. Ize (1989)) have shown, a critical aspect of development policy is to maintain macroeconomic consistency; avoiding "excessive" fiscal (and quasi-fiscal) deficits almost always constitutes a central element of the requisite policy package. The "two-gap" model of the 1960s (savings and foreign exchange) has been reborn as the "three-gap" model of the 1990s, with the third gap being public sector savings.

Of course, the relation between fiscal balance and internal and external economic balance in the real world is by no means as simple as it appears in such models.[9] Such factors as the dependence of revenues on foreign trade and more specifically on the taxation of the main commodity exports (copper in Chile, oil and gas in Mexico, Venezuela, and Ecuador, coffee and oil in Colombia), the specific effects of devaluation on real wages and exports, the prevalence of indexation, and the specifics of exchange rate policy and fiscal adjustments clearly affect the relation between the fiscal deficit, inflation, and the real exchange rate.

A long-standing problem in many countries, for example, has been the inability of governments to refrain from spending temporary increases in revenues during the upswing of trade cycles, whether directly through the budget or indirectly through credit expansion. In the early 1980s, for example, Mexico expanded expenditure so rapidly after an enormous increase in oil revenues that its fiscal deficit actually increased![10]

When the downturn comes, as it inevitably will, governments that have set nothing aside for a rainy day must either drastically cut spending (as prescribed in the usual IMF package) – a course of action that is usually both politically dangerous and, given the fall in export earnings, economically destabilizing – or run up horrendous, and equally destabilizing, deficits. The instability arising from variations in export earnings is thus exacerbated by the cyclical pattern of public spending, and the net result of the ensuing economic uncertainty is generally reduced investment and growth. While measures have been taken in some countries (e.g. through different sorts of stabilization funds in Colombia (for coffee earnings), Chile (copper), and Venezuela (oil)) to ameliorate this situation, in most Latin American countries both exchange rates and public finances remain undesirably vulnerable to fluctuations in external earnings.

Another important problem making both fiscal policy and stabilization difficult in many countries is inflation. In countries with long and hard experience of inflation, such as Argentina, economic agents react quickly to changes in prices so that e.g. devaluation has little, if any, lasting effect on relative prices and hence exacerbates inflationary pressures. In such cases, fiscal adjustment may have to be complemented by fixing the exchange rate and by the application of active wage and price policies to curb inflation. Similarly, specific measures for debt reduction may be needed where countries have accumulated large public debts as a result of repeated fiscal imbalances.

Moreover, although the fiscal systems in such countries are generally adapted to some extent to high and variable rates of inflation, such adaptation is rarely complete.[11] One result of this situation is that the real fiscal picture is often obscured, and the size of the fiscal adjustment needed is far from clear (Tanzi, 1992). More importantly, the effects of particular fiscal measures – e.g. an increase in corporate taxes – may vary sharply, depending upon the level and variability of inflation. For these and other reasons, further measures (e.g. base adjustments) are needed in many countries to reduce the impact of inflation on the tax system – and, in some cases, to increase the (desired) impact of fiscal measures on inflation.

I.2 Fiscal policy and structural reform

In the short run, the most immediate fiscal policy task in many countries in recent years, almost regardless of their longer-run policy goals, has been to reduce the deficit: to lower expenditures, to raise revenues, or both. In the longer run, if fiscal policy is not to be destabilizing, most countries must take measures to reduce the vulnerability of the fiscal system both to external trade cycles and to inflation. At the same time, however, most countries in Latin America need to restore the conditions for sustained economic growth – to "restructure", in the jargon – thus imposing additional demands on fiscal policy.

An essential element of economic restructuring in almost every country, for example, has been trade liberalization. Trade liberalization programmes generally include at least four distinct components:

(1) converting non-tariff barriers (NTBs) to tariffs;
(2) reducing the dispersion of tariffs (including exemptions);
(3) lowering average tariffs; and
(4) removing export taxes.

Unfortunately, the fiscal implications of these measures have too often been neglected. Eliminating or converting NTBs, for example, in itself is likely to increase fiscal revenues, and the revenue effects of reducing tariff dispersion obviously depend on the composition of imports, but the other two measures listed are almost invariably revenue losers.[12]

The overall effects on budgetary revenues of trade liberalization will clearly vary sharply from country to country, as will the importance of these effects for fiscal policy as a whole. In some of the larger Latin American countries, the initial effect of trade reforms was actually to increase the average effective tariff (e.g. Chile in 1974–5, Argentina in 1976–81 and Mexico in 1985–7). Combined with higher imports and, in some instances (Chile and Mexico), real devaluations, the result was increased tariff revenues. In other instances, however, as in Argentina since 1988 and Colombia since 1990, there has been a drastic decline in taxes on trade. In the longer run, of course, as is commonly recommended (World Bank, 1991; Nashashibi *et al.*, 1992), trade taxes need to be replaced by domestic indirect taxes – usually the VAT – if revenues are to be maintained. As noted later, this has already happened in most countries in the region.

The negative revenue effects of trade liberalization have been most important in some of the smaller countries of Latin America, which tend to be more dependent upon foreign trade taxes and to use tariffs (and NTBs) less for protective purposes.[13] Moreover, given the high administrative and compliance costs of most domestic tax alternatives (and their less than general coverage of economic activity) in such countries, it is by no means clear that simply replacing trade taxes by domestic internal taxes is necessarily either desirable or possible. Nonetheless, reduced dependence on trade taxes is almost certainly as desirable in most Latin American countries from the perspective of restructuring for growth as it is for stabilization.

More broadly, the main fiscal component of most economic restructuring programmes (apart from reducing expenditures) is usually taken to be the removal (or at least reduction) of the distortions to economic incentives that result from existing tax (and subsidy) policy. The development of the financial system, for instance, is frequently impeded by explicit and, especially, implicit taxes (Thirsk, 1991). The same is true of foreign investment and indeed of investment in general: it is easy to show, for example, that tax factors often distort the choice of organizational form, the financial structure of enterprises, the level and type of real investment, and so on.[14]

An essential component of the more market-oriented economic policy that has been the aim of most economic restructuring is therefore a less distorting tax system. As the World Bank (1991) has argued, such a system is usually understood to be one with broader bases and lower rates, where the broader bases both reduce the scope for tax-induced behavioural changes and produce sufficient revenue to permit the lower rates which lead to smaller tax-induced distortions.

II   TAX REFORM IN THE 1980s

II.1   The substance of tax reform

In the last decade, major tax reforms have taken place in Mexico, Bolivia, Argentina, and Colombia; somewhat similar reforms took place earlier in the 1970s in Chile and Uruguay, and tax reform has been high on the policy agenda in countries as diverse as Guatemala, Venezuela, Paraguay, and

Ecuador. As with the interaction of fiscal adjustment and macroeconomic and structural policy, it is not possible here to depict adequately the nature and significance of the many diverse tax changes that have occurred in recent years at different times, for different reasons, in these and other Latin American countries. Detailed analysis of some of these countries, however suggests that four general points may perhaps be made with respect to the substance of tax reform in Latin America in the 1980s:[15]

(1) The objectives and nature of tax reform have changed substantially from those that dominated in earlier years. In particular, both because of changing intellectual fashions and, more importantly, increasing evidence of the relative ineffectiveness of redistributive tax policy on the one hand and the efficiency costs of taxation on the other, equality as a goal is now "out" and neutrality is "in". The nature and role of income taxes has thus changed in many countries.

(2) As already indicated, there has been increasing acceptance of the view that the essential role of taxation in a market-oriented development strategy is negative, that is, to reduce distortion, not to direct investment. Tax incentives, once the policy of choice in many Latin American countries, are thus out of fashion, both because they do not fit the new policy emphasis and because of mounting evidence of the extent to which they have weakened the public finances.

(3) Value added tax is now the central fiscal instrument in most countries. Not only has this tax become the dominant form of indirect taxation, but it is now also often the tax of choice when additional revenues are required.

(4) Finally, there is much greater awareness than before of the important constraints imposed by the administrative dimension of tax reform, as evidenced both by the simplification of income taxes and by the renewed emphasis on presumptive and minimum taxes and on withholding as a central feature of tax policy.

The balance of this section develops these points a little more extensively.

II.1.1 Income taxes

Perhaps the most dramatic changes have taken place in income taxes. The move to lower marginal rates of income taxation, particularly in the top brackets, is widespread: since 1979, for example, Colombia has lowered its top personal rate from 56 per cent to 33 per cent, Argentina from 45 per cent to 30 per cent, Mexico from 55 per cent to 35 per cent, and so on. The average top rate of personal income tax in Latin America fell from 48 per cent to 35 per cent during the 1980s. At the same time, the average corporate rate fell from

43 per cent to 36 per cent (Shome, 1992). Bolivia, which nominally has a flat rate of 10 per cent on income, has gone further and effectively abolished both the personal and the corporate income taxes, while Colombia and Ecuador have moved to a gross (rather than net) income basis for most taxpayers. In most countries, the personal exemption level has risen, while the level at which the (now lower) upper bracket is applied has gone down. This marked change in the orientation of personal income taxes appears to have occurred for a number of related reasons.

In the first place, there has clearly been a move away from the use of the tax system to redistribute income. The time when the tax system was considered to be a principal means of correcting inequalities in income and wealth is long gone. One reason for this reversal in attitude is perhaps clearer recognition of the severe constraint imposed on redistributive taxation by the administrative factors discussed below (Bird, 1989). Another may be simply the downgrading of the equity objective relative to incentive concerns that characterized the 1980s more or less around the world.[16]

Secondly, disillusion with the ability of the tax system to redistribute income was matched by scepticism about the ability of tax measures to redirect and reallocate resources – to, as it were, fine tune the economy. Tax incentives have gone out of style almost everywhere, at least for the moment. Indeed, in some countries the reduction of incentives has been the preferred method to expand tax bases and finance rate reductions, owing to their pernicious effects on revenues, combined with their demonstrated ineffectiveness in producing sounder and stronger patterns of growth.

In any case, heavy reliance on tax incentives is no longer in tune with the dominant policy trend. The interventionist policies of the 1960s were, for better or worse, largely replaced in the 1980s by more market-oriented policies. The supply-side emphasis on the disincentive effects of income taxes on investment and work effort – although not particularly well supported empirically (Gandhi, 1987) – has also clearly been influential in some instances, notably the Chilean tax reform of 1984 and the Bolivian reform of 1985. More generally, the desire to reverse capital flight and to attract foreign investment has led many countries in the region to harmonize more closely with the tax regime of the United States, especially after the major 1986 tax reform in that country sharply reduced income tax rates.[17]

Another important change in a number of countries has been the progressive recognition of the effects of inflation on taxation.[18] The first stage in this process has generally been to shorten collection lags and to index tax liabilities, as well as to convert specific indirect taxes to an *ad valorem* base. Such measures obviously increase revenues in real terms. Indexation of tax brackets, personal deductions, and (sometimes) the costs of fixed assets (for calculating tax depreciation) is also common in this stage: these measures, of course, reduce revenues.

A second stage of tax adjustment to inflation requires making more fundamental modifications in the base of the income tax. Mexico (1987–9), Ecuador (1991), and Colombia (1992) have, for example, followed the path of so-called "integral" inflation adjustment, pioneered by Chile in 1975, under which virtually the entire base of the income tax on capital is indexed. Although these measures too may reduce revenues, they may equally well increase them, because the revenue gain from allowing the deduction of only real interest may more than offset the revenue loss from taxing only real interest income and real capital gains as well as allowing the deduction of indexed depreciation allowances.

II.1.2   Value added taxes

The centrality of the value added tax in tax reform in Latin America is clear. As in much of the rest of the world, this variant of general consumption tax has come to play a critical role in all attempts to modernize the tax system, in part because of its less distortionary impact on economic activities and in part because reforms engendered by fiscal crisis, which invariably call for increases in revenues, may only be able to attain their revenue goals by relying on the value added tax.

In the first instance, however, the increased revenues required for fiscal balance in Latin America often came from other forms of indirect taxation. While the direct importance of taxes on foreign trade fell in most countries, for reasons already discussed, other indirect taxes, particularly taxes on motor fuel, continue to be extremely important – perhaps especially in countries that are oil importers. In Bolivia, for example, the impressive rapid rise in tax revenues from 1985 to 1986 (by about 6 per cent of GDP) was due almost entirely to increased fuel taxes; the VAT and the new simplified direct tax system really only came into full effect in 1987 and later years (Mann, 1989).

In the long run, however, increased rates and coverage of VAT clearly constitute the major way of maintaining revenue yields. Argentina has recently offered a particularly striking example, as VAT revenues rose from 0.6 per cent of GDP at the end of 1989 to over 9 per cent of GDP at the end of 1992 (Morisset and Izquierdo, 1993). VAT's role in this respect seems likely to continue to grow in the future. The deterioration of the VAT collection in countries such as Bolivia, Argentina and Mexico in the crisis of the early 1980s demonstrates, however, that, contrary to popular belief, VAT is in no way a self-enforcing tax. The administrative problems of applying VAT, like income tax, are considerable in countries with large urban informal sectors and significant levels of small-scale agriculture, especially when tax rates are high. The result is usually the exemption, in law or in practice, of such activities – but such exemption in turn may reduce efficiency and growth by favouring the less "modern" sectors of the economy. Improved VAT yields usually require both expanded coverage (reduced exemptions) and strengthened administration.[19]

II.1.3   Administrative reform

Would-be tax reformers have in recent years become increasingly aware of the constraints on tax reform imposed not only by the obvious political opposition such reform almost invariably engenders (Boylan, 1992) but also by the very real limits of administrative feasibility (Bird, 1989). The real secret of success in raising and sustaining fiscal revenues often lies not in the adoption of fancy new policies, but in the more mundane task of establishing a more credible and effective tax administration. Tax policy changes such as expanding potential tax bases may be necessary and desirable, but unless tax administration becomes more credible and effective, the desired beneficial results, whether in increased revenue or reduced economic distortion, are unlikely to be sustained for long.

Apart from administrative reform itself – including in some countries substantial "privatization" of some aspects of tax administration (Bird and Casanegra, 1992) – there have also been substantial changes in tax structure in a number of countries, largely for administrative reasons. Such changes range from the abolition of family deductions in Colombia, to the adoption of minimum corporate taxes in twelve Latin American countries by 1991 (Shome, 1992), extensive use of other "presumptive" (estimated) tax bases, and increased use of "final" withholding.

Such proven administrative techniques as withholding, the replacement of complex taxes by simple taxes, improved use of available information, and more visible enforcement activity, have resulted in significant improvements in tax yields in a number of countries. On the other hand, some of the other changes that have been made – notably the exemption of dividends from personal income taxes – while certainly simplifying tax administration (and arguably improving the neutrality of the tax system) may have cost (a little) revenue and reduced even further the already slight redistributive impact of the tax system.

II.2   The process of tax reform

The experience of the last decade also offers some useful lessons with respect to the process of tax reform in general. Perhaps the most obvious lesson is that even the best-designed tax reform, which takes the administrative dimension fully into account, will become reality only if it is politically acceptable. "Good" reforms that will not be accepted or that, if accepted, cannot be implemented, are useless. Designing a successful tax reform thus requires both economic expertise and considerable skill in handling both the administrative and political dimensions of tax reform. This task is especially difficult because, unlike the case with many other economic reforms, there are seldom any clear "winners" from revenue-raising tax reforms.

From this perspective, perhaps the most important lesson of recent tax reform experience in Latin America is simply that a "good" tax reform is one that satisfies three conditions:

(1) It solves the problems that gave rise to the demand for reform in the first place – for example, it increases revenue or reduces barriers to investment.
(2) It is accepted – though rarely welcomed – by those (both taxpayers and tax administrators) who have the power to ensure its success or failure.
(3) It can in fact be implemented reasonably well with the resources at hand.

The timing of tax reform may also be critical. With – as always – some exceptions (e.g. Colombia in 1986, where the revenues from increasing oil exports and a coffee boom permitted a substantial reduction in income tax for other sectors), for the most part major changes in tax structure and administration are possible only when times are bad, that is, in a crisis of some sort. Only then is it possible to overcome the coalition of political opposition and administrative inertia that normally blocks significant change in such "quasi-constitutional" matters as the distribution of the cost of government.[20] Unfortunately, at the very time when tax reform may be most politically feasible, it is also likely to prove most difficult to do well – unless, of course, the government is already prepared to act.

The successful implementation of major tax reforms in times of crisis requires careful preparation and planning. Such planning need not take a long period of time – witness the rapid and successful reform in Bolivia in 1986 (Bird, 1992) – but it must be based on a clear conception of the objectives of reform. Moreover, even the best-laid plans of technicians will come to naught unless key political and administrative figures are involved in the planning from the beginning, so that when the time comes to act they will both be ready and committed to the reforms they have had a hand in formulating. Both of these conditions for success were, to a greater or lesser extent, satisfied in, for instance, Bolivia, Colombia, and Mexico by the mid-1980s, as well as in Chile earlier. In Argentina, however, it was not until the beginning of the 1990s that economic conditions were sufficiently bad, and political conditions sufficiently stable, for meaningful tax reform to occur.

In short, the unsurprising conclusion is that countries which are in crisis, in which politicians are committed to reform, and in which the objectives of reform are clear-cut are those most likely to be able to introduce major tax reforms. These same factors will also go a long way towards ensuring that such reforms can be successfully implemented. Other ingredients required for success in this respect, however, are a sufficiently competent "technical" group to design sensible reforms and, above all, sufficient attention to the critical task of administration, both in the sense of designing reforms that can be administered and in the sense of ensuring that the tax administration is strengthened and supported enough to enable it to implement the reformed system. With political will, sufficient effort and resources, and a clear strategy, success in tax reform is possible; in the absence of any of these ingredients, success is much less probable.

II.3   Conclusion

Even when all the necessary elements identified above are present, the sorts of tax reform that have been adopted in recent years in even the most sophisticated countries of Latin America have been quite different from the increased reliance on the (nominally) progressive income tax that was urged in the past by most would-be fiscal reformers. The first concern of serious tax reformers in most developing countries these days is almost invariably to put an effective general sales tax (generally a VAT) in place as the cornerstone of an improved revenue system.

Accompanying the rise of VAT throughout the continent has been a move away from (nominally) progressive income taxation. As noted above, in part, this move may reflect the lesser emphasis placed in most countries in recent years on redistribution through the fiscal system as a policy objective. In addition, the reduced emphasis on direct and progressive personal taxes also reflects the increasing realization that such taxes have not been, and probably cannot be, effectively administered in the context of most Latin American countries. For better or for worse, the highly progressive "global" income tax that once constituted a key instrument in every tax reformer's tool kit seems no longer to be considered feasible even in the most sophisticated countries of the continent. Nevertheless, by the end of the decade most large Latin American countries had again begun to increase collections from income taxes both through closing loopholes and strengthening administration (Mexico, Argentina) and, in some instances (Chile, 1990; Colombia, 1992), through rate increases.

III   ISSUES FOR THE 1990s AND BEYOND

What does the future hold? Will the direction of fiscal reform continue to be towards simpler, broader-based taxes with lower rates? Will VAT become an even more dominant feature of the tax systems of Latin America? Will fiscal incentives and attempts to tax the rich remain out of favour? Or will new factors, not yet mentioned, come into play and produce a rather different picture than might be suggested by simple extrapolation of the events of the 1980s?

In response to such questions, it must first be noted that many of the old problems have not been solved: indeed, some of them may even have been exacerbated by recent developments. As noted earlier, for example, a number of countries have taken measures to insulate their fiscal systems from inflation, both in the sense of protecting real tax yields from inflation-induced declines and by reducing the economic distortions resulting from the interaction of inflation and the tax system. Other countries, however, still have a long way to go in this respect. Even more important, while some countries have reduced – or are in the process of reducing – their fiscal dependence on trade taxes, no country in Latin America has yet taken sufficient measures to reduce its vulnerability to the export-fiscal "boom-bust" cycle described earlier.

Similarly, with respect to administration, while much has been done in some countries both to make the tax structure more administrable and to administer it better (Bird and Casanegra, 1992), others have as yet made little progress in either of these directions. Moreover, it is far from clear that all the policy changes that have been made for administrative reasons are either desirable or sustainable. For example, recourse to crude "gross assets" taxes on corporations in lieu of corporate income tax does not, on its face, appear to be particularly desirable on any except purely administrative grounds.[21]

The extent to which Latin American countries have adopted and expanded value added taxes, undoubtedly the administratively most demanding form of sales tax, is striking. Some might see this as sort of a backhand way of switching from income to consumption taxes – a move that has been viewed with increasing favour by much of the academic tax literature of recent years. In fact, however, no country (apart from Bolivia and, to some extent, Uruguay) has so far rejected the income tax as such, nor has there been much public discussion in any country of the desirability or otherwise of substituting VAT for income tax. Moreover, as already noted, such countries as Chile and Colombia have actually increased their reliance on income taxes in the last few years.

Value added tax will undoubtedly continue to play a critical role in Latin American tax policy in the immediate future. Over the long run, however, the revival of interest in income taxation just mentioned seems likely to spread, for four reasons. First, it is not at all unlikely that the political pendulum in the developed countries will swing back towards a little more concern with inequality in the near future – a trend that is likely to manifest itself also in at least some of the countries of Latin America. Second, the academic infatuation with consumption taxation, though visible now among some of the more technically oriented policy-makers in Latin America (who tend to be younger than their counterparts in Europe or North America), is already fading in the economic academy and may, in the end, not exert much influence at the policy level anywhere. Third, as VATs become better administered, it becomes possible, indeed in some respects relatively simple, to improve the administration of income taxes also. Finally, the perceived need for increased revenue continues to be pressing in most countries. If the economic case against income taxes becomes weaker, the political case for them stronger, their administrative feasibility greater, and the revenue is needed, it would not be at all surprising by the end of the century to see increased reliance on income taxes in still more Latin American countries.

On the other hand, the increased openness of many Latin American economies provides a reason for expecting the turn-away from income taxes already evident throughout the continent to be more than a passing fancy, at least in the absence of a much greater degree of international co-operation in taxation than seems likely to be evident in the near future. To the extent that economic integration becomes more of a reality in Latin America, whether among Latin American countries themselves or in the broader North American Free Trade Area (NAFTA) currently being negotiated by Mexico, the United States, and Canada, the influence of international competitive factors on domestic tax policy is of course likely to increase.

But even in the absence of such developments, the globalization of financial markets is not just a fashionable slogan: it is also a reality that will make it increasingly difficult for any country, developed or developing, to tax capital income much more heavily than other countries. International factors will thus undoubtedly continue to keep top rates relatively lower (and relatively closer to corporate income tax rates) than the levels imposed in some countries in the heyday of the 1960s, when all things seemed possible.[22] The need to increase revenues, perhaps coupled with a renewed interest in equity, when combined with the need to maintain low marginal rates in the more open economies now found in the region will continue to exert pressure both to broaden the tax base and to improve the enforcement of income tax and of VAT alike.

As with respect to income tax, several reasons may be suggested for expecting a revival of interest in the near future in the non-fiscal role of the tax system. First, Latin America is as subject to environmental pressures as anywhere else, and there is therefore likely to be increasing interest in the possible environmental (and revenue) benefits of "green" taxes. Second, endogenous growth theory, like East Asian experience, suggests that there may, under the right circumstances, be more to be said for the right kind of fiscal interventionism than the purely *laissez-faire* approach of recent years would suggest (Barro and Sala-i-Martin, 1992). Bad governments can do bad things with or without fiscal incentives; but good governments may, it appears, put such incentives to good use in some instances, and it is not beyond the realm of possibility that such governments may – or already do – exist in some Latin American countries.[23]

Finally, and most generally, it may be useful at a conceptual level to think of taxation as a single policy instrument with a single objective (revenue), but this is not the world we live in. Every government, particularly in developing countries, has far more to do than it has instruments to operate with, so all real world policy instruments have multiple objectives. And of course, a tax system is really a complex of instruments, some of which are almost certainly going to be used, and in some instances appropriately so, as the most efficient way either of achieving particular policy goals or at least of supporting, rather than working against, other instruments.

In the future, as in the past, tax policy in Latin America will undoubtedly continue to reflect both the changing set of economic and political forces that shape economic policy in general and the intellectual and technological factors that shape perceptions of the desirable and feasible role of taxes in particular. In this perspective, the past decade has been especially interesting, both because of the dramatic nature of the external circumstances – the debt crisis, the move to democracy, and so on – and the coincidence of these circumstances with changing intellectual notions (e.g. with respect to redistribution) and administrative realities (computerization).

Over the course of the last decade, in response to such pressures, tax policy in a number of Latin American countries began to converge on the pattern sketched above, although at different paces in response to different circumstances. In the future, global and regional pressures will no doubt continue to exert similar pressures, particularly with respect to the taxation of mobile factors (e.g. capital). At the same time, however, it would be surprising if some countries did not break out of the pattern established recently and move either in the direction of (slightly) more progressive or more interventionist tax policy. The fiscal systems in most countries in the region responded, albeit sometimes slowly and erratically, to the policy needs in the 1980s. They will continue to do so in the future: times change, and so do taxes.

NOTES

1 For a useful overview, see Tanzi (1992). Since it is obviously not possible to discuss the widely varying situations in all the different countries in the region, we focus on the experience of the larger countries and draw in particular on the more detailed treatment of some of the major countries in Perry (1992).

2 More detailed discussions of tax policy changes in the region may be found in Bird (1992) and Shome (1992). Changes in tax administration are discussed in detail in Bird and Casanegra (1992). For other recent reviews of tax reform in Latin American countries, see Boylan (1992), Gillis (1989), Jenkins (1991), and Thirsk (1992).

3 For related discussions, see Bahl (1992) and Mintz and Tsiopoulos (1993).

4 This section follows closely the argument in Perry (1992); see also Tanzi (1992).

5 No simple summary, verbal or quantitative, can do full justice to the complex and changing developments in these and other countries in recent years: for a more detailed statistical description of the interaction between fiscal adjustments and macroeconomic and structural policy changes in each period in Argentina, Chile, Colombia, and Mexico, and briefer treatment of other countries, see Perry (1992), which is the source of all data cited in this section unless otherwise indicated.

6 As Seade (1990) emphasizes, the full revenue effects of a devaluation depend not only on its direct impact on trade-related taxes (tariffs and domestic indirect taxes)

but also on its indirect effects on wages and capital incomes as well as on the tax mix (the balance between direct and indirect taxes). It seems unlikely, however, that fuller analysis would alter the conclusion stated in the text.

7 For a detailed analysis of Bolivia in the mid-1980s, see Mann (1989); Nashashibi *et al.* (1992) carry the analysis through to 1990. Morisset and Izquierdo (1993) analyse in detail the decline and subsequent rise of Argentina's tax revenues in the 1983–92 period.

8 For a detailed analysis of this process in Chile, see Boylan (1992), as well as the discussion of Bolivia in Bird (1992). As David Felix (1992) – by no means an unqualified supporter of conventionally "sound" fiscal policy – has rather colourfully put the argument, as matters get worse "desperation will generate a deeper sense of commitment to the larger society. In a sort of symbolic Bonfire of the Vanities, the elites will temper their rent-seeking and tax avoidance and the masses their quick-fix populism in order to regain some developmental momentum."

9 This is not the place to set out the role of public finance in either standard or non-standard macroeconomic theory – see, for example, Blanchard and Fischer (1989) and Taylor (1983) – or growth theory – see Barro and Sala-i-Martin (1992). For a brief introductory discussion of the role of public finance with respect to development in a macroeconomic setting, see Bird (1993).

10 For earlier analysis of such "fiscal cycles" in Colombia, see Bird (1970) and Perry and Cardenas (1986). Of course, the temptation to spend in fine weather (good revenue years) what should in principle be saved for rainy days (bad revenue years) is by no means confined to Latin America, as amply illustrated by the course of recent events in all too many countries, both developed and developing.

11 The details of this issue are too complex to discuss here: see McLure (1990) for an extensive treatment of the effects of inflation on tax policy, and Bird and Casanegra (1992) for its effects on tax administration.

12 For a useful general analysis of the fiscal impact of trade liberalization, see Blejer and Cheasty (1990). Feltenstein (1992) provides a detailed applied general equilibrium analysis of Mexican experience since 1985.

13 It should be remembered that the fiscal importance of foreign trade is often much larger than indicated by the proceeds from export taxes and customs duties alone. In some countries, for example, half or more of VAT revenues are collected from imports, and in most countries much corporate and payroll tax revenue is also collected from companies heavily engaged in trade.

14 See World Bank (1991) for a general discussion of these factors, McLure *et al.* (1990) for a detailed treatment of their interaction with inflation, and Mintz and Tsiopoulos (1993) for an estimate of their quantitative importance in a number of important Latin American countries.

15 See Bird (1992) for a more detailed argument in support of these conclusions, Thirsk (1992) for extensive studies of tax reform in several Latin American countries, and Shome (1992) for a useful quantitative presentation, country by country, of the many changes in tax rates and revenues that have occurred in different countries over the last decade.

16 For documentation of this phenomenon, see, for example, Boskin and McLure (1990).

17 On the importance of US taxation for Latin America, see McLure (1989a, 1989b) and Mintz and Tsiopoulos (1993).

18 See McLure *et al.* (1990) and Bird and Casanegra (1992) for further discussion.
19 In the case of Argentina, Morisset and Izquierdo (1993) estimate that the potential VAT base was raised from little more than 50 per cent of GDP in 1989 to close to 80 per cent of GDP in 1992, but that nonetheless over half the striking increase in VAT yield was attributable to improved administration.
20 See Urrutia, Ichimura and Yukawa (1989) for a comparison of Latin American and Asian experience that emphasizes this point. See also Boylan (1992) for a study of the "constrained populism" that has characterized recent tax reform in Chile.
21 For a more favourable analysis of such taxes, see Sadka and Tanzi (1992).
22 This point is stressed, for example, in Mintz and Tsiopoulos (1993) with respect to direct foreign investment, but it is also a factor with respect to capital flight (see McLure, 1989b).
23 Of course, cynics may note that it is perhaps even more likely that bad governments will adopt bad incentives for the usual bad political reasons, with the usual bad economic results.

REFERENCES

Bacha, E.L. (1992) "External Debt, Net Transfers, and Growth in Developing Countries", *World Development* 20, 1183–92.
Bahl, R. (1992) "Trends in the World Economy: Implications for Fiscal Choices", Research Paper No. 26, Policy Research Center, College of Business Administration, Georgia State University, Atlanta GA.
Barro, R.J. and X. Sala-i-Martin (1992) "Public Finance in Models of Economic Growth", *Review of Economic Studies* 59, 645–61.
Bird, R.M. (1970) *Taxation and Development: Lessons from Colombian Experience*, Harvard University Press, Cambridge MA.
Bird, R.M. (1989) "The Administrative Dimensions of Tax Reform", in Gillis (1989), pp. 315–46.
Bird, R.M. (1992) "Tax Reform in Latin America: A Review of Some Recent Experiences", *Latin American Research Review* 27, 7–36.
Bird, R.M. (1993) "Public Finance in Developing Countries", in P.M. Jackson (ed.) *Current Issues in Public Sector Economics*, Macmillan, London.
Bird, R.M. and M. Casanegra de Jantscher (eds) (1992) *La administracion tributaria en los paises del CIAT*, Instituto de Estudios Fiscales, Madrid.
Blanchard, O.J. and S. Fischer (1989) *Lectures on Macroeconomics*, MIT Press, Cambridge MA.
Blejer, M. and A. Cheasty (1990) "Fiscal Implications of Trade Liberalization", in Tanzi (1990), pp. 66–81.
Boskin, M.J. and C.E. McLure, Jr. (1990) *World Tax Reform: Case Studies of Developed and Developing Countries*, ICS Press, San Francisco CA.
Boylan, D.M. (1992) "Taxation and Transition: The Politics of the 1990 Chilean Tax Reform", Stanford University, January.
Felix, D. (1992) "Privatizing and Rolling Back the Latin American State", *CEPAL Review* 46, 31–45.
Feltenstein, A. (1992) "Tax Policy and Trade Liberalization: An Application to Mexico", International Monetary Fund Working Paper, WP/92/108, December.
Gandhi, V.P. *et al.* (1987) *Supply-Side Tax Policy: Its Relevance to Developing Countries*, International Monetary Fund, Washington DC.
Gillis, M. (ed.) (1989) *Tax Reform in Developing Countries*, Duke University Press, Durham NC.

Ize, A. (1989) "Savings, Investment, and Growth in Mexico: Five Years after the Crisis", International Monetary Fund Working Paper 89/18, Washington DC.

Jenkins, G. (1991) "Tax Reform: Lessons Learned", in D.H. Perkins and M. Roemer (eds) *Reforming Economic Systems in Developing Countries*, Harvard University Press, Cambridge MA.

Mann, A.J. (1989) "Economia politica de la reform tributaria en Bolivia", *Desarrollo Economico* **29**, 375–97.

McLure, C.E., Jr. (1989a) "Lessons for LDCs of U.S. Income Tax Reform", in Gillis (1989), pp. 347–90.

McLure, C.E., Jr. (1989b) "U.S. Tax Laws and Capital Flight from Latin America", *InterAmerican Law Review* **20**, 321–57.

McLure, C.E., Jr. *et al.* (1990) *The Taxation of Income from Business and Capital in Colombia*, Duke University Press, Durham NC.

Mintz, J.M. and T. Tsiopoulos (1993) "Latin American Taxation of Foreign Direct Investment", Paper for Foreign Investment Advisory Service, World Bank Group, Toronto, February.

Morisset, J. and A. Izquierdo (1993) "Effect of Tax Reform on Argentina's Revenues" WPS 1192, Working Papers, World Bank, September.

Nashashibi, K. *et al.* (1992) *The Fiscal Dimension of Adjustment in Low-Income Countries*, International Monetary Fund, Washington DC.

Perry, G. (1992) "Finanzas publicas, estabilizacion y reformas estructurales en America Latina", Banco Interamericano de Desarrollo, Washington DC, October.

Perry, R., G. and M. Cardenas S. (1986) *Diez anos de reformas tributarias en Colombia*, Empresa Editorial Universidad Nacional de Colombia, Bogota.

Sadka, E. and V. Tanzi (1992) "A Tax on Gross Assets of Enterprises as a Form of Presumptive Taxation", *Bulletin for International Fiscal Documentation* **46**, 66–73.

Seade, J. (1990) "Tax Revenue Implications of Exchange Rate Adjustment", in Tanzi (1990), pp. 54–65.

Shome, P. (1992) "Trends and Future Directions in Tax Policy Reform: A Latin American Perspective", *Bulletin for International Bureau of Fiscal Documentation* **46**, 452–66.

Tanzi, V. (ed.) (1990) *Fiscal Policy in Open Developing Countries*, International Monetary Fund, Washington DC.

Tanzi, V. (1992) "Fiscal Policy and Economic Reconstruction in Latin America", *World Development* **20**, 641–57.

Taylor, L. (1983) *Structuralist Macroeconomics*, Basic Books, New York.

Thirsk, W.R. (1991) "Financial Institutions and their Quasi Taxes – A Little Bit of Craziness", in R.M. Bird (ed.) *More Taxing than Taxes? The Taxlike Effects of Nontax Policies in LDCs*, ICS Press, San Francisco CA.

Thirsk, W.R. (ed.) (1992) "Reforming Taxation in Developing Countries", World Bank, Washington DC.

Urrutia, M., S. Ichimura and S. Yukawa (eds) (1989) *The Political Economy of Fiscal Policy*, The United Nations University, Tokyo.

World Bank (1991) *Lessons of Tax Reform*, Washington DC.

7 | Privatization and Social Welfare in Latin America

ROBERT DEVLIN*

I   INTRODUCTION

The economic crisis of 1982 detonated a process of radical economic policy change throughout Latin America. It was the worst such crisis since the 1930s and one which proved to be relatively unresponsive to traditional conjunctural stabilization and adjustment policies.[1] Moreover, the magnitude and protracted nature of the crisis proved to be a fatal blow to the dominant economic strategy in the region, which had typically been characterized by an emphasis on inward-looking import substitution and ample direct state intervention.[2]

What emerged to take its place, gradually at first, but with ever-greater intensity as the decade proceeded, was a new paradigm inspired by the traditional liberal market principles that were especially fashionable in certain industrialized countries during the 1980s.

In effect, the policy focus of most Latin American countries broadened so that adjustment and stabilization efforts included major liberal-oriented structural changes focusing on internal and external liberalization/deregulation and the promotion of a subsidiary role for the state in the domestic economy. One of the cornerstones of the new approach (coined the "Washington Consensus") was the privatization of public enterprises (Williamson, 1990).

This chapter provides an overview of privatizations in the region, and focuses on certain socio-economic dimensions of the process which have not

* Although the analysis presented in this chapter has emerged from my work in the Economic Development Division's project on the Reform of the State, the opinions expressed here are personal and may not reflect those of the UN Economic Commission for Latin America and the Caribbean (ECLAC). I am grateful for the comments of some colleagues in ECLAC and CIEPLAN. In particular I want to thank J. Martin, J. Ramos, R. Ffrench-Davis, F. Jiménez, J.A. Fuentes, and R. Sáez. I also want to thank Rosella Cominetti for her collaboration in the preparation of data.

been given much attention to date. The first section discusses the magnitude of privatizations in Latin America. That is followed by an analysis of some of the apparent motives behind the countries' decision to privatize. The third section focuses on one objective which has sometimes been too easily traded off in the privatizations – social equity – and suggests ways in which the net social benefits of the process could be enhanced. The last section presents the conclusions.

The subject of privatization in developing countries raises a vast number of potential issues which undergo further complexities when examined in the fast-moving context of individual countries. For this reason the overview is relatively general in its focus and selective in its content. It also should be mentioned that my remarks concentrate on divestment, which so far has been the most prevalent technique in the region.[3]

II THE MAGNITUDE OF PRIVATIZATIONS

Public enterprises (PEs) have typically had a high profile in the economic activity of the region. Ironically, consistent and comprehensive data on the region's PEs are hard to come by. Nevertheless, their importance can be illustrated by reference to a few countries. For instance, just before the crisis, the value added of PEs as a percentage of GDP was about 5 per cent in Brazil, 14 per cent in Chile, 8 per cent in Mexico and 30 per cent in Venezuela. Likewise, the region's PEs were major investors in fixed capital, their activities in this area often being equivalent to a quarter or more of total gross investment (Table 7.1). Each country's story on the origin of its PEs is different, but in practically all cases one can find a combination of factors related to, among other things, the deliberate promotion of investment and development, nationalizations derived from unexpected political or financial events, the support of macroeconomic stabilization objectives, and employ-ment and distributional considerations.[4]

Data for a considerable number of the countries in the region indicate that just before the crisis, the overall financial performance of the region's PEs was almost uniformly associated with important financing requirements (Table 7.2). The picture improves markedly for a few countries when the PEs' balances are adjusted for transfers between the firms and central government. Nevertheless, one notices that even after that adjustment, important pre-crisis financing requirements were registered for the PEs of Argentina, Brazil, Colombia, Costa Rica, Ecuador (non-oil) and Mexico (non-oil).

During the crisis years, PEs confronted a very complex operational environment as central governments tried to stabilize domestic prices and reduce the public sector's financing requirements. The serious fiscal problems induced adjustments in the region's PEs and a reduction of their demands for financing: between 1981–2 and 1986–7, the countries with initial deficits either

Table 7.1 Latin America: selected indicators of the participation of public enterprises before the crisis.

	Value added as a % of GDP	Fixed investment as a % of gross investment (1980)	Participation (%) in domestic credit (1978)	Employment as a % of total (1980)
Argentina	4.6[a]	15.4	—	3.1
Brazil	4.7[b]	25.8[d]	11.2	3[g]
Chile	14.2[c]	15.8	—	2.5[d]
Colombia	2.6[a]	12.7	—	—
Costa Rica	—	23.2	12.8	—
Ecuador	—	21.1	—	—
Guatemala	1.1[a]	13.3[e]	—	—
Honduras	—	14.6[f]	—	—
Mexico	8.2[c]	23.1	18.9	—
Paraguay	3.1[a]	6.5[e]	—	—
Peru	—	10.4	26.4	—
Uruguay	—	18.3[e]	—	—
Venezuela	30.9[c]	35.7	1.6	—

Source: Nair and Felippides (1988) and Floyd *et al.* (1984).
[a] 1978–80 (factor cost).
[b] 1982 (market prices).
[c] 1980 (market prices).
[d] 1981.
[e] 1978–80.
[f] 1978–9.
[g] 1982.

lowered their negative balances or converted them into surpluses, and with the exception of Venezuela, those with initial surpluses increased their positive balance. Excluding Chile, Venezuela and the oil-producing PEs of Mexico and Ecuador, the total improvement in the PE balances for the countries in Table 7.2 was equivalent to 2 per cent of GDP. It should be noted, however, that while significant, the financial balancing nevertheless had an artificial component, because it included the effects of sharp and unsustainable cutbacks in investment activity. This is seen in column DH of Table 7.2, which calculates financial balances using pre-crisis investment levels.

Expenditure cutbacks and tariff adjustments were initially the most important instruments for reforming the financial performance of public enterprises. However, sooner or later almost all of the countries in the region began to opt for the more drastic reform of outright divestment or liquidation of their PEs.[5] The scope of most of these privatization programmes has been extremely ambitious, including in almost all the cases major public services. The countries with the greatest experience are Chile and Mexico, followed by Argentina, Venezuela and Brazil.

Table 7.2 Latin America: financing of public enterprises, 1980–1981 and 1986–1987[a] (percentages of GDP).

Country	D 1980–1 (1)	D 1986–7 (2)	D* 1980–1 (3)	D* 1986–7 (4)	DH (5)	Absolute variation in D* (6) = (4) − (3)
Argentina	−2.49	0.43	−3.61	−2.04	−2.32	1.57
Bolivia	0.10	−2.90	3.65	7.95	7.70	4.30
Brazil	−1.69	0.10	−3.10	−2.10	−4.22	1.00
Chile[b]	−1.33	0.78	5.47	10.33	11.93	4.86
Colombia	−2.00	−1.41	−3.16	0.08	−0.21	3.24
Costa Rica	−2.37	0.97	−1.55	3.46	4.11	5.01
Ecuador	−0.63	−1.77	4.60	4.09	4.46	−0.51
(Non-oil-exporters)	(−1.6)	(−0.55)	(−1.92)	(−0.67)	(−1.44)	(1.25)
Mexico	−1.30	0.25	1.49	4.62	3.53	3.13
(Non-oil-exporters)	(−1.57)	(−0.26)	(−6.22)	(−4.97)	(−5.77)	(1.25)
Uruguay	0.26	0.10	2.69	3.14	3.00	0.45
Venezuela	−2.33	−2.62	11.08	5.16	−0.05	−5.92
Total[c]	−1.38	−0.76	1.34	2.71	1.78	1.36
Sub-total[d]	−1.02	−0.34	−0.63	1.31	1.01	1.95

Source: ECLAC, Economic Development Division.
[a] The symbols used in this table are the following:
D = Total income less total expenditure of public enterprises.
D* = D − T (T = net transfers with the central government, registered in its accounts).
DH = D* plus difference in net capital account between 1980–1 and 1986–7.
[b] For the period 1986–7, the values used were those for 1985, which is the last year for which figures are available.
[c] Simple average, excluding Chile.
[d] Simple average excluding Chile, Venezuela, and the petroleum enterprises of Ecuador and Mexico.

II.1 Chile

Chile was the region's pioneer in privatization. In the period 1975–82, Chile's military government "reprivatized" more than 200 firms (mostly in the tradable goods and finance sectors, worth more than $1.2 billion) which had been nationalized or operationally taken over in the special circumstances of the controversial policies of Chile's previous democratic government. Many of these reprivatized firms fell back into the government's hands in 1982–3 as a consequence of a gigantic systemic collapse of the Chilean economy (Ffrench-Davis, 1982); however, these firms were quickly transferred back once again to the private sector, in 1984/85 (Saéz, 1991; Hachette and Lüders, 1992). Then in 1985 the military government announced the beginning of the privatization of many of the country's large traditional PEs, which so far had been considered untouchable. Between 1985 and 1989 thirty public enterprises – producing both tradable goods and major public services – were divested in whole or in part, generating sales equivalent to $1.3 billion (Table 7.3). At its peak in 1987–8 the value of sales were equivalent, on average, to 2 per cent of GDP and 7 per cent of current revenues of the consolidated public sector. At the end of 1989, there remained forty-five public enterprises in the country, compared to more than 200 in 1974 and seventy-five in 1970 (Sáez, 1991). These remaining PEs included the giant copper firm CODELCO, petroleum refining, and water and sanitation facilities.

Table 7.3 Latin America: the value of privatization transactions for major countries.[a]
Mexico

Year	Amount[b]	GDP (%)[c]	Fiscal income (%)[d]
1983	40	—	—
1984	5	—	—
1985	115	0.1[e]	0.4
1986	100	0.1	0.4
1987	170	0.1	0.4
1988	520	0.3	1.2
1989	730	0.4	1.6
1990	3,205	1.6	5.2
1991	10,831	5.1	17.0
1992	7,000	3.1	10.3

Chile

Year	Amount[b]	GDP (%)[c]	Fiscal income (%)[d]
1983	...	...	...
1984	...	...	...
1985	10	0.1	0.3
1986	230	1.4	4.0
1987	310	1.7	5.6
1988	560	2.5	8.1

Table 7.3 *Continued*

Chile Continued

Year	Amount[b]	GDP (%)[c]	Fiscal income (%)[d]
1989	235	0.9	3.0
1990	...	...	...
1991	...	...	...
1992	...	...	...

Argentina

Year	Amount[b]	GDP (%)[c]	Fiscal income (%)[d]
1983	—	—	—
1984	—	—	—
1985	—	—	—
1986	—	—	—
1987	—	—	—
1988	—	—	—
1989	—	—	—
1990	2,105[f]	1.5	11.2
1991	2,592[f]	1.4	9.0
1992	6,094[f]	2.7	14.4

Brazil

Year	Amount[b]	GDP (%)[c]	Fiscal income (%)[d]
1983	—	—	—
1984	—	—	—
1985	—	—	—
1986	—	—	—
1987	—	—	—
1988	—	—	—
1989	—	—	—
1990	—	—	—
1991	1,658[g]	0.3	1.9
1992	2,340[g]	0.5	2.4

Venezuela

Year	Amount[b]	GDP (%)[c]	Fiscal income (%)[d]
1983	—	—	—
1984	—	—	—
1985	—	—	—
1986	—	—	—
1987	—	—	—
1988	—	—	—
1989	—	—	—
1990	9	...	0.1
1991	2,285	4.4	14.5
1992	20	...	0.1

Table 7.3 *Continued*

Colombia

Year	Amount[b]	GDP (%)[c]	Fiscal income (%)[d]
1987	—	—	—
1988	—	—	—
1989	52	0.1	0.3
1990	72	0.2	0.5
1991	670	1.6	4.2
1992	82	0.2	0.6

Peru

Year	Amount[b]	GDP (%)[c]	Fiscal income (%)[d]
1983	—	—	—
1984	—	—	—
1985	—	—	—
1986	—	—	—
1987	—	—	—
1988	—	—	—
1989	—	—	—
1990	—	—	—
1991	3	—	0.1[h]
1992	264	1.0	7.4

Sources: Calculated from the following sources: Gerchunoff and Colma (1992); Hachette and Lüders (1992); Ruprah (1992a); System BNDES, Brasil; Fondo de Inversiones de Venezuela (1992), COPRI (1992) and CEPAL, Economic Development Division.
[a] Reference is made to value of sales and not necessarily cash flow.
[b] Millions of dollars.
[c] Equivalent in dollars.
[d] Current income of the non-financial sector.
[e] Equivalent in pesos.
[f] Includes foreign public debt paper valued at secondary market rates, and for 1992 there is an undisclosed amount of domestic debt paper valued at market prices. Includes original terms of the sale of Aerolineas Argentinas, which were modified in 1992.
[g] Payment was almost exclusively in domestic debt paper.
[h] Current income of the central government only.

In 1990, Chile's new democratic government slowed the pace and altered the content of the privatization programme. Only a limited number of small public firms would be sold to the private sector, while a few other PEs would sell minority shareholdings. The government also planned to allow private participation in new public infrastructure projects, especially those sponsored by the public water and sewerage companies. In 1991 a small state shipping firm was sold and minority shares in the Iquique free trade zone were offered on the local stock market. There also is a scheme to privatize EDELNOR, an electrical power company in the north.

II.2 Mexico

Mexico followed Chile in pioneering privatizations in the region. The de la Madrid government initiated the process in 1983 and it was intensified in 1989 by the new Salinas administration. The policy of reform caused the number of public firms to decline from 1,155 in 1982 to 280 in 1990 (Secretaría de Hacienda y Crédito Público, n.d.). About a third of this reduction was due to outright sale and the rest to liquidations, mergers and transfers to local authorities (Ruprah, 1992a; Tandon, 1992). The process initially focused on relatively small tradable goods firms; however, the size of the firms increased with time (Aeromexico; Mexicana Airlines) and the programme eventually included major public services, of which TELMEX is the most important. Road networks and commercial banks have also been subject to privatization.

The total value of sales over the period 1983–92 was more than $20 billion, most of this being concentrated in 1990–2 (Tables 7.3 and 7.4). The concentration reflects the large size of the privatized firms in this period and the greater importance of outright sales, relative to earlier years. In any event, the value of the sales in this latter period was huge, on average equivalent to more than 3.0 per cent of annual GDP and 10 per cent of current fiscal revenue. Unless the petroleum and electrical sectors are to be privatized (the constitution deems them to be strategic), it appears that the Mexican process of divestment could soon wind down.

II.3 Argentina

Argentina began its privatization programme in late 1989 under the new Menem government. In 1990–2, more than twenty publicly-owned firms involved in tradable goods, including oil production, and major public services were wholly or partially privatized; moreover, the most heavily trafficked highways were transformed into private concessions with rights to charge tolls. The value of sales in the period exceeded $10 billion, on average equivalent to about 2 per cent of annual GDP and 12 per cent of current fiscal revenue (Table 7.3).[6] The Argentine scheme is probably one of the most ambitious in all Latin America, and the government planned to privatize all its remaining PEs and many services during 1992–3.

Table 7.4 Latin America: sectorial distribution of privatizations, 1989–92 (percentages).

Sectors	Argentina	Mexico	Brazil	Venezuela	Chile[a]	Colombia	Peru
Electricity	11	—	—	—	39	—	—
Finance	—	61	—	5	—	9	2
Manufacturing	3	7	96	1	14	67	6
Mining	14	3	—	—	11	—	48
Telecommunications	34	28	—	86	30	—	—
Air transport	6	1	—	6	4	—	20
Other	32	1	4	1	2	24	24
Total	100	100	100	100	100	100	100

Source: Latin Finance (1991 and 1992) and the Economic Development Division of CEPAL. Minor discrepancies between individual figures and totals are due to rounding.
[a] Reflects Chilean privatizations between 1985 and 1989.

II.4 Brazil

Brazil began to privatize under the Collor administration in October 1991. Five firms were sold during that year for a value of $1.7 billion, equivalent to about 0.3 per cent of GDP and 1.9 per cent of current fiscal income. A further twelve firms were sold in 1992 for a value of $2.3 billion.[7] The government's initial list focused exclusively on tradable goods. It was expected that the new administration of Itamar Franco would introduce some important modifications in the programme.[8]

II.5 Venezuela

Venezuela had about 370 state entities in a very wide array of sectors (Fondo de Inversiones de Venezuela, 1992); moreover, some of the firms were mixed capital ventures with foreigners. The government began a privatization process in late 1990 with a small bank. Then seven firms producing tradable goods and major public services were sold in 1991. The sales produced $2.3 billion, equivalent to more than 4 per cent of GDP and almost 15 per cent of fiscal revenue. Originally a further twenty-nine firms in tradable goods sectors and tourism services were scheduled to be sold in 1992. This list rapidly expanded, as forty-three additional firms were prepared for privatization, including the Caracas water supply (Fondo de Inversiones de Venezuela, 1992). Notwithstanding these ambitious plans, the pace of the country's privatizations in fact stagnated in 1992, due to the emergence of serious political instability.

Most other countries in the region are much less advanced in the privatization process than those mentioned above. However, by 1992 virtually every government in the region, except for that of Cuba, had announced a major privatization programme, and most had at least begun some minor sales of public firms.

III WHY ARE THE COUNTRIES PRIVATIZING?

In the theoretical framework of Jones, Tandon and Vogelsang (1990), a government should privatize a public firm if there is a positive net change in the social welfare of the country. This occurs when the social value of that firm under private ownership, plus the net social value of the public sector's sale receipts, is greater than the social value of the firm under public ownership.[9]

Of course few governments have had the time or inclination to use a purely technical cost-benefit analysis. Indeed, governments have typically relied on a more intuitive approach rooted in broader-based political economy. Nevertheless, even in a more informal framework, the number of factors potentially supporting a privatization are often perceived to be so large that it is not surprising that so many governments have decided to initiate a privatization programme. Indeed, the scope of privatizations is becoming so massive that most governments seem in practice to be mimicking the strategy of Mexico's Salinas government: with respect to individual PEs, the Mexican authorities changed the initial ministerial question from the de la Madrid administration's "Should we privatize?" to "Why shouldn't we privatize?". This reformulated question has been behind the accelerated pace of privatizations in that country (Ruprah, 1992a).

Below, I try to outline some of the major factors that seem to be explicitly or implicitly driving the privatizations in the region. The list is by no means exhaustive, but rather reflects those factors, or arguments, which I perceive to be of a broad influence in the decision to privatize. The weights for each factor, of course, differ among the countries. It is also important to point out that the following review does not attempt to systematically evaluate the validity of the arguments. This latter task goes beyond the scope of the article, due to the great specificity of many aspects of a privatization, the difficulty in isolating many of the relevant causal factors, the limited experience of privatized enterprises and the almost meta-economic character of some of the more enthusiastic statements on the subject.

III.1   Structural factors

III.1.1   *Ideology*

As mentioned above, there has been an ideological shift in the region that lays stress on private sector initiative. The central idea is the "subsidiary state", i.e., the public sector should be limited to essential commercial activities that the private sector cannot or will not perform. The new focus has had growing theoretical support (summarized nicely by Killick, 1989) and the encouragement of the political success of the UK's ambitious privatization programme under successive Conservative governments. The interpretation can be subtle and selective. It also can be more emphatic and quantitative, picturing government failure as nearly always worse than private market failure; hence the requirement to drastically reduce the size of the state in absolute terms, irrespective of the theoretical merits of public intervention. The benefits of the new strategy are purported to be greater efficiency through the freeing-up of market forces, and greater equity and social participation through the democratization of capital (Hanke, 1987).

The new ideology can be identified in virtually all the governments of the region, but it has not always been a first- or even second-order consideration in the decision to privatize. Nevertheless, it was clearly the main motivation of the Chilean privatizations of 1985–9 (Hachette and Lüders, 1992); moreover, the programme had the hard-hitting edge of the military government's "Chicago boys". Mexico's programme also has had ideology as a first-order consideration. In effect, the emergence of a new, young generation of US-educated government bureaucrats, less emotionally linked to the statist tradition that emerged out of the Mexican Revolution, brought with it the perception that the state-dominated economy needed fundamental rebalancing (Ruprah, 1992a). The tone of Mexico's reform has been subtle and selective, however, with the government emphasizing that the state would redeploy its efforts to the social sector (Khanna, 1992).

III.1.2 Internal efficiency

Experience in the region suggests that the public sector often has difficulty playing the dual role of principal and agent. It is generally accepted that the principal–agent problem can be more difficult when ownership is disperse due to the limited access to information and the free-rider problem. In this situation the exercise of "voice" (to echo Hirschman, 1970) bears high costs, while a large part of the potential benefits of effective voice are bestowed on third parties. It is because of this that "exit", again borrowing from Hirschman, is often the preferred response; indeed, it reflects an old Wall Street dictum: "If you don't like the management you should sell your stock".

The traditional problem could be considered potentially much more serious for a public enterprise, because in this case the dispersion of ownership is extreme: the public sector is permeated by society at large. In this environment the principal's potential objectives cover the entire spectrum of interests that can be effectively "voiced" by that society. However, the use of voice and the monitoring of performance have high costs; consequently, voice is likely to be exercised only by those groups which perceive the existence of enough benefits to pay the costs that are needed for that effective voice. Since the benefits of greater efficiency in a public firm are dispersed very widely throughout society, the exercise of voice for this objective can be neutralized by the stronger voices of groups with objectives that have more tangible and concentrated benefits for them. This intensified principal–agent problem of public firms is by no means insurmountable, as demonstrated by a number of countries with a tradition of efficient public enterprise management. Indeed, there is evidence that what really matters for efficient firm management is market structure, more than ownership *per se* (Vickers and Yarrow, 1988). Nevertheless, it could plausibly be argued that, all things being equal, the social cost (effort) of exercising the voice of efficiency is relatively less for the principals of a privatized firm than for those of a public firm.

Exit (privatization) and the reallocation, or reduction, of the state's net worth therefore could be proposed as an attractive and less costly option for the achievement of greater efficiency. In effect, the privatization of PEs creates substantially more concentrated ownership, which in turn narrows the principal's potential objectives and enhances its power to monitor the performance of management and labour. In sum, it is assumed that the voice of profit maximization will face fewer competing voices (and hence lower monitoring costs) when the firm is in private hands.

Where monopoly power is involved, allocative efficiency will require some type of public regulation of the privatized firm. However, since public monitoring must now take place "outside" the firm itself, there will be a rise in the public cost of gathering the relevant information needed for effective regulation. Nevertheless, a decision to privatize must mean that the new public costs of external regulation are perceived to be less than the sum of the public costs that must be assumed if the state is to effectively play the triple role of principal, agent and public regulator of an enterprise. At least theoretically, the privatization creates a more transparent division of labour, which makes for potentially better accountability: simplified, the private principals and agents must only pursue some mode of profit maximization while public regulators must only pursue allocative efficiency. Meanwhile, the state can reallocate its receipts from privatization to other activities with returns that are socially high, but privately too low to attract private capital. Alternatively, the receipts can be allocated to the reduction of public debt. Roughly speaking, in either case the government's net worth remains constant (assuming no undervaluation of the firm sold). Or the state can retreat and reduce net worth by using sale receipts to finance current government outlays.

All of the governments of the region have appealed to efficiency to justify the privatization of their firms. It is generally accepted that most PEs have traditionally confronted a proliferation of conflicting public objectives; e.g., investment, conduits for foreign savings, low prices to aid the poor or to support stabilization efforts, creation of demand for domestic capital goods industries, regional development strategies, political largess of different types, corruption, etc. Some of the objectives were consistent with development, while others were not. But clearly the institutional arrangement was often inefficient as one instrument (the PE) was invariably used to accomplish multiple, and often conflicting, social objectives.

In practice, efficiency criteria seem to have been an especially important motivating factor in countries like Argentina, Peru, and Venezuela, which have had notoriously inefficient PEs and governmental apparatuses that have been judged to be too weak to effect the reform needed to raise the voice of efficiency. In other words, authorities have perceived "exit" as the only plausible option to overcome the principal–agent problem. On the other hand, the efficiency factor may have been less of a driving force in a few countries with strong governmental apparatuses and the potential ability to reform PEs, or those where the PE performance was already generally at least acceptable. The best example is Chile, where the military government had the power and demonstrated capacity to reform enterprises; aided by an extremely authoritarian setting, authorities effectively created greater concentration of decision-making power in PEs – lowering the costs and raising the benefits of exercising the voice of efficiency – even though the principal remained nominally public. As a consequence, Chilean PEs were generally relatively efficient and financially viable well before the decision to privatize them.[10]

III.1.3   Changes in what is considered to be a "strategic" sector

In conjunction with the decision of almost all the countries in the region to dramatically and rapidly liberalize trade (Table 7.5), governments have assumed that deregulated markets are now contestable and that foreign competition will cause the number of domestic monopolies and oligopolies in the tradable goods sectors to decline markedly. In effect, regulation of rents by market forces in principle reduces the need for direct regulation via public ownership.

Many authorities are of the opinion that changing technology and innovative administrative techniques have eroded, or at least put into question, the presence of natural monopolies in many public services. Indeed, some technical support has emerged for depackaging certain major domestic public services, as has occurred in the Chilean and Argentine electrical sectors; for subdividing former monopolies, as in the case of Argentine telephones (that make it possible, at least in principle, to regulate externally via "yardstick competition" between the two firms[11]); and for the building and management of public infrastructure through regulated private concessions, as in the case of the Argentine and Mexican road networks. These technical developments, coupled with deregulation and the formation of contestable markets, has reduced the perceived need for PEs.

Monopolistic and oligopolistic control of traded goods (including technologies) in the international market, as well as the dominant position of the US economy, has been sharply reduced by the great post-war expansion of the world economy. In effect, Latin American countries objectively face a more competitive world economy and complex geopolitical matrix than they did in the interwar period and in the 1950s and 1960s. The active participation of European firms, including those from Spain, in the privatizations of Argentina, Chile, Mexico and Venezuela,[12] as well as that of the privatized Chilean electrical distribution and generation companies in Argentina's divestment of its electrical sector, is a testament to the dispersion of international economic power. In these circumstances it could be argued that there is less need for a strong countervailing force in the form of state ownership of productive enterprises.

III.1.4   Repositioned private sectors

One origin of the public entrepreneur was the immaturity of domestic private sectors and markets. After considerable post-war growth and integration of world economies and cultures, there is now some sentiment in the region that the domestic private sectors have matured to a point where they are capable of successfully operating in many sectors formerly dominated by PEs.

Developments in the world economy also have strengthened the apparent attractiveness of transferring property to the private sector. The state's debt crisis, plus its forced absorption of private sector debts,[13] have combined to help make the latter a superior player in world capital markets. There is also some perception that more competitive world markets have also shifted advantage to the private sector in terms of quickly accessing and adapting changing technology and forming alliances with foreign partners. These developments have caused governments to seek opportunities for realignment of public investment portfolios.

III.1.5   A perceived need to project consistency

In the context of a transition to a model which grants priority to private capital, an important state presence – even an efficient one – in economic sectors that are attractive to local entrepreneurs can create a degree of conflict and uncertainty which ultimately leads to a decision to privatize. For instance, when the state maintains a commercial presence in a sector that has been largely privatized, it could be a disincentive for private investment there because of the private firms' fear that they cannot effectively compete with the state entity, which potentially can receive favours from public policy. On the other hand, the value of the state's patrimony in the sector also can effectively deteriorate if the government withholds new investment in order to avoid being accused of squeezing out private initiative. In these circumstances, political pressures can eventually develop to a point where even potentially useful state firms are sacrificed in order to preserve or promote the new consensus about the division of labour between the public and private sectors.[14]

III.2   Conjunctural factors

III.2.1   Political credibility

Governments have often used privatizations as a signal of their commitment to the new ideological model and thereby have attempted to improve the expectations of domestic and international economic agents. While this motive is widespread in the region, it has been especially important for newly elected governments which have become committed (by conviction or circumstances) to a liberal economic strategy, but which have initially lacked the ideological credentials of the Washington Consensus and/or have encountered difficulties in pushing forward liberal reforms on other fronts.

Credibility was of a first-order importance in the emergence of Argentina's first round of privatizations in 1989/90. Assuming power in the middle of an economic crisis, the government's surprise announcement of the privatization of ENTEL and Aerolíneas Argentinas was motivated in part by the need to transform a formerly populist image and stabilize expectations.[15] Credibility also seems to have been a first-order consideration in the Brazilian Collor

Table 7.5 Latin America: process of trade liberalization.

Country	Beginning of programme	Maximum tariff			Number of brackets			Average tariff	
		Initial	Present	Programmed	Initial	Present	Programmed	Initial	Present
Argentina	1987	115	22			4	4	43[a]	9[a]
Bolivia	1985	150	10			1	1	12[b]	10[b]
Brazil	1988	105	85	40	29	7	7	51[c]	25[c]
Colombia	1990	100	23	15	14	4	4	37[b]	14[b]
Costa Rica	1986	220	40	20				27[c]	20[c]
Chile	1973	220	11		57	1	1	94[c]	11[c]
Ecuador	1990	290	35					53[c]	25[c]

Non-tariff barriers	Notes
In 1987–8, the value of industrial output subject to restrictions was reduced from 62% to 18%. In 1989–90, the remaining licensing restrictions were eliminated. The deregulation decree at the end of 1991 reduced non-tariff requirements to security and sanitation controls and removed the "buy Argentinean" restriction.	Liberalization began in 1987 and accelerated in 1989. Besides tariff reductions, other temporary and specific duties were eliminated. At the end of 1991, tariffs were raised from 0% to 5% for foodstuffs and raw materials, and from 11% to 13% for intermediate goods. The initial tariff included a surcharge.
All prohibitions and licence requirements on imports were abolished, with the exception of controls on sugar and wheat, and on goods that affect health and endanger state security.	Before liberalization, quantitative restrictions and the differentiated tariff structure represented high barriers against imports.
In 1990, the list of prohibited imports (annex C) was abolished. Nevertheless, 47 computer-related products could not be imported until 1992, and local-content rules for intermediate and capital goods will be maintained.	Tariffs began to be restructured in 1988–9. The present programme was introduced in 1990; it will gradually reduce tariffs until it reaches a maximum tariff of 40%, a mode of 20% and a median of 14% in 1994.
Prior-licensing restrictions were almost completely eliminated at the end of 1990, except for certain products produced by State monopolies (arms) or covered by international treaties (inputs related to drug traffic) and certain agricultural products).	The process of tariff reduction initially programmed for 1993 was advanced to August 1991. This tariff includes the surcharge, which is now 8% (it was previously 10%) and it was to be eliminated in 1992. The tariff for motor cars is 75%.
Gradual elimination of import permits and other restrictions in the 1990–4 period.	Tariffs above 40% are still applied to some items (among them, motor cars, with a tariff of 100%), but they are small percentage of the total. The maximum tariff will be reduced to 20% in 1992 for most products.
Quantitative import restrictions were eliminated in the 1970s, with the exception of those on second-hand automotive vehicles, and sanitation and phytosanitation controls on a broad range of agricultural products.	In response to a balance-of-payments crisis, the uniform tariff of 10% was raised to 20% in 1983 and 35% in 1984. It was then reduced in successive stages to 15% in 1988 and 11% in 1991.
Quantitative import restrictions are in the process of being eliminated, with the exception of those on vehicles and on chemical substances that can be used to produce illicit drugs. Prior deposits for imports were abolished.	The tariff for vehicles is 40%, but the prohibition to import them is being maintained.

Table 7.5 *Continued*

Country	Beginning of programme	Maximum tariff			Number of brackets			Average tariff	
		Initial	Present	Programmed	Initial	Present	Programmed	Initial	Present
El Salvador	1989		30	20	20	7			
Mexico	1985	100	20		10	5	5	24[a]	12[a]
Peru	1990	110	25	15	53	3	1	66[c]	17[c]
Uruguay	1974	346	30		>30	3	3		22[c]
Venezuela	1989	135	40	20	41	6	3	35[b]	10[b]

Source: ECLAC (1992a).
[a] Weighted by domestic production.
[b] Weighted tariff on imports.
[c] Simple average based on tariff items.

government's decision to privatize; in effect, it produced some concrete forward movement in a troubled economic setting that had not been receptive to across-the-board reforms. Credibility also appears to have had large weight in the privatizations of the newly-elected governments in Venezuela and Peru,

Non-tariff barriers	Notes
Prior deposits for imports and several laws favouring certain sectors were abolished.	The maximum tariff will be gradually reduced to 20% in 1994 (with a few exceptions).
Coverage of import licences was reduced from 92.2% of production in June 1985 to 17.9% in December 1990, and government import prices were eliminated. Prior licences were maintained for some agricultural and food products, petroleum and its by-products and some products used in industrial development programmes.	The surcharge of 5% was eliminated in December 1987. The customs system was reformed.
Licences, controls, import permits, quotas and prohibitions were eliminated in March 1991.	The programme began in August 1990 when the maximum tariff of 50% was established. It went further in March 1991, when the maximum tariff was reduced to 25% for consumer goods and 15% for the rest (80% of all imports). The initial tariff includes the surcharge.
Import quotas and licences were abolished in 1975 and requirements on terms of financing and controls on imports of capital goods in 1977. Benchmark prices were maintained for some products.	Tariffs have been slowly coming down since 1974. This process speeded up in 1979, but stopped between 1982 and 1986. The most recent reductions were made in September 1991.
The number of headings subject to restriction was reduced from 2,204 in 1988 to 200 at present.	Specific duties were eliminated; in some cases they carried the maximum tariff of 940% before the liberalization programme was put into effect. The tariff reduction programme will be completed in 1993.

which also assumed power in the middle of severe economic crises. In the former government it was part of a reform programme that erased an initially populist image and in the latter it helped to give definition to a new political party that had lacked a clear image upon assuming power.

III.2.2   Fiscal crisis and stabilization

The sale of state assets can temporarily close macroeconomically destabilizing fiscal gaps. The sale itself creates an immediate financial transfer to the government. It also affects future fiscal flows. If a firm was losing money, an annual negative fiscal transfer could be converted into a positive flow of tax revenue, assuming private ownership is profitable. If the public firm was already profitable, the net future flow depends on the trade-off between taxes and dividends of the public firm and taxes paid by the privatized firm.

The privatization option becomes tempting when possibilities for fiscal expenditure reduction have been exhausted; revenue cannot (or will not) be raised through increased tax collection, or non-inflationary sources of public finance have become exhausted. In these circumstances there is the option of capitalizing the potential future receipts of a public enterprise through its privatization. This might be termed a "Pan Am effect", as financial distress induces the selling of potentially profitable assets to finance expenditures which cannot be compressed without threatening the short-term viability of the entity in question.

A fiscal deficit which generates serious inflation and balance of payments problems obviously is a socially costly phenomenon: the situation can inhibit reforms, bring unwanted conditionality from the IMF, paralyse investment and growth, and have regressive distributional effects. Hence, a peso of additional revenue today, employed to close the fiscal gap, should have a very high social rate of return. Moreover, in a situation of severe macroeconomic disequilibrium and recession, a peso of fiscal revenue will usually have a higher shadow price than a peso of private consumption or investment.

In these circumstances, an increase in tax collection could be an attractive option, especially if the taxes involved are not regressive in character. However, in an open, highly deregulated economy with an economic recession and a weak political and institutional setting, greater tax collection, especially of a progressive type, could be very difficult to effect. Indeed, in today's fragile political settings, an increased tax burden can intensify capital flight and deepen the recession, with negative net consequences for fiscal income and stabilization. A more assertive tax policy also will frequently be accused of sending the wrong signals to the private sector; after all, the liberal strategy that is fashionable today views most taxes as distortionary and welfare-reducing (Atkinson and Stiglitz, 1980).[16]

Privatizations clearly are an expedient way of bypassing the above dilemma. But using the privatization receipts to finance expenditure is analogous to borrowing. Thus, when financing current outlays, privatizations reduce public sector net worth; moreover, the latter strategy only postpones rather than eliminates the need for further fiscal adjustment in the form of increased taxes or cutbacks in expenditure (Hemming and Mansoor, 1988).

The desire to finance fiscal deficits has been an important consideration in the decision to initiate privatizations. Since money is fungible, it is difficult to isolate the use of receipts derived from divestment. Nevertheless, the existence of fiscal deficits during periods of privatization is indicative of financing via divestment; moreover, deficits on current fiscal balances hint of some financing of current expenditures, inducing a direct loss of public sector net worth.[17] On this basis, privatizations appear to have been a financing instrument in Chile in 1985–6, Argentina in 1989–91, and in Mexico in 1983–90 (Table 7.6).[18] Also, the surpluses registered in Mexico and Venezuela in 1991 would have been deficits without privatization receipts. As for the implicit financing of current outlays, this appears to have occurred in Argentina and Mexico up until 1991. Meanwhile, Marcel (1989), through a more specific tracking of income and outlays, also concluded that 50 per cent of the Chilean privatization receipts in 1985–6 went to finance current outlays, thus reducing the public sector's net worth. Finally it should be mentioned that a primary motive for the recent privatizations in Venezuela and Peru has been the desire to relax severe fiscal constraints.

As a fiscal situation stabilizes, a country has more opportunities to use privatization receipts to finance reductions of public debt and to promote an overall improvement of net worth. In late 1990 Mexico began to earmark privatization receipts for a special fund and a considerable amount of these resources has apparently been channelled to debt reduction: domestic public debt was reduced by $7 billion in 1991 and by $5 billion in the first quarter of 1992. Moreover, in 1992 the government quietly effected buybacks of $7

Table 7.6 Latin America: fiscal balances for selected countries[a] (% of GDP).

	1983	1984	1985	1986	1987	1988	1989	1990	1991
Chile									
Current savings	−0.5	0.3	3.6	4.8	5.3	8.0	7.0	5.6	5.5
Total balance	−3.5	−4.6	−2.9	−2.0	2.6	3.9	5.5	1.5	1.7
Mexico									
Current savings	−2.8	−2.1	−3.4	−9.9	−12.2	−9.8	−5.7	−2.0	0.8
Total balance	−8.1	−7.1	−8.0	−14.5	−14.4	−9.7	−5.1	−2.9	3.4
Argentina[b]									
Current savings	...	...	−1.4	−0.4	−1.3	−2.5	−1.3	−2.2	−1.3
Total balance	...	...	−4.0	−3.1	−5.0	−6.0	−3.8	−3.8	−1.8
Brazil									
Current savings	−1.4	−2.8	−8.1	−7.1	−6.1	−12.6	−20.1	−10.1	−10.0
Total balance	−4.5	−7.6	−12.9	−11.2	−11.4	−17.1	−24.3	−13.5	...
Venezuela									
Current savings	...	...	...	...	8.1	4.0	10.4	12.6	10.7
Total balance	...	...	...	...	−4.4	−8.6	−1.1	0.2	1.2

Source: ECLAC, *Economic Survey for Latin America and the Caribbean*, various issues, and Centro de Estudios de Desarrollo Económico y Social (CEDES), Buenos Aires, Argentina.
[a] Consolidated public sector.
[a] Based on the new GDP series.

billion of public foreign commercial bank debt (equivalent to nearly 10 per cent of the total public foreign debt) through the use of privatization receipts. It is estimated that total public debt, which in 1986 was equivalent to about 80 per cent of GDP was 29 per cent of GDP by the end of 1992.[19] Debt reduction became an important use of Chile's privatization receipts beginning in 1987 (Hachette and Lüders, 1992). The receipts from Argentina's initial round of privatizations (1989/90) involved direct reduction of foreign debt, as a considerable part of the payment was made in promissory notes bought on the secondary market.[20] Much of the country's receipts in the second round of privatization initially went towards the finance of general expenditure, but with a fiscal surplus in 1992 more funds were being earmarked for reduction of public debt.

It usually is not easy to determine whether the privatizations acted as a direct substitute for taxation. However, in Chile it could be that privatizations financed the military government's fiscal reforms of 1984 and 1988, which sharply lowered direct and indirect taxes.[21]

III.2.3 Investment constraints on public enterprises

Simply put, the fiscal crisis during the 1980s is viewed as a serious obstacle to new investment in public firms and social infrastructure. As discussed earlier, when the crisis broke, the investment of PEs could be easily postponed, and was postponed, in order to improve short-term financial balances (Table 7.2). Even profitable public firms became prisoners of the central government's financial crisis. As the decade progressed, the investment lag became intolerable, especially in public services which have a higher degree of visibility. As the public sector's debt problem persisted, privatization came to be perceived as a way to ease the public enterprises' growing investment bottleneck. In effect, through privatization, a public firm could escape the central government's fiscal restraint and thus have greater freedom for investment. Moreover, the receipts from the privatization could potentially allow the state to reinvigorate public social investment, or reduce debt. The investment bottleneck has almost always appeared as a justification for privatization, even in countries like Chile where many PEs were relatively efficient and profitable. As mentioned above, Mexico has laid special stress on the need to sell PEs in order to strengthen social investment.

III.2.4 Catalytic effects

When an economy is in a deep recession, the public sector is traditionally expected to act in countercyclical fashion and stimulate activity through expansive monetary and/or fiscal policy. However, excessively procyclical public policies in Latin America were a major cause of the crisis; hence, when the crisis hit the region there were few degrees of freedom for stimulative public action. Moreover, the new paradigm in the region discouraged public activism. In these circumstances privatization could be interpreted as an unconventional form of "pump priming".

A severe crisis, coupled with the uncertainty generated by a shift to a new economic model and radically different domestic relative prices, can cause the private sector to initially boycott its domestic economy, by refusing to repatriate flight capital, and by withholding taxes and investment. This obviously aggravates the fiscal problem and also is not a very healthy situation for a strategy in which the private sector is supposed to be the primary engine of economic growth. Privatizations seem to have been viewed as a last resort to "stir the pot" and break the stalemate.

As mentioned above, privatizations will generate extraordinary receipts for the government which help it to close the fiscal gap. While a fiscal balancing via privatizations can be only a temporary strategy, it does buy time until more permanent financing can be found. Moreover, since the domestic private sector will purchase state assets by repatriating capital, and foreign participants will bring their own dollars, a significant part of the privatization receipts should be in foreign exchange. This will have the double-barrelled impact of closing the fiscal gap and anchoring the exchange rate, both of which can be conducive to short-term price stabilization and better expectations.

It is also perceived that privatizations can raise the private sector's disposition to save and invest. This is because it can be less risky to buy existing firms (especially if they are undervalued) than to invest in a start-up operation. Moreover, public firms often provide greater and more accurate information than can be found in other sectors of the economy. Another consideration is that many PEs, but especially those that provide public services in monopolistic or oligopolistic markets, are inherently attractive low-risk and cash-rich operations in which shareholders can more easily appropriate a significant part of any efficiency gains. Finally, in view of a crisis environment, the investment activity of highly visible privatized firms – even if not additive – could conceivably create positive externalities and help turn around the private sector's expectations.

Privatizations also can broaden and deepen moribund stock markets, give rise to windfall profits (especially due to undervaluation), new wealth and more optimistic expectations. This, coupled with the externalities of reinvigorated privatized firms and a relaxed external constraint, can contribute to a pick-up in the rate of domestic economic activity. More growth, in turn, will naturally boost fiscal revenue and also provide a better environment for fiscal reforms; consequently, privatization receipts can be gradually replaced with more stable sources of revenue.

Isolating and measuring all the catalytic effects of privatization is clearly an impossible task. Nevertheless, there are some judgements which point to probable catalytic effects. For instance, the World Bank has judged that Mexico's massive return of capital flight and influx of foreign portfolio investment in 1989–91 is largely a derivative of that country's privatization programme (Tandon, 1992). Mexico's stock market, one of the fastest growing in the world, has been stimulated by privatizations, particularly that of Telmex, which accounts for more than a quarter of the market's index (Ruprah, 1990a). Indeed, it has been commented that out of recent stock market developments have emerged a whole new set of entrepreneurs.[22] Investment activity of privatized firms, for example in the telecommunications, air transport and finance sectors, also has generated much publicity and international interest, perhaps contributing to the growing optimism in that country (Ruprah, 1990a; 1992b). The second sell-off of the residual shares of Argentina's ENTEL also stimulated a boom in that country's stock market (Gerchunoff and Castro, 1992).

In Chile, Hachette and Lüders (1992) present a controversial argument concerning the catalytic effects of the second round of privatizations, pointing to the fact that during that period, private savings and investment levels, although relatively low, rose quite sharply. According to these authors, this could have reflected the higher marginal rate of return on investment in privatized firms. The privatizations also are judged to have broadened, deepened and stimulated the stock market, creating a dynamic new source of private wealth in Chile.

III.2.5   Pacifying foreign creditors

Privatizations are strongly encouraged by the international financial community. A programme of this type could therefore enhance external economic relations, especially with the IMF, World Bank and commercial lenders. This consideration was probably important in Argentina's decision to initiate privatizations in 1989.

At that time there was a perceived need to pacify the commercial banks. In early 1988 the country fell into a moratorium, which was relaxed only marginally in 1989 by the initiation of partial debt service payments. A stoppage of payments traditionally raises tensions with foreign creditors. Indeed, in early 1989 the banks were becoming more aggressive in their dealings with countries in a moratorium, as manifested by Citibank's "set-off" of some official deposits of Ecuador, another country limiting debt service payments just like Argentina (Altimir and Devlin, 1993).

A privatization programme like Argentina's, which makes foreign debt paper an eligible means of payment, creates attractive options for the banks, especially the big lenders that make up the Advisory Committee that is in charge of debt renegotiations. On the one hand, the banks gain by the rise in the secondary market price that is the result of the increased demand for debt paper. (In the case of Argentina, that price rose by some 50 per cent during the finalization of the first round of privatizations.) Banks can therefore sell off their bad loans at a smaller loss and also can gain commissions if they are contracted to secure paper for third parties interested in participating in the privatizations. On the other hand, a bank can avoid a loss on its own loan portfolio by capitalizing it through the purchase of a PE. It is no surprise that some very large banks in Argentina's Advisory Committee were attracted to the sale of ENTEL and ultimately two of the country's major lenders, Citibank and Morgan Guaranty, actually bought major shareholdings in the newly privatized company (Gerchunoff and Castro, 1992).

IV IMPROVING THE SOCIAL BENEFITS OF PRIVATIZATIONS

Latin America has had a very difficult ten years of structural adjustment and stabilization efforts, coupled with delicate transitions to democracy. Substantial progress has been made on all fronts. Indeed, in the early 1990s a cautious optimism has emerged about the region's future prospects: Chile seems to have fully turned the corner towards economic recovery;[23] Mexico could be following a similar path, and a number of other countries are to different degrees consolidating their adjustment and transformation processes (ECLAC, 1991). The slow recovery from the crisis of 1982 has, however, been socially very costly as there are signs that income distribution and social equity have deteriorated sharply in many of the countries, most of which were already noted for their serious inequalities of income and opportunities (Altimir, in this volume, and ECLAC, 1992a).

The deteriorated social matrix can be judged worrisome on normative grounds. But it also can be judged troublesome on more positive grounds. On the one hand, the sustainability of the recovery will require social stability, and this in turn requires improvements in social equity. On the other, many dimensions of social equity are functional – indeed necessary – to the construction of the modern institutional and human capitals which are needed to transform the region's economies into truly internationally competitive enterprises (ECLAC, 1990 and 1992a). The recent serious political problems in Venezuela, Haiti, Brazil and Peru have brought international attention to the social plight of the region and contributed to a surge in international concern about the effects of adjustment on social equity. The new focus certainly vindicates some analytical pioneers who argued a number of years ago that adjustment policies needed a more human face (Cornia *et al.*, 1987).

The region's privatizations are an integral part of the adjustment efforts. However, evaluating the effects of privatizations is difficult because of, among other things, the large number of trade-offs that must be considered, the excessively broad nature of relevant counterfactuals, and the difficulty in accounting for the externalities that many attribute to the process. But even more importantly, the privatization experience in developing countries is still relatively immature, even for pioneers like Chile; hence it will be a number of years before we really know all the resulting social benefits, as well as the costs, of the region's decision to privatize.

Notwithstanding the above, the World Bank (Galal *et al.*, 1992) has attempted to grapple with some of these difficult problems. In a study of nine divestments in three developing countries, it found that eight improved world welfare. Thus, to its own question, "Did divestiture make the world a better place, or not?", the Bank answers with a resounding yes.

Needless to say, studies such as that done by the Bank involve numerous subjective judgements which reasonable people could disagree with. For example, in its calculation of the change in welfare, the Bank did not take into account any distributive effects. But one conclusion can be drawn from the study, probably without much debate: whatever the social gains from the region's divestitures have been and will be, from the standpoint of social equity they undoubtedly can be improved upon in future exercises.

In effect, divestment processes have been conditioned by multiple objectives, but as often has been the case in questions of adjustment, social equity has not always carried a large weight. This is unfortunate because the trade-off between social equity and other objectives can be relatively small, and indeed important complementarities would seem to exist. There are many ways that social equity can be enhanced in the privatization exercises. While space is too limited for a comprehensive review, five key areas of consideration are outlined below.

IV.1 Transparency

Transparency improves social welfare because it reduces the possibilities for corruption, collusion, and inside information, all of which create privileged gains from the sale of the public's assets. It also can be complementary with many other objectives. Since transparency opens the process to more public scrutiny, errors can be checked more easily and fairer evaluations can be made as to whether the government's stated objectives – regarding the process of privatization as well as the end product – are being reasonably fulfilled. The closer results are to objectives, the more likely it is that privatization will have a happy ending for the firms, the government, and the general public, which in turn reduces the risk of policy backlash. Transparency also enhances the efficiency of the learning-by-doing process which is an inevitable part of any government's privatization programme. An enhanced flow of information will obviously contribute as well to overall market efficiency and price maximization (see below).

Transparency also can enhance the government's credibility and have catalytic effects, especially when past governments have had a reputation for corruption or cronyism. In addition, the objective of democratization and participation in economic matters, and in society more generally, is consistent with greater transparency.

Of course, transparency trades off with the speed of the privatizations. This could be an important consideration, since some analysts have given top priority to this latter objective; as one highly regarded economist once commented: "privatization should be implemented with less concern about the correct way to do it and more emphasis on getting it done quickly" (Woodrow Wilson Center, 1991). However, most of the objectives that commonly drive privatizations are not necessarily enhanced by speed; indeed many of them, such as productive and allocative efficiency, credibility, government revenue, catalytic effects, etc., not to mention social equity, can be seriously compromised by a hasty privatization process.

Most governments in the region have confronted very heavy external, and sometimes internal, pressure to greatly accelerate their privatization processes. It is encouraging that some have been able to resist excessive pressure, while at the same time proceeding in a deliberate fashion with their objective to privatize. The conflicting pressures that governments face are captured in the remarks of a person who was in charge of Collor de Mello's privatizations in Brazil, a country with one of the more transparent programmes:

> one can always choose urgency, make bad shareholders decisions, leave significant debts pending, reduce the minimum price, etc. These, however, are not good recipes for a successful privatization programme. Indeed, they are detrimental to the principles of openness and transparency, as well as to the public wealth (represented by the assets being sold off). We chose to go about things carefully. Right from the start, we knew that this would result in us having to pay a political price: the ever alert critics, those who are not committed to openness and even analysts of goodwill, yet with academic ingenuity, would condemn the supposed sluggishness of the process. I do not have the slightest doubt, however, that we made the correct choice.
>
> (Marco Modiano, 1992)

While more transparency may be feasible, there is at least one area where the trade-offs can be exceptionally large: fiscal urgency (earlier termed the "Pan Am effect"). Social welfare demands that a country with a highly destabilizing fiscal gap must close it as soon as possible; rapid privatizations conceivably could be the only way to do that. However, experience has shown that rapid processes can be prone to very serious errors (Hachette and Lüders, 1992; Gerchunoff and Castro, 1992); indeed, emerging problems such as corruption, undervaluation, etc., could conceivably neutralize the positive effects of financing the fiscal gap. But the mentioned trade-off is nevertheless very real and is frequently a challenge for the region's policy-makers.

In the face of fiscal urgency, one possible alternative to a rapid privatization is a non-confrontational moratorium on foreign debt payments. However this is a tricky strategy, in which only a few countries have been successful (Altimir and Devlin, 1993). A better public solution is to strengthen the resource base of the World Bank, IMF, and IDB. In effect, this would enable the multilateral organizations to provide more direct compensatory budgetary support to a government formally committed to extensive privatizations. As is true with the adjustment problem in general, adequate compensatory financing will allow a borrower to design a more deliberate, transparent, efficient and socially equitable privatization programme. This should also be of interest to the multilateral lenders, because more efficient and equitable programmes will clearly enhance their borrowers' creditworthiness in the medium term.

What actions could improve transparency? The potential list is long, but a few key policies can be mentioned.

(1) Information: reserved documentation should be the exception rather than the rule. While a limited amount of reserved information may be justified during negotiations for the sale, the public should have easy access to all the information after the transaction is completed, including preparations for the sale of the firm (debt absorptions, labour relations, capital restructuring, etc.), firm valuation reports, preselection and selection processes, administrative and promotional costs, the facts about the buyers and their financing of the purchase.

(2) If sales require subsidies, they should not be hidden in preferential prices and credit terms. Rather, subsidies should be awarded in such a way that they are explicit and easily accountable to the public; e.g., rebates which must be applied for *after* the sale at an unsubsidized price. This is an important consideration, because a double standard has emerged during the period of privatizations: proponents of adjustment rankle at hidden subsidies in the social area, but turn a blind eye to subsidies hidden in underpriced asset sales and below market credit terms.

(3) Earmark sale receipts by putting them in a special account (Mexico has done this). While earmarking is often frowned upon in public finance, it is justified here by the extraordinary nature of the income.

(4) An independent official technical agency (as opposed to just a legal entity) should be responsible for *ex-post* evaluations of individual privatizations, based on *ex-ante* agreed criteria formulated jointly by the congress and the executive branch.

(5) Privatized firms should sometimes be subject to certain special disclosure rules which facilitate the types of information that are needed for effective *ex-post* evaluations of the results of privatization.

(6) An explicit code of conduct could be published for governmental staff as well as for subcontracted technicians involved in the decision to privatize a public enterprise. For instance, central government employees involved in privatization could be prohibited from working in privatized enterprises for a determined period, e.g., five years. Also, these governmental staff – and managers of public enterprises subject to privatization – could be prohibited from owning shares of privatized enterprises for a stipulated period.

IV.2 Price maximization

Referring again to Jones, Tandon, and Vogelsang (1990), it must be remembered that the government's revenues are a key determinant in the welfare gains from a privatization. Thus, when public assets are for sale, prices must be maximized to the greatest extent possible. Price maximization is important because it eliminates hidden subsidies for privileged buyers and keeps public wealth in the public domain where it can be used for consensual public purposes. Unfortunately there is some evidence that privatization processes suffer from a tendency to seriously underprice the state's assets (Vickers and Yarrow, 1988; Seth, 1989; Marcel, 1989; Errázuriz and Weinstein, 1986; Herrera, 1991; Gerchunoff and Castro, 1992). Another possible indicator of underpricing can be indirectly drawn from the aforementioned World Bank study (Galal et al., 1992); of the total of four countries studied, only in Malaysia – a very cautious privatizer – was the government consistently a bigger winner in the privatizations than the new private shareholders.

While there are many ingredients to a price maximization strategy, some central considerations are presented below. Of course, the goal of price maximization is conditioned by some important trade-offs, which are mentioned further on.

(1) When selling a firm, the price is not its value to the public sector, but rather its alternative value as private property. Thus, the point of reference for price maximization should be an estimate of the firm's value to the private sector. This will usually be higher than the value of the firm for the public sector, due to efficiency differentials, synergies, opportunities for diversification, etc.

(2) Approach as much as possible the following sequencing. Among reforms, privatization should be near the end of the adjustment process; after liberalization, correction of relative prices, a settling down of interest rates to their long-term values, introduction of legal frameworks governing property, labour and market behaviour, and the beginning of an economic recovery. This way the real value of the firm will be more apparent, private sector risk premiums will be less distorted, and the privatized firm itself will be more likely to be successful. Among enterprises, privatizations should initially focus as much as possible on the traded goods sector – where learning by doing can have lower costs – and later concentrate on any big public service firms which may be earmarked for privatization.[24] Saving non-tradables for the later stages is also useful because sales will coincide with a period when exchange rates are probably appreciating with respect to levels recorded during periods of adjustment, thereby raising the relative price of these types of services.

(3) Public firms, but especially large ones, should be restructured before

sale, introducing reforms that are reasonably feasible and that enhance efficiency and profitability. This will make the value of the firm more visible to the private sector and also raise the bargaining power of the seller, because it is easier to hold out for a higher price when a firm is commercially viable. Even when no PE reforms are feasible, official valuation exercises should not necessarily take the firm "as is", since at least some of the private sector's reforms can be easily anticipated. Moreover, normal market discount rates should be used in the firm valuation exercises. In this way, the costs of undertaking a sale when private discount rates are distorted (unusually high) becomes explicit to the public. This approach, moreover, could raise political pressure for more optimal preparation, sequencing, and pricing of sales.

(4) Sell to the highest bidder, minimizing as much as possible considerations that go beyond efficiency. Recruit as many bidders as possible, which may sometimes point to the desirability of encouraging foreign participation, including placement of shares in international stock and American Depository Receipt (ADR) markets.[25] Avoid preferential sales; as mentioned earlier, if subsidies are deemed necessary, they should be delivered directly, explicitly and separately from the sale transaction itself.

(5) Since fixing the correct price is often a process of trial and error, there can be an advantage to selling shares off in small packages that are timed to avoid market saturation and capture the best price. Beginning a privatization with the sale of a controlling package has been shown to maximize receipts; in effect, the transfer of control to a good operator, and/or a favourable evolution of the economy, can raise the value of the firm and allow the government to share in the gains through a later contingent sale of its residual shareholdings.[26] Mexico's pursuit of this strategy was indeed clever: it involved prior restructuring of TELMEX's capital so that voting control could be had for as little as 21 per cent of the company's total shares; this raised the number of financially eligible bidders and later helped maximize the price of the government's contingent sell-off of residual shares.

(6) Take payment in cash. Payment in debt paper has several disadvantages. First, it erodes transparency, since it is hard to determine the real value of the debt instrument. Second, payment in foreign debt can narrow the competitive base of bidding, since some potential bidders will not have easy access to the secondary market, while others (especially banks) will have exceptionally good access. Third, if reduction of foreign debt is an important goal, it would seem more efficient to follow Mexico's example: accept only cash sales and use the receipts to negotiate a concerted Brady Deal, and/or

to discretely withdraw debt paper from the secondary market in such a way that it puts minimum pressure on price. Fourth, as far as pacifying banks irritated by arrears, the need to do so on a grand scale may be exaggerated as the banks have shown a limited ability to retaliate beyond the starting of a manageable brush fire (Altimir and Devlin, 1993).

(7) The state can retain a special golden share in a privatized firm, designed to entitle it to share in profits if, in the future, the yield of the enterprise exceeds some mutually agreed level. The golden share is a contingency formula which obliges both parties to share in the risk of privatization. This could be a useful strategy when a PE must be sold in adverse market conditions. The option could initially depress the sale price, but it would also enhance the probability of a happy ending for the firm and a recuperation of property value for the state at a later date.

As mentioned, price maximization must trade off with other objectives. However, once again the trade-offs do not always have to be large, and indeed one can find complementarities.

There obviously can be a serious trade-off between price and efficiency. The highest bidder is not always the most efficient operator (in a dynamic sense, which includes the operator's propensity to invest). Moreover, a higher price will be achieved more easily for a firm with effective monopoly power than for one facing effective competition or external regulation. In sum, it is reasonable to condition price by dynamic internal and allocative efficiency criteria, since efficiency is the other major missing ingredient in Latin America's needed economic transformation (ECLAC, 1992a).

Price is often sacrificed for a specially targetted distribution of shares. Two prevalent target groups have been small investors (popular capitalism) and workers (labour capitalism). The former are ostensibly targetted to democratize capitalism and improve the efficiency of markets. The latter are targetted ostensibly to enhance productivity.

Popular capitalism, at least as sometimes practiced in the region,[27] raises legitimate questions about whether the implicit price subsidy is, socially speaking, really worth it. First, unless there is a virtual giveaway of the public firm to every citizen, there is reason to suspect that in a poor developing country the so-called popular capitalists will not be so popular.[28]

Second, one of the technical justifications for promoting popular capitalism – market efficient takeover threats – is weakened when the main motive for share participation is not risk-adjusted future returns, but rather exploitation of an easy and nearly guaranteed rent.[29] On the one hand, the rent-seekers have less incentive to be well-informed shareholders, making them prone to herd behaviour and exit.[30] On the other hand, uninformed and dispersed shareholders establish conditions for an organized group to emerge with entrenched control of the firm in any event; moreover, the group may well pay a price that is lower than if control had been sold by open bid at the time of privatization.[31] It also should be mentioned that the debate over what is more effective for international competitiveness, concentrated or dispersed ownership, is by no means resolved (especially in the context of a developing country) (Akyuz, 1992; Welch, 1992), making popular capitalism something of a leap of faith.

Third, if monetary incentives are deemed necessary to promote capitalistic values (of course there may be better ways), it is more transparent and equitable to sell the shares at a maximum price and to offer applications for identifiable rebates that make the subsidy explicit and accountable to the general public. Of course, none of these considerations hold if popular capitalism is really a ploy to gain political or ideological advantage; then the hidden subsidy may be a quite effective, if not cynical, tool.[32]

Privatizations have often transferred shares to the firm's workers on preferential terms. Chile probably has the region's most extensive experience in this area, but the strategy has appeared on a lesser scale in most other countries as well.[33] The technical logic behind labour capitalism would seem to make most sense only if the workers gain a large enough block of shares to hold and sustain representation on the board of directors of the privatized firm. But in this case, since workers possess "inside" information about the firm, there obviously would be little reason to subsidize the price of their shares and credit. On the other hand, if workers receive subsidized shares without broad representation, they could conceivably suffer in the medium term as short-term capital gains could erode a union's discipline and effectiveness in collective bargaining.[34]

The preferential distribution of shares to workers in the region has usually not been large enough to grant them sustained board representation. Indeed, the underlying motive of the offer usually seems to have been the reduction of labour's resistance to a privatization. The strategy has tended to work. However, if the main purpose of a subsidized share distribution is to co-opt workers, a more efficient alternative may be to simply link the privatization to the establishment of a profit-sharing arrangement for them and, thereby, reserve the sale of shares for the highest bidders. The approach could improve the net sale proceeds for the state, as one avoids the lower sale price derived from the subsidy on the shares distributed to workers and from the uncertainty that prospective shareholders would face regarding the future role of workers in management of the firm. Moreover, a profit-sharing programme could have larger spread effects in the local economy than a special subsidized sale of shares to workers of certain public enterprises. In effect, it establishes a precedent that other private firms can more plausibly be encouraged to imitate, which in turn opens up prospects of institutionalizing profit-sharing for all workers in the productive sectors of the economy. Finally, as an incentive for productivity, profit-sharing for risk-averse workers may be better than a gratuitous distribution of shares, because it avoids the morale problems that can arise from unfavourable fluctuations in the region's still thin and volatile domestic stock markets.

The objective of price maximization also could conceivably trade off with a subsidy for capitalists, designed to serve as a catalyst for private sector investment and growth. While this particular trade-off finds some support in certain technical circles, the awarding of rents to a select group of domestic capitalists in order to stimulate the overall economy's animal spirits is certainly a controversial hypothesis that is difficult to test. If subsidies are deemed necessary, it is clearly more efficient and equitable to grant them directly in the form of a tax credit or other publicly accountable instrument. In any event, the externalities derived from hidden subsidies in a privatization are probably exaggerated and far less important than those emerging from sound overall public macroeconomic and social reform programmes (which can be aided by a maximum price strategy), astute international bargaining and fortuitous exogenous events.[35]

A maximum price strategy also should be compatible with the objective of projecting political credibility. Where a conflict can emerge is again in cases of great fiscal urgency. This is another reason why more transitory direct compensatory budgetary support should be forthcoming from the international financial agencies.

IV.3 Assign privatization receipts to a social development trust fund

If there were absolutely no alternative role for the state, the outcome of privatizations would be a proportionate shrinking of the public sector. However, even if one were to make the extreme assumption that there is no future direct role for the state in productive activities,[36] there would still be a serious need to strengthen public goods in the social area (including infrastructure). Indeed, after ten years of regressive adjustment in the region, most would concede that the social sector is one area where the state should focus its future efforts. While in some instances support for social development could be provided by imaginative private initiatives, there often will be no good alternative to public production.

In the social area it is not always easy to conceptually distinguish between current and capital outlays. Nevertheless, from an accounting standpoint recurrent social expenditure (particularly non-wage outlays) has suffered the most during the crisis; in relative terms it is here where financial support is most urgently needed in the years ahead (ECLAC, 1992c). Thus, in addition to earmarking privatization receipts for special account, it might be helpful to further earmark all, or at least a significant part, of the income for a national social development trust fund. This type of policy would establish a permanent and flexible base for increased social expenditure on either the recurrent or capital account.[37] Of course, earmarking might be hard to accomplish when there is a general case of fiscal urgency. On the other hand, if authorities were legally required to earmark their extraordinary income for social expenditure, it could serve as a political tool to channel attention on other ways to balance budgets, e.g., tax reforms, cuts in military expenditure or more aggressive debt renegotiation strategies.

IV.4   Fair compensation for PE employees

As an alternative to a strategy for lay-offs followed by new hiring, more effort can be made to exploit possibilities to retrain and reallocate labour within the firm. Shares with board representation, or profit-sharing, can be exchanged for concessions on wages. When systematic lay-offs are necessary in privatization programmes, indemnification is simply not enough.[38] Cash payments can be easily dissipated; hence, distressed workers need counselling, retraining, relocation assistance and follow-up monitoring of their reintegration into the market. Since excess employment in the state firms is a "public problem", it would seem appropriate to finance retraining, counselling and indemnifications with special solidarity taxes or soft lending from international development banks, which incidentally have historically been major creditors of many PEs.[39]

IV.5   Effective regulation

From the standpoint of social welfare, a key assumption of successful privatization is that firms can be regulated externally as well or better than they were under direct public ownership. However, the transfer of property creates new types of problems that must be surmounted.

It is often argued that liberalization of trade is sufficient to regulate traded goods sectors and ensure reasonable internal efficiency. However, this may be only partly true in a developing country, as there will be lags and remaining obstacles to price competition on account of, among other things, the small size of many markets, which creates price inelasticities; the up-front costs of establishing distribution networks; exclusive dealership arrangements; collusion and the considerable transport costs usual in South America. Thus there will be a need for new domestic institutional and legal structures to promote desirable levels of competition and to control arbitrary pricing strategies, especially in durable goods. (Technical norms for quality and consumer safety are, of course, also desirable.)

As far as large public service firms are concerned – an area of intensive privatization (Table 7.4) – the frequent strategy up to now has been to transfer public monopolies to private hands. This is not necessarily a bad decision; in spite of recent ideas which have undermined the strength of the traditional natural monopoly argument, in some sectors there is still legitimate room to debate the effects of deconcentration on dynamic allocative efficiency. In effect, a developing country may not want to assume the risk of experimenting with a break-up of integrated public service systems.

Notwithstanding the above, the new regulatory frameworks which have emerged from the region's privatizations of public service sectors often allow for new entrants, which introduces the assumption of an immediate contestable market. However, when the dominant operator in the market is very large, it, rather than the potential new entrant, is the market threat; hence, in many cases, the practical relevance of contestability as a serious regulatory factor is suspect (Vickers and Yarrow, 1988). Thus, even if a market is contestable in principle, effective direct price/quality regulation of the new privatized industries by public authorities is of paramount importance for allocative efficiency and social equity.

The region's regulatory challenge is a major one, especially in public services. First, effectively regulating powerful monopolies is inherently a difficult and sometimes conflictual task which, as demonstrated by the experience with British Telephone, British Gas, etc. (*The Economist*, 1992), can test the metal of even the most zealous regulators and sophisticated government administrations. Second, the great speed with which new regulatory systems have emerged in Latin America suggests that flaws are likely to be discovered after privatization; when they are serious, countries will have to find ways to correct them without disrupting investment or stock markets, where privatized public service firms usually carry a large weight. Third, regulatory systems also must be flexible in the face of the fast-changing technological developments in some public service sectors. Fourth, regulators may also have to be international diplomats, as many new owners of public services firms are foreign enterprises and many of those are owned by foreign governments.

The signs are that the region's regulatory capacity is lagging far behind the speed of its privatizations. The problem is not so much the lack of formal systems – they often can be quite sophisticated and imaginative, as in the case of the Chilean electricity sector (Banlot, 1993) – but rather that they are emerging with little or no track record and apparently weak or non-existent enforcement systems.[40] The problem is aggravated by the fact that in order to attract buyers and finance their investment commitments, tariffs often underwent prior adjustments which were extremely generous to the privatized firms.[41]

To the extent that regulatory frameworks are permissive, it could mean that authorities have decided to trade off improved internal efficiency of a privatized firm for potentially deteriorated allocative efficiency, based on a veiled bet: that the loss of static allocative efficiency and social equity will be more than compensated for by the catalytic effects of the enhanced profitability of capital in the privatized sector. Unfortunately, from the standpoint of equity this could be another version of the trickle-down approach to development that has tended to dominate thought in the 1980s. Moreover, it assumes that the traded goods sector can prosper even with potentially important distortions in relative prices for important domestic public services.

Success in regulation requires a number of key ingredients, some of which can be mentioned here:

(1) Regulatory systems should emerge well before the privatization of a public service firm (Paredes, 1993) so that a track record can be established and some of the worst operational problems can possibly be ironed out while the firm is still state property. At a minimum, it would be wise to avoid the simultaneous privatization of several public service sectors which still have "virgin" regulatory systems.

(2) Regulatory systems should be based on straightforward impersonal formulae, or rules, that are clearly defined and technically consistent with the administrative skills of the country's prospective regulators, and comprehensible not only to shareholders and management, but also to consumers; indeed, sophisticated regulatory systems which may create a greal deal of theoretical satisfaction may in practice create more regulatory problems than solutions.

(3) Regulatory systems in developing countries must be designed to take into account dynamic and not just static efficiency.

(4) Regulatory bodies should be independent public entities which have their board appointments staggered through the political cycles.

(5) Regulatory personnel should be technically qualified, very well paid relative to the industry that is being regulated, and prohibited from working in the regulated industry for a specified period after their appointments are terminated.

(6) The regulatory board should have fluid channels of communication with its relevant industry, but at the same time maintain final word on the regulatory outcome.

(7) A special legal framework should be established to adjudicate disputes between the firm and the regulator.

(8) The regulator must have a clear, practical, and incrementally-organized set of sanctions at its disposal in case of a firm's non-compliance.

(9) Regulatory reviews among public service sectors should be spread out over an extended period so as to avoid a bunching of review sessions; in this way potential disputes could be less damaging to overall economic confidence.[42]

It also is often overlooked that an essential public service can never be fully privatized, because the operator of last resort will always be the public sector. To avoid moral hazard on the part of private owners, the state should probably consider regulating the privatized firm more comprehensively than is traditionally the case, including its debt accumulation, dividend policy, diversification, and investment. An alternative is to forgo more comprehensive regulation and charge the privatized firm a risk premium for the "public insurance" that covers the contingent costs of state intervention, should the firm enter into a critical operating condition. The moral hazard problem could be more volatile in regulatory frameworks that copy the UK's RPI−X formula, because unexpected shocks − arising from bad management decisions and/or exogenous factors − cannot be passed on to prices.[43] Finding commercially viable ways to control moral hazard is admittedly a difficult task. However, by ignoring the problem, one could be seriously underestimating the costs of privatization.

Finally, it could be argued that effective regulation will lower sale price compared to a firm granted extensive market power. But perhaps the trade-off is not all that large, since astute purchasers will surely discount the effects of excessively permissive regulatory framework that are likely to be subject to serious adjustments at a later date.

V   CONCLUSIONS

Privatization is now a fact of life in Latin America. Moreover, most of the countries' programmes are very ambitious and there is little sign of the trend slowing down before a large part of the region's PEs are divested. The theoretical and practical benefits of divestment in a developing country would seem to be strongest in most conventional tradable goods sectors, where liberalized markets can be counted on to autonomously perform a large part of the regulatory function (and hopefully be complemented by anti-monopoly laws and norms for quality and safety). In contrast, they are more problematic in sectors involving capital-dense public services, or those which have large externalities for macroeconomic management; in these cases, the impact of divestment on social welfare will be intimately linked to the ability of governments to administratively regulate the private firm on a continuous and effective basis. Clearly, the poorer a country and the less sophisticated its public administration, the greater the need for caution in the decision to divest large public service firms.[44] In any event, only time will tell the degree to which the actual process and end-product of divestment improves social welfare. But, whatever benefits are to be had from privatization, they can be improved upon if more attention is given to the objective of social equity.

We have focused proposals on five key areas that can raise the social benefits of privatization: more transparency; more systematic efforts to maximize sale price, fair and more integral compensation for displaced workers, the earmarking of sale receipts for social development and effective public regulation.

Of course, social equity must trade off with other objectives. However, the trade-offs with many of the commonly stated objectives of privatization are not necessarily large or important; indeed, many complementarities would seem to exist. In fact, the most threatening trade-off seems to be fiscal urgency. Thus, it would be helpful if multilateral organizations strengthened, or at least front-loaded, their budgetary support for developing countries willing to initiate a careful and socially equitable divestment programme. This can be justified on grounds which these organizations understand: the improved medium-term creditworthiness of their borrowers.

In sum, reform of public enterprises through privatization is necessarily a complicated task that must balance real trade-offs. However, the starting point of privatizations should be social equity and dynamic efficiency, and these considerations should be traded off for other objectives only reluctantly and in ways which make not only the benefits, but also the social costs of the decision explicit to the public. Latecomers clearly can learn lessons from more advanced programmes on how to improve the net social benefits of the process. Nevertheless, even the best privatization schemes will probably leave some problems that will have to be mopped up by later governments. In this light, privatization should be interpreted not so much as an "event" but rather as a "process" in which one can expect that the divestment of PEs will produce the need for other new reforms, especially in the regulatory area. The success of governments in managing this latter transition will also be an important determinant of the net social benefits of privatization.

NOTES

1 Apart from the sheer magnitude of the crisis, and the fragility of new democratic political regimes, the slow response was also undoubtedly related to the very serious shortcomings in the construction of multilateral conditionality and the official management of the debt problem, which tended to underfinance the adjustment process. See Ramos (1992), Devlin (1989), Killick et al. (1984) and Ground (1984).

2 The financial crisis was also a setback for the monetary approach to the balance of payments and proponents of "self-regulated" credit markets. See Ramos (1986), Ffrench-Davis (1982), and Devlin (1989).

3 There is a gamut of privatization techniques, of which divestment – the total or partial transfer of state-owned enterprises to the private sector – is only one. For a discussion of this, see ECLAC (1992b).

4 For an excellent history of public enterprises in Chile, see Ortega (1989).

5 From here on, "PEs" will be used broadly to include also those public entities that are not necessarily classified as enterprises.

6 About $3.8 billion of the total amount represents the market value of foreign debt paper which was used as a means of payment in several transactions.

7 Almost all the sales were paid for in domestic debt instruments.

8 It is already known that the new government plans to modify some aspects of the privatization programme; in particular, by drastically lowering the amount of debt paper that can be used as a means of payment.

9 In other terms, the government should sell the public enterprise if $V_{sp} + (\alpha_g - \alpha_p)P > V_{sg}$ where V_{sp} is the social value of the enterprise under private ownership, V_{sg}

is the social value of the enterprise under public ownership, P is the sale price and α_g and α_p are the "shadow" prices of public and private revenue, respectively. Of course, the social value of the enterprise under public or private ownership is evaluated through the use of a wide range of indicators of what constitutes net benefits for society. (See Jones, Tandon, and Vogelsang, 1990.)

10 Moreover, many of the remaining inefficiencies were imposed by the military government's ideological preferences, which induced explicitly restrictive policies on the expansion of PE activity. For instance, the public telephone company was not allowed to diversify into new services; new investment was limited; profits were siphoned off to the central government budget and the capacity to borrow was very restricted. The public telephone company was also seriously hurt by the 1982/83 economic collapse, induced in part by the government's macroeconomic policy. See Castillo (1991).

11 For a discussion of yardstick competition, see Vickers and Yarrow (1988).

12 Ironically, some of the European firms like Telefónica, Iberia and France Telcom are public enterprises.

13 During the international debt negotiations, creditors frequently required the public sector to absorb the private sector's unguaranteed debts with foreign banks. This was a highly arbitrary policy, with no real economic justification (Devlin, 1989).

14 This problem seems to have emerged in Chile, especially in the electrical power sector, where private and public firms compete in a sometimes conflictual setting. There has been a dispute between a state power generation firm (EDELNOR) and privatized generators over an investment in a thermal plant in Northern Chile. As part of a solution, the government finally decided to privatize the firm.

15 Prior to being elected into government, the Peronist Party had opposed a partial privatization of ENTEL which had been earlier proposed by the Alfonsin government (Gerchunoff and Castro, 1992).

16 This latter argument would seem to be less relevant for Latin America, which already confronts huge disequilibria and distortions due to the crisis. Indeed, in such a "second-best" world, it is difficult to assert that direct taxes will be distortionary.

17 It has been argued that privatizations are analogous to emitting bonds and therefore should be a "below line" item in the fiscal accounts. Governments, however, tend to put privatization receipts above the line, which thus causes the published accounts to understate deficits or overstate surpluses (Mansoor, 1987).

18 There was an overall deficit in Brazil in 1991, but its privatizations were paid for almost entirely in domestic public debt instruments. The Argentine privatizations of 1989/90 also were paid for to a large degree with foreign public debt instruments.

19 The Minister of Finance of Mexico, as quoted in *Latin American Weekly Economic Report* (1992a).

20 The privatization of ENTEL and Aerolíneas Argentinas generated only $300 million of cash, for assets valued at $1,500 million. This was due in part to the government's decision to receive payment in foreign bank debt, the nominal sum of which was $7 billion (Gerchunoff and Coloma, 1992). The retirement of the debt had little effect on fiscal cash flow because the government was in a moratorium (Altimir and Devlin, 1993).

21 Some have characterized the reform as regressive. (Marfán 1984).

22 See Moffett (1992).

23 Standard and Poor's has given Chile an investment grade rating (BBB).

24 Mexico, but especially Chile (taking into account its first round of privatizations), followed this sequencing. Brazil and Peru so far also have been broadly following this path.

25 This latter strategy was used by Mexico and Chile in their placement of residual TELMEX (Ruprah, 1990a) and CTC shares, respectively. For more information on ADRs, see West (1991).

26 This strategy has worked in Argentina and Mexico (Ruprah, 1990a; Gerchunoff and Castro, 1992).

27 A number of countries in the region have had preferential distributions, but Chile clearly has been the main practitioner of this strategy. During the military regime, preferential sales to the general public and public sector workers (including the armed forces), created some 120,000 popular capitalists (Sáez, 1991). For a study on the official logic and effects of the Chilean programme, see Valenzuela Silva (1989).

28 Our examination of the addresses of 46,000 popular capitalists in one of the largest Chilean privatizations (ENDESA) is suggestive of a high probability of a disproportionate participation by upper income groups. This conclusion is based on the distribution of popular capitalists in the different municipalities of Santiago, a highly socially stratified city, with 40 per cent of the country's population. About 45 per cent of the shares sold to the popular capitalists (preferential price and subsidized credit) were purchased by residents of this city. Of that amount, slightly more than 50 per cent were bought by residents of four municipalities, in which nearly 70 per cent of the households were in the upper two deciles of the income distribution. The primary data on popular capitalists come from CORFO. Data on income distribution were provided to me by Arturo León, of ECLAC's Statistics Division.

29 Regarding the preferential sales of ENDESA, the official brochure distributed to public employees stressed that "the offer involves no cost to the workers" (CORFO, 1988).

30 There are signs of erosion of the small shareholders' base in Chile's privatized firms; for example, ENDESA's small shareholders declined by 11 per cent between 1989 and 1991.

31 In 1989, the holding company ENERISIS emerged to gain control of ENDESA with 12 per cent of the company's total shares. The price was quite attractive, since share prices were relatively depressed at the time of purchase. See Sáez (1991).

32 In Chile, authorities also viewed popular capitalism as a way to discourage future renationalizations (Hachette and Lüders, 1992) and to perhaps gain an advantage in the upcoming 1989 plebiscite. Popular capitalism in the UK has also apparently had political objectives (Vickers and Yarrow, 1988).

33 In Chile, at least fifteen privatizations offered shares to workers on preferential conditions. Although the amounts of shares varied, the general pattern was that a few small firms (e.g., subsidiaries of ENDESA) were sold entirely to workers, while employees of large privatized firms were given small blocks of shares, ranging from 6 to 10 per cent. A major exception was CAP, where workers secured more than 30 per cent of the shares in a highly controversial transaction (Errázuriz et al., 1989), IANSA (21 per cent) and LAN Chile (originally 15 per cent, but only 10 per cent

was realized). In a few privatizations, workers on their own initiative joined together to borrow resources in financial markets and purchase additional shares. However, even in cases where workers nominally gained a large block of shares, it is difficult to ascertain to what degree they participated in decision-making; this is because shares often became managed by investment trusts, where share ownership tended to become concentrated. In Mexico workers also have occasionally participated in sales, e.g., they were sold 4 per cent of Telmex, the country's largest privatization. In the case of Aeromexico, the pilots' union secured 35 per cent of the firm (Ruprah, 1992b). In Argentina, 10 per cent of a privatized firm's shares are frequently earmarked for the workers.

34 I thank Hernán Gutiérrez for this latter observation.

35 Privatizations do not seem to have been the decisive factors in economic recoveries. In Mexico, the decisive factor appears to have been the announcement of the North American Free Trade Zone, coupled with a coherent and tough adjustment/ stabilization programme (of which privatization was a part). In Chile, the recovery was underway before the privatizations. This, coupled with a depreciating exchange rate, could be the principal reason behind rising private savings and investment. Meanwhile, recovery in Venezuela was set off by the favourable effects of the Gulf War on the petroleum sector, coupled with a Draconian reform programme.

36 Of course, in practice, there probably is a future role for state enterprises, due to the infant industry argument, considerations about strategic macroeconomic management, regulatory requirements for firm-level information in oligopolistic public service sectors, public choice, etc. Indeed, as Lahera (1992) has commented, there should be a flexible conceptualization of state participation in the economy. If the state's entrance into economic activity is easy and its exit difficult, there are probabilities of eventual inefficiencies and rents. On the other hand, if entrance is impossible and exit easy, the activity of the state will not always be compatible with development.

37 I thank Martine Guerguil for sharing with me her idea about a trust fund.

38 Information on the fate of workers is an area of analysis that needs much more attention. Mexico's latter rounds of privatizations were characterized by the official objective of avoiding lay-offs; for instance, in the privatization of TELMEX, with 49,000 workers, there were no dismissals. This was due in part to the workers' acceptance of changes in labour contracts and the government's decision to establish a retraining facility within the firm for employees displaced by new technology. On the other hand, the peaceful tone of industrial relations also was influenced by demonstration effects: in 1988, as a prelude to privatizing Aeromexico, the government confronted a striking union by suddenly declaring the firm bankrupt. The work-force dropped overnight from 12,000 employees to less than 4,000 (Ruprah, 1992b). Moreover, Mexican unions claim that 100,000 workers have lost their jobs either through direct privatization or through rationalization of state agencies (*Latin American Weekly Report*, 1992b). In Chile, privatizations were not generally associated with massive lay-offs; indeed employment in many firms expanded. However, the work-force of public enterprises had already been drastically reduced in earlier public enterprise reforms; by 1986 the labour force in major public enterprises was 40 per cent less than it had been in 1974 (Saéz, 1991). In Argentina, although there has been a lay-off of workers as part of the preparation of the privatization of a steel complex, the general strategy has been to repeal labour

contracts and let workers renegotiate them with the privatized firms. The outcome of this process should be studied in order to ascertain how workers have fared in their new contractual limbo.

39 The World Bank has financed indemnifications in some countries.

40 For the cases of Argentina and Mexico, see Ruprah (1990a, 1992b) and Gerchunoff and Castro (1992), respectively. The Chilean systems have a track record since they were first established in the early 1980s; even so, there has been much confusion in the interpretation and enforcement of the different systems (Bitrán and Saavedra, 1993).

41 See Gerchunoff and Castro (1992) and Ruprah (1990a). In Chile, rates underwent severe adjustment well before the privatizations. It should be mentioned that the investment constraint argument for privatizations is weakened when the main source of finance for new investment is government-authorized tariff increases.

42 Long periods between review sessions could create the need for very large adjustments. An alternative to be considered is a continuous review process which induces mini adjustments much like a crawling peg exchange rate system.

43 The formula means that regulated prices rise on average by less than the rate of domestic inflation. This is supposed to be an incentive for innovation and cost reduction. However, there may be little room to absorb shocks, for example, a failed project, debt refinancing problems, etc. The telecommunications sectors in Mexico and Argentina will be regulated by variants of the RPI−X formula. In the case of Argentina, there are adjustments for adverse movements of the exchange rate. See Gerchunoff and Castro (1992) and Ruprah (1990a).

44 Other alternatives might be explored, such as performance contracts for public firms or payment of fees to an experienced private operator which pursues publicly outlined objectives.

REFERENCES

Altimir, O. and R. Devlin (1993) "Una reseña de la moratoria de la deuda en América Latina", in O. Altimir and R. Devlin (eds), *Moratoria de la deuda en América Latina: experiencia de los países*, Fondo de Cultura Económica, México City, forthcoming.

Akyuz, Y. (1992) *Financial Reform and the Development Process*, UNCTAD, Geneva.

Atkinson, A. and J. Stiglitz (1980) *Lectures on Public Economics*, McGraw-Hill, New York.

Banlot, V. (1993) "La regulación del sector eléctrico: la experiencia chilena", in O. Muñoz (ed.), *Más allá de las privatizaciones: Hacia el Estado regulador*, Ediciones CIEPLAN, Santiago, Chile.

Bitrán, E. and E. Saavedra (1993) "Algunas reflexiones en torno al rol regulador y empresarial del Estado", in O. Muñoz (ed.), *Más allá de las privatizaciones: Hacia el Estado regulador*, Ediciones CIEPLAN, Santiago, Chile.

Castillo, M. (1991) *Privatizaciones de empresas públicas en Chile: el caso del sector de telecomunicaciones*, CEPAL, Santiago, Chile (unpublished).

CORFO (1988) *Ponga su futuro en acción*, Santiago, Chile.

Cornia, A., R. Jolly and F. Stewart (1987) *Adjustment with a Human Face*, Clarendon Press, Oxford.

Devlin, R. (1989) *Debt and Crisis in Latin America: The Supply Side of the Story*, Princeton University Press, Princeton NJ.

ECLAC (1990) *Transformación con equidad*, Santiago, Chile.

ECLAC (1991) *Balance Preliminar de la Economía de América Latina y el Caribe, 1991*, Santiago, Chile.

ECLAC (1992a) *Equidad y transformación productiva: un enfoque integrado*, Santiago, Chile.

ECLAC (1992b) *La reestructuración de empresas: el caso de los puertos de América Latina y el Caribe*, Cuadernos de la CEPAL, 68, Santiago, Chile.

ECLAC (1992c) *Education and Knowledge: Basic Pillars of Changing Productive Patterns with the Social Equity*, Santiago, Chile.

The Economist (1992) "Ofwiththelot", 15 August.

Errázuriz, E., R. Fortunatti, and C. Bustamante (1989) *Huachipato*, Programa de Economía de Trabajo (PET), Academia de Humanismo Cristiano, Santiago, Chile.

Errázuriz, J. and J. Weinstein (1986) "Capitalismo popular y privatización de empresas públicas", Santiago, Chile, PET, Academia de Humanismo Cristiano, Working Paper 53.

Ffrench-Davis, R. (1982) "El experimento monetarista en Chile: una síntesis crítica", *Colección Estudios CIEPLAN* 9, December.

Floyd, R., C. Gray, and R. Short (1984) *Public Enterprises in Mixed Economies*, International Monetary Fund, Washington DC.

Fondo de Inversiones de Venezuela (1992) *Política de privatizaciones y restructuración*, Caracas, June.

Galal, A., L. Jones, P. Tandon and I. Vogelsang (1992) "Synthesis of Cases and Policy Summary", paper presented to a Conference on the Welfare Consequences of Selling Public Enterprises, Washington DC, World Bank, 11–12 June.

Gerchunoff, P. and L. Castro (1992) "La racionalidad macroeconómica de las privatizaciones: El caso Argentino", paper presented to the Regional Seminar on Reforms of Public Policy, CEPAL, Santiago, Chile, 3–5 August.

Gerchunoff, P. and G. Coloma (1992) "Privatizaciones y reforma regulatoria en la Argentina", paper presented to the Regional Seminar on Reforms of Public Policy, CEPAL, Santiago, Chile, 3–5 August.

Ground, R. (1984) "Orthodox Adjustment Programs in Latin America: A Critical Look at the Policies of the International Monetary Fund", *CEPAL Review* 23, August.

Hachette, D. and R. Lüders (1992) *La privatización en Chile*, ICS Press, San Francisco CA.

Hanke, S. (1987) "Introduction", in S. Hanke (ed.) *Privatización and Development*, ICS Press, San Francisco CA.

Hemming, R. and A. Mansoor (1988) "Privatization and Public Enterprises", IMF, Occasional Paper 56, Washington DC.

Herrera, A. (1991) "Privatización de los servicios de telecomunicaciones: El caso Argentino", New York, Columbia Business School, August.

Hirschman, A. (1970) *Exit, Voice and Loyalty*, Harvard University Press, Cambridge MA.

Jones, L., P. Tandon and I. Vogelsang (1990) *Selling Public Enterprises*, MIT Press, Cambridge MA.

Khanna, V. (1992) "Mexico's Economic Resurgence Highlighted at World Bank Conference", *IMF Survey*, 25 May.

Killick, T. (1989) "A Reaction Too Far", Overseas Development Institute, London.

Killick, T., G. Bird, J. Sharpley, and M. Sutton (1984) "The IMF: Case for a Change in Emphasis", in Richard Feinberg and Valeriana Kallab (eds), *Adjustment Crisis in Third World*, Transaction Books, New Brunswick NJ.

Lahera, E. (1992) "Un sector público con entrada y salida", *El Diario*, Santiago, Chile, 29 April.

Latin American Weekly Economic Report (1992a), "Aspe Announces Big Debt Mop-Up", London, 18 June 1992.

Latin American Weekly Economic Report (1992b) "Counting the Cost of Privatization", 13 August.

Latin Finance (1991) "Privatization in Latin America", March.

Latin Finance (1992) "Privatization in Latin America", March.

Mansoor, A. (1987) *The Budgetary Impact of Privatization*, IMF, Washington DC.

Marcel, M. (1989) "La privatización de empresas públicas en Chile 1985–8", Santiago, Chile, CIEPLAN, Notas técnicas 125.

Marco Modiano, E. (1992) Speech to a Seminar on the Politics and Economics of Public Revenues and Expenditures, sponsored by the World Bank and Ministry of Economic Affairs, Brasilia, 10–12 June.

Marfán, M. (1984) "Una evaluación de la nueva reforma tributaria", *Colección Estudios CIEPLAN* 13, June.

Moffett, M. (1992) "Mexico's Bull Market Lifts New Generation Into the Wealthy Elite", *Wall Street Journal*, 6 May.

Nair, G. and A. Filippides (1988) "How Much Do State-Owned Enterprises Contribute to Public Sector Deficits in Developing Countries – And Why?", Washington DC, World Bank, Working Paper 45, December.

Ortega, L. (1989) (ed.) *CORFO: 50 años de realizaciones, 1939–1989*, University of Santiago, Department of History, Santiago, Chile.

Paredes, R. (1993) "Privatización y Regulación: Lecciones de la Experiencia Chilena", in Oscar Muñoz (ed.), *Más allá de las privatizaciones: Hacia el Estado regulador*, Ediciones CIEPLAN, Santiago, Chile.

Ramos, J. (1986) *Neo-Conservative Economics in the Southern Cone of Latin America, 1973–1983*, Johns Hopkins Press, Baltimore MD.

Ramos, J. (1992) "Equilibrios Macroeconómicos y Desarrollo", in Osvaldo Sunkel (ed.) *El desarrollo desde dentro*, Fondo de Cultura Económica, Mexico City.

Ruprah, I. (1990a) "Privatization: Case Study Teléfonos de México", Mexico City (unpublished).

Ruprah, I. (1990b) "Privatization: Case Study Compañía Mexicana de Aviación", México City, CIDE, (unpublished).

Ruprah, I. (1992a) "Divestiture and Reform of Public Enterprises: The Mexican Case", Mexico City (unpublished).

Ruprah, I. (1992b) "Aeromexico", México City, (unpublished).

Sáez, R. (1991) "An Overview of Privatization in Chile: The Episodes, the Results and the Lessons", Santiago, Chile (unpublished).

Secretaría de Hacienda y Crédito Público (n.d.) "El Proceso de Enajenación de Entidades Paraestatales", México City.

Seth, R. (1989) "Distributional Issues in Privatization", *Federal Reserve Bank of New York Quarterly Review* 14, Summer.

Tandon, P. (1992) "México", Vol. 1, paper presented to a Conference on the Consequences of Selling Public Enterprises, Washington DC, World Bank, 11–12 June.

Valenzuela Silva, M. (1989) "Reprivatización y capitalismo popular en Chile", *Estudios Públicos* 33, Summer.

Vickers, J. and G. Yarrow (1988) *Privatization: An Economic Analysis*, MIT Press, Cambridge MA.

Welch, J. (1992) "The New Finance of Latin America: Financial Flows, Markets, and Institutions in the 1990s", Federal Reserve Bank of Dallas, Dallas TX.

West, P. (1991) "El regreso de América Latina al mercado crediticio privado internacional", *CEPAL Review* 44, Santiago, Chile, August.

Williamson, J. (1990) *The Progress of Policy Reform in Latin America*, Institute for International Economics, Washington DC.

Woodrow Wilson Center (1991) *Noticias*, Spring.

8 | Is the Market-Friendly Approach Friendly to Development: A Critical Assessment?

JOSÉ MARÍA FANELLI,
ROBERTO FRENKEL
and
LANCE TAYLOR*

Development experience in different countries appears to vary widely. A sensible question with which to approach the issue could be: is it possible to have a general and single approach to development policy? There are those who would answer "yes". For example, in its 1991 *World Development Report* (WDR), the World Bank affirms that "a consensus is gradually forming in favour of a 'market-friendly' approach to development" (1991, p. 1). Throughout this chapter, the WDR 1991 is taken as representing a clear statement of the market-friendly approach.

This chapter assesses the internal consistency and credibility of the "emerging consensus", concentrating on a critical evaluation of the claim that outside forces are relatively insignificant by comparison with domestic policy in affecting developing countries' growth rates and income distributions.

Our central critique is that the market-friendly approach to development (MFAD) is not fully consistent. Our own approach is essentially macro-economic, emphasizing how the foreign resource constraint interacts with other key aggregate variables (mainly the fiscal constraint, investment, and saving) and with economic policy in determining patterns of distribution and growth.

The exposition is organized under three broad headings. In the first, we

* Comments by Gerry Helleiner on a previous draft are gratefully acknowledged. This chapter is based on a critical assessment by the authors of the World Bank's World Development Report, 1991, and is an edited version of their report.

review and criticize the MFAD's typical characterization of paths to development. In the second, we examine the consistency of the macro-economic model(s) behind the MFAD. Finally, we take up structural reform.[1]

I   DEVELOPMENT AND GROWTH

A basic tenet of the MFAD is that countries that have achieved rapid development share two characteristics: they invested in the education of men and women and in physical capital; and they achieved high productivity from these investments by giving markets, competition, and foreign trade leading roles. The argument expands upon these "stylized facts" about development, and derives several policy lessons.

The rationale for such stylized facts goes as follows: growing productivity is the engine of development, and productivity is driven by technical progress. There is strong evidence[2] linking productivity increases to investment in human capital and the quality of the economic environment, i.e. the extent to which markets are not distorted. History shows that policies and institutions largely determine how much is invested in human capital and the extent of market distortion: hence, it follows that policies and institutions are crucial in explaining the difference between success and failure with regard to development. In accordance with these theses, the MFAD focuses on the relationship between government and markets.

Our view is that the protagonists of the MFAD have presented a case which has both loose ends and missing information. The MFAD usually attempts to explain that part of economic growth unaccounted for by the combinations of capital and labour in terms of the efficiency with which inputs are used. It then attempts to explain variations in this residual efficiency in terms of the market friendliness of economic policy.

Other factors are also singled out as determinants of the income growth rate:

(1)   Education is one such factor, where the returns on investment are claimed to be high.

(2)   Domestic policies are seen as affecting both the quantity of inputs and their productivity. Specifically, a strategy of import-substituting industrialization (ISI) may artificially increase investment at the outset, but will have grave long-term costs in terms of low efficiency and slow technical progress, i.e. low productivity growth.[3]

(3)   External openness and competition are associated with high growth and productivity. These linkages are said to hold for various measures of greater openness, e.g. movements of domestic prices for traded goods towards international prices, and increases in trade shares.

(4)   Country studies suggest that macroeconomic instability diminishes the return on investment and the growth of output.

(5)   The effects of external factors such as changes in the terms of trade, growth of the OECD economies, international interest rates, and capital flows are asserted not to account for differences in performance of individual countries.

I.1   Determinants of output growth

Comparing the 1960–73 and 1973–87 periods, the WDR 1991 argues that slower output almost everywhere after 1973 was "due" to a lower residual – there was no significant change in the total contribution of capital and labour growth.

However, the evidence that is claimed to support this is presented at an aggregated level. At a more disaggregated level it is revealed, for example, that Latin America experienced a 1.8 percentage point fall in the growth rate of capital stock between the two periods. By contrast, South Asia experienced a much more moderate decline of 0.8 percentage points.

Similar doubts apply to claims regarding the growth effects of education and ISI. With regard to the former, it is a truism that the labour share – or the estimated elasticity of output with respect to labour in growth analysis – is somewhat lower in developing than in industrialized countries. But should it be deduced from this that more education enhances productivity? There are at least two problems with this logic.

First, if the "labour share" means the share of wage payments in value-added at factor cost, then it will automatically be lower in poor countries, since the incomes of independent proprietors such as peasants and small tradespeople are not imputed to labour. As market economies grow richer, institutions change and proprietors tend to be proletarianized. Their income share declines, while that of wage-earners and corporate enterprises goes up, a point which has little to do with education (Kuznets, 1966).

Second, the equivalence of the labour share to the elasticity of output with respect to labour holds only under assumptions of perfect competition. Yet the MFAD stresses that development problems occur precisely because of strong distortions in product and factor markets. If the counter-argument is that the factor productivity results should be interpreted as good approximations to reality using the "as if" clause, then an obvious question is: How is it that departures from perfect competition so weakly affect econometrics and so strongly explain differences in development performance?

When it takes up the effects on productivity of market distortions, the MFAD treats import substitution as a major culprit, especially in Latin America. It is explicitly blamed for the fall in total factor productivity (TFP) growth observed in the region after 1973. Yet the evidence suggests that while TFP accounted for 25 per cent of output growth in Latin America during 1960–73, it took away 48 per cent during 1973–87. The ISI strategy can scarcely account for this shift, since in one form or another it guided Latin development thinking throughout the *entire* post-war period.

The biggest difference between the sub-periods before and after 1973 is not the dominance or gradual weakening of ISI doctrines, but rather the impact of two international earthquakes: the oil shock and the debt crisis. In trying to manage external instability in the late 1970s and throughout the 1980s, successive Latin American economic teams combined the remnants of ISI with an array of new, and often market-friendly, policy packages. On the whole, the results for development were disappointing.

1.2 The advantages of investing in people

It is a long jump from arguing that more educational attainment is associated with larger personal income at the micro level, to the contention that more education is a sufficient condition for faster overall output growth.

No one denies that in most societies, people's years of schooling and their earned incomes are positively correlated, but the relationship is not easy to explain. There is a long-standing, unsettled debate in the US as to whether school attainment is a strong explanatory factor for income itself, or more of a proxy for family background, "ability", and "luck". This inconclusiveness no doubt carries over to the developing world.

Moreover, even if more school years do increase an individual's potential productivity at the margin, there is no assurance that that person will get a job. Jumping from micro evidence to a more macro relationship between extra education and faster growth requires buying into strong assumptions. The "new" theories of economic growth that underlie the emphasis on human capital typically postulate that output is determined solely by supply factors, and that all resources are fully employed.[4] Especially after the poor countries' dismal performance over the past decade, many economists would prefer not to presume so much.

A less radical analysis starts from the observation that both public and private actions condition the availability, remuneration, and skill content of jobs. In particular, an economy in chronic recession, as in Latin America, is not likely to be starved for skills. Even if there are bottlenecks, job requirements can often be modified accordingly; more generally, labour market structures vary across nations and strongly influence the nexus among years and type of education, personal characteristics, and payment for work.

These observations do not deny experience in South Korea and elsewhere, where increased skills and education have been associated at the micro level with technology acquisition, productivity increases, and growth, nor can one quarrel with the worldwide social consensus that better health and schooling are desirable in and of themselves. But human capital accumulation is not a sufficient condition for higher productivity; it is more a necessary or accommodating factor which cannot be absent in the long run.

I.3   Profits and growth

Another common theme of the MFAD is that market liberalization will increase the profitability of physical capital. In the WDR 1991, *ex-post* rates of return on World Bank investment projects at the country level are regressed on the parallel market premium, the fiscal deficit, the real interest rate, and the degree of trade restriction (a subjective index). Profits are found to decrease as these measures of distortion worsen, but as usual the causal linkages are unclear. If a country gets into macroeconomic trouble, for example, profitability will suffer at the same time as the black market premium increases, the fiscal deficit widens, inflation speeds up, and the authorities impose import quotas. Under such circumstances, distortions look less like causes than simple correlates of low rates of return induced by economy-wide disorders. We are back to the macroeconomic shocks that many developing economies received after the mid-1970s as the underlying determinant of performance.

Moreover, regression results that show a strong positive effect of public investment on the rates of return on World Bank projects suggest that, by increasing profitability, public investment can "crowd in" capital formation by the private sector.

Unfortunately, during the 1980s this potentially beneficial linkage operated in reverse. Latin American nations (and other LDCs) ran into fiscal duress as their export proceeds (from both public firms and taxation of the private sector) declined and foreign interest obligations went up. As discussed in country studies sponsored by the World Institute for Development Economics Research (Taylor, 1992), the resulting cutbacks in public investment combined with high interest rates and low capacity utilization to provoke a fall in capital formation.

I.4   Integration with the world economy

Is there a causal linkage between economic openness and the rate of output growth? Defining openness by high trade shares in GDP, for example, Syrquin and Chenery (1989) split a sample of countries into four groups by size and primary/manufactured goods export specialization. Over the period 1950–83, they compare growth rates in the halves of each group with low and high export shares.

The median GDP growth rate per capita for small countries with primary product specialization and high export shares is 1.1 per cent per year higher than that of similar countries with low shares, a striking difference. However, the obvious conclusion to be drawn from the experience of nations such as Chad, Ghana, and Madagascar (the three slowest growers in the sample) is that both growth and exports will be low when the entire socioeconomic system is in the fire. The policy implications are that somehow overcoming internal disruption and searching out plausible export lines are prior conditions for economic viability; not that liberalizing an economy will miraculously open it to growth through trade.

In the other three groups, the differences in *mean* growth rates between the high and low export sub-groups substantially exceed differences in medians, suggesting the presence of outliers. Sure enough, dropping Japan and the rapidly growing East Asian industrializing economies from the appropriate classes makes the differences in means tend towards zero. Yet again, one of the basic tenets of the MFAD is called into question.

Other cross-country studies such as that of McCarthy *et al.* (1987) also point to an agnostic conclusion about the effects of high or rising trade shares on growth. Nor do exports appear to lead output expansion in time; a recent study of forty-seven African economies finds that there is no "Granger causality" link between more exports and faster growth (Ahmad and Kwan, 1991).

Among individual countries, there are numerous counter-examples: Jamaica, Uruguay, and Portugal historically have combined high manufactured trade shares with slow growth; corresponding shares in Colombia and Brazil have averaged two or three per cent and they historically have grown fast. Despite the East Asian examples of simultaneous expansion of exports and output (backed by steadfast import substitution, heavy state intervention, and big capital inflows at critical junctures), counter-cases all over the globe rule out strong trade/growth associations.

The same conclusion carries over to the weak and tenuous statistical associations between trade distortions and growth that have been found in regression analyses. Similar findings are the rule for individual economies. A World Bank-sponsored study of Chile found *no* changes in sectoral productivity levels after external liberalization; the rationale being that improvements may have been masked by macroeconomic shocks (Tybout *et al.*, 1991).

II MISSING ISSUES IN THE MARKET-FRIENDLY APPROACH

The argument that slow expansion boils down to zero or negative growth rates of TFP, or the "residual", omits or underestimates crucial factors affecting economic performance in developing countries.

Key elements missing include: the sources of and incentives for capital accumulation; the difficulties of building up a domestic capital market in an increasingly integrated financial world; and the difference between allocative and productive efficiency.

II.1   Investment and saving

Economic growth entails three related but distinct problems. To sustain growth, it is necessary to generate sufficient savings – the feature of the process emphasized by the classical or Smithian tradition of thought. The "wealth of nations" is explained by the thrift of their populations. Parts of available resources should always be put into savings in order to increase wealth.

Furthermore, it is necessary to ensure that the non-consumed flow of income is invested, because one cannot count on savings being automatically channelled into capital formation. This problem is highlighted by the Keynesian tradition,[5] which focuses on two determinants of growth. One is the state of investors' animal spirits, primarily affected by their expectations regarding the future evolution of the economy. The other takes the form of marginal productivity decisions in the allocation of a given flow of savings between real and financial assets. These choices among different possible components of asset-holders' portfolios heavily influence the degree of capital-deepening and hence the long-term rate of growth.

A third important factor influencing the growth rate is the efficiency with which given real resources are allocated. This can be called the neoclassical approach to the theory of growth. It should be underlined that neoclassical models concentrate on *allocative* efficiency, implicitly assuming that it leads to productive efficiency as well. We expand on this distinction below.

The MFAD frequently tends to dismiss the Smithian and Keynesian traditions. Its policy proposals understate the need to generate more savings and reinforce the linkages between savings and investment in order to restore growth. This stance is consistent with the neoclassical philosophy underlying the approach which presupposes that market forces can simultaneously resolve the classical, Keynesian, and efficiency problems. Saving cannot be scarce *per se*, because the market-determined interest rate will call forth the optimal flow. Animal spirits/portfolio decision bottlenecks will not occur because neoclassical growth models postulate that investment and saving are instantly equalized by the market. Likewise, money is sometimes viewed as the only asset competing with real holdings in an economy closed to foreign wealth.

This approach has several flaws when it comes to addressing linkages between savings, investment, and growth in developing economies:

(1)   There is no empirical evidence of a strong relationship between the interest rate and the supply of savings.[6]

(2)   Nor are there many observable examples of a scenario tracing back to McKinnon (1973) whereby a higher interest rate leads to a portfolio switch toward bank deposits. The increased financial intermediation

       implicit in a higher deposit/output ratio is supposed to cause the
incremental capital/output ratio to decline. As we argue below,
adjustments in the opposite direction are more likely to take place.

(3) The neoclassical model assumes that the substitution effect of an
increase in the interest rate is stronger than the income effect.[7]
However, the existence of a significant amount of public debt, both
domestic and external, implies that any increase in private savings
due to a higher interest rate could be more than offset by the
decrease in public sector savings due to the increased cost of debt
service. Even supporters of the market-friendly approach recognize
that public dissaving due to higher debt service could have explosive
macro implications.[8]

(4) Many developing economies are open to external capital movements.
The corresponding portfolio decision between local real and foreign
financial assets (the "capital flight" phenomenon) is a crucial
determinant of investment and therefore growth.

(5) The importance of institutions in determining the national saving
rate is not addressed in neoclassical models, because they emphasize
the equilibrating role of movements in the interest rate. Likewise,
institutional determinants of investment are underrated. These
omissions are particularly striking with regard to the state as a
generator of both savings and investment. Mainstream models
emphasize the importance of the government budget constraint in
inflation/stabilization questions, but not with regard to growth.

II.2   External shocks

National saving and investment performance in developing countries has
proven to be highly sensitive to external shocks.

       Average annual total saving in LDCs exceeded investment (representing a
net resource transfer from South to North) by 0.7 per cent of world GDP
during 1981–5 and by 0.5 per cent during 1986–8 ($94 billion in 1988). This
"perverse" transfer surely is related to the fact that annual average GDP
growth rates in Sub-Saharan Africa and Latin America dropped by about 2.5
percentage points between 1973–80 and 1980–9. The sustained external shock
represented by these transfers amounted to approximately 3 per cent of total
developing countries' GDP (now about $3.1 trillion) per year. It is scarcely
surprising that their output growth rates slowed.

       The simplest explanation for the low growth rates of total factor
productivity in developing economies, noted above, is that after the mid-1970s
lagging output expansion reduced the estimated residual, not the other way. In
many developing economies capital/output ratios rose in response to capacity
underutilization as they adjusted in contractionary fashion to increasingly
severe external strangulation.

Similarly, when the effects of external shocks are integrated into an analysis of macroeconomic disequilibria, it becomes natural to take account of the Smithian (or saving) constraint on growth. The observed decreases in national saving rates in many developing countries have been closely correlated with reductions in real national incomes induced by higher external payments flows after the early 1980s.

II.3 Capital flight and financial intermediation

Thinking of capital flight as only a consequence of "macroeconomic mismanagement", as the MFAD is apt to do, trivializes the Keynesian problem that many countries face. Adverse private capital movements are a symptom of structural weaknesses of the financial system – they are the counterpart of demonetization and the shrinkage of domestic asset markets. In Argentina, Mexico, the Philippines and Venezuela, private capital outflows approximated the increase in the nation's foreign debt. Alienation of national wealth and assignment of a substantial fraction of the flow of domestic savings toward foreign holdings means that many developing economies face local financial disintermediation as a direct consequence of liberalization. Foreign governments and investors reap the gains, while domestically there is a liquidity squeeze.

This financial barrier between local economic actors whose savings exceed investment flows and firms and households with saving insufficient to finance desired levels of capital formation stems from the portfolio preferences of the domestic private sector and the credit policies of foreign institutions. In countries like Argentina and Brazil, the demand for domestic financial assets can be as low as a few percentage points of GDP. If the government seeks to finance a small increment in its deficit locally (its only possible choice, since the foreign credit market is rationed), the induced excess demand will spill over into rapidly escalating real interest rates and/or a "panic" which leads to capital flight.

Unfortunately, the possibility of panicky reactions is real. Perceived macroeconomic instability increases wealth-holders' preferences for liquid foreign assets as opposed to physical capital. By the same token, foreign financial institutions tighten credit rationing and try to reduce their exposure in the country concerned. During the 1980s, capital outflows worked against domestic equilibrium: they reversed or reduced during relatively stable periods, but intensified with macroeconomic shocks.

By ignoring these destabilizing feedbacks, the MFAD denies the existence of a major market failure. By themselves, "sound" macroeconomic policies cannot eliminate international disintermediation of funds.

It is certainly true that a more stable environment would increase demand for domestic financial assets, thereby reducing the outflow of internal savings. But it is also true that flight capital may represent a permanent reallocation of private agents' portfolios. Recent technological and institutional changes have made it easier for wealth-holders to store funds abroad at the same time as they see foreign financial institutions as being safer and more efficient than domestic ones.

Even if macroeconomic stability were attained, the restoration of growth calls for higher investment. In other words, repatriated flight capital should finance capital formation. But if animal spirits are weak, the outcome could be a stagnant equilibrium of self-fulfilling pessimistic expectations as private agents assume a wait-and-see attitude before taking the risk of immobilizing their funds in productive assets. The government cannot "prime the pump", because restricted local markets mean that it cannot place its own liabilities. Even worse, the private sector may enter into speculation in local financial paper, as happened in Chile, Turkey, the Philippines, and elsewhere during market liberalization experiments before and after 1980.

These difficulties suggest that financial liberalization alone is not likely to be a successful policy option. The case of Chile is instructive in this regard. After its internal financial boom and crash (discussed in more detail below), Chile's official donors increased their exposure in the country, supplementing commercial bank credit and relaxing the external liquidity constraint. There were two direct beneficial consequences.

In the first place, increased external credits allowed the central bank to transfer non-performing loans from the commercial banks' to its own portfolio. Subsequently, this transaction was refinanced by a "big bond" exceeding $7 billion (in an economy with a GDP of $25 billion) from the national treasury to the central bank, thereby making debt service a taxpayers' obligation. Bad debts still exist within the financial system, but for the moment their destabilizing effects have been neutralized.

Second, foreign financing permitted a high level of public investment. Beyond more pump-priming, substantial copper export capacity was created and animal spirits were buoyed up. Chile enjoyed a steady inflow of official multilateral credits which forestalled the worst aspects of international financial disintermediation. By 1991, the country had attained renewed access to international financial markets, but only on the basis of previous donors' lending sustained over a long period of time.

II.4 Allocative vs. productive efficiency

In the contexts of industry and finance respectively, Hjalmarsson (1991) and UNCTAD (1991) show how the irrelevance of liberalization to growth can be dissected in terms of distinct notions of "allocative" and "productive" efficiency: the latter is by no means assured by putting the former into place. Market and capital stock structures, forms of financial intermediation, resource "endowments" as defined by changing technology and tastes, the size of the economy, historical fetters from colonialism, access to geopolitically determined capital inflows and penetrable markets affect productive efficiency in numerous and complex ways not appreciated by the MFAD.

Nor is the MFAD clear about how removing wedges separating prices, especially between international and national valuations of potentially tradable goods, is supposed to generate productivity gains. Meeting external competition, for example, may reflect low real wages as much as the high labour productivity which is essential for a high per capita GDP. Similarly, if capital markets, are reasonably competitive and stable, then getting rid of distortions is supposed to stimulate productive efficiency within firms. Enlightened neoclassical economists recognize that even this contingent guarantee breaks down under conditions typical of developing countries or those undertaking the transition from socialism (Tirole, 1991).[9]

If productive efficiency is not assured by liberalization, then how can it be enhanced? There are no foolproof stimulants, but intriguing possibilities can be inferred from historical experiences. One example is the model of accumulation followed by the Nordic economies after 1930 and South Korea two decades later. This emphasized the advantages of workers' productivity growth when they were employed by firms big enough to benefit from best practice technology and economies of scale. Such enterprises were consciously sanctioned by Nordic and Korean authorities as monopolies or oligopolistic participants in export trade. After relatively short learning periods, governments sought allocative efficiency by supporting their local champions in competition with counterparts abroad (the Nordics, though not the Koreans, also opened their national markets to foreign competition). They learned to meet world prices of commodities and services with elastic export demands, so that labour productivity increases could be absorbed into foreign sales.

Pressures toward productive efficiency came not from capital markets, but from Scandinavian trade unions and the South Korean state. The Nordic workers promoted higher productivity on the understanding that it would be translated rapidly into real wages; without underwriting wage growth, the South Korean economic bureaucracy followed their Japanese mentors in adopting a pro-productivity line. Given the tightly held nature of (say) the Swedish Wallenberg bank-centred "group" of companies and the Korean *chaebol*, stock market discipline did not figure in production or investment decisions. Cross-financing of investment within the groups, industrial subsidies, and targetted, cheap credit in restricted national capital markets, however, certainly did (Kosonen, 1991; Amsden, 1989).

Another missing link has to do with countries' size. It is natural for small and large nations to pursue different lines of industrial strategy to gain productive efficiency. Differences in development patterns between small and large economies have been studied for a long time; Syrquin and Chenery (1989) provide a recent summary. A dividing line between the two types of economy is most conveniently drawn on the basis of population, somewhere between 20 and 50 million.

Katzenstein (1985) and Pekkarinen *et al.* (1991) suggest that economically successful small countries prospered along Nordic/Korean lines, with close state/capitalist/labour collaboration in supporting "thrust" sectors under an open trade (although not necessarily capital market) regime. Extended to incorporate active government dealing with transnational corporations, and more or less explicit labour repression, this approach has worked recently in small, growing raw material exporters like Malaysia and Chile. It is fair to ask how long the former country can successfully court potentially footloose TNC assembly operations without a coherent national industrial structure, or how long the latter can defer distributional strife (Taylor, 1992).

While small countries necessarily concentrate on a limited number of export industries in the search for profitable niches, large ones usually follow a more uniform pattern of industrial change. They enter earlier into import substitution and have higher manufacturing shares of GDP than do small nations at the same per capita income level; they pursue import substitution further into intermediate and capital goods and producers' services. The statistically "typical" large country's import and export shares of GDP are likely to be around 10 per cent (with a standard deviation of about the same size), while a small country's share may be more than one-half.

The basic premise of large economy strategies is that protected markets at home can permit economies of scale and scope. At the same time, they allow the luxury of allocative inefficiency for extended periods of time – high-cost production need not represent a binding restriction on inward-oriented growth. Ultimately, a statically inefficient industrial sector may become the base for breaking into world trade with import-substituted products, as suggested by Turkey's example during the 1980s.

Big countries have an internal economic space which it is socially efficient to explore, even if there are welfare losses in the form of distortions from world prices and limited access to a variety of goods. In the long run, confrontation with external competition makes sense (as the Turkish experience demonstrates), but large countries have the freedom to pick a place and time. In the medium term, intelligent use of multi-tiered pricing systems and targetted incentives along Indian lines (Alagh, 1991) can help transform an industry with an unbalanced capital stock into something closer to a potential world competitor. With a few hundred million people making up a potentially dynamic internal market, there is no compelling reason to jump into external liberalization *tout court*.

III   THE MACROECONOMIC FOUNDATION

Internally generated imbalances are mostly attributed to policy mismanagement and are seen as the centrepiece of a macroeconomic disequilibrium in the MFAD. Excessive government spending in Brazil in the 1970s and the surge of private spending during the import/speculative finance boom in Chile in the early 1980s are presented as typical examples.

Shifts in the terms of trade are emphasized as causes of disequilibria originating outside the national economy with commodity booms inducing governments to raise expenditures, drive up the price of non-traded goods relative to that of traded ones, and draw labour and capital away from production of tradables. The real value of the currency appreciates[10] and the economy starts to suffer "Dutch disease". There is also the tendency for increases in state spending to outrun revenue gains from a trade windfall.

The advice coming from the MFAD on how to avoid boom and bust episodes is to pursue policies that do not give rise to big macro imbalances, adjust quickly, respond cautiously to shifts in the terms of trade and keep spending consistent with permanent income. The conclusion that naturally follows is that independently of whether the origin of macroeconomic problems is internal or external, all disequilibria express themselves as excesses of domestic absorption over income. Taking into account caveats regarding adverse short-run consequences on growth and inflation the MFAD recommends the usual IMF package to restore equilibrium.

This vision of the macroeconomic problems of developing countries suffers from conceptual inconsistencies; moreover, country experiences that are supposed to support the MFAD's macro framework in fact do not easily fit into it. As a consequence, the recommendations for stabilization policy that follow on from it are unpersuasive.

III.1 Macroeconomic disequilibrium

While the macroeconomics underpinning the MFAD recognizes that an adequate supply of external capital is essential, international capital market conditions are not given a significant role in accounting for macro disequilibrium. For instance, in discussions of Latin American macroeconomic strategies, the abrupt jump in international interest rates and rationing of credit markets in the early 1980s are often not even mentioned. Nor is any emphasis placed on the easy credit conditions of the 1970s, when commercial banks so aggressively pushed loans that they created a Dutch disease problem throughout the developing world.[11]

When imperfections (the existence of rationing) and volatility in international capital markets are seriously taken into account, advice to keep spending in line with permanent income borders on being vacuous. While policy advice to smooth the cycles caused by fluctuations in the terms of trade and to save export excesses may be prudent, the question is how to do it.

If the domestic financial market is thin, an attempt on the part of the central bank to sterilize reserve inflows resulting from a favourable shock could create serious imbalances; on the real side of the economy, it would be virtually impossible to avoid higher absorption. If a seriously indebted country attempts to place extra funds in the international capital market, commercial banks are likely to exert pressure on it to retire debt. The obvious question is whether it would be permitted to borrow when times turned bad. With rationed credit markets, that option may not be at hand.[13]

It *is* true that internal imbalances tend to be associated with policy mismanagement, not excluding past reform attempts along market-friendly lines. The latter "mistakes" are, however, studiously ignored by the MFAD's interpretation of internal shocks. For example, a veil is often drawn over the Chilean crisis of 1980–1 which followed the failure of a financial liberalization exercise in the late 1970s. Indeed, the Chilean case merits careful study by market-friendly scholars, since the economy went into external imbalance when the public sector was running a surplus of 5 per cent of GDP and reforms of the sort they recommend had been put into place.

The problem was that despite "sound" policy, the private sector chose to run a deficit of 16 per cent of GDP, leading via a speculative financial boom to a major crash. As already discussed, public debt from state intervention in the financial system plus lender-of-last resort activities still amounts to 30 per cent of GDP, while a good part of the government's foreign debt has the same origin.[13] *Mutatis mutandis*, a similar story could be told about countries like Argentina and the Philippines.

Thinking of macro disequilibria as problems of excess absorption is not always wrong, but it can be distracting; this mindset blocks the MFAD from seeing aspects of imbalance created by the debt crisis. Excess absorption clearly did *not* create large trade surpluses (as percentages of GDP) in highly indebted countries during the 1980s – as illustrated by the numbers in Table 8.1, they simply had to make the corresponding external transfers. Countries such as Argentina and Brazil which did not receive external finance slipped into macro disequilibrium; countries like Chile which did receive external donor support fared much better.

In order to highlight how interlinkages among external shocks, internal (especially fiscal) factors, and the structural features of developing economies can lead to macroeconomic imbalance, many economists have recently started using a variant of the dual gap model, but adding a third fiscal/financial constraint to the specification.[14]

The liberalization literature postulates that if institutional obstacles are removed, a market economy will attain an equilibrium position by itself. The new gaps approach, on the contrary, considers that disequilibrium phenomena may or may not persist after barriers to the free working of market forces are taken away.[15] The outcome will depend on whether or not market signals by themselves induce economic actors to close the gaps; this in turn will be determined by structural features of the economy.

For instance, liberalizing the foreign exchange market might lead to hyperinflation if the stock/flow disequilibrium between foreign liabilities and national income is large. Gap models do not *a priori* disregard explosive paths

Table 8.1 Developing country trade, investment and savings flows (percentages of GDP).

	Investment					Saving			
	Intermediate imports	Foreign capital goods	Domestic capital goods	Public sector	Private sector	Total	Public sector	Private sector	Trade deficit
Argentina (1988)	6.0	1.8	12.6	7.6	6.8	14.4	0.8	15.6	−2.0
Brazil	3.8	2.1	17.9	6.2	13.8	20.0	6.2	18.3	−4.5
Chile (1988)	14.9	6.8	11.6	7.9	10.5	18.4	5.7	15.6	−2.9
Colombia (1988)	5.4	3.5	14.6	7.1	11.0	18.1	4.0	16.7	−2.6
India (1988)	4.5	2.4	20.8	12.7	10.5	23.2	2.4	18.9	1.9
S. Korea (1987)	24.7	15.7	13.9	6.2	23.4	29.6	11.1	28.5	−10.0
Malaysia (1988)	22.1	11.5	11.7	9.3	13.9	23.2	5.9	27.5	−10.2
Mexico (1988)	7.9	2.5	18.1	6.4	14.2	20.6	4.2	20.1	−3.7
Nicaragua (1989)	17.5	12.1	12.1	2.1	22.1	24.2	−2.0	9.5	16.7
Nigeria (1986)	1.7	3.8	8.1	7.6	4.3	11.9	3.1	8.9	−0.1
Philippines (1988)	11.4	4.4	13.8	3.0	15.2	18.2	0.0	19.2	−1.0
Sri Lanka (1987)	11.5	6.5	19.9	14.9	11.5	26.4	4.4	18.0	4.0
Tanzania (1986)	5.7	11.9	15.0	8.3	18.6	26.9	5.6	11.8	9.5
Thailand (1987)	9.8	8.6	15.0	6.7	16.9	23.6	5.4	19.7	−1.5
Turkey (1987)	13.5	1.0	24.4	13.3	12.1	25.4	8.2	19.5	−2.3
Uganda (1987)	5.6	8.6	8.4	3.9	13.1	17.0	−5.6	16.0	6.6
Zambia (1987)	30.7	8.0	2.7	7.7	3.0	10.7	−16.7	32.5	−5.1
Zimbabwe (1986)	11.1	7.1	15.4	11.9	10.6	22.5	−5.1	30.9	−3.3

Source: WIDER.

that may occur during adjustment processes, or the possibility that free markets could lead to a "bottom of the well" equilibrium with stagnant growth and persistent unemployment.

Indeed, gap models are designed explicitly to incorporate the diverse structural characteristics of developing economies. At least five sets of factors often contribute to macroeconomic imbalance, as pointed out in the recent WIDER country studies summarized in Taylor (1992). Table 8.1 presents numerical evidence for the following conclusions:

(1) The public sector plays an important role in capital formation in all the countries, from free market bastions like Chile and Malaysia to statist India, Turkey, and Zimbabwe. As we have already noted, public investment typically facilitates or "crowds in" private capital formation. For macro programming, public capital formation may be the only vehicle for stimulating investment after adverse shocks. Unless export growth pulls investment demand up in a cumulative process along Korean lines (certainly an outlying case among developing economies), it is hard to see how private capital formation will recuperate in and of itself.

(2) The public sector is typically a strong net saver. The only exceptions are macroeconomically distressed Nicaragua, Uganda, and Zambia, along with Zimbabwe where for historical reasons the private saving rate is abnormally high. Saving by the public sector reflects its activity in capital formation, as well as the unique ability of the state to gather resources. This developing country pattern resembles that in some industrialized nations, which historically have arrived at diverse institutional means for generating savings (Kosonen, 1991).

(3) Private savings flows are also large. They must be intermediated into capital formation and/or loans to the state to cover the public sector borrowing requirement (PSBR). This process can lurch into imbalance if a fall in the demand for domestic assets squeezes credit to the public sector or for private investment projects.

(4) Most economies in the WIDER sample have negative trade deficits, i.e. surpluses. In many cases, these reflect foreign shocks suffered in the 1980s. Latin American and other countries had to run surpluses to meet foreign interest obligations at the same time as their governments needed fiscal surpluses, since they had nationalized foreign debt. This "double transfer" problem crippled stabilization efforts and fiscal rectitude.

(5) The last point to be noted is the extreme import-dependence of developing economies. Taking into account the negative effect of a nation's size on its trade shares, which was discussed above, the proportions of both intermediate and capital goods imports in GDP are large, especially in East Asian economies such as Korea, Malaysia, Thailand, and the Philippines.

In all LDCs, capital goods and intermediate imports are essentially "non-competitive", in the sense that they and similar products are not produced nationally, but they can play different strategic roles. Malaysia and Thailand, for example, increasingly are serving as platforms for assembly of exportable final goods by Japanese firms. Korea's big import shares reflect poor natural resource endowments and a hypertrophied industrial sector. Elsewhere, as in India and Brazil, intermediate imports shares are low because they are large countries which have long pursued ISI.

The dynamic macroeconomic behaviour of developing economies is strongly affected by these features, especially when they are hit by external shocks. A sudden cut-off of credits or a significant fall in the terms of trade, besides leading to devaluation and inflation, is likely to cause reductions in both output and investment. Three-gap models emphasize the following channels:

(1) The data in Table 8.1 suggest that by limiting imports, scarce foreign exchange squeezes either current production or capital formation, since local commodity production requires imported intermediates while foreign-made capital goods are an essential component in most investment projects.

(2) At the same time, capital inflows are a source of saving, which has to be replaced domestically if it is curtailed. As discussed in detail below, the required reduction in aggregate demand is often realized through an acceleration in inflation.

(3) Fewer funds will be flowing through the financial system, reducing the supply of credit and therefore capital formation.

Precisely because international capital markets are imperfect, the economy tends to adjust to reduced point-in-time availability of foreign exchange via output reductions mediated by faster inflation and domestic credit rationing.[16] For the time being, the much more efficient possibility of smoothing this dynamic by temporarily increasing external indebtedness is not available to most developing economies – regardless of whether policy-makers have clear perceptions of their countries' permanent incomes or not.

III.2 Stabilization policy

The International Monetary Fund has a responsibility for stabilizing economies that turn to it. Despite recent rhetorical softening, its programmes have not fundamentally changed: they still aim at cutting the inflation rate and the trade deficit by restraining aggregate demand through fiscal and monetary austerity. Without fundamental changes in international credit conditions, there is a risk that IMF-inspired adjustment policies will drive their recipients toward prolonged "stabilized stagnation", because they ignore crucial macroeconomic factors such as linked foreign exchange and fiscal constraints, financial fragility, and the dynamics of the inflation process.

III.2.1   *Austerity and the linkages between the fiscal and foreign constraints*

Not untypical of the market-friendly approach, the WDR 1991 states that:

> experience shows that when government spending has expanded too far, the result has often been large deficits, excessive borrowing or monetary expansion which has been quickly followed by inflation, chronic overvaluation of the currency, the loss of export competitiveness. Excessive borrowing can also lead to domestic and external debt problems and to crowding out of private investment.
>
> (World Bank, 1991, p. 8)

This view of the causes and effects of fiscal duress presupposes that macroeconomic disequilibrium uniquely results from an imbalance between domestic income and absorption; it implies that adjusting the fiscal deficit is sufficient to restore stability. It is wrong, because it ignores structural features linking the saving, external, and fiscal gaps, and it thereby understates the complexity of stabilization, especially if stagnation is to be avoided.

The analysis is particularly inappropriate for highly indebted economies, where policy is constrained by two new stylized facts that emerged during the past decade. The first is that the nature of the external constraint has changed. Before the debt crisis, periodic external imbalances caused short-run instability but did not impede growth in the long run. From time to time, scarce foreign exchange did induce misalignment between income and absorption; IMF-style policies helped restore foreign balance without completely stopping accumulation over time.

Since the debt crisis, however, external disequilibrium has become structural. It is not being generated by differences between flows of income and spending, but from a stock-flow disequilibrium between foreign obligations and current income as reflected by a high debt/GDP ratio. While, previously, scarce foreign exchange used to create liquidity squeezes in the short run, during the 1980s chronic trade surpluses reflected a solvency as opposed to a liquidity problem. The result is negative long-run growth, rather than a recession for a limited period of time.

The second stylized fact is that the external crisis assumed a fiscal form. In most highly indebted economies, governments hold nearly all the external obligations; therefore, solvency problems fall into the hands of the public sector. The impact effect of the crisis was to raise ratios of the stock of public debt to current revenue to unsustainable levels.

In order to reduce their exposure, governments reacted by slashing expenditures, including public investment. This fall in capital formation still "crowded-in" private investment – but in reverse. Via the third gap, the government budget constraint became an independent restriction on growth. An essential question for the 1990s will be how to restore public investment in physical and human capital with associated externalities, while at the same time maintaining fiscal responsibility.

Because of the strong linkage between fiscal weakness and external solvency, the two problems have to be addressed simultaneously. Using three-gap models simulated over time, it is easy to see that if fiscal and solvency difficulties are not jointly resolved, then the economy is almost certain to stagnate due to inadequate capital formation at the same time as ratios of external and internal debt to potential GDP shoot up toward infinity (Fanelli and Frenkel, 1992). Bolivia, Uruguay, and numerous other small, primary exporting economies are observable examples.

Countries that had severe external shocks but succeeded in restoring growth all utilized foreign exchange up front – examples in Latin America are Colombia, Chile, and Mexico – and benefited from other favourable circumstances, which included the ability of the state to tap natural resource rents, as in Colombia, Chile and Mexico.

Countries that avoided major disruptions (mostly in Asia) were relatively balanced in fiscal terms and in some cases lucky. Exchange rates in ASEAN countries, apart from the Philippines, weakened against the yen after the mid-1980s, since they were pegged to the dollar. They also received ample DFI from Japan and the diversifying newly industrialized economies. This foreign investment financed capital goods and intermediate imports, which fed into export growth.

Continuing inflows even permitted repeated botched stabilizations while adjustment proceeded apace: Chile between 1973 and 1985 and Turkey in the early 1980s are cases in point. The stabilize-then-adjust sequence recommended by the MFAD may be common, but is not essential; such a smooth progression is certainly unlikely if a country is expected to attempt reform entirely by itself.

III.2.2 Demonetization

Another problem for national economies is the disarticulation of finance. Debt and terms of trade shocks led to demonetization, as inflation accelerated and capital flight increased. The natural consequence was "dollarization" of financial relationships, which in turn created an inconsistency between the demand for and supply of financial assets (i.e. it created excess demand for external assets and excess supply of domestic ones). Movements of the relevant rates of return were unable to restore equilibrium without driving both the public and part of the private sector toward insolvency.[17]

Since the main source of supply of domestic assets is the government, these portfolio adjustments made it extremely difficult to finance the public deficit . . . for a given national propensity to save, dollarization and the denationalization of savings put a tighter financial limit on the public sector than would otherwise have occurred. Solving this problem will take more than mere remonetization, if and when inflation is contained; there has to be renewed access to foreign finance. Official lenders can play a fundamental role in providing credits to restore growth before (and to assist) the restoration of creditworthiness and the reversal of capital flight. That is, they can decisively support government investment and restructuring of the public finances.

III.2.3   Anti-inflation policy

Although inflation may have negative effects on information, income distribution, and the efficiency of the financial system, there are risks involved in stopping inflation on the basis of a fixed exchange rate.

Inflation may act as a disequilibrium process that plays a crucial role in closing (*ex-post*) the gaps in a highly imbalanced macroeconomic setting. This issue is essential precisely because in one developing country after another, inflation has accelerated as the economy has sought some sort of macro balance after suffering an adverse foreign shock.

Steady price increases amount to a crude but effective means of cutting aggregate demand to an externally constrained level of supply, via the "inflation tax" on money balances (which ultimately proves self-defeating, as people and firms reduce cash holdings to a few per cent of GDP) and "forced saving" resulting from inflation-induced income redistribution against low savers (real wages have fallen by more than 50 per cent in economies all over Africa and Latin America). In Argentina and elsewhere, unexpected accelerations in inflation helped stave off massive bankruptcy by reducing the real liabilities of heavily indebted economic actors in both the public and private sectors.

In several Latin American countries, the "equilibrating" role of faster inflation had major institutional implications. Because of the spread of implicit or explicit contract indexation, a high inflation regime came to be established, making anti-inflation policy a central social question.

Broadly speaking, there are only five ways to break a cumulative inflation process:

(1) Relative prices can be manipulated – for example, the exchange rate can be allowed to appreciate in real terms or the real wage to fall. Ultimately the nominal wage and/or exchange rate has to be held fairly stable as an anchor against further price increases.

(2) Imports can be increased to ease local supply bottlenecks, at least for internationally traded goods. Often, purchases abroad (and capital flight) must be financed by the central bank as it spends reserves to support an exchange rate pegged as a price anchor.

(3) Incomes policies and other forms of market intervention can be deployed to muffle the most acutely conflicting social claims. The most obvious example is a "social pact" to reduce wage inflation while holding profit claims in line.

(4) In a more extreme case, a price freeze plus contract de-indexation can be attempted as a policy "surprise".

(5) Austerity can be applied, a cut in the public sector borrowing requirement coupled with monetary restriction based on increased interest rates and credit restraint.

As noted above, the MFAD leans toward austerity, but successful anti-inflation packages always combine several of the listed measures. Each economy's inflation process is unique, making it difficult to generalize about which policies will be effective in any specific case. However, a few observations are worth making.

Austerity is likely to work better when "most" market transactions occur in a regime of flexible prices, in circumstances where mark-up pricing and contract indexation are not widely spread. In practice, the IMF often combines austerity with real wage cuts, reductions in income support programmes and subsidies. All these measures reduce demand, so that the outcomes include output contraction and a lower trade deficit (via import cuts) along with slower inflation.

The relative impacts of austerity and associated measures on inflation, output, and the external deficit are of obvious importance; experience, unfortunately, suggests that regressive income redistribution and output losses may come rapidly, while inflation reduction can be slow. An unpublicized aspect of the orthodox Bolivian stabilization of the mid-1980s was its heavy-handed repression of public sector wages and of the tin-miners' union (Pastor, 1991).

Combining austerity with incomes policies has been a recipe for success in other circumstances. Mexico, for example, blended a modicum of demand restriction with heterodox shocks in successful packages. A social pact was included which was more or less democratically ratified and there was massive foreign exchange support from reserves built up over several years of austerity. These conditions are somewhat unusual – to say the least – and also underline the difficulties of co-ordinating several policies simultaneously in the fight against inflation.

III.2.4   The external gap and exchange rate policy

Within the MFAD, maintaining a competitive exchange rate is seen as one of the most important guarantees for achieving a sound closure of the external gap. The problem is that the pre-stabilization situation often includes an overly strong exchange rate, making it necessary to devalue early on.

Devaluation has complicated, economy-wide effects. By increasing import costs, it may be price inflationary and output contractionary. However, if foreign exchange is a severe constraint, the outcomes may go the other way; *any* net export response to depreciation generates scarce dollars which can be used to reduce excess demand by allowing intermediate imports and production to rise, with a corresponding reduction in inflation.

A reasoned judgement about the likely effects of devaluation is essential to the design of stabilization programmes. If any rule applies, it might be that small, open economies which are externally constrained are more likely to respond favourably to a devaluation/capital inflow package than are large, closed ones.

Problems also arise in co-ordinating devaluation with other policies, in both stabilization and adjustment contexts. For anti-inflation purposes, the exchange rate may be frozen as a nominal anchor. But then if inflation continues, there will be real currency appreciation. Imports will rise and export growth decline, upsetting the real side of the economy, as in numerous failed stabilization attempts in Latin America over the past two decades.

With regard to fiscal policy, if depreciation is expansionary, then it can usefully be combined with austerity. The exchange rate change improves the trade balance, while fiscal policy helps avoid inflationary excess demand. If devaluation is contractionary, on the other hand, combining it with austerity can lead to a sort of policy overkill.

A further question is whether devaluation will by itself markedly improve trade performance. A considered answer might well be in the negative. Getting rid of extreme price distortions appears to be a necessary condition for (or at least is correlated with) greater "tradability" of domestic activities. However, as argued below, price incentives are never sufficient. A real exchange rate with a reasonable and stable value is an invaluable stimulant to net exports, but it must be supplemented with directed trade promotion, policies such as tax drawbacks, export subsidies and cheap credits, as well as state interventions to improve infrastructure and the economic environment more generally.

Finally, how should the real exchange rate be held stable? Crawling peg policies involving frequent nominal mini-devaluations to keep the exchange rate in line with the domestic price level have a fairly respectable track record in all corners of the developing world. The outcomes of exchange auctions have been spotty, since they lead at times to speculative surges of consumer imports.

Besides the exchange rate itself, one also has to consider the implications for stabilization of commercial and capital market policy. Import quotas can be intelligently deployed to offset external shocks; they can also play a pivotal role in industrial policy. Changes in trade regimes can bring substantial benefits, effectively widening forex bottlenecks and perhaps reducing incentives for smuggling, but removing exchange controls in general can prove an open invitation to capital flight. All such possibilities have to be weighed in terms of the history and institutions of the specific economy under consideration.

IV   STRUCTURAL REFORM AND THE PRIORITIES
FOR ACTION

According to MFAD, there is a neat division of labour between stabilization and structural reform. Stabilization policies work mainly on the demand side to reduce inflation and external deficits. Structural policies focus on addressing the efficiency of resource use and emphasizing reforms in specific sectors, especially trade, finance, and industry. Generally it is believed that reforms should be implemented in a specific order. Macroeconomic stabilization comes at the outset and can either precede or accompany structural reform. This is followed by liberalization of product markets, and trade. In the area of the liberalization of the external sector, the trade account is seen as best preceding the capital account. Asset markets adjust faster than good markets, so the premature deregulation of capital flows can lead to speculation and financial instability.

The arguments supporting these recommendations, however, are not neat and tidy, and signal that the task of stabilizing and reforming an economy is much less a science than an art.

IV.1 The art of policy sequencing

Are there really any solid arguments supporting the inevitability (and thereby "desirability") of the sequence of steps from stabilization via reform to growth outlined above? In principle, the answer to any such question has to be ambiguous, on both theoretical and empirical grounds.

In the first place, the implicit division of labour between the IMF and the World Bank, with the former dealing with stabilization and the latter designing the policy package for growth, has no firm basis in theory. The only attempt to combine the Bank's and the Fund's approaches that Fischer (1987) quotes in his survey of policies for development is by Khan et al. (1986).[18] The problem is that while the market-friendly strategy heavily relies on adjustment of relative prices to get a better resource allocation, this mechanism is scarcely mentioned by Khan and associates.

Secondly, as Michalopoulos (1987) clearly recognizes in a paper advocating World Bank programmes for adjustment and growth, great uncertainty is unavoidable when reforms are implemented, precisely because little is known about their likely dynamic effects.

At least two sets of considerations are relevant here, regarding (i) the sequencing of policy measures aimed at stabilization and those that focus on adjustment, and (ii) the optimal sequence of reforms to remove distortions when they are present throughout the economic system. We are back to the question of how stabilization and adjustment interact. If economic theory offers scant guidance about an optimal sequence for removing market distortions, then why should one assume a priori that the dynamics of the process will never be explosive? How can one even evaluate the benefits and costs of policy reform?

With regard to the dynamics question, recent experience in Latin America suggests that one cannot a priori rule out rapidly rising debt/income ratios, inflation rates, and other indicators of instability when orthodox packages are imposed. Costs and benefits are no less relevant. "Mistakes" in sequencing financial, trade, and capital account liberalizations in the Southern Cone in the late 1970s cost countries in the region tens of billions of dollars in terms of increased foreign debt. Was it wiser to pay the price of these failed liberalizing "global shock treatments" than to move away gradually from repressed economic structures? More successful adjustment in Colombia over the 1980s relied upon piecemeal changes, as opposed to immediate eradication of the ISI development model. These examples suggest that a degree of risk aversion may be advisable with regard to massive changes in policy design.

Then there is the question of whether "sound" domestic policies will call forth external financing, from official sources or even from commercial lenders via Brady-like initiatives. In Latin America, countries like Uruguay, Bolivia, and even Mexico undertook deep reforms but external money arrived in amounts too limited to restore growth and only after long delays. Latin American external debt now totals over $500 billion, while inflows under the Brady Plan at most will amount to $20–25 billion. In 1991–2 international interest rates were far more important than concessionary support from international creditors. Argentina could, for example, receive a reduction in interest payments of about $1 billion under the Brady Plan, while each percentage point fall in international interest rates saves the country $0.6 billion, or 5 per cent of its total exports.

The fact remains that countries which received financial support *and* were successful in boosting saving (especially public saving) were able to grow. In Korea, Turkey, and Chile, for example, resources were reallocated with an ample savings flow at hand from domestic sources or abroad.[19] But elsewhere, Uruguay and Bolivia sought to liberalize markets but have very low savings and investment levels. Fully in accord with the Smithian and Keynesian analytical traditions discussed above, until there was an upward blip in capital movements toward Latin America in 1991, these countries did not resume growth.[20]

IV.2 Structural reforms

Not only are there doubts about the sequencing of MFAD reforms but there are also major unsettled questions about the content of reforms.

IV.2.1 Trade policy reform

Sustained growth in many countries has taken place with distorted trade regimes, trade policy shifts were overwhelmed by macroeconomic forces in the determination of LDC growth rates during the 1980s, and most formal models show that eliminating distortions is likely to be of second-order significance anyway: "trade policy orientation, while important, may not be a dominant determinant of growth and may not therefore deserve the attention that the World Bank and others have given it" (Helleiner, 1990).

Despite all these objections, liberalizing trade is an essential component of the MFAD. It is interesting to explore the intellectual rationale, and inquire whether the underlying economic model can be restated to make it more relevant to historical developing country experience.

The MFAD position basically rests on textbook theorems about how interventions should be designed. If an economy is initially very distorted (say from an extended period of ISI with a high and complicated tariff structure and/or strict import quotas), most economists agree that steps should be taken to simplify and perhaps cut back on the interventions. There *is* professional consensus in this regard; the problem is that different authors' policy remedies diverge. Evans (1991) suggests that the market-friendly pharmacopoeia can be listed as follows:

(1) The mainstream recognizes arguments for intervention, such as nurturing infant industries, attempts to repel foreign dumping (however defined), and optimal export taxes. However, in terms of complexity, red tape, and inflexibility, quotas and tariffs aimed at correcting these problems may well proliferate beyond reason under ISI.

(2) When there is a market imperfection, the corrective policy should be applied as "closely" to it as possible – for example, a subsidy for an infant industry makes more sense than a tariff, since the latter will induce a by-product consumption distortion.

(3) Under competition in the standard Heckscher-Ohlin model, an import quota has an "equivalent" tariff, which will let the same quantity of foreign goods enter. Since the government gets the tariff's proceeds, while producers benefit from quota rents, the tariff may be preferable.

(4) If producers have market power, they can squeeze extra rents from a quota. If they go in for rent-seeking (directly unproductive profit-seeking) by devoting productive resources to lobby for more quotas, this form of protection looks even less desirable.

(5) All this leads to standard sequence of recommended policies: first, there should be macroeconomic stabilization; thereafter, quotas should be "tariffized", and the tariff schedule simplified to two or three rates in the 10–50 per cent range, sufficient to provide some protection and generate revenue.

(6) As part of the exercise, there will probably have to be real exchange depreciation to hold the trade deficit constant as quota/tariff protection is cut back. For this reason, capital market liberalization which may lead to appreciation should be postponed.

It is impossible to refute these arguments on their own terms; as often in neoclassical formulations, they sound like limpid practical reason. Their deficiencies lie in incompatibilities between their underlying assumptions and the world as it really functions. One clear example is the implicit orthodox presumption that rent-seeking activity is solely a response to state interventions, although the private sector readily generates its own distortions and rents through the monopolization of markets.

Secondly, the model treats its "distortions" as small perturbations to an economy assumed to be at full employment with investment determined by available saving (perhaps mediated by a variable interest rate). When these hypotheses are relaxed in investment-driven growth models, protection to a given sector can easily lead to faster overall expansion if it leads to a spurt in investment demand and/or endogenous technical advance. In a fully neoclassical framework, the saving counterpart can come from reshuffling intertemporal budget constraints (Buffie, 1991) and in a Kaleckian model from increased output, or else income and wealth redistributions under inflation.

Finally, this approach does not incorporate the LDC trade patterns pointed out in connection with Table 8.1. Yet programming the level and composition of non-competitive intermediate and capital goods imports has been key to the success of developmentalist states. Brazil used protection and licensing to build an automobile sector, which flourished until the economy was derailed macroeconomically in the 1980s (Shapiro, 1991).

Pack and Westphal (1986) emphasize that interlinked factors underlie such examples of successful state intervention at the micro level. Technology is imperfectly tradable, since local producers and workers have to gain know-how to operate physical capital goods which are not produced at home. There are economies of scale in both production and technology acquisition, and externalities among output levels, prices, and technical choice. Room is created for intervention, which can be rationalized in neoclassical terms, especially if it creates two-way information flows among regulators and producers, which raise productivity efficiency as they expand. Evans (1991) underlines the following implications:

(1) Protection is justified, and may be programmed more effectively if it is based on quotas. Quota rents on strategic, technology-bearing imports can help subsidize export activity. Quotas on competitive imports turn the national market into a place for profitable learning. Costs can be held down if firms are exposed to foreign competition on the export side; real wage increases force the cost reductions to come from productivity advance.

(2) Rent-seeking may characterize the process of allocating quotas, but ultimately they can be tied to export and output performance. Ideology and public pressure can help keep DUP within "reasonable" bounds.

(3)   Two-way flows of information between firms and policy-makers are essential.

If a well-designed quota allocation system under this second line of policy action leads firms to use strategic inputs to acquire technology and expand non-traditional exports, it may well raise potential output faster than MFAD trade reform (especially if investment responds). Moreover, it allows for more decentralized decision-making than liberalization imposed from the top. Guessing tariff equivalents of quotas, phasing the liberalization to avoid bankrupting viable domestic producers by taking away effective protection, and getting the exchange rate "right" are not easy tasks. Policy-makers can never be in a practical position to solve realistically dynamic computable general equilibrium models to reprogramme the price system in a liberalization "shock".

The implication is that interventionist policies have been and can be effectively utilized, which is more than can be said for orthodox reforms such as that in Argentina in the late 1970s which got its effective protection and other incentive signals all wrong. As we have already observed, this neo-liberal "mistake" aborted economic growth for at least a decade.

By contrast, on the other side of the Andes, a rhetorically *laissez-faire* government's public investments in copper mines and quiet promotion policies for fruits, forestry products, and fisheries laid the base for Chile's export boom after 1985. These interventionist steps were taken while the economy reeled through a twelve-year sequence of disastrous stabilization experiments amply supported by the Bank and Fund. The stabilize-then-adjust sequence was exactly reversed (Meller, 1991).

Of course, there have been interventionist failures as well. The implication for both sides is that there is room for debate about such questions, while the World Bank asserts that convincing support exists for "a general statistical association between less intervention and lower price distortions on the one hand and higher productivity growth on the other" (World Bank, 1991, p. 99). Rodrik's (1992) summary of the evidence is that "if truth-in-advertising were to apply to policy advice, each prescription for trade liberalization would be accompanied with a disclaimer: 'Warning! Trade liberalization cannot be shown to enhance technical efficiency; nor has it been empirically demonstrated to do so.' "

IV.3   Financial reform

Financial restructuring is another broad plank in the market-friendly platform, although the routes by which savings flows are intermediated into capital formation through financial markets are often ill-defined. Their basic policy suggestions are just to increase interest rates and deregulate the system. As observed by UNCTAD (1991), the goal again is to enhance allocative efficiency, in the sense that returns on financial saving instruments and investment projects should tend toward equality, presumably with the marginal product of physical capital.

Just as price liberalization does not ensure that firms will efficiently produce commodities, there is no particular reason to expect that removing wedges separating rates of return will guarantee a low-cost supply of financial services. Usually when it has been applied, in fact, this reform package has *reduced* productive efficiency in finance, leading to increased credit costs. The outcomes also included stagflation (lower capacity utilization, coupled with faster inflation), a fall in investment demand, and a speculative flurry ending in a financial crash.

The MFAD model of finance has the same basic shortcoming as its counterpart for trade and industrial policy: it ignores existing market structures. In most developing economies, the "formal" financial sector comprises public institutions, large private enterprises, and banks. Financial claims typically have short maturities, and the ratio of the outstanding value of either assets or liabilities to GDP is a fraction of those observed in industrialized economies. Although their size is difficult to judge, informal markets may account for as much as one-half of total credit outstanding. Loans to the private sector from both formal and informal intermediaries to a large extent pay for working capital; investment finance comes from internal funds, the state, or informal sources.

The typical initial conditions for a high interest rate/deregulation package include ceilings on nominal interest rates, and directed formal sector credit allocations by sector and form of use. Immediately imposing a reform gives the following sorts of results:

(1) Getting rid of ceilings on bank deposit rates removes a nominal anchor on the pricing system. Particularly if the external capital account has been deregulated, the alternative to a bank deposit in a citizen's portfolio is a foreign holding. The equivalent domestic return equals the foreign interest rate plus the expected rate of exchange depreciation plus a premium for higher risk. Such an alternative puts a floor under the local deposit rate which is usually strongly positive in real terms. Deposit institutions have to pass on their higher costs into interest rates on their loans.

(2) Eliminating credit targets in the absence of effective prudential regulation leads banks towards high-risk/high-return loans (a moral hazard made more acute if the government implicitly promises that failing banks will be rescued). The proportion of non-performing loans in bank portfolios rises; the implicit cost has to be carried by debtors still meeting their obligations.

(3) Higher interest rates on loans for working capital tend to be passed

on by firms into higher prices (especially if they have market power, common enough under ISI). Since production costs rise, supply may also be reduced, giving rise to stagflation. Higher lending rates and lower output constrict investment demand.

(4) More attractive deposit rates can also pull funds from the informal market, reducing its credit flows and raising kerb or bazaar borrowing costs with unfavourable effects on output and prices.

(5) Although banks can (up to a point) protect themselves from these developments by raising the spread between borrowing and lending rates, the same is not true of their borrowers. The financial position of the private productive sector becomes more precarious, while a higher proportion of the government's fiscal receipts must be dedicated to interest payments on its internal liabilities outstanding. Refinancing these flows can reach manic dimensions as in the "overnight" market in Brazil during the 1980s. Profits on turning over the federal debt made bankers partisans of inflation in that country, a peculiar and risky situation.

(6) The Brazil example suggests that with high interest rates and low investment, speculative holdings become attractive. Turkey had Ponzi schemes[21] around bank CDs, Chile a stock market boom for shares of prematurely privatized public firms (financed by loans from banks central to economic "groups" whose owners used the money to bid up prices of their own companies' equity) and Argentina destabilizing flows of foreign exchange. In all cases, speculation went together with deteriorating enterprise balance sheets to pave the way for a crash. As we have seen, the taxpayers ended up with bills amounting to tens of per cent of GDP to put the financial system back together.

During the past ten to fifteen years, scenarios along these lines have played out in other countries as well as providing a substantial list of neo-liberal "mistakes" to be added to those involving trade policy. A more gradual reform in South Korea avoided a débâcle, while after presiding over a stock market boom and crash around the early 1980s, the Chilean government later took advantage of ample support from its donors to privatize once again, restructure its internal debt, and set up an effective pension fund programme to capture savings flows. From these experiences and those of now developed economies, can anything sensible be said about productively efficient directions for LDC financial evolution?

One option that immediately presents itself is that of modernizing the development bank institution with due care to avoid rent-seeking and inflationary finance for the benefit of chronically derelict parastatals. Since (especially after fiscal restructuring) development banks can tap public savings flows, they fit naturally with the public/private patterns of saving and capital formation set out in Table 8.1.

Another idea worth pursuing is effective regulation and support of the bank-centred conglomerates which are common in the Third World, so that internal economies of scale and information flows can lead to low credit costs within the group.

IV.3.1 Privatization

Across nations, different historical divisions among public, local, private, and foreign ownership of productive enterprises have emerged. Although the MFAD favours privatization, there is no solid evidence that firms of one type are consistently more efficient in static terms than those of another. Dynamically, scholars such as Amsden (1989) argue that Korea's home-owned but publicly-subsidized private conglomerates are more adept at indigenizing technology than TNC affiliates, while in Brazil before the last decade public enterprises were effective motors for capital accumulation and technical change (Shapiro, 1991; Carneiro and Werneck, 1992).

In economic terms, the effects of privatization on savings and investment flows will be the only ones amenable to evaluation for years – changes in productive efficiency will be difficult to trace, and in any case do not seem likely in the absence of financial market reforms and joint public sector/labour/ management efforts to raise productivity growth. Finally, despite vigorous declarations of intent, outside Chile, Mexico, and Turkey, not much privatization has in fact taken place.

Even calculations of savings and investment effects are tricky, when discounting is taken into account. Marcel (1989) argues, for example, that in Chile's 1985–8 second go at privatization, firms were sold at below their present value, and half the receipts were allocated to uses such as tax reduction. In other words, there were probably no positive impacts on capital formation, along with a flow portfolio shift from public liabilities toward enterprise equity on the part of the private and external sectors.

More generally, local private sectors can finance acquisitions of public firms in just four ways:

(1) an increase in private saving;
(2) a fall in private investment;
(3) a decrease in private sector flow demand for financial assets;
(4) an increase in private sector flow demand for credit.

Alternative (1) could be helpful for growth if accompanied by a jump in investment. The public sector would probably have to be the motor, taking into account the crowding-in effects discussed above. In other words, privatizing governments should reinvest the proceeds, instead of following

Chile's example of cutting the current fiscal deficit. This observation becomes doubly relevant if under alternative (2) the private sector cuts its own capital formation to take over public firms.

Alternative (3) is more likely than (4), especially in countries where financial markets have contracted in the wake of adverse shocks. But then the government will find it increasingly difficult to place its own liabilities, provoking it to create money or bear higher interest burdens or both. As in the Chilean case, there will be strong pressures to use the proceeds of privatization to cover the public sector borrowing requirement, with no spill-over to capital formation.

Finally, if public firms are sold to foreigners, is their direct foreign investment "additional" to what would have arrived otherwise? What about remittance obligations in the future? It *is* true that TNCs which are doing more than simple sourcing do not readily leave a country once they have entered and built up sunk capital, and that they can serve as vehicles for technology acquisition. But can the same be said of debt-swapping banks? Even in terms of current financial flows, privatization need not produce great benefits.

V   CONCLUDING REMARKS:
THE RISKS OF REFORM

The discussion in this chapter suggests that the apparent simplicity and universality of a market-friendly approach to development is misleading. Developing economies such as those in Latin America are complex, and it is unlikely that any one simple solution such as that advocated by the MFAD will provide an answer to their economic problems. Moreover, to ignore the relevance of domestic and external financing constraints, as well as the budgetary constraints which are themselves interlinked with external influences, will lead only to the pursuit of ineffective and/or costly policies.

Appropriate policy will vary from country to country depending on individual circumstances, and, while scientific analysis helps, the job of reforming economies is perhaps more of an art than a science. It can also be a highly risky endeavour.

To what extent will the pursuit of market-friendly policies actually require the state to be autocratic and undemocratic? There are clearly political risks here. Moreover, it is hardly reassuring that advocates claim that the best chance of successfully adopting market-friendly policies occurs at a time of economic crisis with a new government in place which is prepared to go for "shock therapy" across a wide range of economic reforms, rather than gradualist policies which may be undermined by the limited credibility enjoyed by many governments in developing countries.

The risks of failure would appear to be rather high for any policy where the greatest probability of success requires comprehensive shock therapy reform to be implemented by a new government with limited credibility in the midst of an acute economic crisis.

Who walks where angels fear to tread?

NOTES

1 The arguments presented in this chapter draw on many sources (see the references). Some of the arguments have been presented previously in Fanelli, Frenkel, and Rozenwurcel (1990) and in Taylor (1991a).

2 The evidence adduced for the importance of market-friendly development policy comes from comparative studies starting with Bhagwati (1978) and Krueger (1978) and continued by numerous teams at the World Bank. The WDR 1991 indicates that experience ranging from that of the Nordic countries starting in the 1870s to East Asian economies after the Second World War demonstrates that education, openness, and competition are the best roads to development, while import substitution strategies have shown disappointing results.

3 Nonetheless, it is recognized that theory is ambiguous with respect to the net effects of tariffs on technical advance.

4 Although arguably they add little to the insights of Nicholas Kaldor and his colleagues working twenty years ago, "new" growth models proliferated in neoclassical economics during the latter part of the 1980s. They have heavily influenced thinking in the research complex of the Bank. Romer (1989) provides a favourable, semi-technical review.

5 Especially by Harrod's "real" growth model and Tobin's "monetary" one.

6 Dornbusch (1990) discusses the empirical evidence on the relationship between interest rates and saving. See also the 1989 edition of the *World Development Report*.

7 See, for example, Blanchard and Fischer (1989), Chapter 2.

8 This possibility is mentioned by Williamson (1990) and in Chapter 6 of the WDR. Its consequences, however, are not integrated into the Report's macroeconomic analysis of the highly indebted countries.

9 Tirole's main arguments are: (1) because of the instabilities we have discussed, prices in asset markets are noisy and do not convey much information about firms' performance (especially since many enterprises in developing economies are closely held); (2) a noisy economic environment facilitates rent-seeking; as a counterpoise, firms' incentive payments to managers may be kept low, meaning that they will not actively search for ways to raise efficiency.

10 We follow standard but confusing terminology about the exchange rate. If the nominal peso/dollar conversion factor is increased, the local currency becomes weaker or depreciates. If the peso/dollar ratio is increased less rapidly than domestic inflation, then there is real strengthening or appreciation of the peso.

11 In a foreign credit-starved economy, any capital inflow can trigger symptoms of Dutch disease. A very recent example is Argentina, where in 1991 the privatization process plus low US interest rates led to large inflows of funds.

12 The point of these arguments is not that using assets to offset cyclical shocks is wrong. The problem is that managing intertemporal constraints is not easy for a

country facing an imperfect capital market. It is well known that permanent income theories break down when liquidity constraints and market imperfections abound.

13 On the quasi-fiscal activities of the Chilean government, see Eyzaguirre and Larranaga (1990).

14 Chenery and collaborators such as Bruno (1962) set up models with internal and external balance relationships specified to capture the structural peculiarities of developing economies. This approach is dismissed in Chapter 2 of the WDR, but no mention is made of the three-gap formulations which add a fiscal/monetary balance to the original two restrictions. The omission is striking, considering the issues to which the Report is devoted.

15 See Bacha (1990), Fanelli, Frenkel, and Winograd (1987), Fanelli (1988), Carneiro and Werneck (1990), and Taylor (1991b) for interpretations of developing country disequilibria in terms of gaps.

16 On the importance of point-in-time restrictions as opposed to neoclassical intertemporal budget constraints, see Chisari and Fanelli (1991).

17 On this topic see Fanelli and Frenkel (1989) and Fanelli (1988). Broadly speaking, insolvency can be modelled as rapidly rising debt/income ratios for the parties concerned.

18 These authors are all associated with the Bretton Woods institutions.

19 Corden (1990) discusses the cases of Turkey and other successfully stablizing countries that received strong support from abroad.

20 Our stress on the need to raise investment to restore growth does not deny that there is broad scope for improving efficiency. However, capital is not fully malleable and externalities and indivisibilities are always present – a minimum level of gross investment is unavoidable if the economy is to adjust to a new set of relative prices. Moreover, since technical progress is not manna from heaven, efficiency gains require new capital formation.

21 Charles or Carlo Ponzi operated in Boston in 1920. He promised to pay 50 per cent interest on 45-day deposits, to use in arbitrage operations between depreciated foreign currencies and International Postal Union coupons which could be exchanged for US stamps. He took in $7.9 million and held only $61 worth of stamps when he was arrested. His ingenuity in using newly-borrowed money to pay his prior obligations did not exceed that of more recent financial manipulators in developing economies – their imaginations have repeatedly been stimulated by liberalization experiments.

REFERENCES

Ahmad, J. and A.C.C. Kwan (1991) "Causality between Exports and Economic Growth: Empirical Evidence for Africa", *Economics Letters* 27, 243–8.

Alagh, Y.K. (1991) *Indian Development Planning and Policy*, Vikas, New Delhi.

Amsdem, A. (1989) *Asia's Next Giant: South Korea and Late Industrialization*, Oxford University Press, New York.

Bacha, E.I. (1990) "A Three-Gap Model of Foreign Transfers and the GDP Growth Rate in Developing Countries", *Journal of Development Economics* 32, 279–96.

Bhagwati, J. (1978) *Foreign Trade Regimes and Economic Development: Anatomy and Consequences of Exchange Control*, Ballinger, Cambridge MA.

Blanchard, O.J. and S. Fischer (1989) *Lectures on Macroeconomics*, MIT Press, Cambridge MA.

Buffie, E.F. (1991) "Commercial Policy, Growth, and the Distribution of Income in a Dynamic Trade Model", *Journal of Development Economics* 37, 1–30.

Carneiro, D. and R. Werneck (1992) "Brazil", in Taylor (1992).

Chenery, H. and M. Bruno (1962) "Development Alternatives in an Open Economy: The Case of Israel", *Economic Journal* 72, 79–103.

Chisari, O.O. and J.M. Fanelli (1991) "Three-Gap Models, Optimal Growth, and the Economic Dynamics of Highly-Indebted Countries", *Quaderni del Dipartimento di Economia Politica* 101, Siena.

Corden, W.M. (1990) "Macroeconomic Policy and Growth: Some Lessons of Experience", *Proceedings of the World Bank Annual Conference on Development Economics*, Washington DC.

Dornbusch, R. (1990) "Policies to Move from Stabilization to Growth", Proceedings of the World Bank Annual Conference on Development Economics, Washington DC.

Evans, D. (1991) *Institutions, Sequencing, and Trade Policy Reform*, University of Sussex, Institute of Development Studies, Brighton.

Eyzaguirre, N. and O. Larranaga (1990) *Macroeconomica des las Operaciones Cuasifiscales en Chile*, CEPALC, Santiago.

Fanelli, J.M. (1988) "Disequilibrio Macroeconomico Restricciones Financieras y Politicas de Estabalizacion", Buenos Aires, unpublished doctoral dissertation.

Fanelli, J.M. and R. Frenkel (1989) *A Growth Exercise for Argentina*, CEDES, Buenos Aires.

Fanelli, J.M. and R. Frenkel (1992) "Argentina", in Taylor (1992).

Fanelli, J.M., R. Frenkel and G. Rozenwurcel (1990) *Growth and Structural Reform in Latin America: Where We Stand*, CEDES, Buenos Aires.

Fischer, S. (1987) "Economic Growth and Economic Policy", in V. Corbo et al. (eds) *Growth-Oriented Adjustment Programs*, International Monetary Fund and World Bank, Washington DC.

Helleiner, G.K. (1990) "Trade Strategy in Medium-Term Adjustment", *World Development* 18, 879–97.

Hjalmarsson, L. (1991) "The Scandinavian Model of Industrial Policy", in M. Blomstrom and P. Meller (eds) *Diverging Paths: Comparing a Century of Scandinavian and Latin American Economic Development*, Johns Hopkins University Press, Baltimore MD.

Katzenstein, P. (1985) *Small States in World Markets: Industrial Policy in Europe*, Cornell University Press, Ithaca NY.

Khan, M., P. Montiel and N.U. Haque (1986) *Adjustment with Growth: Relating the Analytical Approaches of the World Bank and the IMF*, World Bank, Washington DC.

Kosonen, K. (1991) "Saving and Economic Growth in a Nordic Perspective", in Pekkarinen et al. (1992).

Krueger, A. (1978) *Liberalization Attempts and Consequences*, Ballinger, Cambridge MA.

Kuznets, S.S. (1966) *Modern Economic Growth*, Yale University Press, New Haven CT.

Marcel, M. (1989) "Privatizacion y Finanzas Publicas: El Caso de Chile", *Colecion Estudios CIEPLAN* 26, 5–60.

McCarthy, F.D., L. Taylor and C. Talati (1987) "Trade Patterns in Developing Countries: 1964–82", *Journal of Development Economics* 27, 5–39.

McKinnon, R.I. (1973) *Money and Capital in Economic Development*, The Brookings Institution, Washington DC.

Meller, P. (1991) *Review of the Chilean Liberalization and Export Expansion Process (1974–90)*, CIEPLAN, Santiago.

Michalopoulos, C. (1987) "World Bank Programmes for Adjustment and Growth", in V. Corbo et al. (eds) *Growth-Oriented Adjustment Programs*, International Monetary Fund and World Bank, Washington DC.

Pack, H. (1988) "Industrialization and Trade", in H.B. Chenery and T.N. Srinivasan (eds) *Handbook of Development Economics* (Vol I), North-Holland, Amsterdam.

Pack, H. and L.E. Westphal (1986) "Industrial Strategy and Technological Change: Theory vs Reality", *Journal of Development Economics* **22**, 87–128.

Pastor, M. Jr (1991) "Bolivia: Hyperinflation, Stabilisation, and Beyond", *Journal of Development Studies* **17**, 211–37.

Pekkarinen, J., M. Pohjola and B. Rowthorn (eds) (1991) *Social Corporatism – A Superior Economic System?*, WIDER, Helsinki.

Porter, M.E. (1990) *The Competitive Advantage of Nations*, Free Press, New York.

Rodrik, D. (1991) "Closing the Productivity Gap: Does Trade Liberalisation Really Help?" in G.K. Helleiner (ed.), *Trade Policy, Liberalisation, and Development: New Perspectives*, Clarendon Press, Oxford.

Romer, P.M. (1989) "Capital Accumulation in the Theory of Long-Term Growth", in R.J. Barro (ed.), *Modern Business Cycle Theory*, Harvard University Press, Cambridge MA.

Shapiro, H. (1991) *The Public–Private Interface: Brazil's Business–Government Relations in Historical Perspective, 1950–1990*, Harvard Business School, Boston MA.

Shapiro, H. and L. Taylor (1990) "The State and Industrial Strategy", *World Development* **18**, 861–78.

Syrquin, M. and H.B. Chenery (1989) "Patterns of Development: 1950–1983", World Bank Discussion Paper No 41, Washington DC.

Taylor, L. (1988) *Varieties of Stabilisation Experience*, Clarendon Press, Oxford.

Taylor, L. (1991a) "Polonius Lectures Again: *The World Development Report*, the Washington Consensus, and How Neoliberal Sermons Won't Solve the Economic Problems of the Developing World", Department of Economics, Massachusetts Institute of Technology, Cambridge MA.

Taylor, L. (1991b) *Income Distribution, Inflation and Growth*, MIT Press, Cambridge MA.

Taylor, L. (ed.) (1992) "The Rocky Road to Reform", in press.

Tirole, J. (1991) *Privatization in Eastern Europe: Incentives and the Economics of Transition*, Department of Economics, MIT, Cambridge MA.

Tybout, J., J. de Melo and V. Corbo (1991) "The Effect of Trade Reforms on Scale and Technical Efficiency: New Evidence from Chile", *Journal of International Economics* **31**, 231–50.

UNCTAD (United Nations Conference on Trade and Development) (1991) *Trade and Development Report 1991*, United Nations, New York.

Williamson, J. (1990) "What Washington Means by Policy Reform", in J. Williamson (ed.) *Latin American Adjustment: How Much Has Happened?*, Institute for International Economics, Washington DC.

World Bank (1991) *The Challenge of Development: World Development Report 1991*, published for the World Bank by Oxford University Press, New York.

9 | Income Distribution and Poverty Through Crisis and Adjustment

OSCAR ALTIMIR*

Most Latin American countries are painfully recovering from the protracted crisis they suffered during the 1980s and from the traumatic adjustments they undertook to extricate themselves from it and to lay the basis for a new phase of sustained growth.

The net transfer of resources to the region, which represented more than 2 per cent of its GDP before the crisis, suddenly became negative. Between 1982 and 1989, Latin America's net export of capital was equivalent to almost 4 per cent of its aggregate GDP. The turnaround of the net transfer of resources was thus tantamount to a permanent loss of 6 per cent of domestic output along the period.

After the external adjustment that brought regional per capita product down 10 per cent between 1980 and 1983, most Latin American economies wavered between recession and inflation, muddling through the debt tangle and its domestic sequels for most of the decade. At its closing, per capita product was still at the 1983 level and real national income per capita was 15 per cent lower than in 1980. However, in 1991/92 growth has been steadier; there have been signs of reanimation in private investment, along with the return of significant capital flows; the trend toward price stabilization has generalized; and most of the huge fiscal adjustments of the previous years have held fast.

Although in some cases stabilization processes remain fragile, most Latin American economies are now resting on new foundations. These are characterized by a firmer orientation towards exports (which volume has, in many cases, at least doubled during the past decade), trade liberalization, fiscal

* Director of Economic Development at the U.N. Economic Commission for Latin America and the Caribbean. The views expressed are my responsibility and do not necessarily reflect those of the Organization. I wish to thank Robert Devlin, Norberto García and Arturo León for valuable comments, as well as Gloria Bensan and Guillermo Mundt for skilful assistance, without making them responsible for the end results.

austerity, more prudent management of monetary policy, and greater reluctance to resort to public regulation of economic activity.

For the poor and the lower-middle income groups, the severe economic crisis of the 1980s involved damaging declines both in real incomes and in access to and quality of social services. Almost all countries experienced an acute redistribution of income among households during the decade of crisis, in most cases with regressive net outcomes at the end of the decade. Regressive changes in relative incomes and the fall of real per capita income during the first half of the decade, when most economies suffered recessionary adjustments, or had just begun to recover, involved significant increases in absolute poverty. Only in a few cases were these increases partially reversed with the stabilization and growth processes of the latter years.

Estimates for Latin America as a whole (CEPAL, 1991 and CEPAL, 1992) put the population living in poverty at 41 per cent in 1980, increasing to 43 per cent in 1986 and reaching 46 per cent in 1990. Corresponding estimates of poverty incidence among households increased from 35 per cent in 1980 to 37 per cent in 1986 and to 39 per cent in 1990. This deterioration, however, is almost entirely attributed to the aggravation of urban poverty, which affected 25 per cent of urban households in 1980, 30 per cent in 1986 and 34 per cent in 1990. This almost doubled the absolute numbers living in poverty in the urban areas, to 22.7 million households and 115.5 million people in 1990. (See Table 9.1.)

In contrast, the incidence of rural poverty in the region as a whole remained more or less stable during the decade. Close to 54 per cent of households and 60 per cent of the rural population live in poverty, with absolute numbers increasing by slightly more than 1 per cent a year, to 80 million people. Consequently, around 60 per cent of the Latin American poor now live in urban areas, compared with less than half in 1980.

Recovery and the abatement of inflation are bringing relief on the poverty front, but there is increasing concern that the new modality under which the economies are functioning and the new rules of public policy involve greater income inequalities and more precarious employment conditions than in the past, in a certainly tighter fiscal environment.

I THE APPROACH

I.1 The data base on income distribution and poverty

Income distribution statistics in Latin America are of varied reliability and are not straightforwardly comparable.[1] Among the many factors distorting their comparability, the under-estimation of income affects income levels and their concentration in different ways. In order to somehow sidestep this obstacle, the analysis of changes in the relative distribution of income is based on pairs of available estimates (see in Table 9.2), selected for being similar – and,

Table 9.1 Latin America:[a] estimates of poverty and destitution, 1980, 1986 and 1990.

Area	Poverty[b]						Destitution[c]					
	1980		1986		1990		1980		1986		1990	
	Mill.	%	Mill.	%	Mill.	%	Mill.	%	Mill.	%	Mill.	%
	(Households)											
National	24.2	35	32.1	37	37.0	39	10.4	15	14.6	17	16.9	18
Urban	11.8	25	18.7	30	22.7	34	4.1	9	7.0	11	8.7	13
Rural	12.4	54	13.4	53	14.3	53	6.3	28	7.6	30	8.2	30
	(Persons)											
National	135.9	41	170.2	43	195.9	46	62.4	19	81.4	21	93.5	22
Urban	62.9	30	94.4	36	115.5	39	22.5	11	35.8	14	44.9	15
Rural	73.0	60	75.8	60	80.4	61	39.9	33	45.6	36	48.6	37

Sources: 1980 and 1986: CEPAL (1991); 1990: CEPAL (1992).

[a] Nineteen countries. Based on data for: Argentina, Brazil, Colombia, Costa Rica, Guatemala, Mexico, Panama, Peru, Uruguay, and Venezuela, for 1980 and 1986, and also for Chile, Honduras, and Paraguay for 1990.

[b] Corresponds to household per capita incomes below poverty lines equivalent to the double of country-specific minimum food budgets, which range from 22 to 34 dollars of 1988 per person a month, for the urban areas.

[c] Corresponds to household per capita incomes below the value of the country-specific minimum food budgets used to draw the poverty lines.

Table 9.2 Latin American countries: changes of income distribution in selected periods.

Country	Period	Source	Coverage[a]	Income concept[b]	Change of concentration (%) Gini	Change of concentration (%) Rel. 10h/40l	Change of shares of income groups (% of total income) 40 low	Change of shares of income groups (% of total income) 50 int	Change of shares of income groups (% of total income) 10 high
Argentina	1970–4	Altimir (1986)	MA	HI	4	9	−0.7	−0.7	1.4
	1974–80	Altimir (1986)	MA	HIPC	10	28	−2.1	−1.2	3.3
	1980–6	CEPAL (1991b)	MA	HIPC	11	27	−1.5	−3.2	4.7
	1980–9	Psacharopoulos et al. (1992)	MA	HIPC	17	47	−2.9	−3.0	5.9
	1985–90	Beccaria (1991)	MA	HIPC	...	33[c]	−1.4[d]	−3.4[e]	4.8
Brazil	1979–87	CEPAL (1991b)	MA	HIPC	4	32	−2.3	−1.3	3.6
			RU	HIPC	7	9	2.7	−5.5	2.8
	1979–89	Psacharopoulos et al. (1992)	N	HIPC	7	28	−1.3	−2.4	3.7
	1987–90	Hoffmann (1992)	U	RI	8	31[f]	−2.1[g]	−2.8[h]	4.9
	1987–90	Hoffmann (1992)	U	RI	2	9	−1.0	—	1.0
	1987–90	CEPAL (1991b; 1993)	MA	HIPC	−6	−18	0.4	6.3	−6.7
			RU	HIPC	1	53	−5.1	5.2	−0.1
Colombia	1978–88	Londoño (1990)	N	RI	−1	−3	−0.2	0.3	−0.5
	1980–6	CEPAL (1991b)	MA	HIPC	−3	−12	0.2	0.8	−1.0
			RU	HIPC	−5	0	0.4	3.0	−3.4
	1980–9	Psacharopoulos et al. (1992)	U	HIPC	−9	−27	1.9	3.2	−5.1
	1986–90	CEPAL (1991b), CEPAL (1993)	MA	HIPC	−2	−1	−0.4	2.7	−2.3
			RU	HIPC	−9	−2	1.9	1.4	−3.3
Costa Rica	1981–8	CEPAL (1991b)	MA	HIPC	7	22	−1.5	−1.6	3.1
			RU	HIPC	14	3	−1.9	−3.2	5.1
	1981–9	Psacharopoulos et al. (1992)	N	HIPC	−3	−10	1.4	−1.9	0.5
	1988–90	CEPAL (1991b; 1993)	MA	HIPC	−6	−13	1.1	1.1	−2.2
			RU	HIPC	−6	−15	0.4	3.0	−3.4

Country	Period	Source							
Chile	1968–74	Heskia (1980)	MA	HI	−10	−23	2.0	1.8	−3.8
	1974–80	Heskia (1980), Riveros (1985)	MA	HI	21	60	−2.8	−6.2[h]	9.0[i]
	1981–3	Riveros (1985)	MA	HI	2	14	−1.1	−0.5[h]	1.6[i]
	1968–83	CEPAL (1979), Rodríguez (1983)	N	HI	23	38	−1.6	−6.2	7.8
	1969–78	Ffrench-Davis-Raczynski (1990)	MA	HE	…	54[j]	−4.9	−1.6[h]	6.5[i]
	1978–88	Ffrench-Davis-Raczynski (1990)	MA	HE	…	23[j]	−1.9	−1.7[h]	3.6[i]
	1987–90	CEPAL (1991b; 1991c)	U	HIPC	−2	−3	0.4	−0.4	—
Mexico	1977–84	CEPAL (1988b), Lustig (1992)	N	HI	−9	−41	2.8	0.7	−3.5
	1984–9	Lustig (1992)	N	HI	…	28	−1.4	−3.7	5.1
Panama	1979–89	Psacharopoulos et al. (1992)	N	HIPC	16	66	−3.5	−2.8	6.3
Peru	1985/6–90	Psacharopoulos et al. (1992)	MA	HIPC	2	5	−0.7	0.5	0.2
Uruguay	1973–9	Melgar (1981)	MA	HPI	32	100	−4.7	−8.3	13.0
	1979–81	Melgar (1981), Melgar-Villalobos (1987)	MA	HPI	−2	−4	−1.2	6.3	−5.1
	1981–6	CEPAL (1991a; 1991b)	MA	HIPC	7	20	−1.2	−2.4	3.6
	1986–9	CEPAL (1991a; 1991b)	RU	HIPC	−9	−19	1.4	3.1	−4.5
	1981–9	Psacharopoulos et al. (1992)	U	HIPC	−7	−12	1.5	0.1	−1.6
			U	HIPC	−3	−7	0.8	−0.2	−0.6
Venezuela	1981–6	CEPAL (1991b)	MA	HIPC	8	19	−2.5	−1.7	4.2
			RU	HIPC	18	46	−2.6	−3.1	5.7
	1981–9	Psacharopoulos et al. (1992)	N	HIPC	3	8	−0.4	−1.3	1.7
	1986–90	CEPAL (1991b; 1993)	MA	HIPC	−4	−7	0.8	−0.4	−0.4
			RU	HIPC	—	3	—	−0.6	0.6
	1987–9	Marquez-Mukherjee (1991)	N	HIPC	6	11	−0.2	−3.5	3.7
	1989–90	Marquez-Mukherjee (1991)	N	HIPC	−4	−14	0.9	1.8	−2.7

[a] MA: Metropolitan area; RU: rest of urban areas; U: urban areas; N: national.
[b] HI: household income; HPI: household primary incomes; HIPC: household income per capita; HE: household expenditure; RI: recipients income.
[c] Relation 10h/30l.
[d] Corresponds to the low 30%.
[e] Corresponds to the intermediate 60%.
[f] Relation 10h/50l.
[g] Corresponds to the low 50%.
[h] Corresponds to the intermediate 40%.
[i] Corresponds to the higher 20%.
[j] Relation 20h/40l.

therefore, apparently comparable – with regard to the income concept, the technique for measuring income, the geographical coverage of the surveys used to collect the data, as well as the units and criteria used by the respective authors in processing or adjusting the survey data.[2] However, proven or assumed differences in any of these aspects in many cases invalidate going beyond these pair-wise comparisons into simply pooling estimates.

Poverty estimates for the 1980s are those produced by CEPAL (1991 and 1992). They are the result of cutting estimated distributions of households by per capita income, previously adjusted for income underestimation,[3] by means of country-specific poverty lines representing minimum normative budgets of private consumption based on minimum food budgets that adequately cover nutritional requirements.[4] The poverty lines used for different years of the 1980s were held constant in real terms, a criterion that is acceptable for a period of recession and recovery.[5]

This chapter uses headcount ratios as the poverty measure, which are available for several years of the past decade, for each country considered.[6] These are displayed in Table 9.3, which also includes the incidence of extreme poverty or destitution, defined as the proportion of households with a per capita income less than the value of the minimum food budget.

These estimates actually build up national measures of poverty from urban and rural estimates. However, it should be borne in mind that headcount estimates for the rural areas are considerably less reliable than those for the urban areas. On the one hand, the norms used to draw rural poverty lines have an unavoidable urban bias, in spite of taking into account price and consumption rural–urban differences. On the other hand, available measures of rural incomes and of their distribution are usually even less accurate than those of urban incomes from the same survey. Finally, some of the rural estimates are no more than educated guesses, based on relevant but indirect data.[7]

The set of countries considered in this chapter includes the major ones in Latin America as well as some others for which comparable inequality and poverty measurements are available both at the beginning of the decade and at some later point of time. It excludes predominantly rural countries, like Guatemala and Honduras, for which poverty estimates were also produced by CEPAL, because the method of analysis used here and the variables on which it rests capture mainly urban phenomena, and the mere dimensions of rural poverty according to those estimates (affecting four-fifths of the rural population and representing at least three-quarters of all the poor) both underline the irrelevance of a urban-centred analysis and suggest that poverty measurement and analysis in such cases should be based on surveys, poverty yardsticks and explanatory variables more closely related to rural conditions.

Income in this data base generally measures household disposable cash income,[8] including primary income (wages and salaries and entrepreneurial

Table 9.3 Latin American countries: incidence of poverty and destitution in the 1980s (% households).

Country and years	Poverty			Destitution		
	Urban areas	Rural areas	National level	Urban areas	Rural areas	National level
Argentina						
1980	7	16[b]	9	2	4[b]	2
1986	12	17[b]	13	3	6[b]	4
1990	19[c]					
1991	15[c]					
Brazil						
1979	30	62	39	10	35	17
1987	34	60	40	13	34	18
1990	39	56	43	17	31	20
Colombia						
1980	36	45[b]	39	13	22[b]	16
1986	36	42	38	15	22	17
1990	35			12		
Costa Rica						
1981	16	28	22	5	8	6
1988	21	28	25	6	10	10
1990	22	25	24	7	12	10
Chile						
1980	32[a]	41[a]	33[a]			
1987	37	45	38	13	16	14
1990	34	36	35	11	15	12
Mexico						
1977			32			10
1984	23	43	30	6	19	10
Panama						
1979	31	45	36	14	27	19
1986	30	43	34	13	22	16
1989	34	48	38	15	25	18
Peru						
1979	35	65[b]	46	10	38[b]	21
1985/86	45	64	52	16	39	25
Uruguay						
1981	9	21[b]	11	2	7[b]	3
1986	14	23[b]	15	3	8[b]	3
1989	10	23[b]	15	2	8[b]	3
Venezuela						
1981	18	35	22	5	15	7
1986	25	34	27	8	14	9
1990	33	38	34	11	17	12

Source: CEPAL (1991a, 1991b, 1992).
[a] Author's estimate, based on Pollack and Uthoff (1987). See Altimir (1991).
[b] These estimates should be considered educated guesses based on relevant but indirect information.
[c] Author's estimate, based on Beccaria and Minujin (1991).

incomes) and other money income (pensions, transfers, rentals, interest, etc.) after direct tax payments. It therefore excludes imputed income from public goods and services rendered free of charge or heavily subsidized and, hence, the redistributive effects of such public expenditure. Nor do these income measurements capture the incidence of indirect taxes on real incomes.

1.2   The method of analysis

The above caveats should warn us not to confuse the map for the territory. Although our ultimate concern is with changes in social stratification and with distinguishing changes that are permanently reshaping Latin American societies from those related to transitory accommodation to hard times, we are able here to focus only on aggregate changes in the relative distribution of welfare and the incidence of poverty, leaving out changes in the composition of households and their economic strategies, including their manner of participating in the labour market.

Moreover, the analysis is limited to changes in the distribution of private income, excluding the distribution of social incomes (i.e., those accruing to households in the form of public goods or subsidies), thus focusing on the distributive results of participation in the productive process and institutionalized entitlements. This focus ignores the immediate redistributive consequences of social policies implemented through public expenditure (except entitlements to social security payments). However, it captures both the short-term effects of economic policy on the distribution of income and the eventual influences of public policy on the structure of incomes, mingled as it may be with structural changes beyond the influence of policy.

Within these limitations, I try to assess the distributive costs of the crisis and adjustment, which is more than "social costs" measured as losses in aggregate welfare, but is far less than total social costs, as soon as we recognize that the social structure is more than the distribution of welfare and that living conditions are not determined only by income.

Costs of what process, is another matter. The distributive changes recorded by available income distribution data incorporate the effects of adjustment, institutional changes involving policy reform, and underlying restructuring processes. However, since the crisis of the 1980s is the counterpart of an epochal transformation of Latin American development, measured distributive losses are attributable to a transformation that included the periods of instability and inflation, and failed policies or policies involving over-adjustment.

The focus is not on the interaction of macroeconomic variables (which has been analyzed elsewhere[9]) but on the relationships between changes of income distribution and poverty and processes of adjustment, policy reform and structural mutation underlying the changes of those macroeconomic variables.

Nonetheless, neither the depth nor the characteristics of productive restructuring are adequately revealed by changes in the set of macroeconomic variables used, and their permanent distributive consequences can only be hinted at by considering distributive situations after stabilization and adjustment. Likewise, the association of distributive changes with policy reforms is explored in a broad way, given the methodological problems for linking both.

Even though the distributive costs of external adjustment, stabilization, fiscal adjustment and economic restructuring are intertwined, the characteristics and sequencing of policy packages certainly make a difference in the magnitude and duration of distributive losses.[10] Unfortunately, income distribution and poverty estimates in our data base are too scanty to obtain more than very broad hints in this regard.

In many instances the periods of analysis imposed by the data include adjustment or stabilization policies followed by their failure and the acceleration of inflation, thus encompassing the distributive costs of both kinds of processes.

The basic assessment criteria I use here are, on the one hand, to compare distributive changes and changes in macroeconomic and labour market variables during similar macroeconomic phases along the adjustment process in different countries and, on the other hand, to compare the distributive situations before and after adjustment in each country.

Thus the analysis is carried out for different macroeconomic phases of each economy during the 1980s, the underlying hypothesis being that different relationships between distributive changes and macroeconomic changes may hold during instability, recession, recovery and growth close to the production frontier. This stance, given the scarcity of distributional measurements for each country and the lack of uniformity in their correspondence to similar macroeconomic phases, precludes a formal econometric exercise.

The selection of macroeconomic variables has taken into account both availability and analytical relevance. The implicit conceptual model links changes in inequality with those of real national income per capita,[11] the real exchange rate as a proxy for relative prices, public consumption expenditure at constant prices[12] as a proxy for government employment and real wages, inflation, real urban wages and urban labour under-utilization (i.e. urban unemployment and informal employment). Changes in urban poverty are, in turn, related to variations of real income per capita, inequality and the real minimum wage. Changes in rural poverty, on the other hand, are linked to changes of real income per capita, agricultural product and the real exchange rate.

There are a number of measurement limitations that hinder a rigorous association between observed changes of income distribution and poverty and observed changes of macroeconomic variables. Foremost among them is that observed income distributions from household surveys of the type generally used for these estimates (i.e. labour surveys) measure income in a specific month of the year, whereas measures for most of the relevant macroeconomic variables are made available on a yearly basis, with quarterly data being much more difficult to obtain.

On the other hand, the years for which income distribution or poverty measurements are readily available do not always correspond to relevant phases of the conjunctural movements of the economy – which in many cases have been numerous and often of different direction – or to spells when a specific policy package was in force.

The analysis of associations between distributive changes and macro-economic variables focuses on the distribution of income and poverty in the urban areas, with only a summary analysis of changes in rural poverty. There are various reasons for disaggregating the analysis. For one, as noted above, income distribution and poverty measurements at the national level incorporate or mix urban and rural measurements of very different degrees of reliability or accuracy, making the "constant bias over time" assumption less tenable. Most macroeconomic variables available also have a different relationship with either urban or rural incomes (e.g. the exchange rate) or a tenuous or remote relationship with rural incomes (e.g. unemployment or informal employment), or almost no bearing at all on them in the short run (e.g. urban wages). Hence, analysis based on aggregate income distribution or poverty at the national level blurs the differential explanatory value of these variables.

Furthermore, for some countries or periods, only measurements for urban areas are available. To be sure, this is a hindrance in distributional analysis. However, it is a less serious one than in other developing regions, since in most of the Latin American countries considered here, more than 60 per cent of the population is urban (and more than 80 per cent is urban in the Southern Cone countries and Venezuela), while less than half the poor are rural (20 per cent or less in the Southern Cone and Venezuela).

Finally, the distributive changes of the 1980s are assessed in the context of the previous trends of the 1970s, before the crisis, when different growth processes were in place and – in some countries – policy reforms were undertaken.

II   THE RECORD OF THE 1970s

II.1   Inequality

The analysis of changes in income distribution and growth in the main countries of the region during the 1970s (Altimir, 1992) suggests, as summarized in Table 9.4, that:

(1)   Countries which had very different degrees of income concentration at the beginning of the decade, but which experienced slow and

Table 9.4 Changes in income distribution and poverty in the 1970s.

Countries	Changes in income concentration[a]	Changes in poverty incidence[a]		
		National	Urban	Rural
I. *Slow growth* (≤ 1%)				
Argentina	I	M	I	D
Chile	I	I	I	I
Peru	I	D	I	D
II. *Moderate growth* (2–3%)				
Costa Rica	I	D	M	D
Panama	—	M	I	D
Uruguay	I		I	
III. *Rapid growth* (> 3%)				
Brazil	M	D	M	D
Colombia	D	D	D	D
Mexico	D	D	D	D
Venezuela	D	D	D	D

Source: Altimir (1992).
[a] I: increased; M: maintained; D: decreased.

unstable – or even disrupted – growth, like Argentina, Chile or Peru, suffered significant increases of inequality.

(2) In countries with moderate average per capita growth rates (between 2 per cent and 3 per cent) over the decade and in which income concentration, at its beginning, was intermediate, like Costa Rica or Uruguay, inequality increased.

(3) Three countries (Colombia, Mexico and Venezuela) with solid average – and, therefore, sustained – per capita growth rates (over 3 per cent a year), significantly improved their previously high (Gini over .5) income concentration.

(4) On the contrary, the intense growth (close to 6 per cent per capita a year) of Brazil during the 1970s was not accompanied by a reduction of the very high income concentration (Gini about .6) established during the previous decade.

II.2 Poverty

Changes in the incidence of absolute poverty are dependent upon growth of average real income, changes in the distribution of income, and the change of poverty norms over time.[13] Using comparable estimates of the incidence of poverty for 1970 and around 1980, with poverty lines both constant and shifting over time (Altimir, 1992), the following highlights (summarized in Table 9.4) emerge, for the sample of countries:

(1)   Argentina, Chile and Peru, a group of countries with increasing
      inequality and low and unstable growth during the decade – as a
      consequence of economic shocks and institutional disruptions –
      experienced either discouraging or outright dismal results on the
      poverty front. In Argentina the incidence of poverty at the national
      level may have increased slightly and in Peru even decreased, if the
      respective "educated guesses" about the decrease in rural poverty are
      accepted, but in both countries urban poverty tended to increase. In
      Chile, the virtual explosion of poverty took place both in urban and
      rural areas.

(2)   In the two countries (Costa Rica and Uruguay) which experienced
      moderate growth and increasing inequality, urban poverty either
      remained unchanged or increased, with rural poverty decreasing or
      about constant, respectively.

(3)   Those countries which attained high rates of per capita growth and
      decreasing inequality (Colombia, Mexico and Venezuela) show
      significant reductions of absolute poverty, both in the urban and
      rural areas.[14]

(4)   Brazil's intense growth resulted in the reduction of poverty, even in
      spite of the lack of improvement of the relative income distribution;
      however, if some shifting of the poverty line is accepted, to allow for
      the eventual effects of such a growth process on the prevailing style
      of living, the incidence of poverty in urban areas would have roughly
      remained constant.

(5)   The incidence of poverty in rural areas showed a downward trend
      during the 1970s in almost all of the countries considered,
      irrespective of the rate or stability of their growth, with the
      noticeable exception of Chile.

(6)   Rural–urban migrations, which were particularly intense in the
      seventies, may have been more important than the improvement of
      economic conditions in the rural areas in explaining the absolute
      reduction of the rural poor in Argentina, Brazil and Venezuela. On
      the contrary, the last factor has been weightier than migrations in
      abating absolute rural poverty in Colombia, Mexico and Panama and
      the incidence of rural poverty in Costa Rica and Peru. In Chile,
      rural–urban migrations merely cushioned the rise of the incidence of
      poverty.

III   THE 1980s: A TALE OF TEN COUNTRIES

Income concentration and poverty increased in the urban areas of almost all
Latin American countries during the 1980s, as is evident from Tables 9.2 and
9.3. Colombia is the only unambiguous exception, while Mexico and Costa

Rica appear to have somehow cushioned distributive deterioration caused by the adjustments of the decade, and Panama only suffered when disrupted by political and international conflict. Highly unequal Brazil has also undergone relatively less additional deterioration. Chile, Argentina and Uruguay experienced severe distributive losses, in the course of different phases of their reform and adjustment processes during the last two decades, and their record of the 1980s has to be considered in this context. Peru and Venezuela also suffered heavy distributive losses, from different combinations of shocks and policy failures. Changes of income concentration[16] and urban poverty in each country and period are compared with changes of relevant macroeconomic and labour market variables in Table 9.5.

III.1   Colombia

The exceptional case is that of Colombia, where all available data show improvement of the income distribution during the decade; between 1978 and 1988, a relatively slight reduction of income concentration among earners (Londoño, 1990); between 1980 and 1986, a significant decrease in the share of the upper decile of households, mainly in favour of the middle strata; moreover, up to 1990, that improvement deepened, favouring also the lower four deciles of households. However, the incidence of urban poverty in 1990 was roughly similar (around 35 per cent) to the 1980 and 1986 marks.

These results are roughly consistent with the initial conditions before the crisis, the macroeconomic trends of the period and the traditionally prudent style of Colombian economic policy. When the systemic financial crisis of the 1980s broke, Colombia was not heavily indebted; adjustment did not take place until 1984–5 and then policy managed it gradually and deliberately aimed at minimizing wage and employment losses. In fact, during the rest of the decade economic policy included among its objectives job creation and sustained wages (García, 1991).

In 1986, the country's comparatively mild external adjustment had just been completed, real income per capita was already 5 per cent higher than in 1980 and real wages were 12 per cent higher. However, urban unemployment was 4 points (i.e., almost half again) higher than in 1980 and 2 per cent more of the urban labour force (i.e., 27 per cent of it) was employed in informal activities. The 1986–90 period has been one of growth with stability, of sorts, for the Colombian economy, with the macroeconomic situation deteriorating somewhat in 1990. Real income per capita expanded more than 4 per cent over the period, with exports, public consumption expenditure and private consumption leading the expansion. Unemployment correspondingly decreased (by more than 3 points) as did the importance of informal employment, but real wages increased slightly up to 1989 and decreased significantly only in 1990.

Table 9.5 Changes in macroeconomic and labour variables and distributives changes in different phases of the eighties (% over each period).

Country	Period	Macroeconomic variables[a]			Labour market[b]						Distributive changes[c]	
		RNIpc	RER	INF[d]	RW	RMW	NALU	NALI	UU	CGpc	Concentration (Gini)	Urban poverty
I. Periods of recessive adjustment to external shocks												
Argentina	1980–83	−23	77	I	−1	37	10	1	81	−19	I?	I+?
Brazil	1979–83	−13	26	I	−18	−5	20	24	8	−7	M	I
Colombia	1980–83	−5	−12	D	8	7	12	9	21	7	D	M?
Costa Rica	1980–83	−26	40	I/D	−18	−1	12	12	42	−30	I?	I+
Chile	1981–83	−22	34	I	−11	−19	32	5	111	−8	I	I
Mexico	1981–84[e]	−12	40	I	−30	−32	12	7	36	−14	I?	I?
Peru	1982–84	−12	14	I	−25	−20	32	31	35	−22	...	I+
Uruguay	1981–86	−19	55	I	−13	−14	...	...	60	−14	I	I+
Venezuela	1981–86	−30	51	—	−19	6	24	6	78	−21	I	I+
II. Periods of recovery after external adjustment												
Argentina	1983–86	—	—	D	8	7	10	8	19	14	I	I?
Brazil	1983–87	19	13	D/I	37	−23	−11	−1	−45	42	I	D
Colombia	1983–86	10	67	I	4	6	4	−2	18	−3	D	M
Costa Rica	1983–88	8	15	I	8	16	−4	8	−25	11	I?	D?
Chile	1983–87	12	72	—	−3	−27	−25	−16	−37	−23	I	...
Panama	1982–86	10	—		16	13	...	...	26	−3	...	M?
Peru	1984–87	16	—	D/I	40	−3	−15	−7	−46	28	...	D?
Uruguay	1986–89	13	12	M/I	6	−12	...	...	−20	−20	D	D
Venezuela	1986–89	−6	52	I	−38	−15	−5	4	−20	−20	I	I

III. Periods of recession due to internal imbalances

Argentina	1986–89	-13	34	I/H	-19	-62	14	8	36	...	I	I+
Brazil	1987–89	-1	-31	I	-11	-1	-6	-6	-11	17	I	I
Mexico	1984–87	-8	44	I	-16	-17	21	36	-32	-20	I?	...
Panama	1986–89	-22	—	I/H	-1	-1	...	...	61	-21	I?	I
Peru	1987–90	-30	-49	I/H	-69	-64	...	...	73	-58	I?	I

IV. Periods of disinflation and recovery

Argentina	1990–91	5	-24	D	-7	39	...	...	-13	...	...	D
Mexico	1987–89	2	-11	D	-2	-16	9	14	-7	-10	I?	...

V. Periods of growth beyond recovery

Colombia	1986–90	4	31	I	-5	-5	-13	-7	-25	20	D	D
Costa Rica	1988–90	—	-4	D/I	2	5	-4	1	-14	20	D	I
Chile	1987–90	18	5	I	11	27	-15	1	-45	-3	D	D
Venezuela	1989–90	10	4	D	1	-5	2	—	8	-9	D	...

Source: Changes in macroeconomic and labour variables, CEPAL and PREALC. Distributive changes: Tables 3 and 4.

[a] RNIpc: real national income per capita; RER: real effective exchange rate; INF: inflation.

[b] RW: real urban or industrial wages; RMW: real minimum wage; NALU: non-agricultural labour force underutilization (per active person) equal to NALI+UU; NALI: Non-agricultural labour force in informal activities (PREALC definition); UU: urban unemployment rate; CGpc: real per capita government consumption expenditure.

[c] I: increased; I+: increased a lot; D: decreased; M: maintained; "?" indicates most likely presumption for the phase (see text) in the context of the changes observed in Tables 9.2 and 9.3 for a longer period.

[d] I: increased; D: decreased; M: maintained.

[e] I: increased; D: decreased; M: maintained; H: entered into hyperinflation.

* This period includes a transient recovery.

III.2   Mexico

In Mexico, available measurements show a significant decrease of inequality, accompanied by a reduction of poverty at the national level, between 1977 and 1984, and a subsequent deterioration between 1984 and 1989, a period during which the government's policy stance changed radically.[17] The 1984 observation falls in the midst of the first programme of adjustment and stabilization, at a time when a moderate economic recovery from recessionary adjustment was taking place (Lustig, 1992). However, the real wage had dropped almost 30 per cent in two yers, and per capita public consumption expenditure had decreased 14 per cent. It is likely that the improvement in concentration with respect to 1977 – beyond the ever-present possibility that the two measurements are not comparable – conceals a deterioration from a substantially better distributive situation reached during the period of vigorous growth (6 per cent a year) prior to the crisis, particularly in the urban areas.

Be that as it may, there is evidence of an increase in inequality between 1984 and 1989. At this time, the Mexican economy was recovering moderate growth, with inflation under control, after absorbing an oil shock (real national income per capita was still 7 per cent lower than in 1984), and fiscal discipline and policy reforms were progressively gaining ground. Over this period, per capita public consumption expenditure was reduced by more than 30 per cent in real terms and urban real wages declined a further 26 per cent. At the same time, unemployment dropped to levels below those during the oil boom and informal employment increased 10 points, to more than 30 per cent of the non-agricultural labour force. Both developments, consistent with the remarkable flexibility of real wages, must have cushioned the impact on the incomes of poor and lower-middle class households (Lustig, 1992).

III.3   Costa Rica

Costa Rica has traditionally been characterized by political and economic stability, and the adjustment of its economy during the 1980s was significantly aided by official transfers from the United States. Nevertheless, the distribution of urban incomes worsened between the beginning and the end of the decade, although higher rural incomes may have helped to preserve the previous concentration of income at the national level.[18] The deterioration that took place between 1981 and 1988 was reversed only partially during the later biennium, the reversal having favoured the middle strata more than the poor. Consequently, urban poverty increased significantly between 1981 and 1988, and advanced somewhat further up to 1990.

During the recessionary external adjustment of 1981–2, there is evidence that impoverishment was acute, while later stabilization and recovery in 1983–6 brought about a decrease of absolute poverty, to levels of incidence close to those prior to the crisis (Trejos, 1991). At least, this appears to have happened at the national level; real devaluation may have increased the incomes of the rural poor, as argued by Morley and Alvarez (1992), and the real rise – after the adjustment – of wages in formal activities may have improved the situation of the lower-middle strata. On the other hand, the deterioration of real incomes in informal activities – which had expanded – may have increased the number of the urban poor.[19]

In the later period, marked by policy reform (especially trade liberalization) and unstable expansion, available evidence indicates a relative stabilization of poverty incidence at the national level,[20] but also – as already indicated – a tendency for urban poverty to increase, in the context of a reduction of the real wage, lower real income per capita, and a relatively constant real exchange rate. On the other hand, expansion of public consumption expenditure in real terms (20 per cent per capita) contributed to the observed improvement of the relative position of middle income groups.

III.4 Panama

The external shocks that ignited the crisis in other Latin American countries had a lagged and milder impact on the economy of Panama, which only suffered a brief stagnation of economic activity in 1983–4. In spite of a 23 per cent rise of real income per capita and a 14 per cent increase of real wages, between 1979 and 1986 urban poverty fell only slightly, to less than 30 per cent of households. The political crisis-cum-international conflict that pushed the Panamanian economy into recession in 1988–9, brought real income per capita to 5 per cent below the 1979 level, although this was not so with real wages. It also reduced per capita public consumption expenditure more than 20 per cent and widened open unemployment by 10 percentage points of the urban labour force. With this, the concentration of income significantly increased, as did poverty, to 34 per cent of urban households.

III.5 Brazil

The already highly unequal income distribution of Brazil, which had not improved during the previous decade of high growth, worsened further during the 1980s. Inequality in the distribution of household income remained relatively stable during the 1981–3 recession and later recovery, having improved slightly and briefly in 1986, in the milieu of growth and temporary stability created by the Cruzado Plan. Between 1986 and 1989, with the acceleration of inflation and the onset of the present recession, income concentration increased. However, there is evidence (Hoffman, 1992) that in 1990 inequality of household income improved somewhat.

Consequently, the distribution of income in 1989 was more concentrated than in 1979, and poverty affected 5 per cent more of urban households. Real national income per capita and industrial wages were at about the same level as at the end of the previous decade, but unemployment had risen by more than 3 percentage points, as did also informal employment. On the other hand, expansion of public consumption expenditure (55 per cent per capita, between 1979 and 1989) must have helped to cushion the relative deterioration felt by middle income groups. The fall of economic activity and incomes in 1990, accompanied by a 20 per cent real reduction of industrial wages, increased urban poverty by 4 additional points, to almost 39 per cent of households.

III.5   Chile

External shocks and policy reforms under the authoritarian rule of the Pinochet regime, along with ensuing instability and low average growth, caused major changes of income distribution and poverty in Chile, both during the 1970s and the 1980s. Income distribution suffered a significant deterioration; not only was the short-lived redistribution that lasted up to 1974 reversed, but the distributive pattern of Chilean society underwent a metamorphosis.

By 1980, after the recovery from a deep recession (per capita GDP was only 6 per cent higher than in 1970), the implementation of a radical trade liberalization programme, the reversal of agrarian reform, and institutional reforms that allowed for greater labour market flexibility but also for labour repression (Ffrench-Davis and Raczynski, 1990), the upper decile of households was receiving at least five points more of total income than in 1968, to the detriment of the shares and real incomes of both the middle and lower strata. Real wages were still more than 10 per cent lower than in 1970, 17 per cent of the labour force was unemployed and 28 per cent was in informal activities. Absolute poverty virtually exploded, both in the urban areas – from 12 per cent in 1970 to around 28 per cent in 1980 – and in the rural areas, bringing the incidence of poverty at the national level to about 30 per cent of the households (Altimir, 1991).

During the 1982–3 crisis, existing inequality was further aggravated – although perhaps marginally, with respect to the overturn of the previous period – and urban poverty increased even more.[21] Deterioration may have continued until 1987, when real income per capita and real wages were respectively still 12 per cent and 5 per cent lower than in 1980, per capita public consumption expenditure had shrunk more than 30 per cent and unemployment still affected 17 per cent of the labour force, even while the share of informal activities had been reduced. Under those circumstances, urban poverty had risen by about 4 points (14 per cent on a per capita basis) and the distribution of income had become further concentrated in favour of the upper quintile, whose share of expenditure increased by almost 4 per cent of the total with respect to 1978, to the detriment of those of the middle and lower strata, the latter having suffered a relative greater loss.

Only between 1987 and 1990, with the Chilean economy reaching full capacity utilization and progressive reforms of the labour laws, did the distributive picture improve somewhat. Real per capita income increased 18 per cent, real wages 11 per cent, and unemployment was reduced by almost 6 points, to about 7 per cent of the labour force. Notwithstanding this performance, urban income concentration decreased slightly, in favour of the lower income groups, and urban poverty was reduced by 2 points; rural poverty decreased more significantly, bringing the incidence of poverty at the national level to less than 35 per cent of households.

III.6 Argentina

Major distributive changes have also taken place in Argentina since the seventies, under successive spells of economic instability and political disruption. After the advent of a military regime in 1976, policy reforms were introduced to liberalize prices, trade and the financial market, but not employment and wages (which were repressed for most of the period). Economic activity followed a stop-go pattern in the context of a high inflation regime, in spite of the overriding anti-inflationary policy stance which permeated three successive programmes (Canitrot, 1981).

Between 1970 and 1980 income concentration significantly increased: the upper decile of households enlarged its share of total income by almost 5 points, while the lower strata lost almost 3 points. Urban poverty increased by 2 points, to 7 per cent. Most of this deterioration, however, took place after 1974.[22] In 1980, real income per capita was roughly similar and real wages in manufacturing were still 11 per cent lower than in 1974, while unemployment was very low.

The magnitude of the external shocks and ensuing adjustments and swings in relative prices, associated with high and accelerating inflation during the 1980s, were accompanied by movements of the relative distribution of income, although perhaps not as intense as macroeconomic ebb and flow (Beccaria, 1991). By 1986, income concentration had further increased with respect to 1980, with a dramatic change from the beginning of the 1970s: the share of the upper decile had been enhanced about as much as it had been in the previous decade, but this time at the expense mainly of the middle-level strata. Urban poverty had increased 6 points (i.e., it almost doubled), to more than 12 per cent of households. Although the economy was recovering under a successful stabilization programme, real per capita income was 22 per cent below the 1980 level, unemployment was 3 points higher and informal employment 2 points higher; on the other hand, the real wage was 6 per cent higher than at the beginning of the decade.

After 1986, the acceleration of inflation and the fall in real wages led to a further deterioration in the relative income distribution. This culminated in 1989 with the burst of hyperinflation and the trough of recession.

Concentration then stood at its peak. In 1990, income concentration among individual recipients receded to the still high level reached in 1988 (Beccaria, 1991). Between 1986 and 1990, poverty may have involved an additional 6 per cent of urban households (an increase of more than 50 per cent on a per capita basis). It only improved in 1991, when prices stabilized and economic recovery began.

III.7 Uruguay

Uruguay is the other Southern Cone country in which policy reforms were already undertaken in the 1970s, under authoritarian rule, with significant distributive consequences. Starting in 1974, the financial market was liberalized and price controls were gradually eliminated, while wages continued to be administered; in 1979, a trade liberalization programme was put into effect. The 1973–81 period was one of relatively high growth (3.4 per cent per capita a year). Nevertheless, the distribution of income deteriorated sharply between 1973 and 1979 – at the expense of both the middle and lower strata – and improved somewhat later, but only to the benefit of the middle income strata. This evolution closely followed that of the relationship between real national income per capita and real wages: the former increased by 12 per cent between 1973 and 1979, while the latter dropped 32 per cent. Between 1979 and 1981, real income expanded 4 per cent, but real wages rose about 17 per cent. On the other hand, urban poverty increased by 4 percentage points (40 per cent on a per capita basis) between 1970 and 1981.

External shocks and ensuing adjustments slashed real per capita income by 19 per cent between 1981 and 1986. The real wage fell 8 per cent and unemployment increased 4 points, while per capita public consumption expenditure was reduced more than 30 per cent. Income concentration increased again, and urban poverty expanded by 5 additional percentage points, to 14 per cent of households. As a result of economic recovery and later stagflation, real per capita income in 1989 was 13 per cent higher than in 1986 and the real wage was 6 per cent higher, while unemployment had decreased by 2 percentage points. Consequently, the distribution of urban incomes improved and urban poverty decreased by 4 percentage points. Thus, at the end of the decade, the relative distribution of income and the incidence of absolute poverty were roughly similar to those at its outset, while real wages were substantially lower and unemployment somewhat higher than in 1981.

III.8 Venezuela

Continuing deterioration of real national income in Venezuela between 1980 and 1986, caused by the fall of oil revenues, and the ensuing reduction (by around 20 per cent) of real wages and per capita public consumption expenditure, were accompanied by a significant worsening of distribution.

Between 1981 and 1986 urban poverty increased 7 percentage points (to almost 40 per cent on a per capita basis) while the relative distribution of income also became more unequal.

Economic policy failed to adjust to the fall of oil prices in 1986; external and fiscal imbalances widened and the rate of inflation tripled. The orthodox stabilization programme was implemented at the beginning of 1989, along with the first trade and price liberalization measures of a programme of policy reform. This brought a recession and sharp fall in public consumption expenditure and real wages, while previous gains in employment were reversed and informal activities expanded. Consequently, poverty increased[23] and income distribution apparently "equalized downwards". The rise in oil earnings caused by the Gulf conflict in 1990, and ensuing public expenditure in 1991, fuelled an extraordinary – and unsustainable – expansion of economic activity. This, however, was mainly to the advantage of the upper-middle strata: urban poverty in 1990 was still 9 percentage points higher than in 1986 and 16 points above (i.e., almost double) that of 1981. On the other hand, there is evidence indicating that by 1991, poverty – at least at the national level – may have receded somewhat.[24]

III.9 Peru

The worsening income distribution in urban Peru in the 1970s was aggravated during the 1982–5 crisis and subsequent adjustment, as well as by increasing violence. By the end of 1985 and early 1986, when the economy was recovering under the drive of an unsustainable heterodox stabilization programme implemented by the Garcia government, real national income per capita and real wages in the private sector were still 9 per cent and 6 per cent lower than in 1979, and an additional 10 per cent of the non-agricultural labour force was employed in informal activities (reaching more than 40 per cent). At the time, urban poverty still affected 45 per cent of urban households, 10 percentage points more than in 1979.

Although there are not comparable observations for later years, there is some evidence that by 1990, in the midst of hyperinflation and economic collapse, poverty may have expanded by more than half with respect to 1985–6, and worsened even further in 1991, when the Fujimori government implemented the present stabilization programme.[25]

IV   RURAL POVERTY

For most of the countries in our sample there is evidence of a decrease – albeit only slight, in some cases – in the incidence of rural poverty during the 1980s, thus at least inertially continuing the trend towards abatement of rural poverty manifested in the previous decade. The only clear exceptions are Panama and Venezuela, where that trend appears to have been reversed by the end of the 1980s, and possibly Argentina, for which a slight increase of rural poverty has been estimated. Chile is a special case, where the rural impoverishment of the 1970s continued well into the following decade, only to be reversed in the latter years. (See Table 9.3.)

The exceptional increases in rural poverty are associated with declining real per capita income, but the reverse does not hold: of nine recorded spells of rural poverty reduction, real national income per capita increased in only four cases;[26] in the remaining five, rural poverty decreased along with real national income. By contrast, there is a close association of rural poverty reduction with expanding agricultural output, which holds in eight of the nine spells, suggesting that peasants somehow share general rural prosperity. However, going against conventional wisdom,[27] the association is weaker with real devaluation of the exchange rate, since it is observed only in four of the cases, and in most of them with low parameters. (See Table 9.6.)

All this suggests that, in the absence of major institutional reform,[28] slow-

Table 9.6 Changes of rural poverty and of relevant macro variables in the 1980s (% over each period).

Country	Period	Change of rural poverty[a]	Variations of:[b]		
			RNIpc	Agric GDP	RER
Argentina	1980–6	4	−23	12	75
Brazil	1979–87	−3	4	41	43
	1987–90	−6	−7	—	−38
Colombia	1980–6	−7	5	11	47
Costa Rica	1981–8	−3	−5	18	−6
	1988–90	−10	—	10	−4
Chile	1980–7	11	−13	33	89
	1987–90	−19	18	14	5
Panama	1979–86	−4	23	11	—
	1986–9	11	−22	7	—
Peru	1979–85/86	−2	−9	12	−9
Venezuela	1981–6	−3	−30	23	51
	1986–90	12	3[c]	1	59

Source: ECLAC.
[a] From estimates in Table 9.3.
[b] RNIpc: real national income per capita
  Agric GDP: agricultural product
  RER: real exchange rate.
[c] 1986–9: −6%.

moving structural changes in the rural milieu affect rural poverty more than short- or even medium-term changes in macroeconomic variables, although these may be able to slow down or even temporarily reverse trends.

Those slow-moving changes are in part reflected in the continuous transfer of rural poverty to the urban areas through migrations. In the 1980s, this was less intense than in the previous decade, but it was still substantial. In most of the countries, rural–urban migrations were the main force sustaining the trend toward the reduction of poverty in the rural areas, although they may not have been sufficient – as it had been in the 1970s – to prevent an absolute increase of the rural poor (Altimir, 1991).

V   TRANSIENT AND PERMANENT CHANGES OF INCOME DISTRIBUTION

To shed some light on the extent to which changes of inequality during the decade of crisis and adjustment may be permanent, it is crucial to consider the different macroeconomic phases through which Latin American countries have passed and the structural circumstances that prevail at present, as well as the nature and depth of policy reforms undertaken. Changes of macroeconomic and labour variables and distributive changes in selected periods corresponding to different macroeconomic phases of the 1980s are summarized in Table 9.5.[30]

V.1   Income distribution and poverty in different phases of adjustment processes

Recessive adjustment to external shocks at the beginning of the decade has had adverse effects on inequality and devastating effects on urban poverty across Latin America. Income concentration certainly increased in Argentina, Chile, Uruguay and Venezuela, and perhaps in Costa Rica and Mexico, while in Brazil inequality apparently remained invariant through the rapid adjustment of 1981–4.[29] In all these cases urban poverty increased during adjustment, along with under-utilization of the urban labour force[31] (which rose between 10 per cent and 20 per cent, depending on the country) and with sizeable declines in per capita real income, real average wages[32] and real per capita public consumption expenditure.

Colombia stands out as an exception, in part due to its lesser initial debt burden. The economy went through a smooth external adjustment – even with real currency appreciation – and reduction of inflation, which allowed for real rises in minimum and average wages, and even for the real expansion of per capita consumption expenditure. This was the background for a likely improvement in income distribution and apparent stability in absolute poverty. Although Panama also underwent a mild adjustment in 1982–4, with rising real wages but higher unemployment, in this case we have no evidence of distributive changes over the period.

Recovery after external adjustment brought relief on the poverty front only in some countries. In Brazil, reduced poverty may have been associated with the cumulative rise of real per capita income (close to 20 per cent) and real wages (37 per cent), and with decreasing labour under-utilization, in spite of a probable increase of inequality.[33] If Peru also experienced a slackening of urban poverty during this phase – which is not really known, but just plausible – it may have been due to a similar configuration of changes in the level of activity and the labour market. The decrease in poverty in Uruguay (along with inequality) and perhaps in Costa Rica and Panama, and the possible maintenance of an already reduced poverty incidence in Colombia, are also associated with improvements in income and the labour variables, although less spectacular in magnitude.[34]

By contrast, recovery in Argentina, Chile and Venezuela was accompanied by further increases of urban poverty, although for different reasons. In Argentina, the unsteady and only partial recovery and the increase of unemployment and informal labour apparently outweighed the modest rise of the real wage and the temporary abatement of inflation. In Venezuela, until 1989, the recovery had also been partial and subject to adverse external shocks, with accelerating inflation; on the other hand, shrinking (−38 per cent) real wages and per capita consumption expenditure (−20 per cent, in real terms) prevailed over a very modest decrease of labour under-utilization. In this setting, increases of inequality and of urban poverty occurred. In the case of Chile, complete labour market flexibility allowed for equity deterioration in the medium-run; the 1983–7 recovery was vigorous, and under-utilization of the labour force fell significantly – although it still remained above a third of the urban labour force – but the real wage and per capita public consumption expenditure barely held, in a context of moderate and roughly constant inflation. Here, both inequality and absolute poverty increased.

After the initial recovery from external adjustment, those countries which again plunged into recession, due to pervasive internal imbalances, additional external shocks, and accelerating inflation-cum-stabilization efforts, experienced even further increases of inequality and absolute poverty.

In Argentina and Peru, such imbalances drove the economies to hyperinflation, and in Brazil to the brink of it; real income and wages plunged, and labour under-utilization increased, as did absolute poverty and income inequality. Controlling hyperinflation in Argentina in 1990 stopped the fall and even brought about some marginal improvement of inequality, although it did not prevent a further increase of poverty. The acceleration of inflation in Brazil took place along with some economic expansion and higher per capita public consumption expenditure, although real per capita income stagnated and real wages fell. The 1990 stabilization package brought about disinflation with recession, which then apparently increased poverty further.

External shocks in 1985–6 and stabilization efforts in Mexico also led to a new recessionary spell. The increase in informal employment and the drop in real wages suggest the possibility of greater urban poverty. This recession, together with the fall in per capita public consumption expenditure, indicate that part of the observed increase of inequality up to 1989 may have taken place during this period. Panama's deep recession of 1988–9, triggered by political and international conflict, increased urban poverty and possibly also inequality.

The two cases of stabilization and recovery from high inflation and recession in the late 1980s (Argentina in 1990–1 and Mexico in 1987–9) included moderate increases of real income and higher urban labour force utilization, with moderate reductions of real wages. In the case of Argentina, urban poverty decreased from the high incidence attained during the previous spells. In the case of Mexico, there is no evidence of a similar abatement of poverty or a decrease of inequality.

In the few observable instances of sustained or even unsustainable growth after recovery, such circumstances tended to bring about an improvement of the relative income distribution and some decrease in urban poverty. However, in Costa Rica in 1990 urban poverty rose, with the acceleration of inflation and particularly the elimination of subsidies and the increase of public services rates. Both in Colombia and Chile inequality and poverty decreased; in the last case the rises of real incomes and wages were more substantial, but in Colombia real per capita public consumption expenditure expanded. In Venezuela, there are indications of a reduction of income concentration in 1989–90, in spite of falling real wages and increasing unemployment.

V.2   Policy reforms and income distribution

Economic policy reforms intended to facilitate or promote sustainable growth on the basis of freer trade and private investment may play a role in the income distribution consequences of stabilization and adjustment packages. Some of these effects may have been imposed politically to enable reforms to take root. In the longer term, the consequences of reform can have negative distributive effects if a trade-off between growth and a more equitable distribution of income is observed, or expected on the basis of the pattern of growth promoted by the particular reforms undertaken.

Moreover, while there is a blueprint for market-oriented reforms, broadly reflected in the *World Economic Report 1991* (World Bank, 1991), which has a pervasive influence, there is not in fact a common model of policy reform being applied by all countries of the region. All Latin American countries pursue goals of macroeconomic stability and international competitiveness, but they have shown wide differences in their strategies of reform with respect to the institutional content and the style of state intervention involved, as well as the mix and sequencing of particular reforms.

Policy reforms carried out in Southern Cone countries in the 1970s, in combination with stabilization programmes,[35] coincided with increases of income concentration and the aggravation of urban poverty. However, their longer-term associations with growth and income distributions are blurred by the ensuing crisis and the course of adjustment in each case.

In Argentina, trade and financial liberalization reforms were reversed or suspended at the beginning of the crisis (Canitrot and Junco, 1992). The complex later story of instability with recurring efforts to adjust the economy and stabilize prices includes the continuing deterioration of distributive equity, underlined above. A new programme of stabilization and policy reform was put in place in 1989 and consolidated in 1991.

In Chile, reforms were resilient enough to be maintained, with only a partial reversal of trade liberalization during the 1983–4 crisis (Meller, 1992), and a second wave of reforms took place after 1984. The structural effects of the sweeping policy reforms undertaken in this country are manifold, but they can fairly be summarized as having eventually resulted in a stable and growing outward-oriented economy with substantially greater income inequality.

In Uruguay, financial liberalization in 1974–9 was consolidated and supplemented by trade liberalization in 1979–81. Over the medium-term, these reforms appear to have facilitated growth under a regime of "controlled instability", while income distribution has tended to regain its previous (relatively) low concentration pattern.

After a shock stabilization policy, in 1985 Costa Rica started a gradual programme of structural reforms, along with measures to reduce the attendant social costs. These costs appear to have been mainly transient, as far as the relative income distribution is concerned, now that the economy is back on a medium-term growth path to recover the pre-crisis level of per capita income.

In 1987, after renegotiating its external debt, Mexico stepped up its gradual policy reform strategy, enhancing trade and financial liberalization while implementing fiscal reform. Until 1989, inequality had contemporaneously increased, as already noted, although apparently not to a greater degree than in the late 1970s.

Market-oriented policy reforms were launched much more recently in the other countries – in 1989 in Argentina and Venezuela and in 1990 in Colombia and Peru. This hinders any assessment of their association with changes in income concentration, beyond those related to the macroeconomic evolution of each economy during the period.

Whether economic restructuring promoted by these policy reforms and by the new structural circumstances involves a more unequal distribution of income is a matter which must wait for full empirical verification of their long-term effects. For the moment, we can only consider what appear to be the "normal" or more or less "stable" distributive structures once each economy regains a sustained growth path.

V.3   Permanent changes in income concentration

Consider first the countries that have already attained a stage of full-capacity growth. Colombia is the only one in which income concentration at that stage is lower than before the crisis. On the other hand, in Costa Rica in 1990 urban inequality was only slightly higher than in 1981. In both countries, the real wage and per capita public consumption expenditure were higher than at the beginning of the decade (see Table 9.7).

On the contrary, in Chile, after regaining a medium-term growth path, the structure of income is significantly more concentrated than prior to the crisis and certainly much more concentrated than that prevalent at the end of the 1960s, before the socialist populist experiment and the authoritarian structural reforms of the 1970s (see Table 9.1). This is in spite of an almost recovered real wage. In Venezuela, income concentration is also higher than before the crisis, after recovery evolved into rapid albeit unsustainable growth; in this case, both real wages and per capita public consumption are substantially lower than before the crisis.

Although not yet on a full-capacity growth path in 1989, Mexico and Uruguay, were approaching the culmination of their respective recoveries; at that stage, income inequality had nearly returned in both cases to lower pre-recession levels.[36] In Mexico, this was in spite of drastic reductions of real wages and public consumption expenditure, while in Uruguay both variables were more moderately eroded.

The countries that at the end of the 1980s were still labouring under recession and instability (Argentina, Brazil, Panama and Peru), showed degrees of inequality substantially higher than those prevailing before the crisis. Stabilization and recovery in Argentina only brought some improvement of income inequality. Yet inequality remained at a high degree relative to the pre-crisis level, which was substantially higher than the level that prevailed before the disruptions of the 1970s. On the other hand, in the spells of recovery after external adjustment, income distribution improvements – where they existed – only took place along with real wage increases, as outlined above; these are less likely during the stabilization processes still faced by Brazil and Peru, and did not occur during the current Panamanian recovery.

Therefore, one should not expect significant equity improvements in these countries as a consequence of stabilization and recovery. Even more, full deployment of policy reforms and associated adjustment measures – particularly on the fiscal front – may still bring some medium-term increase in income inequality. Furthermore, if the experiences of Colombia and Chile are taken as examples, all these countries can only expect a modest attenuation of income inequalities later, when they attain a sustained growth path.

In sum, "normal" distributive patterns in the coming phase of sustained growth, once most Latin American countries have recovered from the crisis and its sequels, completed structural adjustments and deployed policy reforms,

Table 9.7 Inequality, urban poverty and macroeconomic variables[a] at the end of the 1980s, relative to pre-crisis levels (indices).

Country	Year	Base year	Macro phase[b]	Policy reform[c]	Inequality (Gini)	Urban poverty	GDP	RNIpc	CGpc	NALF	RW	RMW	TCRE
Argentina	1990	(1980 = 100)	ST/RY	R	113	205	93	69	...	88	77	40	185
Brazil	1990	(1979 = 100)	RNU	P	108	130	127	97	158	98	85	55	89
Colombia	1990	(1980 = 100)	SDG	P	91	96	135	110	125	99	106	108	192
Costa Rica	1990	(1981 = 100)	SDG	Y	103	138	128	95	115	103	102	134	90
Chile	1990	(1981 = 100)	SDG	Y	113	107	126	104	69	108	96	76	240
Mexico	1989	(1977 = 100)	ST/RY	Y	100?	>95	147	106	76	89	54	41	111
Panama	1989	(1979 = 100)	RNU	N	116	111	116	95	99	...	108	93	...
Peru	1990	(1979 = 100)	RNU	R	...	190	94	72	62	...	36	24	40
Uruguay	1989	(1981 = 100)	RVY	Y	98	109	100	92	86	...	93	76	173
Venezuela	1990	(1981 = 100)	UNG	R	110	188	105	72	68	93	48	63	240

Source: Table 9.5.

[a] For notation, see Table 9.5. NALF: index of the proportion of the non-agricultural labour force employed in formal activities (inverse of NALU).

[b] ST/RY: stabilization (from high inflation) and recovery; RVY: recovery; RNU: recession due to internal imbalances/inflation; UNG: growth with instability; SDb: sustained medium-term growth.

[c] Y: yes, a policy reform package has been put in place; R: reform package recently in place; P: partial reform; N: no significant policy reform.

will tend to be more unequal – at least in the urban areas – than those prevailing in the last stages of the previous growth phase, during the 1970s.

Only Colombia, Costa Rica and Uruguay – and, just possibly, Mexico – have managed to restore their previous degrees of inequality (see Table 9.7). It is hardly by chance that such a thing happened in countries in which social justice values have traditionally impregnated institutions, equity objectives have been consistently incorporated in policy design throughout the adjustment phase, and both adjustment and policy reforms have been approached gradually and pragmatically.[37] This suggests that the factors that increase inequality of primary earnings (before the eventual corrections involved in public social spending) can be positively corrected by economic policy design and implementation.

VI PROSPECTS FOR POVERTY ALLEVIATION

Even with no significant changes in the relative distribution of income,[38] absolute poverty will be reduced by economic growth; more quickly – at least in economists' estimates – if constant poverty lines are used, more parsimoniously if shifting poverty yardsticks are deemed normatively more appropriate.

The record of the 1970s, outlined earlier, shows urban poverty decreasing only in rapidly growing economies, which either maintained or reduced the concentration of their household income. In Colombia, Mexico and Venezuela, where equity improved, the reduction of urban poverty showed elasticities of −.5 to −1 with respect to the increase in real per capita income and of −.4 to −2 with respect to real wages. In Brazil, with no significant improvement of income concentration, such elasticities were much lower. (See Table 9.8.)

Recession and recovery in the 1980s left most Latin American countries with a – sometimes gapingly – higher incidence of poverty in urban areas than before the crisis. Only Colombia and possibly Mexico were able to end their respective recovery phases with less urban poverty than before the recession, in both cases because of a decrease of inequality. (See Table 9.7.)

Available poverty estimates seldom allow a sharp differentiation between recessive spells and recovery spells. However, the beneficial effects of recovery on poverty appear weaker than the negative effects of the previous recession. In Uruguay, the elasticity of poverty with respect to real income in the 1986–9 recovery was −2, while during the recession it had been −3. In Argentina, disinflation-cum-recovery abated poverty as elastically (−4) as recession had increased it, but recovery itself was then only incipient. In Venezuela, on the other hand, the completion of recovery did not prevent a further widening of poverty.

In other instances (Brazil 1979–87, Costa Rica 1981–8, Chile 1980–7 and Peru, 1979–86) the recovery phase left the economy with a greater degree of

Table 9.8 Changes of urban poverty and their relationship with changes of concentration and real incomes, in different spells.

Country	Period	Change of income concentration[a]	Change of (%):[a]				Elasticity of urban poverty w/respect to:		
			Urban poverty	RNIpc	RW	RMW	RNIpc	RW	RMW
I. Growth spells in the 1970s									
Brazil	1970–9	M	−14	67	48	−1	−0.2	−0.3	14
Colombia	1970–80	D	−21	44	17	27	−0.5	−1.2	−0.8
Mexico	1970–84	D	−30	31	15	−20	−1.0	−2.0	1.5
Venezuela	1970–81	D	−30	71	—	−3	−0.4	−0.4	10
II. Recession and recovery spells in the 1980s									
Argentina	1980–6	I	71	−23	7	47	−3.1	10	1.5
	1986–90	I	52	−15	−22	−64	−4.0	−2.4	−0.8
	1990–1	...	−22	5	−7	39	−4.4	3.1	−0.6
Brazil	1979–87	I	13	3	19	−27	4.2	0.7	−0.5
	1987–90	I	15	−6	−29	−26	−2.5	−0.5	−0.6
Colombia	1980–6	D	—	5	12	13	—	−0.1	—
Costa Rica	1981–8	I	31	−5	16	27	−6.5	1.9	1.1
Chile	1980–7	I	14	−13	−5	−31	−1.1	−2.8	−0.5
Mexico	1977–84	D	−6[b]	14	−34	−40	−0.4	−0.2	0.2
Panama	1979–86	I	−3	23	14	−6	−0.1	−0.2	0.5
	1986–9	...	13	−22	−1	−1	−0.6	−13	−13
Peru	1979–86	I	29	−7	−5	−39	−4.1	−5.8	−0.7
Uruguay	1981–6	I	56	−19	−13	−14	−3.0	−4.3	−4.0
	1986–9	D	−29	13	6	−12	−2.1	−4.8	2.4
Venezuela	1981–6	I	39	−31	−19	6	−1.3	−2.1	6.5
	1986–90	D	32	3	−41	−19	9.4	−0.8	−1.7
III. Growth spells at the end of the 1980s									
Colombia	1986–90	D	−3	4	−5	−5	−0.7	0.6	0.6
Costa Rica	1988–90	D	5	−2	2	5	−2.8	2.5	1.0
Chile	1987–90	D	−8	18	11	27	−0.4	−0.7	−0.3

Source: Table 9.5.
[a] For notation, see Table 9.5.
[b] Corresponds to national poverty.

inequality and a higher incidence of urban poverty. In Costa Rica, not even sustained growth after 1988 was able to prevent the increase of urban poverty, as a consequence of price deregulation. (See Table 9.8.)

In most cases, real wages at the end of recovery were lower than prior to the crisis, which helps to explain the weaker effect of recovery on poverty. Although in Argentina and Brazil, at the culmination of the respective heterodox stabilization programmes, and in Costa Rica, real wages were higher, that fact alone appears to have been offset by other factors increasing inequality and, in the first case, particularly by the fall of real income per capita. By contrast, in Colombia and Panama higher real wages have reinforced the recovery of real income, thus preventing the eventual increase of urban poverty. Not so in Mexico, where the real wage in 1984 was substantially lower than before the crisis. (See Table 9.8.)

On the other hand, the few observable growth spells at the end of the 1980s (Colombia 1986–90 and Chile 1987–90) show similar elasticities with respect to real per capita income ($-.7$ and $-.4$, respectively) than those recorded in the 1970s in rapidly growing economies where income inequality was decreasing. Only in Chile, however, has poverty reduction been more elastic with respect to real wages than to real incomes, as was true in all cases in the 1970s. (See Table 9.8.)

Rural–urban migrations will continue to strain the ability of the economies to alleviate urban poverty. If the experience of the last two decades (Altimir, 1991) is an indication of what might happen, in the relatively less urbanized countries with high incidence of poverty in the rural areas, the migrating rural poor may enlarge the urban poor at a rate equivalent to 1.3–2.0 per cent a year of absolute increase.

To summarize this evidence, it is likely, on the one hand, that countries accomplishing their recovery into full-capacity growth will change gear in their ability to reduce urban poverty in the short run, requiring relatively more expansion of economic activity than in the recovery phase for each percentage point of poverty reduction. On the other hand, medium-term growth with no improvement of income inequality would represent a slow process of poverty abatement: slower than in the cases of high growth and equity improvement of the 1970s, and slower than during recent growth spells in Colombia and Chile, when income distribution also improved.

VII   CONCLUSIONS

After turning the corner of the 1980s, Latin American countries are venturing into a new era of potential growth under a different pattern of development and a new style of state intervention. The adjustments and structural changes still under way have imprinted most Latin American societies with a more unequal distribution of income and a higher incidence of poverty among their people. The few exceptions are the result of a deliberate and persistent care for equity in economic policy design and implementation. Moreover, the prospects for poverty alleviation only through growth, without improvement of the relative distribution of incomes and vigorous social policies, appear so parsimonious as to be disheartening, counterproductive for social integration and, ultimately, for sustained growth.[39]

Given the weak prospects for lowering inequality in primary earnings, even under the deliberate care of economic policy, equity improvements and the abatement of absolute poverty will have to lean much more on social policy and its effectiveness. But with fiscal resources reduced or still strained by the burden of debt, the scope for welfare transfers will be restricted to providing all but a basic social safety net, ceding more space to social expenditures that can be considered as investment in human resources.

Eventual equity gains in the structure of income distribution will depend on the spread of productivity improvements and their actual appropriation by households. Structural transformations under way tend to increase the productivity of capital and total factor productivity, thus enhancing labour productivity in the economy at large. However, for income distribution to improve on the basis of differential productivity gains, three developments are required. First, employment in formal or modern activities must expand (along with productivity increases), as a proportion of the labour force, thus absorbing under-employment. Second, productivity increases have to actually translate into proportional wage rises. Third, capital per worker in the informal, small business and traditional sectors of the economy should increase dramatically.[40]

Such developments, as well as higher capital productivity, require an increase in the skills of different segments of the labour force, and a restructuring of the available skills to enhance the technological capabilities of the productive system at large. To achieve this, heavy investment in human resources (education, training and retraining, nutrition and health) is needed to supplement investment in fixed capital.[41] Even more, there is some ground for substituting investment in human capital for investment in physical capital, as a greater contribution to total factor productivity can be expected from the former in the long term.

Fulfilling these requirements involves substantial investment resources, to be partly generated and handled in the market-place, but in some part to be raised and allocated by the state. On the other hand, for higher skills to be reflected in the income of earners, pay structures have to face the double challenge of being both institutionalized and flexible.

The efficient absorption of capital by the under-employed, the effective widespread acquisition of skills and their efficient application to production, and the correspondence between productivity and earnings, all call for substantial organizational improvements at the firm level and deep institutional reforms of public policy.

Abating structural poverty runs along these same tracks, but poses different obstacles than improvements of income distribution for policies to be effective. On the one hand, physical capital required may be lower than in modern activities, but the skills gap is greater. On the other hand, effective public policies are more demanding of organizational requirements and institutional creativity. Finally, the remedies have to address the whole vicious circle of circumstances that reproduce poverty from one generation to another.

Strategies for equity improvement must take into account these differences. Designing social policy according to the usual practice, in a way that actually restricts access to the strata above poverty and thus "dumps" the poor, may ratify the disintegration of the poorer strata into a segregated underclass. On the other extreme, a unilateral strategy focusing only on the poor, may debilitate further low and middle strata of the population, where a rich reservoir of skills, social cohesion and political dynamism is located. What is required is a two-tier strategy, that recognizes existing differences between the poor and the non-poor working population and aims at integrating both universes into a single society.

NOTES

1 See Altimir (1987) for a review and discussion of the reliability of income measurements from different types of surveys in Latin America and of their comparability problems.

2 For a detailed compilation of the income distribution statistics available for each country and the selection of comparable pairs, see Altimir (1992). In particular, the selection based on the similarity of data and their treatment permits comparison of Gini coefficients and calculation of their variations as in Table 9.2 which has been computed on the basis of similarly grouped data.

3 For the method of adjustment applied, see Altimir (1987) and for the details of the adjustments CEPAL (1991).

4 See CEPAL (1991a) for details on these country-specific minimum food budgets and how they were set. Minimum food baskets were drawn on the basis of the composition of food consumption of those strata of households that in each country attained with some latitude the minimum nutritional requirements, although such reference baskets were adjusted to those minima as well as to mean national availability of each foodstuff and depurated of high-price-per-calorie or nutritionally superfluous items. Therefore, the criterion to establish the minimum food baskets was one based on habits, taking into account availability and cost rather than one of minimum cost, taking into account availability and habits used in Altimir (1979) for the 1970 estimates.

5 For a discussion of the case for shifting poverty lines over periods of economic growth, see Altimir (1991).

6 CEPAL (1991) also includes estimates of the poverty gaps, but only for 1986.

7 See Altimir (1991).

8 Incomes in kind and imputed incomes, such as receipts from family subsistence

activities of rent of owner-occupied dwellings, are either explicitly excluded or so poorly measured as to be considered excluded in most of the surveys in the data base, which are labour or incomes surveys, only a minority of them being income and expenditure surveys, which may somehow measure such items (see Altimir (1987)).

9 See, for example, Bianchi, Devlin and Ramos (1985, 1987) and CEPAL (1986).

10 See, for example, García (1991).

11 This is per capita product after net factor payments and the effect of terms of trade variations; therefore, this variable incorporates the direct (i.e., accounting) effect of external shocks represented by changes of the terms of trade and of accrued interest on the foreign debt.

12 That is, public consumption expenditure at current prices deflated by the GDP deflator, which is different from public consumption expenditure in real terms as estimated in national accounts, which in Latin American practice reflect, at best, government employment.

13 Contrary to the widespread fashion of using poverty lines constant over time in real terms, there is a strong argument for shifting even *absolute* poverty lines over time, in a context of growth and societal progress (see Altimir, 1991).

14 Even with shifting poverty lines – because of high growth – poverty would have declined, although to lesser degrees.

15 This is found in a simulation done by the author (Altimir, 1991).

16 Even reliable income distribution measures are not able to capture income of the country's residents accrued on assets abroad. Capital flight during the initial years of the crisis has been substantial, particularly in Argentina, Mexico and Venezuela (see Cumby and Levich, 1987). With yields current at the time, property income on assets accumulated abroad by the private sector of those countries may have represented around 3 per cent of household disposable income in Argentina and Mexico and as much as 5 per cent in Venezuela. These proportions have most likely increased the share of the upper decile or quintile on total household income, adding to the changes recorded in Table 9.2 for the first half of the decade. Similarly, the later fall of the international interest rate and related yields should have represented an inverse change (of about half the previous one) of the "total" (i.e. from domestic and foreign sources) share of the upper-income groups.

17 On this subject, see Lustig (1992).

18 Morley and Alvarez (1992) argue that the real devaluation that was required for external adjustment presumably increased agricultural wages after 1981, although the bulk of the devaluation occurred in that year. They also verify that between 1981 and 1989 rural nominal incomes in the lower deciles of the national distribution increased more than those of urban households in the same deciles (cf. their Tables 7b and 7c).

19 Morley and Alvarez (1992) indicate a sharp deterioration of nominal wages in non-basic services relative to industry, among urban households, between 1981 and 1986 (see their Table 7h).

20 See Trejos (1991) and CEPAL (1992).

21 Pollack and Uthoff (1987) estimate an 8 percentage points (from 40 per cent to 48 per cent) increase of absolute poverty in the Greater Santiago area.

22 See: Altimir (1986), for the evolution of income distribution, and Beccaria and Minujin (1991), for the evolution of absolute poverty during the period.

23 Márquez (1992) estimates poverty at the national level at 28 per cent of households in 1985, 32 per cent in 1987 and 41 per cent in 1989.

24 Márquez (1992) puts poverty incidence at the national level at 35 per cent of households, compared with 41 per cent in 1989, a point where it was no doubt higher than in 1990.

25 See Figueroa (1992), Table 2 and Abugattas and Lee (1991), Table 4. On the other hand, the comparison of the distributions of Lima households by size of per capita consumption expenditure, from the 1985/86 and 1990 LSMS surveys (Psacharopoulous *et al.*, 1992), shows little increase of inequality between the two observations; this may reflect another case of "downward equalization" by recession, with the real consumption of the poor falling by almost 7 per cent a year and that of the richer decile by almost 6 per cent a year.

26 Brazil 1979–87, Colombia 1980–6, Chile, 1987–90 and Panama 1979–86.

27 At least, without allowing for time-lags between real devaluation, reallocation of resources to tradables, ensuing expansion of agricultural output, and the eventual participation of peasants and labourers in such an expansion.

28 Such as agrarian reform, as in Peru, or its reversal, as in Chile, both in the 1970s.

29 See Hoffmann (1992).

30 The macroeconomic phases corresponding to the periods selected according to the availability of comparable income distribution or poverty measurements included in Tables 9.2 and 9.3, and changes of macroeconomic and labour variables recorded over those periods are indicated in Table 9.5.

31 The indicator of under-utilization of the urban labour force used here is the sum of the rate of open (urban) unemployment and the proportion of the non-agricultural labour force in informal activities, estimated by PREALC.

32 In Argentina, however, the real wage recovered and the minimum wage jumped in 1983, at the end of the disintegrating military regime, even with accelerating inflation. In Chile, the real average wage (in formal activities) rose up to 1982, in the context of moderate inflation, high labour under-utilization (almost half of the non-agricultural labour force) and a new labour regime that granted total flexibility in the labour market (García, 1991).

33 However, the conspicuous increase of real per capita public consumption expenditure (42 per cent) must have improved the relative position of some middle income strata.

34 Mexico's brief and mild recovery in 1984 did not significantly alter the results of the previous recessive phase, although "the very circumstances that triggered [it] contributed in part to its demise", along with worsening terms of trade in 1985 (Lustig, 1992, pp. 34–6).

35 For a comparative analysis of those reforms, see Corbo and de Melo (1987).

36 However, if pre-recession (*ca.* 1981) inequality in Mexico was even lower than the degree observed in 1977, as suggested earlier, post-recovery inequality would have been somewhat higher than that previous mark.

37 The gradual approach has been abandoned in Mexico in the last phase of the reform process, but then this process has been incorporated in the country's preparation for NAFTA, a strategic jump that, when fulfilled, will radically change the structural conditions of the Mexican economy, including its distributive structures.

38 Including, to be sure, no changes either of the composition of households and of their work and resource utilization strategies – a highly artificial assumption.
39 See ECLAC (1990).
40 Perhaps doubling, for those remaining in such activities, which nevertheless would demand much less capital than the amount required for each job created in the more modern or "bigger business" activities.
41 See ECLAC (1992).

REFERENCES

Abugattas, J. and D.R. Lee (1991) "The Economic Crisis, Policy Reforms and the Poor in Peru During the 1970s and the 1980s", paper presented to the Seminar on Macroeconomic Crises, Policy Reforms and the Poor in Latin America, Cali, October 1–4.

Altimir, O. (1979) "La dimensión de la pobreza en América Latina", Cuadernos de la CEPAL 27, Santiago.

Altimir, O. (1982) "The Extent of Poverty in Latin America", World Bank Staff Working Paper 522, Washington DC.

Altimir, O. (1986) "Estimaciones de la distribución del ingreso en la Argentina, 1953–1980", Desarrolla Económico 26(100), Buenos Aires.

Altimir, O. (1987) "Income Distribution Statistics in Latin America and their Reliability", Review of Income and Wealth 33(2).

Altimir, O. (1991) "Latin American Poverty in the Last Two Decades", paper presented to the Seminar on Macroeconomic Crises, Policy Reforms and the Poor in Latin America, Cali, October 1–4.

Altimir, O. (1992) "Cambios en las desigualdades de ingreso y en la pobreza en América Latina", paper presented at the Fifth Interamerican Seminar on Economics organized by the National Bureau of Economic Research, the PUC of Rio and the Instituto Torcuato Di Tella, Buenos Aires, May 8–9.

Beccaria, L.A. (1991) "Distribución del ingreso en la Argentina: Explorando lo sucedido desde mediados de los setenta", Desarrolla Económico 31(123), Buenos Aires.

Beccaria, L. and A. Minujin (1991) "Sobre la medición de la pobreza: Enseñanzas a partir de la experiencia argentina", UNICEF, Working Paper 8, Buenos Aires, November.

Bianchi, A., R. Devlin and J. Ramos (1985) External Debt in Latin America. Adjustment Policies and Renegotiation, Lynne Rienner Publishers Inc., in cooperation with the UN Economic Commission for Latin America, Boulder CO.

Bianchi, A., R. Devlin and J. Ramos (1987) "El proceso de ajuste en la América Latina, 1981–1986", El Trimestre Económico LIV(4), No 216.

Canitrot, A. (1981) "Teoría y práctica del liberalismo. Política antiinflacionaria y apertura económica en la Argentina, 1976–1981", Desarrolla Económico 21(82), Buenos Aires.

Canitrot, A. and S. Junco (1992) Apertura y condiciones macroeconómicas: el caso argentino, BID, Serie de Documentos de Trabajo 108, Washington DC.

CEPAL (1979) América Latina en el umbral de los años 80, (E/CEPAL/G.1106), Santiago.

CEPAL (1986) "The Economic Crisis: Policies for Adjustment, Stabilization, and Growth", Cuadernos de la CEPAL 54 (LC/G.1408/Rev.2), Santiago, October.

CEPAL (1988) "Antecedentes estadísticos de la distribución del ingreso. Mexico, 1950–1977", Serie Distribución del Ingreso 7, Santiago.

CEPAL (1991a) "Magnitud de la pobreza en América Latina en los años ochenta", Estudios e Informes de la CEPAL 81, Santiago.

CEPAL (1991b) La equidad en el panorama social de América Latina durante los años ochenta, (LC/G. 1686), Santiago, October.

CEPAL (1991c) *Una estimación de la magnitud de la pobreza en Chile 1990*, (LC/R. 1069), Santiago.
CEPAL (1991d) *Estabilización y equidad en América Latina en los ochenta*, (LC/R. 1132), Santiago.
CEPAL (1992) *El Perfil de la Pobreza en América Latina a comienzos de los años 90*, (LC/L. 716), Santiago.
CEPAL (1993) *Panorama Social de América Latina*, (in press).
Corbo, V. and J. de Melo (1987) "Lessons from the Southern Cone Policy Reforms", The World Bank, *Research Observer 2*, 2, July, Washington DC.
Cumby, R. and R. Levich (1987) "On the Definition and Magnitude of Recent Capital Flight", in D. Lessard and J. Williamson (eds), *Capital Flight and Third World Debt*, Institute for International Economics, Washington DC.
ECLAC (1990) *Changing Production Patterns with Social Equity* (LC/G.1601 (SES. 23/4)), March, Santiago de Chile.
ECLAC (1992) *Social Equity and Changing Production Patterns: an Integrated Approach* (LC/G. 1701 (SES. 24/3)), February, Santiago.
Fanelli, J.M., R. Frenkel and G. Rozenwurcel (1990) *Growth and Structural Reform in Latin America. Where We Stand*, CEDES, Buenos Aires.
Ffrench-Davis, R. and D. Raczynski (1990) *The Impact of Global Recession and National Policies on Living Standards: Chile, 1973–89*, CIEPLAN, Notas Técnicas No. 97, Third Edition, Santiago.
Figueroa, A. (1992) "Social Policy and Economic Adjustment in Peru", paper presented at the Brookings Institution and Inter-American Dialogue's Conference on Poverty and Inequality in Latin America, Washington DC, July.
García, N.E. (1991) *Reestructuración, Ahorro y Mercado de Trabajo*, PREALC, Investigaciones sobre Empleo **34**, Santiago.
Heskia, I. (1980) "Distribución del ingreso en el Gran Santiago 1957–1979", Dpto. de Economía, Universidad de Chile, *Documento Serie Investigación* **53**, October, Santiago.
Hoffmann, R. (1992) *Crise Economica e Pobreza no Brasil no Periodo 1979–90*, Universidade de Sao Paulo, Escola Superior de Agricultura "Luiz de Queiroz", Departamento de Economia e Sociologia Rural, Brazil, July.
Londoño, J.L. (1990) "Income Distribution During the Structural Transformation. Colombia 1938–1988", PhD thesis, Harvard University (mimeo).
Lustig, N. (1992) *Mexico: The Remaking of an Economy*, The Brookings Institution, Washington DC.
Márquez, G. (1992) "Poverty and Social Policies in Venezuela", Instituto de Estudios Superiores de Administración. Paper presented at the Brookings Institution and Inter-American Dialogue's Conference on Poverty and Inequality in Latin America, Washington DC.
Márquez, G. and J. Mukherjee (1991) *Distribución del ingreso y pobreza en Venezuela*, Instituto de Estudios Superiores de Administración, Noviembre 1991, Caracas.
Melgar, A. (1981) "Distribución del ingreso en el Uruguay", *Serie Investigaciones* **18**, CLAEH, Montevideo.
Melgar, A. and F. Villalobos (1987) "La desigualdad como estrategia", Argumentos del CLAEH.
Meller, P. (1992) *Economía política de la apertura comercial chilena*, Proyecto Regional de CEPAL "Reformas de Política para Aumentar la Efectividad del Estado en América Latina y el Caribe", diciembre, Santiago.
Morley, S.A. and C. Alvarez (1992) "Poverty and Adjustment in Costa Rica", Department of Economics, IDB, Preliminary version, January, Washington DC.
Pollak, M. and A. Uthoff (1987) *Pobreza y mercado de trabajo en el Gran Santiago. 1969–1985*, PREALC, Documentos de Trabajo, **299**, Santiago.
Psacharopoulos, G. et al. (1992) *Poverty and Income Distribution in Latin America. The Story of the 1980s*, Report No. 11266-LAC, The World Bank, November, Washington DC.
Riveros, L.A. (1985) "Desempleo, distribución del ingreso y política social", *Revista del Centro de Estudios Públicos* **20**, May, Santiago.

Trejos, J.D. (1991) "Crisis, Ajuste y Pobreza: la Experiencia de Costa Rica en los Ochenta", paper presented to the Seminar on Macroeconomic Crises, Policy Reforms and the Poor in Latin America, Cali, October 1–4.

Williamson, J. (1990) "The Progress of Policy Reform in Latin America", Institute for International Economics, *Policy Analyses in International Economics* 28, January, Washington DC.

World Bank (1991) "The Challenge of Development", *World Development Report 1991*, Oxford University Press, Washington DC.

10 | Sustaining Economic Recovery in Latin America: State Capacity, Markets, and Politics

MERILEE S. GRINDLE

Latin America's economic recovery from the crisis of the 1980s will depend in part on the quality of the reform measures adopted by governments throughout the region. As other chapters in this book show, individual policy measures and packages of policy reforms must satisfy two conditions related to their substance. First, they must be the right policies: do they identify the appropriate steps to take for resolving specific problems of debt, inflation, economic stagnation, trade, and lagging social welfare indicators? Second, they must be well-designed policies: Are the measures crafted so they accomplish the ends sought? During the past decade, much was accomplished in terms of the research and analysis necessary for satisfying these two conditions, and much of the energy of Latin America's policy-makers was directed towards this goal.

Unfortunately, passing these two tests is not enough to ensure economic growth and recovery in the future. As Puyana argues in an earlier chapter, these achievements will be directly affected by conditions in the international economic environment, conditions that may be only modestly supportive for many countries during the 1990s (World Bank, 1991, ch. 1). Unlike concerns about the quality of the economic reform measures, passing the test of viability in an international context is largely out of the hands of the policy-makers, policy managers, and citizens of Latin American countries, who so desperately seek brighter economic and political futures.

Even allowing for a more dynamic and supportive international context for growth and development in Latin America, a fourth test is central to effective economic reform: how capable is the Latin American state of managing and sustaining economic restructuring?[1] This question points to the importance of redefining long-standing relationships between the state and the economy and the state and civic society, if economic restructuring is to succeed. New relationships to the economy and civic society require states that are capable in a variety of ways. In this chapter, I explore the dimensions of state capacity

that are central to economic recovery and consider the impact of the crisis of
the 1980s on various dimensions of state capacity.

I DEVELOPMENTAL STATES, MINIMALIST STATES, AND CAPABLE STATES

Accumulating evidence of misguided development policies and mismanagement of public institutions and public functions in the 1970s and 1980s raised
serious questions about the capacity of existing states to manage tasks of
economic development. In development economics, for example, issues related
to state capacity dominated a considerable amount of research, analysis, and
discussion. A field that had pioneered research and analysis on "market
failures" in the 1950s and 1960s began to focus increasing attention on
"government failures" by the mid-1970s (see Bhagwati, 1978; Colander, 1984;
Krueger, 1974; Lal, 1984 and Srinivasan, 1985). As a result, scholarly
literature of the 1980s increasingly scored actions by governments that
distorted markets and created disincentives for productive use of private and
public resources. Similarly, explanations for poor development performance,
high levels of debt, and extensive fiscal deficits focused on the regulatory,
investment, and distribution decisions of states that had grown too large,
intervened in economic interactions too energetically, and mismanaged policy-
making and implementation too regularly (see, for example, World Bank,
1984).

For a number of analysts of economic stagnation and decline, the state
became the single most important culprit in explaining a decade or more of
poor economic performance, extensive rent-seeking, and widespread inefficiency, mismanagement, and corruption (see especially Colander, 1984).
Policy prescriptions derived from this analysis emphasized the importance of
radically diminishing the scope of state activities and state intervention in the
market, simultaneously diminishing opportunities for rent-seeking and
opening up greater scope for private economic agents to make efficient
decisions about the allocation of resources (see, for examples, Buchanan,
Tollison, and Tullock, 1980). This perspective was important in influencing a
decade of policy recommendations and central in negotiations of Latin
American countries with international financial institutions.

By the mid-1980s, however, other voices began to insist on the importance
of the state to effective economic development (see, for a review, Killick, 1989;
see also Callaghy, 1989 and Krasner, 1984). While acknowledging the
problems created by over-centralized decision-making, extensive regulation,
inefficient state-owned enterprises, and disincentives to productive use of
resources by private economic agents, they argued that a minimalist approach
to the state failed to recognize that states were also central to creating

conditions under which sustained economic development could occur. In this view, states were uniquely able to establish and maintain basic conditions of law and order, enforce the rules of the game for economic competition, manage macroeconomic policy, invest in appropriate physical and social infrastructure, and respond to deeply embedded issues of inequity and poverty (see Berry, 1990; Boeninger, 1991; Hopkins, 1990; Israel, 1990; Killick, 1989; World Bank, 1991, pp. 128–47). The reaction against the state, according to some, had been "a reduction too far" (Killick, 1989). Supporting this perspective was a significant amount of research on the East Asian "success stories" that emphasized the important role of strong and interventionist states in the development of countries such as Korea, Japan, Taiwan, and Singapore (see especially Haggard and Moon, 1983 and Wade, 1990). By the end of the 1980s, economists increasingly noted the importance of "governance" to sustainable economic development.

Economists were not alone in reconsidering the role of the state in development during the 1980s. Political scientists, political economists, and other social scientists exploring issues of regime type, regime transition, and civic society also focused on issues of governance. A considerable literature emerged exploring the legitimacy of institutions of government, participation in government decision-making, and the responsiveness of politicians and governments to societal demands and aspirations (see Bright and Harding, 1984; Colburn, 1990a). Each of these factors were demonstrated to be important to the ability of states to marshall support for economic policy reforms and new departures in development strategies. Empirically, political institutions such as parties and trade unions, grass-roots social and political organizations, as well as elite pressure groups, helped define new relationships between the state and civic society and establish norms for holding public officials accountable for their actions.[2] In some cases, these initiatives sought to contest the right of government to make decisions under existing rules of the game for representation; in other cases, the principal purpose of the mobilization of civic organizations was to increase the capacity of such groups to negotiate effectively with the state; in still other cases, local groups sought to provide services that existing states were either too weak or too unresponsive to provide. Central to all such efforts was an implicit recognition that states, to be effective managers of economic development, must be legitimate, enjoy some popular support, and be capable of resolving economic and social conflict on an ongoing basis.

Criticism of existing state activities, growing realization of the positive contributions that states could make to economic development, extensive evidence of deteriorating relationships between states and civic societies, and increasing interest in the importance of civic society to economic development encouraged considerable rethinking of the role of the state among both scholars and development practitioners. The dominant view during the 1950s and 1960s was that the "developmental state" should play a central role as the engine of national development, and during the late 1970s and 1980s that the "minimalist state" should exit as much as possible from economic interactions. The late 1980s and early 1990s saw the emergence of interest in the "capable state", whose role was to contribute institutional, technical, administrative, and political skills to the task of managing economic development (see Boeninger, 1991; Hopkins, 1990; Israel, 1990; World Bank, 1991).

Drawing on the diverse literatures of economics, political science, and political economy, I consider four dimensions of state capacity that are central to the effective management of economic development.[3] I define these dimensions in the following ways:

(1) "Institutional capacity" is the ability of states to make and maintain effective rules of the game for regulating economic and political interactions. These are broad sets of legal norms and institutional relationships that govern interactions among economic agents (such as property rights and contracts) and that determine relationships of power and responsibility in political society (such as constitutional and administrative rules that set standards of behaviour for public servants and that establish procedures for authoritative decision-making, conflict resolution, and the conduct of public affairs).

(2) "Technical capacity" refers to the ability of states to set and manage effective macroeconomic policy, including the ability to assess economic policy options and to utilize technical information and technical advice in decision-making.

(3) Administrative capacity refers to the ability of governments to carry out the normal administrative functions of government, to develop and maintain physical infrastructure, and to deliver basic social services. This means the ability to carry out such basic tasks as collecting taxes, delivering the mail, building and maintaining roads, and ensuring the effective performance of education, health, and public health services.

(4) Political capacity is the ability of governments to provide effective channels for demands made by citizens, to allow for the representation of diverse interests, to include citizen participation in decision-making, and to respond to societal needs and aspirations. This dimension of state capacity requires that political leaders and societal groups be jointly involved in the allocation of public resources and the mediation of economic and political conflict. Political capacity differs from institutional capacity in that it deals not with the broad rules of the game but with the everyday interactions between citizens and public officials within contexts in which the rules are assumed to be clear and equitable.

This list focuses on what ought to be in place if states are to contribute positively to economic development. Existing states never achieve any of these dimensions fully and they will vary in their ability to demonstrate these capacities. In addition, individual states will vary over time in how well they are able to achieve specific dimensions of capacity. Evidence from Latin America indicates that the combination of economic and political crises during the 1980s affected existing characteristics of state capacity in many countries. In brief, most states were able to strengthen their technical capacity, but saw their institutional, administrative, and political capacities seriously jeopardized. In the remainder of this chapter, I suggest that using increased technical capacity and rebuilding diminished institutional, administrative, and political capacities will be critical to sustaining policy reforms and restructuring economies in the future.

II   STATE CAPACITY AND THE CRISES OF THE 1980s

The 1980s and early 1990s were a period of economic and political crises of historical dimensions in Latin America. Throughout the region, economies that had grown relatively well in earlier decades were severely weakened and even destroyed by massive debt burdens, sky-rocketing rates of inflation, low commodity prices, and high interest rates. Political systems that had been entrenched for years faced severe challenges to their right to govern. Regime changes, political violence, repression, civic protest, and demands for accountability of officials and protection of civil rights are well-documented characteristics of this era. As a result of these circumstances, long-established relationships between state and economy and state and society were called into question in economic, political, and social arenas. These conditions also had significant implications for the dimensions of state capacity outlined earlier.

II.1   Institutional capacity

Sustained economic development requires relatively stable rules of the game for regulating economic and political relations. Such rules, when effectively enforced, encourage predictability in a variety of economic and political interactions and inspire individuals and groups to make current decisions in the context of longer-term expectations. In Latin America, institutional capacity was severely affected by the economic and political crises of the 1980s.

Compared to other regions of the developing world, Latin American states had achieved substantial institutional capacity by the 1970s. States such as those that emerged in Argentina, Brazil, Chile, Venezuela, Mexico, and Costa Rica had long been institutionalized in terms of their coercive and administrative infrastructure and had penetrated deep into social systems through government-sponsored programmes, patronage networks, corporatist interest representation, and military and police presence. Then, the emergence in the 1960s and 1970s of bureaucratic authoritarian regimes, identified particularly with Argentina, Brazil, Chile, and Uruguay, further emphasized the notion of strong and coercive states in the region (see O'Donnell, 1973; Linz and Stepan, 1978). Although not conforming to the bureaucratic authoritarian model, the Mexican state was also noted for its strong capacity to set the rules for economic and political interaction (Hamilton, 1982; Bennett and Sharpe, 1985; Grindle, 1977). States such as those in Colombia, Costa Rica, and Venezuela, while less autonomous and more penetrated by societal interests, nevertheless maintained considerable capacity to govern authoritatively (see Berry, Hellman, and Solaún, 1980; Karl, 1986; Winson, 1989). The institutional capacity of such states did not ensure equity or the effective representation of interests in national decision-making, but did, for considerable periods, ensure the maintenance of order and relatively stable rules of the game for economic interactions, even in the context of inequity.

Given the economic and political upheaval of the decade, it is not surprising that during the 1980s, many governments in Latin America lost the ability to set the broad rules of the game for regulating economic, political, and social behaviour. State authority collapsed for extended periods in Bolivia and Peru, was severely challenged through the exposure of official corruption in Argentina, Brazil, Mexico, and Venezuela, was confronted by the countervailing power of drug barons and military chieftains in Colombia and Panama, and threatened by civil war in El Salvador and Nicaragua. Indeed, in Colombia, Bolivia, Peru, and parts of Central America, national governments charged with the task of enforcing rules and ensuring order at local and regional levels were often less able to do so than local strongmen, drug cartels, military commanders, and revolutionary groups.[4] Military regimes, no longer able to sustain high rates of growth in the face of economic crisis, also lost their ability to claim legitimacy based on the ability to "produce results".[5] In economic interactions, some states were overwhelmed by the emergence of parallel and informal markets and their own inability to enforce contracts or property rights in the face of powerful informal arrangements among economic actors.[6] Under stress of the sort experienced in the 1980s, judicial systems were also undermined or exposed as corrupt, weak, and inequitable.

Latin America's economic recovery will be affected by the extent to which governments respond to weakened institutional capacity. In fact, the 1980s and early 1990s are replete with evidence of efforts to rewrite and renegotiate the rules of the game for economic and political interactions (see Williamson, 1990). In almost all countries of the region, efforts to introduce neo-liberal economic development strategies implied initiatives to redefine the relationship between state and economy. Privatization of public enterprises was undertaken in most countries, accompanied by initiatives to define the limits of public authority over private economic interactions and the limits of private property rights. Similarly, deregulation efforts in many countries incorporated significant attention to rethinking the rights of property and the power of the state to affect such rights. Extensive efforts to revamp judicial systems were undertaken in part to strengthen the rule of law and the ability of the state to enforce contracts and obligations.

Measures to re-establish the institutional capacity of the state were most apparent in moves to redefine the relationship between the state and civic society. For many countries, redefining the rules of the game for political interactions implied developing a consensus on the need to return to democratic regimes after extended periods of military rule. Throughout the region, civilian elites – often representing the political parties, unions, and groups that had been suppressed by military regimes – met to negotiate "pacts" that would ease the transition to civilian and democratic regimes (see especially Karl, 1990; O'Donnell, Schmitter, and Whitehead, 1986). This generally involved not only reaching agreement about the rules of the game for political competition and policy decision-making, but also overcoming long-standing animosities and policy divisions among diverse groups of politicians and economic interests.[7] Overall, the decade witnessed the widely celebrated resurgence of democratic systems in the region and the return of the military to the barracks. In 1980, ten of nineteen Latin American countries were ruled by the military; in 1992, there remained only one such country, although the military continued to have a large informal political power in at least eight more. By 1992, there were at least eleven genuine multiparty political systems with competitive and periodic elections.

The durability of these newly installed democracies was not a foregone conclusion, however. While the broad legitimacy of democratic processes was accepted widely, more general agreements about institutional roles and relationships of power among institutions continued to divide political society in country after country. In particular, executives and legislatures argued over the distribution of power between them and the right to initiate public action; disputes over electoral rules and the fairness of results were equally apparent (Grindle and Thoumi, 1992; Conaghan, 1989). Allegations of fraud, corruption, and abuses of power were also frequent, suggesting that effective rules for holding public officials accountable for their actions were still wanting. In Brazil, Argentina, and Venezuela, allegations of corrupt behaviour by presidents and their close advisors lessened public support for newly installed democratic governments and diminished their prestige (see Keck, 1990; Schneider, 1991). In Peru, a quasi-coup by President Alberto Fujimori in 1992 was a direct attack on the formal procedures of the democratic institutions set up in 1980. In Mexico, the extent to which the government was willing to allow the rules for electoral contestation and political representation to be rewritten, and therefore possibly to undermine the long-standing hegemony of the PRI, was ambiguous at best. Thus, considerable efforts to renegotiate the basic rules governing economic and political interaction were

apparent in many Latin American countries, but newly established relationships between state and economy and state and society remained fragile in
many of them in the early 1990s.

II.2   Technical capacity

Economic development requires the capacity to manage macroeconomic policy
and to have skilled personnel and appropriate institutions to analyse policy
options and advise decision-makers accordingly. Indeed, a large policy-focused
literature exploring the origins of lagging industrial and agricultural productivity, debt, inflation, balance of payments crises, and budget deficits calls
attention to flawed macroeconomic policies and their management in Latin
America. (See, for example, Dornbusch and Edwards, 1991.)

Despite evident limitations that continued to plague efforts at macroeconomic policy-making, technical capacity to establish and manage this aspect
of economic development increased significantly in most countries in the
region during the 1980s. In part, increased technical capacity was a response to
the need to design stabilization and structural adjustment programmes insisted
upon by the IMF, the World Bank, and other international agencies as
conditions for lending. Over the course of the 1980s and early 1990s, evidence
of increased technical capacity in central economic ministries was almost
universal. Prominent economists became ministers and their advisers, and
often the closest advisers to presidents, in Argentina, Bolivia, Chile, Colombia,
Ecuador, Mexico, Peru, Venezuela, and elsewhere. In these and other
countries, economic advisory teams and top ministerial positions of "independent" technocrats were increasingly recruited from universities, think tanks,
international agencies, and the private sector, rather than from political parties
or the ranks of personal loyalists (see especially Naim, 1991, p. 19; Malloy,
1989). Similarly, policy analysis units increased in number in central economic
ministries and played a more intimate role in national policy decisions.

Presidents of Colombia, Mexico, and Ecuador in the late 1980s and early
1990s were all trained as economists. During the same period, the ministers of
finance in Mexico, Chile, Colombia, Ecuador, and Peru all held PhD degrees
in economics. The influence of technocrats on high-level policy-making,
strategic development planning, and macroeconomic management achieved
new heights in Mexico under the administration of Carlos Salinas de Gortari,
where eight of twenty-six ministerial appointees held post-graduate degrees in
economics, many of them from economics departments in major US
universities. Throughout the tenure of this government, technocrats were
placed in positions of extensive authority, and technical analysis units became
central to policy-making at all levels. In Chile, eighteen members of President
Aylwin's team held post-graduate degrees (Sigmund, 1990). In Peru, four of

six top economic advisors in the Fujimori government held PhDs. In Argentina, Chile, Colombia, Ecuador, and Peru, technocrats assumed ministerial-level positions and transformed their ministries through the introduction of computers, policy analysis units, and young, well-trained economists.

During the decade, central economic ministries, their technocratic leadership, and their technical analysis units became more important in national policy-making, often to the detriment of cabinets, legislative institutions, party leaders, and traditional ministries such as those of the interior, public works, and foreign affairs. Economic policy-making also became more highly centralized and focused around presidents, their economic teams, and the technical units supporting these influential individuals.[8] In a number of countries, "economic cabinets" formed of top economic policy advisors met regularly and frequently with the president. Similarly, in several cases, the minister of finance or the minister of the economy became economic "czars" who, through delegated presidential authority, co-ordinated economic policy-making and strategic planning.

Much of the process of economic policy change that was introduced during the 1980s and 1990s was promulgated through presidential decrees rather than as law debated and passed through congress, indicating the extent to which centralized economic management had come to be defined as a presidential and executive prerogative. Presidents themselves began to be assessed on how well they managed their economic teams and the extent to which such teams developed consensus about the broad direction of national economic policy and the instruments to be used to achieve it (see Grindle and Thoumi, 1992).

Thus, most Latin American states notably increased their technical capacity to set and manage macroeconomic policy during the 1980s and early 1990s. Yet countries differed in the extent to which technocratic elites were insulated from the direct pressure of interest groups and political controversy, and in the extent to which economic teams were able to work effectively together and agree upon the scope, nature, and priorities of stabilization and structural adjustment measures (Grindle and Thoumi, 1992). There were also significant differences in the extent to which political leaders were able to communicate the substance and rationale of policy change to broad sectors of the population.

In explaining these differences, one of the defining characteristics of the relative success of some countries in promoting extensive policy change – Mexico is the best example, but Argentina under Menem, and Chile under Aylwin are also cases in point – was the ability to generate and communicate a vision of what altered economic policy would bring to the country in question. This vision, promulgated primarily by political leaders, set the broad framework for understanding policy errors of the past, indicating remedies for these errors, and putting together coalitions of support around newly defined economic goals. In these cases, the impact of new technical capabilities on the formulation and implementation of economic policy was greater because it was paired with a clear and widely disseminated vision of a new and more promising future if major economic policy changes were introduced and sustained. In these cases, enhanced technical capacity was more fully utilized in policy-making contexts.

II.3   Administrative capacity

The capacity of states to carry out routine administrative functions and to provide for basic services and investment in human resource development is an often overlooked aspect of economic development. It is a critical capacity, however, because it affects the ability of private economic agents to achieve their goals, the availability of a well-trained and healthy work-force, and the satisfaction of basic societal needs. A decade of economic stagnation and decline had significant implications for the administrative capacity of Latin American states. Data on government expenditure and on investment in social and physical infrastructure begin to suggest the extent to which the crisis years of the 1980s were a "lost decade" in terms of human welfare and basic economic infrastructure.

In many Latin American countries, austerity budgets were a clear response to expanding government deficits and inability to borrow additional funds to finance the deficit. Table 10.1 presents an index of current government expenditures for eight Latin American countries. The data indicate that in Argentina, Bolivia, and Peru, budget expenditures in the late 1980s were significantly less than they had been in 1980. Government expenditures in Chile and Ecuador increased only marginally during the decade; only in Brazil and Mexico were significantly more funds available at the end of the period than at its outset.

Even where budgets increased, government funding for national development needs fell in relative terms as increasing proportions of national government expenditures were needed to service the debt (see Bourguignon,

Table 10.1   Index of current expenditures (1980 = 100).

	1980	1981	1982	1983	1984	1985	1986	1987	1988	1989
Argentina	100.0	107.2	96.1	108.8	86.6	129.1	120.8	115.8	85.2	N/A
Bolivia	100.0	94.4	153.3	74.1	233.9	N/A	86.7	80.5	88.8	99.3
Brazil	100.0	94.6	102.6	98.6	105.1	138.3	159.5	152.8	253.3	N/A
Chile	100.0	111.3	109.5	102.5	106.8	103.5	103.8	107.5	133.9	N/A
Colombia	100.0	105.9	118.8	124.3	135.7	120.7	124.7	130.8	N/A	N/A
Ecuador	100.0	137.9	133.7	111.4	113.9	133.3	131.8	121.3	112.8	113.5
Mexico	100.0	132.7	214.0	186.4	172.2	192.3	219.8	179.4	211.8	223.0
Peru	100.0	100.6	86.8	83.6	76.6	79.7	93.9	95.7	67.1	75.8

Source: Adapted from World Bank, *World Tables*.

de Melo, Morrisson, 1991, p. 1500; Meller, 1991). Table 10.2 indicates that in Argentina, Bolivia, Chile, and Mexico, all or part of budgets expended on education services decreased between 1980 and 1989 and per capita expenditures on education declined markedly in all countries except Brazil. Table 10.3 provides similar indices for health expenditure, demonstrating declines in sector budgets in Argentina, Bolivia, Ecuador, Mexico, and Peru and declines in per capita expenditure in six out of seven countries. A study of central government expenditures in Colombia also indicates declining shares for education and health as debt service increased (Hommes, 1990, p. 204).

These figures provide clear signals of decreased ability to provide for basic educational and health services in even the largest countries of the region. They do not allow for insight into the impact of decreased budgets on the quality of educational or health services, but other, more focused studies indicate a disturbing reality with regard to investment in human development during the decade. In education, internal adjustments in sector budget allocations in Chile, Costa Rica, the Dominican Republic, and Venezuela cushioned the impact of budgetary cuts by increasing the share of primary education in overall education expenditures; in Argentina, Colombia, and Jamaica, however, this share fell (Grosh, 1990, p. 40; Hommes, 1990, p. 205). Country studies of educational services refer particularly to cuts in teachers' salaries, by far the largest portion of education budgets in all countries. In the five years between 1983 and 1988, Mexico's primary school teachers' salaries decreased by 34 per cent in real terms; in Costa Rica in 1991, primary teacher salaries were 66 per cent of their 1980 levels (Reimers, 1990, p. 547). In Argentina, Bolivia, Brazil, Chile, Colombia, Costa Rica, Mexico, and Peru, expenditures on teaching materials fell during the decade (Grosh, 1990, p. 49; Reimers, 1990, p. 543). In Bolivia and Costa Rica, the number of students per teacher in primary schools increased, and primary enrolment rates declined in Bolivia, Chile, Costa Rica, and El Salvador (Grosh, 1990, pp. 49, 62). Rural youth suffered more than urban youth through cutbacks in educational budgets. Again, these figures suggest a decreasing capacity of governments to provide for basic education of their populations.

In health care, a similar story emerges from country studies. Drastic reductions in health professionals' salaries in Mexico have been documented, as have cutbacks in investments and routine maintenance of health facilities in Chile. In El Salvador and Jamaica, administrative expenditures were cut and investments in preventive medicine suffered in Venezuela (Grosh, 1990, p. 43). Increasingly unfavourable nurse–doctor ratios affected Argentina, Bolivia, Chile, Costa Rica, and Venezuela (Grosh, 1990, p. 51). These declines in services affected Latin American populations at a time when economic hardship increased the number of poverty-induced conditions like malnutrition, gastro-intestinal illnesses, respiratory diseases, cholera, and tuberculosis, and at a time when health ministries were under increasing pressure to respond to AIDS and AIDS-related illnesses. With growing numbers of households no

Table 10.2 Index of total and per capita educational expenditures.

Total educational expenditures (1980 = 100)

	1980	1981	1982	1983	1984	1985	1986	1987	1988	1989
Argentina	100.0	91.3	67.6	90.6	88.7	76.3	71.4	78.4	77.8	N/A
Bolivia	100.0	88.5	75.3	75.8	103.6	N/A	56.6	70.8	65.1	71.6
Brazil	100.0	109.5	140.7	103.2	91.4	113.0	149.4	200.7	294.8	N/A
Chile	100.0	112.2	107.7	94.2	95.2	94.4	94.0	91.9	88.8	N/A
Colombia	N/A	N/A	N/A	N/A	N/A	N/A	N/A	N/A	N/A	N/A
Ecuador	100.0	137.9	133.7	111.4	113.9	133.3	131.8	121.3	112.8	113.5
Mexico	100.0	127.6	136.0	95.6	99.2	101.9	87.5	88.9	82.7	98.9
Peru	100.0	102.7	143.6	129.8	131.3	125.3	175.1	126.3	108.7	108.6

Per capita educational expenditures (1980 = 100)

	1980	1981	1982	1983	1984	1985	1986	1987	1988	1989
Argentina	100.0	84.8	57.2	78.7	80.6	76.1	103.9	110.5	76.9	N/A
Bolivia	100.0	86.2	71.3	70.0	93.1	N/A	48.1	58.6	52.4	56.1
Brazil	100.0	107.1	134.4	96.5	83.6	101.1	130.9	172.1	247.7	N/A
Chile	100.0	110.3	104.2	89.6	89.0	86.8	85.0	81.6	77.6	N/A
Colombia	N/A	N/A	N/A	N/A	N/A	N/A	N/A	N/A	N/A	N/A
Ecuador	100.0	90.2	80.4	71.3	67.6	68.0	67.2	59.8	50.9	28.3
Mexico	100.0	124.7	130.0	89.5	90.8	91.4	76.9	76.5	69.7	81.5
Peru	100.0	100.2	137.0	121.0	119.7	111.8	152.9	107.9	90.9	88.9

Source: Adapted from World Bank, *World Tables*.

Table 10.3 Index of total and per capita health expenditures.

Total health expenditures (1980 = 100)

	1980	1981	1982	1983	1984	1985	1986	1987	1988	1989
Argentina	100.0	86.1	59.0	82.3	85.5	81.7	113.1	121.8	85.8	N/A
Bolivia	100.0	57.1	24.3	19.5	28.1	N/A	13.0	57.9	54.2	52.0
Brazil	100.0	94.6	102.6	98.6	105.1	138.3	159.5	152.8	253.3	N/A
Chile	100.0	98.1	97.8	80.4	88.7	85.6	85.8	95.2	101.5	N/A
Colombia	N/A	N/A	N/A	N/A	N/A	N/A	N/A	N/A	N/A	N/A
Ecuador	100.0	114.4	109.5	97.2	100.3	104.0	102.2	143.6	117.6	66.4
Mexico	100.0	98.6	101.8	77.8	92.0	92.1	91.6	93.1	92.3	96.8
Peru	100.0	117.5	118.6	113.1	116.5	114.1	123.3	109.1	90.3	71.2

Per capita health expenditures (1980 = 100)

	1980	1981	1982	1983	1984	1985	1986	1987	1988	1989
Argentina	100.0	86.1	74.5	87.7	84.8	92.4	79.7	85.9	96.3	N/A
Bolivia	100.0	55.6	23.0	18.0	25.3	N/A	11.1	47.9	43.6	40.7
Brazil	100.0	105.4	117.7	97.2	102.0	113.1	122.2	176.4	184.2	N/A
Chile	100.0	96.4	94.6	76.4	83.0	78.7	77.6	84.6	88.7	N/A
Colombia	N/A	N/A	N/A	N/A	N/A	N/A	N/A	N/A	N/A	N/A
Ecuador	100.0	111.1	103.4	89.1	89.3	90.0	86.2	117.8	94.1	52.2
Mexico	100.0	96.3	97.3	72.8	84.3	82.6	80.5	80.1	77.7	79.8
Peru	100.0	114.7	113.1	105.4	106.3	101.8	107.7	93.2	75.5	58.2

Source: Adapted from World Bank, *World Tables*.

longer employed in the formal sector, and with a steady decrease in average wage rates, better-off households that had formerly had access to private health care turned increasingly to already overburdened public health care. Everywhere, the impact of austerity budgets for health were felt most among the poor and those living in rural areas.

The capacity to provide for infrastructure is also an investment critical to economic recovery and growth, as well as a general indicator of the extent to which populations are being provided with basic services such as electricity, water, and transportation. Among the most basic investments for infrastructure is that for roads. Table 10.4 indicates that investment in roads in most countries remained near 1980 levels, increasing significantly only in Brazil and Chile. While few studies document the impact of lack of resources directed toward infrastructure investment, much commentary refers to roads fallen into disrepair and those that have become virtually impassible due to neglect, suggesting a backlog of important investments for future economic development.

Economic recovery in Latin America will be affected by the ability of governments to carry out such normal functions of government as providing for an educated and healthy work-force and building and maintaining systems of transportation and communication. The economic crisis of the 1980s hit this ability particularly hard in most countries of the region and created increased need to strengthen the capacity of the state to be both efficient and effective in the activities that have a direct impact on the lives of citizens and the ability of the economy to function well. Building administrative capacity is a difficult task at best, requiring not only significant budgetary outlays but also extensive efforts to alter bureaucratic behaviour and the incentives for performance that affect how organizations deliver services and respond to citizens' needs. This is a challenge that remains to be addressed by most countries in the region.

In Latin America during the 1980s, programmes to target the poor with social services were initiated in some countries and user fees introduced to

Table 10.4 Index of expenditures on roads (1980 = 100).

	1980	1981	1982	1983	1984	1985	1986	1987	1988	1989
Argentina	100.0	87.4	76.7	91.6	89.8	99.2	86.7	94.6	107.4	N/A
Bolivia	N/A	N/A	N/A	N/A	N/A	N/A	N/A	N/A	N/A	N/A
Brazil	100.0	110.1	98.4	100.8	74.8	111.6	111.8	193.4	183.8	N/A
Chile	100.0	153.0	128.9	152.3	193.1	215.2	236.3	243.0	231.2	N/A
Colombia	N/A	N/A	N/A	N/A	N/A	N/A	N/A	N/A	N/A	N/A
Ecuador	100.0	88.8	86.1	67.8	92.4	128.5	111.7	103.8	N/A	62.7
Mexico	100.0	177.2	193.0	223.4	210.3	155.0	102.4	113.8	96.1	90.8
Peru	N/A	N/A	N/A	N/A	N/A	N/A	N/A	N/A	N/A	N/A

Source: Adapted from World Bank, *World Tables*.

ration some social services more effectively (see Zuckerman, 1989). The most frequent response to diminished administrative capacity was the development of "quick response programmes" to address the anticipated short-term consequences of stabilization and structural adjustment, particularly on the poor and unemployed. Generally designed to bypass traditional bureaucracies considered too weak, immobile, or corrupt to distribute resources effectively, programmes such as the Social Emergency Fund in Bolivia, PRONASOL in Mexico, the Social Well-Being Program in Jamaica, PRONATAS in Argentina, the Social Investment Fund in Guatemala, and targetted programmes for the poor in Chile did little to address the pronounced problems of weak administrative capacity that existed in most social welfare agencies and ministries.[9] While such social adjustment programmes were important in providing much needed response to economic crisis and dislocation, and some were interesting as experiments in achieving poverty alleviation goals, in the longer term, central and local government ministries for social and physical infrastructure and those agencies charged with such routine tasks as tax collection and social security administration must be strengthened and streamlined.

II.4   Political capacity

The ability to mediate conflict, to respond to citizens' demands, and to provide opportunities for effective political participation at national, regional, and local levels is important to Latin America's economic recovery. These capacities promote political stability and enhance the basic legitimacy of the rules of the game established for both economic and political interactions. During the 1980s and early 1990s, economic hardship decreased the ability of political leaders in many Latin American countries to use state resources to maintain their core constituencies of support and to provide policy benefits to respond to local and national level conflicts. It also made them more vulnerable to demands for change.

In part, loss of political capacity was reflected in decreased ability to pursue populist policies and the "politics of spoils". Governments in Latin America traditionally used allocations of public goods and services as a political resource. Frequently, public investments in physical and social infrastructure, as well as jobs, were distributed with a sharp eye toward the political capital they could engender, the political conflicts they could resolve, or the loyalties they could cement (see for examples, Grindle, 1977, 1980; Ames, 1987). In addition, large sectors of the populations of many countries, particularly the politically volatile urban working classes, had become accustomed to government-subsidized food, transportation, housing, and health care. In the 1980s, just as such groups were bearing the brunt of economic crisis and adjustment dislocations, governments became less able to call upon state resources to respond to public protest and concerns.

In a number of countries, political dynamics changed as political leaders became more vulnerable to claims for better and more services, wider participation in decision-making, or greater autonomy to address local problems at the community level. Deprived of resources with which to respond to increased demands, political leaders lost legitimacy in the eyes of many, along with the loyalty of their traditional clienteles. Grass-roots political organizations achieved prominence in Brazil, Mexico, Colombia, and Chile, challenging the behaviour of traditional political bosses and authoritarian leaders (see Fals Borda, 1990, p. 115). Here and elsewhere, such movements were part of "a changing political culture, where popular movements no longer make petitions or ask for benefits but make demands and insist on basic rights" (Foweraker, 1990, p. 8; see also Hornsby, 1991).

The pressure for political opening which accompanied most demands for economic redress was fuelled also by the desire to participate more fully in the selection of national and local leaders, to be included in national decision-making, and to reclaim space for autonomous community and individual action. While transitions to democratic regimes meant that participation through the vote was an important and positive development, the simultaneous strengthening of technical capacity and the greater centralization of economic decision-making, by insulating policy decision-making, worked to distance the substance of policy from input from organized groups and legislatures. Economic crisis heightened public dissatisfaction with those in power; at the same time, it weakened their capacity to respond effectively to political dissatisfaction or to shore up political support through the use of state patronage, rents, and access to spoils.

Such diminished political capacity was effectively responded to in some countries. In Mexico, for example, the newly developed quick response programme for social adjustment put increased resources in the hands of the president that were useful in shoring up support for the PRI as well as enhancing the tolerance for introducing policy reforms (see Dresser, 1991). Political leaders such as Alan Garcia in Peru, Alfonsin in Argentina, and Sarnay in Brazil benefited from the generalized euphoria that accompanied the transition to democratic rule, but their popularity was short-lived when it became clear that democracy did not necessarily or immediately translate into better economic conditions (de Pablo, 1990; Keck, 1990). The skills of political leaders were important in Mexico, Colombia, and Costa Rica, where they provided a clear and evocative vision of how current sacrifices would result in future benefits. With these exceptions, however, the task of rebuilding political capacity continues to challenge the possibility for economic recovery in many countries and will need to be addressed through wise investment in human and physical resources, decentralization of decision-making, responsiveness to local demands for basic needs and autonomy, and politically astute leadership.

III   RESPONDING TO NEW REALITIES

Moments of historic crisis, such as those experienced by many Latin American countries in the 1980s and early 1990s, called into question existing state–economy and state–society relations. Space for new initiatives to manage economic and political tasks was created by these interconnected crises of growth and distribution and of power and legitimacy. How these crises are played out in individual countries depends in large part on the strength and durability of existing institutions for conflict resolution and on the skills and orientations of political leaders in using the expanded space available to them to define new strategies for economic development and to build new and durable coalitions of political support.

In doing so, they must address new conditions in the capacity of states to manage tasks of economic and political development. As suggested in previous pages, many Latin American states will need to work with economic and social groups to redefine the rules of the game for economic and political interaction, they will have to find ways to use increased technical capacity wisely and democratically, and they will need to find ways of strengthening administrative and political capacities without over-centralizing, over-promising, or over-spending. Austerity will continue to be a hallmark of the region's recovery, and this means that states will need to accomplish more with less. How or whether this can be done may well depend on the quality of political leadership and political institutions in individual countries.

In this regard, the potential for economic recovery can be assessed, at least in part, on the basis of country responses to altered conditions in the basic dimensions of state capacity outlined earlier:

(1) How have governments responded to weakened institutional capacity? Have they been able to define and negotiate new and more appropriate rules of the game to govern economic and political behaviour?

(2) How have governments responded to increased technical capacities to set and manage macroeconomic policy? Have they developed and implemented alternative strategies for economic development, increased the insulation of policy making from domestic rent-seekers, or altered the attitudes and behaviour of economic interests in society?

(3) How have governments responded to weakened administrative capacity? Have they introduced innovative means for delivering basic services in their societies? Have they addressed institutional weaknesses of traditional social service and physical infrastructure ministries?

(4) How have governments responded to decreased political capacity to mediate and resolve conflict and to respond to societal demands?

Have they worked to increase the problem-solving skills of government, incorporated new groups into decision-making, and allowed for increased political participation and local level problem-solving?

Answers to these questions will contain significant clues about the extent to which states have encouraged the adoption of new definitions of the role of the state, altered opportunities available to private economic agents, and affected the ways in which citizens relate to government and engage in efforts to influence policy outcomes. They therefore affect the durability of efforts to restructure both economic and political relationships. Enhanced state capacities are not sufficient to ensure the durability of economic recovery in Latin American countries, but failure to address the need for legitimate and effective states will certainly diminish the potential for economic development in the future.

NOTES

1 In this chapter, I define states in the tradition of Weberian analysis as sets of institutions for administration and control that claim "the monopoly of the legitimate use of force within a given community" (Weber, 1946, p. 78). I distinguish states from regimes and administrations, but not from governments.

2 This literature is extensive. See, for example, Castells (1983), Eckstein (1989), Fals Borda (1990), Foweraker and Craig (1990), Hornsby (1991), Karl (1990), Migdal (1988), O'Donnell, Schmitter and Whitehead (1986), Tilly (1985).

3 These dimensions of state capacity are drawn from a forthcoming book by the author, *Challenging the State: Crisis and Innovation in Latin America and Africa*.

4 This perspective is fully developed in Migdal (1988).

5 In the 1960s and 1970s, the claim that strong authoritarian governments were required to impose economic and political order to stimulate national economic growth, and that civilian governments had proved themselves ineffective and corrupt in the pursuit of this task, were strong rationales provided by the military for seizing power in Argentina, Brazil, Chile, Peru, and Uruguay.

6 Tokman (1989, p. 1067) indicates that in 1989, 30 million Latin Americans were employed in the informal sector; from 1980 to 1985, the number of people in the sector increased by 39 per cent.

7 Rank and file party and union members were more publicly engaged in efforts to install democracy, organizing protest marches and strikes against the authoritarian regimes. From local communities came pressure from religious organizations, women's groups, and others demanding democratic reforms and greater responsiveness from government. On the negotiation and durability of pacts in Brazil, Peru, Argentina, and the region generally, see Corradi (1990), Hagopian (1990), Mainwaring (1988), McClintock (1989), Nef (1988), Kochon and Mitchell (1989).

8 Economic teams were typically composed of the minister of finance, the head of the central bank, the head of the monetary board, and the minister of planning.

9 For a discussion of these programmes, see Block (1991), Naim (1991, p. 42), Newman, Jorgensen, and Pradhan (1991), PACT (1990), Ribe *et al.* (1990), Zuckerman (1989).

REFERENCES

Ames, B. (1987) *Political Survival: Politicians and Public Policy in Latin America*, University of California Press, Berkeley CA.
Bennett, D.C. and K.E. Sharpe (1985) *Transnational Corporations Versus the State: the Political Economy of the Mexican Auto Industry*, Princeton University Press, Princeton NJ.
Berry, R.A., R.G. Hellman and M. Solaún (eds) (1980) *Politics of Compromise: Coalition Government in Colombia*, Transaction Books, New Brunswick NJ.
Berry, S.K. (1990) "Economic Policy Reform in Developing Countries: The Role and Management of Political Factors", *World Development* 18(8), 1123–31.
Bhagwati, J.N. (1978) *Foreign Trade Regimes and Economic Development: Anatomy and Consequences of Exchange Control Regimes*, Ballinger, Cambridge MA.
Block, M.A.G. (1991) "Economic Crises and the Decentralization of Health Services in Mexico", in M. Gonzalez de la Rocha and A.E. Latapi (eds) *Social Responses to Mexico's Economic Crisis of the 80's*, University of California, San Diego CA.
Boeninger, E. (1991) "Governance and Development: Issues, Challenges, Opportunities and Constraints", paper prepared for the World Bank Conference on Development Economics, April 25–6, Washington DC.
Bourguignon, François, Jaime de Melo and Christian Morrisson (1991) "Poverty and Income Distribution During Adjustment: Issues and Evidence from the OECD Project", *World Development* 19(11), 1485–1508.
Bright, S. and S. Harding (eds) (1984) *Statemaking and Social Movements: Essays in History and Theory*, the University of Michigan Press, Ann Arbor MI.
Buchanan, J.M., R.D. Tollison and G. Tullock (eds) (1980) *Toward a Theory of the Rent-Seeking Society*, Texas A&M University Press, College Station.
Callaghy, T.M. (1989) "Toward State Capability and Embedded Liberalism in the Third World: Lessons for Adjustment", in J.M. Nelson *et al. Fragile Coalitions: The Politics of Economic Adjustment*, Transaction Books, New Brunswick NJ.
Cardoso, E. and A. Helwege (1992) "Below the Line: Poverty in Latin America", *World Development* 20(1), 19–38.
Castells, M. (1983) *The City and the Grassroots*, Edward Arnold, London.
Colander, D.C. (ed.) (1984) *Neoclassical Political Economy: The Analysis of Rent-Seeking and DUP Activities*, Ballinger, Cambridge MA.
Colburn, F.D. (1990a) "Statism, Rationality, and State Centrism", *Comparative Politics* 20(4), 485–92.
Colburn, F.D. (1990b) *Prospects for Democracy in Latin America*, Princeton University Center of International Studies, Princeton NJ.
Conaghan, C. (1989) "Loose Parties, Floating Politicians, and Institutional Stress: Presidentialism in Ecuador, 1979–1988", paper presented at a symposium on "Presidential or Parliamentary Democracy: Does It Make a Difference?", Georgetown University, Washington DC, May 14–16.
Corradi, J.E. (1990) "Argentina", in F.D. Colburn (ed.) *Prospects for Democracy in Latin America*, Princeton University Center of International Studies, Princeton NJ.
Dornbusch, R. and S. Edwards (eds) (1991) *The Macroeconomics of Populism in Latin America*, University of Chicago Press, Chicago IL.
Dresser, D. (1991) *Neopopulist Solutions to Neoliberal Problems: Mexico's National Solidarity Program*, Center for US–Mexican Studies, University of California, San Diego CA.

Eckstein, S. (1989) *Power and Popular Protest: Latin American Social Movements*, University of California Press, Berkeley CA.

Fals Borda, O. (1990) "Social Movements and Political Power: Evolution in Latin America", *International Sociology* 5(2), 114–27.

Foweraker, J. (1990) "Popular Movements and Political Change in Mexico", in J. Foweraker and A.L. Craig (eds) *Popular Movements and Political Change in Mexico*, Lynne Reinner Publishers, Boulder CO.

Foweraker, J. and A.L. Craig (eds) (1990) *Popular Movements and Political Change in Mexico*, Lynne Reinner Publishers, Boulder CO.

Grindle, M.S. (1977) *Bureaucrats, Politicians, and Peasants in Mexico: A Case Study in Public Policy*, University of California Press, Berkeley CA.

Grindle, M.S. (1980) *The Politics of Policy Implementation in the Third World*, Princeton, NJ: Princeton University Press.

Grindle, M.S. and F. Thoumi (1992) "Muddling Towards Adjustment: The Political Economy of Economic Policy Change in Ecuador", in A.O. Krueger and R. Bates (eds) *The Political Economy of Structural Adjustment*, Basil Blackwell, Oxford (forthcoming).

Grosh, M.E. (1990) *Social Spending in Latin America: The Story of the 1980s*, World Bank Discussion Paper No. 106, Washington DC.

Haggard, S. and C. Moon (1983) "The South Korean State in the International Economy: Liberal, Dependent, or Mercantile?", in J. Ruggie (ed.) *The Antinomies of Interdependence*, Columbia University Press, New York.

Hagopian, F. (1990) " 'Democracy by Undemocratic Means'?", *Comparative Political Studies* 23(2), 147–70.

Hamilton, N. (1982) *The Limits of State Autonomy: Post-revolutionary Mexico*, Princeton University Press, Princeton NJ.

Harberger, A.C. (1985) "Economic Policy and Economic Growth", in A.C. Harberger (ed.) *World Economic Growth*, Institute for Contemporary Studies, San Francisco CA.

Hommes, Rudolf (1990) "Colombia and Venezuela", in J. Williamson, ed., *Latin American Adjustment: How Much Has Happened?*, Washington, D.C.: Institute for International Economics.

Hopkins, R.F. (1990) "The Role of Governance in Economic Development", paper prepared for the Task Force on Development Assistance and Cooperation (Agriculture 2000), November 14–15.

Hornsby, A. (1991) "Pushing for Democracy in Colombia: Non-Profit Challenges to Dependence on the State", PhD Dissertation, Department of Sociology, Harvard University, September.

Israel, A. (1990) "The Changing Role of the State: Institutional Dimensions", World Bank Country Economics Department Working Paper no. 495 (August).

Karl, T. (1986) "Petroleum and Political Pacts: The Transition to Democracy", in G. O'Donnell, P.C. Schmitter and L. Whitehead (eds) *Transitions from Authoritarian Rule: Latin America*, Johns Hopkins University Press, Baltimore MD.

Karl, T. (1990) "Dilemmas of Democratization in Latin America", *Comparative Politics* 23(1), 1–21.

Keck, M. (1990) "Brazil", in F.D. Colburn (ed.) *Prospects for Democracy in Latin America*, Center of International Studies, Princeton University, Princeton NJ.

Killick, T. (1989) *A Reaction Too Far: Economic Theory and the Role of the State in Developing Countries*, Overseas Development Institute, London.

Krasner, S.D. (1984) "Approaches to the State: Alternative Conceptions and Historical Dynamics", *Comparative Politics* 16(2), 223–46.

Krueger, A.O. (1974) "The Political Economy of the Rent-Seeking Society", *American Economic Review* 64(3), 291–303.

Lal, D. (1984) "The Political Economy of Predatory State", World Bank Development Research Department Discussion Paper DRD 105.

Linz, J.J. and A. Stepan (eds) (1978) *The Breakdown of Democratic Regimes: Latin America*, Johns Hopkins University Press, Baltimore MD.

Mainwaring, S. (1988) "Political Parties and Democratization in Brazil and the Southern Cone", *Comparative Politics* 21(1), 91–120.

Malloy, J.M. (1989) "Policy Analysts, Public Policy and Regime Structure in Latin America", *Governance: An International Journal of Policy and Administration* 2(3), 315–38.

Malloy, J.M. (1991) "Parties, Economic Policymaking, and the Problem of Democratic Governance in the Central Andes", paper prepared for the Sixteenth International Congress of the Latin American Studies Association, Washington DC, April 4–6.

McClintock, C. (1989) "The Prospects of Consolidation in a 'Least Likely' Case: Peru", *Comparative Politics* 21(2), 127–48.

Meller, P. (1991) "Adjustment and Social Costs in Chile During the 1980s", *World Development* 19(11), 1545–61.

Migdal, J.S. (1988) *Strong Societies and Weak States: State–Society Relations and State Capabilities in the Third World*, Princeton University Press, Princeton NJ.

Milimo, J.T. and Y. Fisseha (1986) *Rural Small Scale Enterprises in Zambia: Results of a 1985 Country-wide Survey*, Michigan State University Working Paper No. 28.

Naim, M. (1991) "The Launching of Radical Policy Changes: The Venezuelan Experience", unpublished manuscript.

Nef, J. (1988) "The Trend Toward Democratization and Redemocratization in Latin America: Shadow and Substance", *Latin American Research Review* 13(3), 131–53.

Newman, J., S. Jorgensen and M. Pradhan (1991) *Workers' Benefits from Bolivia's Emergency Social Fund*, World Bank Living Standards Measurement Study Working Paper No. 77, Washington DC.

O'Donnell, G. (1973) *Modernization and Bureaucratic Authoritarianism*, University of California Institute of International Studies, Berkeley CA.

O'Donnell, G., P.C. Schmitter and L. Whitehead (eds) (1986) *Transitions from Authoritarian Rule: Latin America*, Johns Hopkins University Press, Baltimore MD.

de Pablo, J.C. (1990) "Argentina", in J. Williamson (ed.) *Latin American Adjustment: How Much Has Happened?*, Institute for International Economics, Washington DC.

PACT (1990) *Steps Toward a Social Investment Fund*, PACT, New York.

Reimers, F. (1990) "The Impact of the Debt Crisis on Education in Latin America", *Prospects* 20(4), 539–54.

Ribe, H., S. Carvalho, R. Liebenthal, P. Nicholas and E. Zuckerman (1990) *How Adjustment Programs Can Help the Poor: The World Bank's Experience*, World Bank Discussion Paper No. 71, Washington DC.

Rochon, T.R. and M.J. Mitchell (1989) "Social Bases of the Transition to Democracy in Brazil", *Comparative Politics* 21(3), 307–22.

Schneider, B.R. (1991) "Brazil Under Collor: Anatomy of a Crisis", *World Policy Journal* 8(2), 321–47.

Sigmund, P. (1990) "Chile", in F.D. Colburn (ed.) *Prospects for Democracy in Latin America*, Center of International Studies, Princeton NJ.

Srinivasan, T.N. (1985) "Neoclassical Political Economy: The State and Economic Development", *Asian Development Review* 3(2), 38–58.

Tilly, C. (1985) "Models and Realities of Popular Collective Action", *Social Research* 52(4), 717–87.

Tokman, V.E. (1989) "Policies for a Heterogeneous Informal Sector in Latin America", *World Development* 17(7), 1067–76.

Wade, R. (1990) *Governing the Market: Economic Theory and the Role of Government in East Asian Industrialization*, Princeton University Press, Princeton NJ.

Weber, M. (1946) "Politics as a Vocation", in H.H. Gerth and C. Wright Mills (eds) *From Max Weber: Essays in Sociology*, Oxford University Press, New York.

Williamson, J. (ed.) (1990a) *Latin American Adjustment: How Much Has Happened?*, Institute for International Economics, Washington DC.

Williamson, J. (1990b) "What Washington Means by Policy Reform", in J. Williamson (ed.) *Latin American Adjustment: How Much Has Happened?*, Institute for International Economics, Washington DC.

Winson, A. (1989) *Coffee and Democracy in Modern Costa Rica*, St Martin's Press, New York.

World Bank (1984) *Toward Sustainable Development in Sub-Saharan Africa*, World Bank, Washington DC.

World Bank (1991) *World Development Report 1991*, Oxford University Press, Oxford.

Zuckerman, E. (1989) *Adjustment Programs and Social Welfare*, World Bank Discussion Paper 44, Washington DC.

Index

Note: Figures and Tables are indicated by *italic page numbers*; notes are shown as page number followed by note number (e.g. 45n3 means page 45, note 3)